Short Bike Rides in
Greater Boston
and Central Massachusetts

" . . . Keeps you organized and informed as you pedal through the
back roads."
    —*Women's Sports and Fitness* magazine

"Howard leaves no stone unturned in his books. He describes the
geography of the region, bicycle safety tips, and the basic accessories you should take with you on bike rides; all add to the pleasure
of cycling."
    —The *Rhode Island Herald*

Tobacco farm in Hadley with the Holyoke Range in the background.

Short Bike Rides in Greater Boston and Central Massachusetts

Second Edition

by
Howard Stone

An East Woods Book

Chester, Connecticut

Photographs on pages 11, 13, 67, 75, 81, 93, 311, 365, 387, 409, 415, 463, 485, 491, 519, 525, 545, and 567 were supplied by the Massachusetts Department of Commerce and Development, Division of Tourism.
All other photographs were taken by the author.

Library of Congress Cataloging-in-Publication Data

Stone, Howard, 1947-
   Short bike rides in greater Boston and central Massachusetts / by Howard Stone. — 2nd ed.
      p.   cm.
   ISBN 0-87106-717-X (pbk.)
   1. Bicycle touring—Massachusetts—Boston Metropolitan Area—Guide-books. 2. Bicycle touring—Massachusetts—Guide-books. 3. Boston Metropolitan Area (Mass.)—Description.
   4. Massachusetts—Description and travel—1981- —Guidebooks.   I. Title.
GV1045.5.M42B677 1988
917.44'61—dc 19   88-7060
                                                                             CIP

Manufactured in the United States of America
Second Edition/Second Printing

Acknowledgments

This book could never have come to fruition without a lot of help. Many members of the Narragansett Bay Wheelmen kept me company, while I was researching the rides, by providing good cheer, taking notes, and patiently putting up with endless hours of backtracking and rechecking intersections. Bob Paiva suffered through two straight weeks of this routine. He also loaned me his tape recorder and typewriter after both of mine broke down. Nat Lomas drove me around most of the North Shore to help me reconstruct a pile of lost notes. Sandra Gallup, my supervisor, allowed me to work flexible hours so that I could take advantage of the daylight to research the rides. John Bergeron and Barbara Ryan loaned me cameras knowing that they would be jostled for hundreds of miles on my bike. Brian Daniele, John Wojtowicz, John Bergeron, and Mary Logan developed the photographs. Jeanne LaFazia helped me interpret the intricacies of the laws of Massachusetts. Carla Petersen helped me type the manuscript. Dozens of local residents told me about hidden back roads and interesting places to see. I would also like to thank Kevin and Anita Clifford, Alan Moretsky, and Leesa Mann for putting me up overnight at various times.

Some of the photographs were supplied by the Massachusetts Department of Commerce and Development, Division of Tourism. Mr. Leon White gave me full access to the photo collection and helped me choose scenes that would best capture the various landscapes of the state.

A few of the rides were originally mapped out as a whole or in part by the following members of the Narragansett Bay Wheelmen, to whom I extend my thanks:

Ted Ellis, Ride 69	Phil Maker, Ride 63
Bill McIlmail, Rides 69, 71	Steve McGowen, Ride 67
Ed Ames, Rides 62, 65	Wes Ewell, Ride 68
Chick Mead, Ride 72	

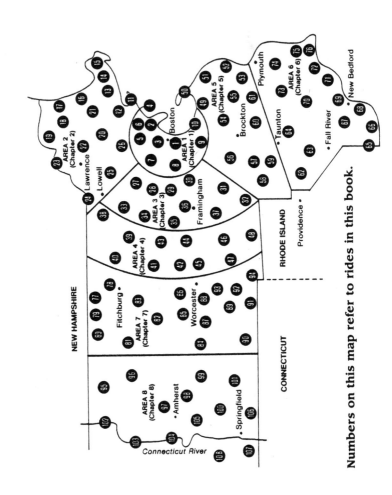

Numbers on this map refer to rides in this book.

Table of Contents

Chapter 3. The Closer Western Suburbs

Chapter 4. The Farther Western Suburbs

Chapter 7. Central Massachusetts

Chapter 8. The Connecticut Valley

Preface to the Second Edition

The second edition of *Short Bike Rides in Greater Boston and Central Massachusetts* follows the same basic format as the first edition, with an introductory description, map, and point-to-point directions for each ride. The directions are somewhat more detailed to make them as easy to follow as possible.

Many of the rides have been modified slightly to improve scenery or to avoid badly deteriorated roads. Some of the starting points for rides in the first edition now have parking "for customers only" or for short time periods. In these cases, I have changed the starting point to a location where parking is no problem.

Introduction

This book is a guide to bicycling in most of Massachusetts, covering the area between the Cape Cod Canal and the Connecticut River. The region, along with the sections of Rhode Island, New Hampshire, and Connecticut just over the state line, offers ideal cycling. Massachusetts is blessed with an impressive network of thousands of back roads, most of them paved but not heavily traveled. Beyond the built-up metropolitan areas, which comprise a very small percentage of the state, the landscape is rural enough to give the cyclist a sense of remoteness and serenity, and yet the nearest town, village, or grocery store is never more than a few miles away. The terrain is refreshingly varied for a relatively small state.

East of Boston lies the seacoast, one of the state's most scenic features. Most of the Massachusetts coast is beautiful and relatively unspoiled, with smooth, sandy beaches, windswept dunes, and extensive salt marshes. Surrounding Boston is a broad belt of affluent suburbs with gracious homes and estates surrounded by acres of gently rolling, open land. Southeast of Boston, toward Cape Cod, is a landscape of cranberry bogs and scrub pine. Beyond the metropolitan area, as the land becomes genuinely rural, lie lake-dotted forests, rolling apple orchards, and old mill villages. Central Massachusetts is an inspiring region of broad sweeps of farmland spreading along rugged hills and ridgetops, eventually sloping down to the broad valley of the Connecticut River.

Bicycling is an ideal way to appreciate the New England landscape's unique intimacy, which is not found in most other parts of the United States. The back roads turn constantly as they hug the minute contours of the land, forcing your orientation down to a small scale. Every turn and dip in the road may yield a surprise—a weathered barn, a pond, a stream, a little dam or falls, a hulking old mill right out of the Industrial Revolution, a ragged stone wall, or a pasture with grazing cattle or horses. Most of the smaller town centers are architectural gems, with the traditional stately white church and village green flanked by the town hall, a handsome brick or stone library, and graceful old wooden homes.

Geography of the Region

Not counting Cape Cod, Massachusetts is basically a rectangle that extends upward and downward at its eastern edge. The eastern side of the rectangle is notched inward by the U-shaped cup of Massachusetts Bay, with Boston lying at the innermost point. The area covered by this book measures about fifty miles from north to south and one hundred miles from east to west, except in the Boston area, where the north-south axis increases to about ninety miles.

In general, the land east of a line drawn between Lowell and the northeastern corner of Rhode Island is fairly flat, and everything else is rolling or hilly. As a result, biking in much of Massachusetts involves some effort. Most of the rides traverse at least one or two hills, sometimes steep or long enough that you'll want to walk them. To compensate, however, no hills are long enough to be really discouraging, except for a few in the mountains near the Connecticut River, and for every uphill climb there's a corresponding downhill run. The large majority of the hills you'll encounter are less than half a mile long, the steepest portion limited to a couple of hundred yards or less.

Culturally, Massachusetts has a long and proud history, beginning with the Pilgrim settlement in Plymouth in 1620. The first armed encounters of the Revolutionary War occurred a century and a half later in Concord and Lexington. The deep and sheltered waters of the harbors bordering Newburyport, Gloucester, Salem, Boston, and New Bedford spawned thriving seaports, fisheries, and maritime commerce in Colonial times and into the nineteenth century. Today these same harbors, along with the many smaller coves and inlets piercing the coast, are filled with motor yachts and sailboats. The Industrial Revolution got a head start in Massachusetts when Lowell and Holyoke, two of the first planned industrial cities in the country, evolved before the Civil War. In later years, culminating between the end of the Civil War and the turn of the century, hundreds of mills were built along the swift-flowing Merrimack, Blackstone, Quaboag, and numerous other rivers, manned by waves of immigrants from Europe and French Canada.

Today, Massachusetts's hundreds of smaller towns and villages comprise some of the state's most appealing and architecturally fascinating hallmarks. As you bike through a town, try to notice each building along the green. First you'll see the graceful white church, generally built before 1850, often on a little rise, standing proudly above the rest of the town. Next look for the town hall, usually a handsome, white-pillared, Colonial-style building or an ornate wooden or stone Victorian one. Near the town hall you'll usually find the library, a gracious brick or stone building dating from the turn of the century or the two decades before it. The small-town library is almost always recognizable, generally built to be impressive looking yet inviting, with wide steps, a portico framing the front door, and often a dome or rounded roof.

Another building worth noticing is the schoolhouse. In the smaller towns, the schools are generally handsome old wooden or brick buildings, sometimes with graceful bell towers. In some towns, like Fairhaven, the high school is an architectural showpiece. Generally as towns get larger the schools get grimmer and more fortresslike, until you get block-long monstrosities from the turn of the century in larger communities like Medford and Quincy that are massive and intimidating enough to drive generations of students to truancy.

Mill towns at first may look depressing, but there is always some architectural beauty to be found. The mills themselves are often fascinating old Victorian structures, foreboding but ornamented with cornices and clock towers. Next to the mill is usually a small millpond with a little dam or falls. Many mill towns have orderly rows of identical two- or three-story wooden houses, originally built for the workers during the late 1800s. Unfortunately, fire, neglect, and vandalism claim several mills each year, but a growing consciousness has arisen about preserving and maintaining these unique and impressive buildings.

Geographically, the state is divided into ten fairly distinct areas, and this book covers all of them except for the Cape and the Berkshires. Boston and its close-in suburbs, lying within the Route 128 semicircle and extending along the coast as far as Lynn to the northeast and Quincy to the southeast, is the most densely populated part of the state. Immediately north of Boston is a cluster of cities that are as densely populated as Boston itself—Cambridge,

Somerville, Everett, Chelsea, Medford, Malden, Revere, and Winthrop. Beyond this urban cluster, Boston itself, Lynn, and Quincy, the area consists primarily of affluent communities with gracious older homes and estates, and a surprising amount of protected, lake-dotted woodland—including the Lynn Woods, Middlesex Fells, and Blue Hills reservations.

I've defined the North Shore as the land between the coast slanting northeastward from Lynn and the west bank of the Merrimack River where it enters New Hampshire. The North Shore has the most extensive concentration of old wealth in the state, expressed by mansions, estates surrounded by acres of gently rolling meadows, and hundreds of tidy horse farms with simple white fences bordering large fields. The coastline is the nicest in the state, with mansions and estates lining most of the stretch between Lynn and Ipswich. North of Cape Ann are extensive salt marshes and Crane's Beach, one of the finest in the state. Salem, Marblehead, Gloucester, and Newburyport are historic communities where you'll find narrow streets lined with old wooden homes and broad avenues boasting the impressive Federal-style mansions of early merchants and sea captains. The wide Merrimack River, which at the turn of the century was the textile center of the country, enters the state from Nashua, New Hampshire, and flows through the three early mill cities of Lowell, Lawrence, and Haverhill, evenly spaced about ten miles apart. East of Haverhill the river flows through an idyllic, undeveloped landscape of gentle green hills.

I've defined the South Shore as the shoulder of coast extending southeastward from Weymouth to Kingston Bay just north of Plymouth, inland to the northeast corner of Rhode Island, and bordered on the south by Route 44 between Providence and Plymouth. The South Shore is more built up and suburban than the North Shore. The coast is a varied mixture of estates and fine homes in Duxbury and Cohasset, summer beach colonies with rows of cottages and more modest homes in Marshfield, Scituate, and Hull, and vast salt marshes along the mouth of the North River between Marshfield and Scituate. Inland from Kingston Bay is a large cluster of lakes and ponds, and here you start to see the cranberry bogs that are a distinguishing feature of the southeastern part of the state. At the western edge of the region is the jewelry capital of the

United States, along the axis from Attleboro to Pawtucket and Providence, Rhode Island.

Southeastern Massachusetts includes everything south of the South Shore, excluding Cape Cod. This region has unique characteristics—sandy soil, scrub pine, cranberry bogs, generally flat and often swampy terrain, and cedar-shingled houses with peaked roofs. In general this area provides the easiest bicycling in the state. The historical center of the region is of course Plymouth, with its collection of landmarks and sites related to the Pilgrim settlement. The southern coast is delightful, with unspoiled beaches and a string of elegant small towns that at one time were shipbuilding communities and are now yachting and sailing centers. In the middle of the southern coast is New Bedford, the nation's prime whaling port during the mid-1800s and today the home of the East Coast's largest fishing fleet.

The western suburbs comprise the broad belt of Massachusetts between the North Shore and the South Shore within commuting distance of Boston. I've divided them into halves separated roughly by Route 495. East of this highway the landscape becomes more suburban and is punctuated by a large number of towns, most of them enjoyable. Many of the closer western suburbs are affluent, with prosperous gentleman farms and spacious homes on large wooded lots. Bicycling in this area is a pleasure, with gently rolling terrain that does not become hilly until you get west of Framingham. The best-known historic sites in this region are the green in Lexington, the Old North Bridge in Concord, and the Wayside Inn in Sudbury. Not far from Route 128 are the two truly rural and unspoiled towns closest to Boston, Carlisle and Dover. West of Concord is the prime apple-growing region of the state, with dozens of orchards stretching along the hillsides in Stow, Bolton, Harvard, and Boxboro.

West of Route 495 the landscape becomes more genuinely rural and hillier. Biking in the farther western suburbs is more challenging, but the superb scenery makes it worthwhile. Most of the small towns are elegant, unspoiled jewels. The Wachusett Reservoir, with its massive dam at the northern end in Clinton, is the second largest lake in the state. The southern half of the region is drained by the Blackstone River, running southeastward from Worcester to Woonsocket,

Rhode Island. A series of fascinating old mill towns right out of the Industrial Revolution lies along the banks of the river and its tributaries. In this area is Purgatory Chasm, a deep cleft in the earth formed by some glacial cataclysm. The Blackstone Valley is currently being developed by the state into a linear historical park.

Central Massachusetts covers the slice of state between Worcester and Fitchburg on the east and the Quabbin Reservoir on the west. This is one of the most rural and inspiringly beautiful parts of the state. The terrain is hilly and challenging for the cyclist, but the scenery more than makes up for it. The region is marked by an endless succession of hills and ridges, many crowned by broad, open farms that provide magnificent views. Almost without exception, the towns are graceful New England classics. The historic highlight of the region is Old Sturbridge Village, a superb reconstruction of a rural community from the early 1800s.

The westernmost area covered by this book is the Connecticut Valley, also called the Pioneer Valley. In the southern third of the state the Connecticut River is heavily urbanized by Springfield, Chicopee, and Holyoke; but north of Holyoke it is delightfully rural as the broad, gracefully curving river winds between rich farms and tobacco fields, with the mountains rising dramatically at the edge of the valley several miles away. At the center of the region is a cluster of five colleges, three of them in Amherst. Ten miles south of the Vermont border is Old Deerfield, a restored community of elegant old homes. East of Amherst the landscape becomes very rural and very hilly—challenging but exciting to bicycle through. At the eastern edge of the region is the immense Quabbin Reservoir, by far the largest lake in the state. As in Central Massachusetts, the towns in the Pioneer Valley are for the most part unspoiled gems. Some of the villages in the northern half of the state, such as New Salem, Wendell, and Warwick, seem unchanged from a hundred years ago except for cars in the driveways and pavement on the road.

Massachusetts is fortunate to benefit from an active heritage of preserving the land and historic sites that began in the nineteenth century, before preservation was even considered in many other parts of the country. The state park system, run by the Department of Environmental Management, is admirable. A unique feature of the state park system is the renovation of old mills and factories, along with their adjacent waterways, into interpretive museums and visitor centers called Heritage State Parks. The names of two organizations, the Trustees of Reservations (TOR) and the Society for the Preservation of New England Antiquities (SPNEA), appear frequently in our descriptions of the rides. The first body is dedicated to acquiring and maintaining scenic areas, and they do the job admirably. A TOR reservation is never shabby or shopworn, as so many public areas are; instead it will be impeccably clean and well landscaped. Some of the finest natural areas in the state, such as Crane's Beach in Ipswich and World's End in Hingham, are TOR properties. The second body aims to acquire, preserve, and open to the public historic homes and mansions. Like TOR, it does a superb job. The only problem with SPNEA properties is that they are open during limited hours, usually afternoons in the summer. Being largely a volunteer and member-supported organization, it simply does not have the funds to keep longer hours. In addition to these two bodies, dozens of other local historical societies and conservationist groups, including the Massachusetts Audubon Society, maintain historic houses and areas of greenspace.

One final geographic feature you'll encounter across the state is the drumlin, a small, sharp hill left behind by the glacier. Most drumlins are elliptical like a football sliced lengthwise across the middle; are less than a mile long and less than 200 feet high; and lie along a northwest-southeast axis, the direction of glacial flow. The biggest concentration of drumlins lies within ten miles of Boston. Most of those near the ocean, such as Orient Heights in East Boston or Great Hill in Weymouth, offer outstanding views. Other clusters of drumlins are scattered across the state. In rural areas such as West Newbury, Groton, Lunenburg, and an extensive region between Worcester and Springfield, they transform the land into a rippling sea of rolling hills with broad pastures and orchards sweeping up and over them, providing some of the most inspiring and scenic bicycling in the state.

About the Rides

Ideally a bicycle ride should be a safe, scenic, relaxing, and enjoyable experience that brings you into intimate contact with the landscape. In striving to achieve this goal, I've routed the rides along paved secondary and rural roads, avoiding main highways, cities, and dirt roads as much as possible. I've tried to make the routes as safe as possible. Hazardous situations such as very bumpy roads or dead stops coming down a steep hill have been avoided except for a few instances with no reasonable alternate route. Any dangerous spot has been clearly indicated in the directions by a • *CAUTION* warning. I've included scenic spots such as dams, falls, ponds, mill villages, ocean views, or open vistas on the rides wherever possible.

Nearly all the rides have two options—a shorter one averaging about 15 miles long, and a longer one that is usually between 25 and 30 miles long. All the longer rides are extensions of the shorter ones, with both options starting off in the same way. A few rides, generally in remote areas, have no shorter option, and several have three alternatives. All the rides make a loop or figure eight rather than going out and then backtracking along the same route. For each ride I include both a map and directions.

If you've never ridden any distance, the thought of riding 15 or, heaven forbid, 30 miles may sound intimidating or even impossible. I want to emphasize, however, that *anyone* in normal health can ride 30 miles and enjoy it if he or she gets into a little bit of shape first. You can accomplish this painlessly by riding at a leisurely pace for an hour several times a week for two or three weeks. If you bought this book and aren't bedridden, you can go out and bike 15 miles right now—guaranteed! If you're already engaged in a physical activity such as tennis, racquetball, swimming, or jogging a couple of times a week, or have a job in which you're walking around or lifting things all day, you can hop on your bike and ride 30 miles right now—guaranteed! You've probably gone on a two- or three-hour ride at some time or other—if so, chances are you rode 15 or 20 miles without even realizing it. If you think of the rides by the hour rather than the mile, the numbers are much less frightening. Then you can tell your sedentary, chain-smoking friends that you biked 25 miles and watch their mouths drop open with astonishment and admiration.

To emphasize how easy bicycle riding is, most bike clubs have a hundred-mile ride, called a Century, each fall. Dozens of ordinary people try their first Century without ever having done much biking, and finish it, and enjoy it! Sure they're tired at the end, but they've accomplished the feat and loved it. (If you'd like to try one, the biggest and flattest Century in the Northeast is held in southeastern Massachusetts on the Sunday after Labor Day—ask at any good bike shop for details.)

Not counting long stops, a 15-mile ride should take about two hours at a leisurely speed, a 20- to 25-mile ride about three hours, and a 30-mile ride about four hours. If you ride at a brisk pace, subtract an hour from these estimates.

A few of the rides in this book have short (half a mile or less) sections of dirt road, or go a block or two along streets that are one-way in the wrong direction. This was occasionally necessary when there was no simple alternate route, or to avoid making the directions needlessly complicated. If you come to a dirt road, get the feel of it first. If it's hard-packed you can ride it without difficulty, but if it's soft you should walk because it's easy to skid and fall. If you encounter a one-way street in the opposite direction, *always* get off your bike and walk, using the sidewalk if there is one. It's illegal and also very dangerous to ride against traffic, because motorists simply aren't expecting you, especially if they are pulling out of a driveway or side street.

For every ride I've recommended a starting point, but you can start anywhere else along the route if it's more convenient. This is the best choice, especially if you live in Boston and don't have a car, and would like to try the rides within biking distance of the city. For some of the rides between Worcester and Springfield you may want to start at the western edge of the ride if you're coming from the Springfield area, or at the eastern edge if you're coming from the Worcester area.

I have intentionally not listed the hours and fees of historic sites because they are subject to so much change, often from one year to the next. If it's a place you've heard of, it's probably open from 10 a.m. to 5 p.m., seven days a week. Unfortunately, many of the less frequently visited spots have limited hours—often only weekday afternoons during the summer, perhaps one day during the weekend. A few places of historic or architectural interest, such as the Rocky Hill Meetinghouse in Amesbury, are open only by appointment. The reason is a matter of funding and manpower.

Most historic sites are maintained by voluntary contributions and effort, and it's simply impossible to keep them staffed more than a few hours a day or a few months a year. If you really want to visit a site, call beforehand and find out the hours.

You may wonder why, with the exception of the Boston area and New Bedford, no cities are on the rides. The reason is twofold. First, most cities just aren't very pleasant to bike through. Do you really want to ride along congested streets lined with businesses and tenements, just to see a few points of interest? Second, once you get to the points of interest there is usually no safe place to keep your bike. The best way to explore a city is on foot, so that you can look at the architecture of each building and visit places without having to worry about traffic or having your bike stolen. If you really want to explore a city—and Lowell, Fall River, Worcester, and Springfield are worth exploring—visit it by car or public transportation and leave your bike at home.

About the Maps

The maps are reasonably accurate, but I have not attempted to draw them strictly to scale. Congested areas may be enlarged in relation to the rest of the map for the sake of legibility. All the maps contain these conventions:

1. Route numbers are circled.
2. Small arrows alongside the route indicate direction of travel.
3. The longer ride is marked by a heavy line. The shorter ride is marked by a dotted line where the route differs from that of the longer ride.
4. I've tried to show the angle of forks and intersections as accurately as possible.

Enjoying the Rides

You'll enjoy biking more if you add a few basic accessories to your bike and bring a few items with you.

1. **Handlebar bag with transparent map pocket on top.**

It's always helpful to have some carrying capacity on your bike. Most handlebar bags are large enough to hold tools, a lunch, or even a light jacket. If you have a map or directions in your map pocket, it's much easier to follow the route. You simply glance down to your handlebar bag instead of fishing map or directions out of your pocket and stopping to read them safely. You may also wish to get a small saddlebag that fits under your seat, or a metal rack that fits above the rear wheel, to carry whatever doesn't fit in the handlebar bag.

Always carry things on your bike, not on your back. A knapsack raises your center of gravity and makes you more unstable; it also digs painfully into your shoulders if you have more than a couple of pounds in it. It may do for a quick trip to the grocery store or campus, but never for an enjoyable ride where you'll be on the bike for more than a few minutes.

2. **Water bottle.** It's nice to be able to take a drink whenever you wish, especially in hot weather. On any ride of more than 15 miles, and any time the temperature is above 80 degrees, you will get thirsty, and it's important to have water with you. On longer rides through remote areas, or on a hot day, bring two water bottles.

3. **Basic tools.** Always carry a few basic tools with you when you go out for a ride, just in case you get a flat or a loose derailleur cable. Tire irons, a six-inch adjustable wrench, a small pair of pliers, a small standard screwdriver, and a small Phillips-head screwdriver are all you need to take care of virtually all roadside emergencies. A rag and a tube of hand cleaner come in handy if you have to handle your chain. If your bike has any Allen nuts (nuts with a small hexagonal socket on top), carry metric Allen wrenches to fit them. Cannondale makes a handy one-piece kit with four Allen wrenches, along with a standard and Phillips-head screwdriver.

4. **Pump and spare tube.** If you get a flat, you're immobilized unless you can pump up a new tube or patch the old one. Installing a brand new tube is less painful than trying to patch the old one on the road. Do the patching at home. Pump up the tire until it's hard, and you're on your way. Carry the spare tube in your handlebar bag, or wind it around the seat post, but make sure it doesn't rub against the rear tire.

If you bike a lot, you'll get flats—it's a fact of life. Most flats are on the rear wheel, because that's where most of your weight is. You should therefore practice taking the rear wheel off and putting it back on the bike, and taking the tire off and putting it on the rim, until you can do it confidently. It's much easier to practice at home than to fumble at it by the roadside.

5. **Dog repellent.** When you ride in rural areas you're going to encounter dogs, no two ways about it. Even if you don't have to use it, you'll have peace of mind, knowing you have something like ammonia or commercial dog spray to repel an attacking dog if you have to. More on this later.

6. **Bicycle computer or odometer.** A bicycle computer or odometer provides a much more reliable way of following a route than depending on street signs or landmarks. Street signs are often nonexistent in rural areas or are rotated 90 degrees by mischievous kids. Landmarks like "turn right at green house" or "turn left at Ted's Market" lose effectiveness when the green house is repainted red or Ted's Market goes out of business. A computer is much easier to read than the traditional odometer, because it sits on top of your stem and has large, clear digits. Most computers indicate not only distance, but also speed, elapsed time, and cadence. The solar-powered models last a long time before the batteries need replacement.

7. **Bike lock.** This is a necessity if you're going to leave your bike unattended. The best locks are the rigid, boltcutter-proof ones such as Kryptonite and Citadel. The next best choice is a strong chain or cable that can't be quickly severed by a normal-sized bolt-cutter or hacksaw. A cheap, flimsy chain can be cut in a few seconds and is not much better than no lock at all.

In urban or heavily touristed areas, always lock both wheels as well as the frame to a solid object, and take your accessories with you when you leave the bicycle. Many a cyclist ignoring this simple precaution has returned to the vehicle only to find one or both wheels gone, along with the pump, water bottle, and carrying bags.

8. **Rear-view mirror.** A marvelous safety device, available at any bike shop, which enables you to check the situation behind you without turning your head. Once you start using a mirror you'll feel defenseless without it. Mirrors are available to fit on eyeglasses, a bike helmet, or the handlebars. If you don't wear glasses, buy a

cheap pair of sunglasses and remove the lenses.

9. **Bike helmet.** Accidents happen, and a helmet will protect your head if you fall or crash. Bike helmets are light and comfortable, and more and more cyclists are using them.

10. **Food.** Always bring some food with you when you go for a ride. It's surprising how quickly you get hungry when you're biking. Some of the rides go through remote areas with no food along the way, and that country store you were counting on may be closed on weekends or out of business. Fruit is nourishing and includes a lot of water. A couple of candy bars will provide a burst of energy for the last 10 miles if you're getting tired. (Don't eat candy or sweets before then—the energy burst lasts only about an hour, then your blood-sugar level drops to below where it was before and you'll be really weak.)

11. **Bicycling gloves.** Gloves designed for biking, with padded palms and no fingers, will cushion your hands and protect them if you fall. For maximum comfort, use handlebar padding also.

12. **Bike rack.** It is easier to use a bike rack than to wrestle your bike into and out of your car or trunk. Racks that attach to the back of the car are most convenient—do you really want to hoist your bike over your head onto the roof? If you use a rack that fits onto the back of the car, make sure that the bike is at least a foot off the ground and that the bicycle tire is well above the tailpipe. Hot exhaust blows out tires!

13. **Light.** Bring a bicycle light and reflective legbands with you in case you are caught in the dark. Ankle lights are lightweight and bob up and down as you pedal for additional visibility.

14. **Roll of electrical tape.** You never know when you'll need it.

Take advantage of your gearing when you ride. It's surprising how many people with ten- or twelve-speed bikes use only two or three of their gears. It takes less effort to spin your legs quickly in the low or middle gears than to grind along in your higher ones. For leisurely biking, a rate of 70 to 80 revolutions per minute, or slightly more than one per second, is comfortable. If you find yourself grinding along at 40 or 50 RPMs, shift into a lower gear. Time your RPMs periodically on a watch with a second hand or your bicycle computer—keeping your cadence up is the best habit you can acquire for efficient cycling. You'll be less tired at the end of a ride, and avoid strain on your knees, if you use the right gears.

You'll find it much easier to climb hills if you get a freewheel (the rear cluster of gears) that goes up to 34 teeth instead of the standard 28 teeth. You may also have to buy a new rear derailleur to accommodate the larger shifts, but the expense will be more than worthwhile in ease of pedaling. You can obtain even lower gears by putting a smaller chainwheel in the front, or converting your bike to a fifteen-speed. This alteration is quite expensive and not necessary for leisurely riding.

When approaching a hill, always shift into low gear *before* the hill, not after you start climbing it. If it's a steep or long hill, get into your lowest gear right away and go slow to reduce the effort. Don't be afraid to walk up a really tough hill; it's not a contest, and you're out to enjoy yourself.

Here are a few more hints to add to your cycling enjoyment: Adjust your seat to the proper height and make sure that it is level. Test for proper seat height by pedaling with your heels. Your leg should barely straighten out (with no bend) at the bottom of the downstroke. If your leg is bent, the seat is too low. If you rock from side to side as you pedal, the seat is too high.

Pedal with the balls of your feet over the spindles, not your arches or heels. Toe clips are ideal for keeping your feet in the proper position on the pedals; they also give you added leverage when going uphill. The straps should be *loose*, so that you can take your feet off the pedals effortlessly. In proper pedaling position, your leg should be slightly bent at the bottom of the downstroke.

Eat before you get hungry, drink before you get thirsty, and rest before you get tired. To keep your pants out of your chain, tuck them inside your socks. Wear pants that are as seamless as possible. Jeans or cut-offs are the worst offenders; their thick seams are uncomfortable. Use a firm, good-quality seat. A soft, mushy seat may feel inviting, but as soon as you sit on it, the padding compresses under your weight, so that you're really sitting on a harsh metal shell.

Using the Maps and Directions

Unfortunately, a book format does not lend itself to quick and easy consultation while you're on your bike. The rides will go more smoothly if you don't have to dismount at each intersection to consult the map or directions. You can solve this problem by making a machine copy of the directions and carrying it in your map pocket, dismounting occasionally to turn the sheet over or to switch sheets. Most people find it easier to follow the directions than the map.

In the directions, I have indicated the name of a road if there was a street sign at the time I researched the route, and I did not indicate it if the street sign was absent. Street signs have a short life span—a couple of years on the average—and are often nonexistent in rural areas. Very frequently, the name of a road changes without warning at a town line, crossroads, or other intersection.

Using a bicycle computer or odometer is virtually essential to enjoy the rides. The directions indicate the distance to the next turn or major intersection. Because so many of the roads are unmarked, you'll have to keep track accurately of the distance from one turn to the next. It is helpful to keep in mind that a tenth of a mile is 176 yards, or nearly twice the length of a football field.

In the written directions, it is obviously not practical to mention every single intersection. Always stay on the main road unless directed otherwise.

In addition to distances and a description of the next intersection, the directions also mention points of interest and situations that require caution. Any hazardous spot—for example, an unusually busy intersection or a bumpy section of road—has been clearly indicated by a • *CAUTION* warning. It's a good idea to read over the entire tour before taking it, in order to familiarize yourself with the terrain, points of interest, and places requiring caution.

In the directions, certain words occur frequently, and so let me define them to avoid any confusion.

To "bear" means to turn diagonally, at an angle between a right-angle turn and going straight ahead. In these illustrations, you bear from road A onto road B.

To "merge" means to come into a road diagonally, or even head-on, if a side road comes into a main road. In the examples, road A merges into road B.

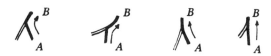

A "sharp" turn is any turn sharper than 90 degrees; in another words, a hairpin turn or something approaching it. In the examples, it is a sharp turn from road A onto road B.

Safety

It is an unfortunate fact that thousands of bicycle accidents occur each year, with many fatalities. Almost all cycling accidents, however, are needless and preventable. Most accidents involve children under sixteen and are caused by foolhardy riding and failure to exercise common sense. The chances of having an accident can be reduced virtually to zero by having your bike in good mechanical condition, using two pieces of safety equipment (a rear-view mirror and a helmet), being aware of the most common biking hazards, and not riding at night unless prepared for it.

Before going out for a ride, be sure your bike is mechanically sound. Its condition is especially important if you bought the bike at a discount store, where it was probably assembled by a high school kid with no training. Above all, be sure that the wheels are secure and the brakes work.

Invest in a rear-view mirror and a bicycle helmet, both available at any bike shop. The mirror attaches to your glasses, your helmet, or your handlebars, and works like a charm when properly adjusted. Its greatest asset is that when you come to an obstacle, such as a pothole or a patch of broken glass, you can tell at a glance whether or not it's safe to swing out into the road to avoid it. On narrow or winding roads you can always be aware of the traffic behind you and plan accordingly. Best of all, a mirror eliminates the need to peek back over your shoulder—an action that is not only awkward but also potentially dangerous, because you sometimes unconsciously veer toward the middle of the road while peeking.

A bicycle helmet is the cyclist's cheapest form of life insurance. A helmet not only protects your head if you land on it after a fall, but also protects against the sun and the rain. More and more cyclists are wearing them, and so you shouldn't feel afraid of being thought a weirdo if you use one. Once you get used to a helmet you'll never even know you have one on.

While on the road, use the same plain old common sense that you use while driving. Stop signs and traffic lights are there for a reason—obey them. At intersections, give cars the benefit of the doubt rather than trying to dash in front of them or beat them through the light. Remember, they're bigger, heavier, and faster than you are. And you're out to enjoy yourself and get some exercise, not to be king of the road.

Several situations are inconsequential to the motorist, but potentially hazardous for the bicyclist. When biking, try to keep aware of these:

1. **Road surface.** Not all roads in Massachusetts are silk-smooth. Often the bicyclist must contend with bumps, ruts, cracks, potholes, and fish-scale sections of road that have been patched and repatched numerous times. When the road becomes rough, the only prudent course of action is to slow down and keep alert, especially going downhill. Riding into a deep pothole or wheel-swallowing crack can cause a nasty spill. On bumps, you can relieve some of the shock by getting up off the seat.

2. **Sand patches.** Patches of sand often build up at intersections, sharp curves, the bottom of hills, and sudden dips in the road. Sand is very unstable if you're turning, and so slow way down, stop pedaling and keep in a straight line until you're beyond the sandy spot.

3. **Storm-sewer grates.** Federal regulations have outlawed

thousands of hazardous substances and products, but unfortunately have not yet outlawed the storm sewer with grates parallel to the roadway. This is a very serious hazard, because a cyclist catching the wheel in a slot will instantly fall, probably in a somersault over the handlebars. Storm sewers are relatively rare in rural areas, but always a very real hazard.

4. **Dogs.** Unfortunately, man's best friend is the cyclist's worst enemy. When riding in the country you will encounter dogs, pure and simple. Even though many communities have leash laws, they are usually not enforced unless a dog really mangles someone or annoys its owners' neighbors enough that they complain—a rare situation because the neighbors probably all have dogs too.

The best defense against a vicious dog is to carry repellent—either ammonia in a squirtgun or plant sprayer (make sure it's leakproof), or a commercial dog spray called Halt, which comes in an aerosol can and is available at most bike shops. Repellent is effective only if you can grab it instantly when you need it—*don't* put it in your handlebar pack, a deep pocket, or any place else where you'll have to fish around for it. For Halt to work you have to squirt it directly into the dog's eyes, but if the dog is close enough to really threaten you it's easily done.

The main danger from dogs is not being bitten, but rather bumping into them or instinctively veering toward the center of the road into oncoming traffic when the dog comes after you. Fortunately, almost all dogs have a sense of territory and will not chase you more than a tenth of a mile. If you're going along at a brisk pace and you're in front of the dog when it starts to chase you, you can probably outrun it and stay ahead until you reach the animal's territorial limit. If you're going at a leisurely pace, however, or heading uphill, or the dog is in the road in front of you, the only safe thing to do is dismount and walk slowly forward, keeping the bike between you and the dog, until you leave its territory. If the dog is truly menacing, or there's more than one, repellent can be comforting to have.

If you decide to stay on the bike when a dog chases you, always get into a low gear and spin your legs as quickly as possible. It's hard for a dog to bite a fast-rotating target. Many cyclists swing their pump at the animal, but this increases the danger of losing

control of your bike. Often, yelling "Stay!" or "No!" in an authorita-
tive voice will make a dog back off.

A word of caution about using commercial dog spray: It can be
legally argued that dog spray comes under the Massachusetts fire-
arms law, which carries a mandatory one-year jail sentence for
carrying an unlicensed firearm. Such a case would probably not
hold up in court, but because of the potential hazard, a zealous
policeman might give you a hassle if he noticed it on your bike. The
law states in Section 10 of Chapter 269 "Whoever . . . carries . . . a
firearm . . . as defined in Section 121 of Chapter 140 . . . shall be
punished by imprisonment. . . ." When you go to the definition in
Section 121 of Chapter 140, it says "Firearm shall mean a pistol,
revolver or other weapon of any description loaded or unloaded,
from which a shot or bullet can be discharged." Dog spray hardly
fits this definition.

Further into Section 10 of Chapter 269 it states: "Whoever,
when arrested . . . for an alleged crime or . . . while committing a
breach or disturbance of the public peace, is armed with . . . a . . .
dangerous weapon . . . shall be punished by imprisonment. . . ."
Then in Section 10C of the same chapter it says, "Whoever uses . . .
any device or instrument which contains a liquid, gas, powder, or
any other substance designed to incapacitate for the purpose of
committing a crime shall be punished by imprisonment. . . ." The
last two sentences imply that the law is intended to apply to crimi-
nal activity. Squirting a dog in self-defense hardly qualifies as a
crime.

5. **Undivided, shoulderless four-lane highways.** This is
the most dangerous type of road for biking. If traffic is very light
there is no problem, but in moderate or heavy traffic the road becomes a death trap unless you ride assertively. The only safe way
to travel on such a road is to stay in or near the center of the right
lane, rather than at the edge, forcing traffic coming up behind you
to pass you in the left lane. If you hug the right-hand edge, some
motorists will not get out of the right lane, brushing past you by
inches or even forcing you off the road. Some drivers mentally
register a bicycle as being only as wide as its tire, an unsettling
image when the lane is not much wider than a car.

Several rides in this book contain short stretches along highways. If traffic is heavy enough to occupy both lanes most of the time, the only truly safe thing to do is walk your bike along the side of the road.

6. **Railroad tracks.** Tracks that cross the road at an oblique angle are a severe hazard, because you can easily catch your wheel in the slot between the rails and fall. NEVER ride diagonally across tracks—either walk your bike across or, if no traffic is in sight, cross the tracks at right angles by swerving into the road. When riding across tracks, slow down and get up off the seat to relieve the shock of the bump.

7. **Oiled and sanded roads.** Many communities spread a film of oil or tar over the roads in the fall to seal cracks before winter. Then they spread sand over the road to absorb the oil. The combination is treacherous for biking. Be very careful, especially going downhill. If the tar or oil is still wet, better walk or you'll never get your bike clean.

8. **Car doors opening into your path.** This is a severe hazard in urban areas and in the center of towns. To be safe, any time you ride past a line of parked cars, stay four or five feet away from them. If oncoming traffic won't permit this, proceed very slowly and notice whether the driver's seat of each car is occupied. A car pulling to the side of the road in front of you is an obvious candidate for trouble.

9. **Low sun.** If you're riding directly into a low sun, traffic behind you may not see you, especially through a smeared or dirty windshield. Here your rear-view mirror becomes a lifesaver, because the only safe way to proceed is to glance constantly in the mirror and remain aware of conditions behind you. If you're riding directly away from a low sun, traffic coming toward you may not see you and could make a left turn into your path. If the sun is on your right or left, drivers on your side may not see you, and a car could pull out from a side road into your path. To be safe, give any traffic that may be blinded by the sun the benefit of the doubt, and dismount if necessary. Because most of the roads you'll be on are winding and wooded, you won't run into blinding sun frequently, but you should remain aware of the problem.

10. **Kids on bikes.** Little kids riding their bikes in circles in the middle of the road and shooting in and out of driveways are a

hazard: The risk of collision is always there because they aren't watching where they're going. Any time you see kids playing in the street, especially if they're on bikes, be prepared for anything and call out "Beep-beep" or "Watch out" as you approach. If you have a loud bell or horn, use it.

11. **Wet leaves.** In the fall, wet leaves are very slippery. Avoid turning on them.

12. **Metal-grate bridges.** When wet, the metal grating becomes very slippery, and you may be in danger of falling and injuring yourself on the sharp edges. If the road is wet, or early in the morning when there may be condensation on the bridge, please walk across.

A few additional safety reminders: If bicycling in a group, ride single file and at least 20 feet apart. Use hand signals when turning—to signal a right turn, stick out your right arm. If you stop to rest or examine your bike, get both your bicycle and yourself *completely* off the road. Sleek black bicycle clothing is stylish, but bright colors are safer and more visible.

Finally, use common courtesy toward motorists and pedestrians. Hostility toward bicyclists has received national media attention; it is caused by the 2 percent of discourteous cyclists (mainly messengers and groups hogging the road) who give the other 98 percent—responsible riders—a bad image. Please do not be part of the 2 percent!

Bicycle Clubs

If you would like to bike with a group and meet other people who enjoy cycling, join a bicycle club. Most clubs have weekend rides of comfortable length, with a shortcut if you don't want to go too far. Usually a club will provide maps and mark the route by painting arrows in the road so that nobody gets lost. Joining a club is especially valuable if you don't have a car, because you'll meet people who do and who'll be able to give you a lift to areas beyond biking distance from home. To find out about clubs in your area, ask at any good bike shop. Addresses of clubs riding in Massachusetts (subject to annual change) are as follows:

Boston Area Bicycle Coalition, Box 1015, Kendall Square Branch, Cambridge, MA 02142 (phone 491-RIDE). A political action group devoted to improving conditions for bicyclists. Recently the BABC lobbied successfully to allow bicycles on some of the Massachusetts Bay Transit Authority lines on Sundays (see next section for details).

Charles River Wheelmen, 19 Chase Avenue, West Norton, MA 02165. The main club for the Boston area.

American Youth Hostels, 1020 Commonwealth Avenue, Boston, MA 02215. Biking in the Boston area, also hiking, canoeing, cross-country skiing.

Appalachian Mountain Club, 5 Joy St., Boston, MA 02108. Mostly hiking, but some bicycle rides in the Boston area.

Northshore Cyclists, 64 McKay Street, Beverly, MA 01915.

Nashoba Valley Pedalers, 133 Pine Hill Rd., Boxboro, MA 01719. Northwestern suburbs between Concord and Fitchburg.

Granite State Wheelmen, 2 Townsend Ave., Salem, NH 03079. Southern New Hampshire and nearby Massachusetts.

Massachusetts Bay Road Club, 48 Sandwich St., Plymouth, MA 02360.

Narragansett Bay Wheelmen, Box 1317, Providence, RI 02901. Rhode Island and nearby Massachusetts.

Seven Hills Wheelmen, Box 24, Greendale Station, Worcester, MA 01609.

Fitchburg Cycling Club, Box 411, Lunenburg, MA 01462.

Cyclonauts Bicycling Club, 29 Brooklawn Road, Wilbraham, MA 01095. Springfield area.

Franklin-Hampshire Freewheelers, c/o Albert Shane, RFD 3, Two Mile Road, Amherst, MA 01002.

Most of these clubs are affiliated with the League of American Wheelmen, which is the main national organization of and for bicyclists. It publishes an excellent monthly magazine and has a dynamic legislative-action program. Address of the league is 6707 Whitestone Road, Suite 209, Baltimore, MD 21207.

There are certainly other clubs in the state that I'm not aware of. Your local bike shop will know about them.

Bicycles and Public Transportation

Thanks to the efforts of the Boston Area Bicycle Coalition, bicycles are currently allowed on some of the routes of the Massachusetts Bay Transit Authority (the T) on Sundays. You must obtain a bicycle permit first from the MBTA Washington Street Concourse Senior Citizen Registration Office (in the downtown Washington Street station), between 8:15 to noon and 12:30 to 4 p.m. on weekdays. The permit costs $5.00 and is good for four years. Bikes are allowed only on the three in-town lines using subway cars: the Red, Blue, and Orange Lines. Bikes are not allowed on trolleys (the Green Line), commuter rail trains, or MBTA buses.

It must be emphasized that this is a trial program which may be either expanded or curtailed at any time. The Boston Area Bicycle Coalition urges cyclists to use the program, so that the MBTA will see that there is continued interest in it. The more cyclists take advantage of the program, the more likely it will be continued or expanded in the future.

The only other public transportation practical for bicycles are the ferries that run from Boston Harbor to Hingham, Hull, Provincetown, and Gloucester. Bikes are allowed on Amtrak trains and most inter-city buses only if boxed. Bikes are currently allowed unboxed on the Cape Cod and Hyannis Railroad, which runs from Braintree to Cape Cod during the summer.

Cyclists who depend on public transportation may wish to consider a folding bicycle that fits into a small bag. Several brands, which are sturdy yet easily assembled and disassembled, are available at better bike shops. Folding bikes are suitable for the rides in this book. It may take a little while to get used to the steering and handling, because of the small wheels.

Bikeways

Bikeways, or bicycle paths, are few and far between in Massachusetts. The best bikeways in the state are on Cape Cod. (Two rides in this book, number 75 and 76, utilize the bikeway along the Cape Cod Canal). In the Boston area, bikeways run along both sides of the Charles River in the Back Bay and in Cambridge. In good weather they are jammed with pedestrians and joggers. The Southwest Corridor Bikeway runs 4 miles from the Forest Hills T station in Jamaica Plain to Back Bay Station, paralleling the new T Red Line tracks and the Amtrak line. It runs through marginal neighborhoods and crosses some busy streets. Two bikeways originate from the Alewife T station in Cambridge, following abandoned railroad lines. One runs east to Davis Square in Somerville, the other (a crushed stone path) runs west to the Belmont city line. Construction continues on the Minuteman Bikeway, which will run from Alewife Station to Bedford, roughly paralleling Massachusetts Avenue and Route 225.

Bikeways are a mixed blessing. If well designated and well maintained, like the Cape Cod Rail Trail or the East Bay Bicycle Path in Rhode Island, they are a pleasure. If poorly designed or maintained, they are much more dangerous than the roads that they're supposed to avoid. Many bikeways are too narrow or have curves that are too sharp, and many have unsafe road crossings. Unless maintenance is vigilant, a bikeway will rapidly fill up with leaves, glass, and debris; and the surface will deteriorate. In good weather, all bikeways in populated areas will be used by pedestrians, joggers, rollerskaters, dogs, and other noncyclists.

The Boston Area Bicycle Coalition is actively striving to improve and increase bikeways. If you'd like to join in their efforts, contact them at Box 1015, Kendall Square Branch, Cambridge, MA 02142 (phone 491-RIDE).

Feedback

I'd be grateful for any comments, criticisms, or suggestions about the rides in this book. Road conditions change, and a road that is safe to ride on now may resemble a lunar landscape in a couple of years. A new snack bar may open up along one of the routes. An intersection may be changed by road construction or improvement, or a traffic light may be installed. I'd like to keep the book updated by incorporating changes as they occur, or modifying a route if necessary in the interest of safety. Please feel free to contact me through the Globe Pequot Press, 138 West Main Street, Chester, Connecticut 06412 with any revision you think helpful.

Further Reading and Resources

Massachusetts and neighboring states are well covered by bicycling guides and maps if you'd like to explore new territory:

Short Bike Rides on Cape Cod, Nantucket and the Vineyard, Third Edition, by Jane Griffith and Edwin Mullen. Chester, CT: Globe Pequot Press, 1988. Thirty-two rides.

Bicycle Touring in the Pioneer Valley, by Nancy Jane. Amherst: University of Massachusetts Press, 1978. Sixteen rides covering the valley in much greater depth than this book does.

Short Bike Rides in Rhode Island, Third Edition, by Howard Stone, Chester, CT: Globe Pequot Press, 1988. Forty-four rides, several of them in nearby Massachusetts.

Short Bike Rides in Connecticut, Third Edition, by Jane Griffith and Edwin Mullen. Chester, CT: Globe Pequot Press, 1989. Thirty rides.

Twenty-five Bicycle Tours in New Hampshire, by Tom and Susan Heavey. Revised edition. Woodstock, VT: Backcountry Publications, 1985.

Twenty-five Bicycle Tours in Vermont, by John Freidin. Revised edition. Woodstock, VT: Backcountry Publications, 1987.

Twenty-five Bicycle Tours in Maine, by Howard Stone. Woodstock, VT: Backcountry Publications, 1986.

New England over the Handlebars: A Cyclist's Guide, by Michael H. Farny. Boston: Little, Brown, 1975.

Boston's Bikemap. Beverly, MA: Great Circle Productions, 163 East Lothrop Street, Beverly, MA 01915. New edition, 1987. Available at many Boston-area bike shops. Shows suggested routes in Boston and nearby suburbs; also tips on safety and riding in traffic; lists bicycle shops.

Massachusetts Bicycle Map. Available free from State Transportation Library, 10 Park Plaza, Boston MA 02116 (phone 973-8000). Indicates selected routes throughout the state; also information on safety, bicycle laws, publications, bicycle and organizations, recreation and conservation, and state parks and forests. Published 1987.

Boston–Cape Cod Bikeway Map. Available free from State Transportation Library, 10 Park Plaza, Boston, MA 02116.

The Other Massachusetts: Beyond Boston and Cape Cod, by Christina Tree. Woodstock, VT: Countryman Press, 1987. This is the best general guidebook to Massachusetts in print, with comprehensive information on things to see and do, historic sites, special events and fairs, parks and reservations, restaurants, and overnight accommodations.

🚲 Chapter 1:

Boston and Immediate Suburbs

Numbers on this map refer to rides in this book.

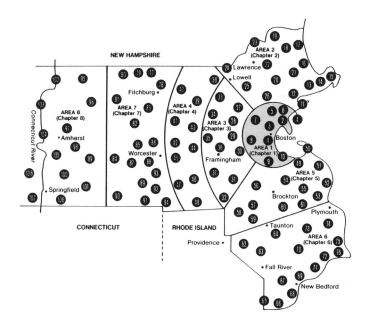

1. Boston

Number of miles: 16 (10 with shortcut omitting South Boston)
Terrain: Flat, with a couple of short hills.
Food: Numerous grocery stores and restaurants.
Start: The most convenient starting point is Northern Avenue in Boston, on the east side of the bridge over Fort Point Channel. There are a couple of parking lots where you can park all day for about $5. For free parking, you can start from the Bunker Hill Monument in Charlestown (start with direction number 18) or from Fort Independence in South Boston (start with direction number 50).
How to get there: From the south, get off the Southeast Expressway at the Atlantic Avenue–Northern Avenue exit, just beyond the tunnel. Turn right at end of ramp onto Northern Avenue and cross the bridge. From the north, take Route 1 or Route 93 into downtown Boston and get off at the High Street–Congress Street exit. Turn left at the bottom of the ramp and then right at end, paralleling the expressway on your left. Make a U-turn to the left at the first opportunity, turn right on Northern Avenue, and cross the bridge.

• *CAUTION:*

1. If traffic is heavy, which it will be if you don't do the ride on a weekend, walk your bike at left-hand turns as a pedestrian. Seasoned bicycle commuters weave around and through traffic in a living game of Space Invaders; don't imitate them.

2. To avoid traffic, several sections of the ride go along areas for pedestrians. Always assume that they don't see you coming and give them a wide berth. On warm, sunny days you'll probably have to walk your bike along the Charles River Esplanade and through Boston Common because of throngs of pedestrians, joggers, and rollerskaters clogging the pathways.

Bunker Hill Momument in Charlestown marks the spot of the famous battle.

Touring Boston by bicycle is a unique visual, historical, and architectural experience. It's also not nearly as hairy as you probably think, especially if you go on Sunday morning, when the downtown streets are amazingly deserted. Saturday morning is almost as good a time to go, followed by Sunday afternoon and Saturday afternoon. During the week, of course, the streets will be clogged with traffic, but even then the city is surprisingly bikeable because the traffic won't be going any faster than you. If traffic is heavy, walk your left-hand turns as a pedestrian and you won't have any trouble. When you bike in Boston, your biggest hazard won't be the traffic, but rather pedestrians and having your bike stolen. If you plan to visit points of interest—which you should, because they help make Boston the special city that it is —ideally you should use an old three-speed or even one-speed clunker, plus a good lock. The land is so flat that you don't need ten speeds; in fact, the extra ruggedness and more cushioned ride of a three- or one-speed bike is an advantage in urban riding. The couple of hills you'll encounter are only a block or two long. If you use a ten-speed and would like to visit places, a boltcutter-proof lock is essential. When you leave the bike, lock both wheels as well as the frame and carry all removable accessories with you—that means pump, water bottle, handlebar bags, and the rest. A knapsack is handy for this purpose.

This is one ride you shouldn't rush through. You could do it in little more than an hour, but take several instead. Notice the architecture of as many buildings as possible; it's one of Boston's most appealing features. Go out onto the wharves along the waterfront, poke around the shoulder-to-shoulder shops and eateries at Quincy Market, clamber down the narrow hatches of *Old Ironsides*, climb the Bunker Hill Monument for a magnificent (and absolutely free) view of the metropolis, relax along the banks of the Charles or on a Swan Boat in the Public Garden.

You'll start off by going along the waterfront. At the beginning you'll pass the New England Aquarium, with the world's largest fish tank, and Quincy Market, which boasts more visitors than Disney World. Most of the old wharves have been tastefully recycled into luxury apartments and trendy shops, with the exteriors of the fine old mercantile buildings kept intact. A few wharves are decaying and still hold ancient warehouses and fish-processing facilities.

4

"Old Ironsides" with the Bunker Hill Monument in the background.

From the waterfront you'll head inland a few blocks through the North End, with its maze of narrow streets lined with unbroken rows of four- and five-story brick buildings. Here you'll pass Old North Church, the famous statue of Paul Revere, and the venerable Copps Hill Burying Ground, filled with gravestones from the 1700s. From the North End you'll cross the mouth of the Charles River into Charlestown, where you'll visit *Old Ironsides* and the Bunker Hill Monument, which provides an outstanding view of the city.

From Charlestown you'll head briefly into Cambridge, where you'll parallel the Charles River. The views of the skyscrapers across the water are impressive. You'll cross back into Boston for a tour of Beacon Hill, the city's most elegant neighborhood, and still a stronghold of the descendants of the city's old and proper families. The hilly streets are lined with gracious brick row houses adorned by ornate doorways, wrought-iron balconies, and dark wooden shutters. At the bottom of Beacon Hill you'll once again head along the Charles through the long, grassy park along its bank. Then you'll head back toward downtown along the broad center island of Commonwealth Avenue, where you can rubberneck without worrying about traffic at the procession of ornate Victorian row houses adorning both sides of the street.

From here you'll cross the Public Garden and Boston Common, two surprisingly well-landscaped, clean, and well-maintained enclaves of greenery in the heart of downtown. The Public Garden is a visual delight, with fountains, flower beds, and the beloved Swan Boats plying up and down its small duck-filled pond. The Common is the oldest public park in the country, dating from 1634, and pleasantly wooded with stately old shade trees. It has a bandstand and maintains an air of grace and elegance despite daily assault by thousands of pedestrians.

From the Common you'll skirt Chinatown and pass South Station. Here you're only a couple of blocks from the starting point if you want to cut the ride short. The long ride heads a mile south into South Boston, affectionately known as Southie, which comprises a triangular peninsula jutting eastward into Massachusetts Bay. South Boston is a blue-collar, highly ethnic residential area that consists primarily of that hallmark of Boston's domestic architecture, the "three-decker" house with a front porch and bay win-

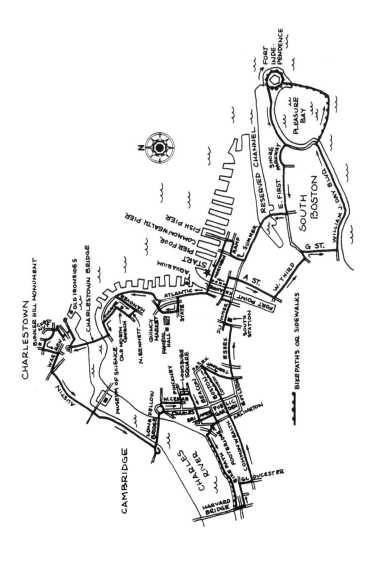

CHARLESTOWN

BUNKER HILL MONUMENT

OLD IRONSIDES

CHARLESTOWN BRIDGE

CAMBRIDGE

WARREN

AUSTIN

MUSEUM OF SCIENCE

OLD NORTH CHURCH

N. BENNETT

HANOVER

QUINCY MARKET

FANEUIL HALL

STATE

ATLANTIC

AQUARIUM

START

PIER FOUR

COMMONWEALTH PIER

FISH PIER

N

RESERVED CHANNEL

E. FIRST

SOUTH BOSTON

SHORE PARKWAY

FORT INDE-PENDENCE

PLEASURE BAY

WILLIAM J. DAY BLVD.

G ST.

W. THIRD

A ST.

SUMMER

RAMP

PORT POINT

KNEELAND

SOUTH STATION

ESSEX

TRACK

BOSTON

LOUISBURG SQUARE

PINCKNEY

BEACON

ARLINGTON

BOYLSTON

COMMONWEALTH

GLOUCESTER

W. CEDAR

CHARLES

PUBLIC GARDEN

BRI

FOOTBRIDGE

BIKE PATH

CHARLES RIVER

HARVARD BRIDGE

LONGFELLOW BRIDGE

BIKEPATHS OR SIDEWALKS

7

dow extending from the first floor all the way up. After a short climb up and over the hill in the center of the peninsula, you'll come to the shore of Dorchester Bay and enjoy a relaxing run along its shore. At the tip of the peninsula is massive pentagon-shaped Fort Independence, a great spot from which to watch the ships passing through Boston Harbor and the jets swooping into and out of Logan Airport. From here it's a short hop back to the start past several more piers. At the end of the ride, you're only a block from the Computer Museum and the Children's Museum.

Directions for the ride: 16 miles

1. Head toward downtown on Northern Avenue to end (Atlantic Avenue). The area on your right, between Pier Four Restaurant and the bridge, is called the Fan Pier. It is about to be developed into an elaborate complex of condominiums, trendy shops, and offices, similar to Copley Place or Quincy Market. Current plans are to build a new bridge but to keep the old one for pedestrians; use the old bridge if possible. • *CAUTION* on metal grating.

2. Turn right on Atlantic Avenue and go 3/10 mile to State Street on left, at traffic light immediately before the Long Wharf Marriott Hotel on right. You'll pass the twin Harbor Towers apartment buildings and then the New England Aquarium on your right.

3. Turn left on State Street, going underneath the expressway, and go one block to Commercial Street on the right. On your left is the tall, slender Custom House, the only tall building in downtown Boston until the early 1960s.

4. Turn right on Commercial Street. This is a pedestrian area, so walk your bike. To your left is Quincy Market, which has been the commercial centerpiece of downtown Boston since 1976, when it was transformed from decaying warehouses. The handsome, domed central market building was built in 1826. At the far end of Quincy Market is Faneuil Hall, and just beyond that is the futuristic New City Hall and Government Center. Just beyond Quincy Market, go underneath the highway. Turn right immediately beyond the highway on Cross Street, and go one short block to end (Atlantic Avenue).

5. Turn left on Atlantic Avenue. On your right is the Waterfront Park, a great place to relax and enjoy the view of Boston

Harbor between T Wharf on the right and Commercial Wharf on the left. Follow Atlantic Avenue 4/10 mile to Hanover Street on the left, after building number 414. The wharves along the waterfront are fascinating to go out onto.

6. Turn left on Hanover Street, main street of the North End, a predominantly Italian neighborhood that is one of Boston's oldest and safest areas. Go almost 2/10 mile to your third right, North Bennett Street. You'll pass the Paul Revere statue on your right, set in a narrow little park called the Paul Revere Mall or the Prado. Opposite the statue on your left is magnificent Saint Stephen's Church, designed by Charles Bulfinch in 1804.

7. Turn right on North Bennett Street, which is typical of the mazework of narrow lanes threading through the North End. Go 1/10 mile to end (Salem Street).

8. Turn right on Salem Street and go 1/10 mile to end (Charter Street). You'll pass Old North Church on your right.

9. Turn left on Charter Street and go 1/10 mile to end (Commercial Street). You'll pass Copps Hill Burying Ground on your left, filled with headstones from the 1700s.

10. Turn left on Commercial Street and go 1/10 mile to the Charlestown Bridge on right, at traffic light.

11. Turn right and go 4/10 mile to far end of bridge. It is safest to use the sidewalk. • *CAUTION* on metal grating at top of bridge.

12. Turn sharply right at end of bridge, toward the water, and go one short block to end (Constitution Road).

13. Turn left on Constitution Road and go 2/10 mile to the Charlestown Navy Yard on right. Here the *USS Constitution*, better known as *Old Ironsides*, is located. In addition to the ship, you can visit the Bunker Hill Pavilion, which recreates the Battle of Bunker Hill, the visitor center, and a Navy destroyer docked next door.

14. From *Old Ironsides*, backtrack 1/10 mile to your first right, opposite the Bunker Hill Pavilion.

15. Turn right and go underneath the highway to end (Chelsea Street).

16. Turn right at end and just ahead bear left on Chestnut Street, following the Freedom Trail signs to the Bunker Hill Monument. If the signs are missing, go up Chestnut Street 100 feet to crossroads (Adams Street), turn left to end (Winthrop Street), and right to monument. There are 294 steps to the top, but the view is fantastic, and it's free. At the base of the monument are exhibits.

17. Leaving the monument, walk down the stairs heading toward the city (Bunker Hill Museum opposite bottom of stairs). Turn right at bottom of stairs and go one block to crossroads (Monument Square on right, Pleasant Street on left).

18. Turn left at crossroads and go one block to the first crossroads (Warren Street), at bottom of hill.

19. Turn right on Warren Street and go 1/10 mile to Austin Street on left, at traffic light. Just before the intersection, notice the marvelous stone Victorian building on your right, built in 1875 as a Masonic Hall.

20. Turn left on Austin Street and go 1/2 mile to second traffic light, at end of long overpass. At the first traffic light you'll see the ultramodern, sterile campus of Bunker Hill Community College. If you turn right at the first light and go two blocks you'll come to the Phipps Street Burying Ground, with more than 100 gravestones from the 1600s. At the second light the ride goes straight, but if you turn left the Museum of Science is just ahead on your right.

21. Continue straight at light onto Commercial Avenue and get on the sidewalk on the left-hand side of the road, going alongside the Charles River. (If you cannot get down to the river, stay on Commercial Avenue to the Longfellow Bridge.) Go 6/10 mile to the Longfellow Bridge, which you'll take back into Boston. To get onto the bridge, cross the road just before it and go underneath the bridge with the traffic. Immediately beyond the bridge, bear right on the ramp (sign may say to Government Center, Boston).

22. Cross the bridge and go to West Cedar Street, which is your second right, at the far end of the rotary.

23. Turn right on West Cedar Street and go to your third left, Pinckney Street, at stop sign. The first block of West Cedar Street is one-way in the wrong direction, and so walk your bike. You are now on Beacon Hill.

24. Turn left on Pinckney Street and go 1 block to Louisburg (pronounced Lewisburg) Square on right. Walk your bike, because Pinckney Street is one-way in the wrong direction. You really don't want to pedal up that hill, anyway.

View of downtown Boston including Custom House.

25. Turn right on Louisburg Square and go 1 block to end. Continue to walk your bike because this street is also one-way. This delightful block, built between 1833 and 1837, is the heart of Brahmin Boston. Notice the statues at both ends of the green in the middle. Only residents of the Square have keys to the green.

26. Turn right at end (Mount Vernon Street) and go 2/10 mile to Brimmer Street, just before end.

27. Turn left on Brimmer Street and go 1/10 mile to end (Beacon Street).

28. Turn right on Beacon Street and go 1/10 mile to traffic light (Embankment Road on right).

29. Turn right at traffic light, and walk your bike onto the sidewalk. Immediately ahead is a footbridge crossing the highway. Walk your bike over the footbridge, and then over a smaller footbridge to the bike path along the Charles.

30. Follow the Charles River on your right 8/10 mile to Massachusetts Avenue, which crosses the river. Watch for pedestrians, joggers, and rollerskaters. Carry your bike up the stairs to Massachusetts Avenue. (There are fewer pedestrians on the path between the lagoon and the highway. Recross the small bridge over the lagoon if you prefer a smoother ride.)

31. Turn left at top of stairs on the sidewalk. Go 100 yards to an alley on your left immediately after the overpass.

32. Turn left into the alley, paralleling the highway on your left. Go 2/10 mile to second right.

33. Take your second right (Gloucester Street) and go three blocks to Commonwealth Avenue, which has a broad, grassy center island.

34. Turn left on Commonwealth Avenue, using the center island, and go 8/10 mile to end (Arlington Street). At most of the cross streets you'll have to walk your bike over curbs.

35. Cross Arlington Street and continue straight across the Public Garden to Charles Street, at the far end. Walk your bike through the Garden. Riding a bike here is prohibited and police enforce this regulation. Midway through the Garden you'll cross the little pond with the Swan Boats.

36. Cross Charles Street into Boston Common. Here you can ride if pedestrian traffic permits, which it probably won't. Go 3/10

12

Swan Boat in the Public Garden, Boston.

mile to end, at the junction of Park Street and Tremont Street. You'll pass a bandstand on your right. If you wish you can chop off a few hundred feet by bearing right before the end, coming into Tremont Street at the Boston Visitor Information Center.

37. Turn right on Tremont Street and go 3/10 mile to traffic light at end of Common (Boylston Street). Tremont Street is very busy, and so use the sidewalk unless there's no traffic.

38. Turn left on Boylston Street and go 4/10 mile to end (Atlantic Avenue). After one block you'll cross Washington Street onto Essex Street. This is the Combat Zone, with its dense cluster of topless bars, adult bookstores, and pornographic movie theaters. It's perfectly safe in the daytime so long as you stay outdoors. Just beyond on the right is Chinatown. The heart of Chinatown is one block to your right, on Beach Street. Just before the end is a wide, diagonal crossroads; go straight here.

39. Turn left on Atlantic Avenue and go one block to traffic light. On your right is South Station, one of the two main train stations for Boston.

40. Turn right at light and go one block to Dorchester Avenue, at traffic light just before the bridge.

41. Turn left on Dorchester Avenue and go one block to end.

42. Turn right at end and cross bridge. On the far side of the bridge the short ride turns left and the long ride goes straight. Midway across the bridge on the left is a replica of one of the Boston Tea Party ships. As soon as you cross the bridge, you'll see a giant white milk bottle on the left containing an ice cream stand. It was a landmark in Taunton for many years before being moved to Boston in 1977. Next to the milk bottle, in the same building as McDonald's, are the Computer Museum and the Children's Museum.

43. Continue straight at far end of bridge 1/10 mile to A Street, your first right.

44. Turn right on A Street and go 6/10 mile to West Third Street, immediately after traffic light. • *CAUTION*: A Street is bumpy.

45. Turn left on West Third Street and go 6/10 mile to end (Dorchester Street).

46. Turn left at end and then immediately turn right on G Street, up steep hill. Follow G Street 4/10 mile to end, at water. The first block of G Street is one-way in the wrong direction, and so you'll have to walk up that hill anyway. At the top of the hill on your right, behind South Boston High School, is the Dorchester Heights Monument, a graceful white tower in a park. Unfortunately it's locked. The street that goes around the monument, Thomas Park, is lined with graceful houses on the south side. • *CAUTION*: The end of G Street is at the bottom of a very steep hill.

47. Turn left at end of G Street, going alongside Dorchester Bay on your right. Go 1.1 miles to a pedestrian walkway on your right leading out onto a breakwater with the sea on both sides. The breakwater starts where the main road curves sharply left.

48. Follow the breakwater 1 mile to end, at parking lot just past Fort Independence.

49. Turn right at end, going clockwise around the fort with the ocean on your left. Go 6/10 mile back to parking lot.

50. Turn left at parking lot and go 4/10 mile to Shore Parkway, your first right. It is a small road.

51. Turn right on Shore Parkway and go 2/10 mile to fork, at stop sign (East First Street bears right).

52. Bear right at stop sign on East First Street and go 1/2 mile to traffic light (Summer Street). • *CAUTION*: Diagonal railroad tracks at beginning.

53. Turn right on Summer Street and go 8/10 mile to your second right, Viaduct Street. It is an overpass with the World Trade Center (formerly the Commonwealth Pier) at the far end.

54. Turn right across overpass and go 2/10 mile to Ramp Street, which turns right and goes down to ground level.

55. Turn right on Ramp Street and go 1/10 mile to your first left, at bottom of ramp.

56. Turn left at bottom of ramp and go one block to end (Northern Avenue). In front of you is the Fish Pier, the longest and finest in architecture of all the Boston Harbor piers. An unbroken row of fish companies line both sides of the pier. From the end is a splendid view of the harbor. On the pier is the No-Name Restaurant, a great place to eat fresh fish at reasonable prices.

57. Turn left on Northern Avenue (right if you're coming off the Fish Pier), and go back to starting point. You'll pass Anthony's Pier Four, one of the most famous restaurants in Boston. It's expensive but totally worth it.

Directions for the ride: 10 miles

1. Follow directions for the long ride through number 42.

2. Turn left immediately after the bridge between the milk bottle and McDonald's, going along Fort Point Channel on left. Go 2/10 mile to end (Northern Avenue).

3. Turn right on Northern Avenue back to start.

2. Winthrop-Revere

Number of miles: 9 (19 with Revere extension)
Terrain: Flat. The long ride has one tough climb to Orient
    Heights, which can be omitted.
Food: Numerous grocery stores and snack bars.
Start: Osco Drug, opposite 1159 Saratoga Street (Route 145) in
    East Boston, just west of the Winthrop line. From the
    Sumner-Callahan Tunnel, take expressway to the Route 145
    exit. Bear right after 1 mile on Saratoga Street (still Route
    145) and go 1/2 mile to drug store on left. If you're coming
    from the north on Route 1, exit west onto Route 16 (Revere
    Beach Parkway). Make a U-turn at first opportunity and go
    underneath Route 1. After 1.1 miles, bear right on Route 145
    (still Revere Beach Parkway). Go 7/10 mile to where the
    main road curves left and a smaller road, Winthrop Avenue,
    goes straight. Go straight on Winthrop Avenue 2/10 mile to
    traffic light (Bennington Street). Turn right on Bennington
    Street and go 1 mile to Saratoga Street, at traffic light. Turn
    left and go 1/2 mile to drug store on left.

The coastline immediately northeast of Boston is surprisingly
scenic and pleasant for biking. The short ride loops around Winthrop, a pleasant middle-class community along a peninsula just
north of Logan Airport that narrows to a point at its southern end.
As you bike around the rim of the peninsula on quiet streets, you'll
first head along the boat-filled harbor, passing the handsome old
Cottage Park and Winthrop Yacht Clubs, with the Boston skyline
always visible across the water. The jets taking off and landing over
the harbor present a dramatic sight. At the southern tip is Deer
Island (now part of the mainland), which contains the Suffolk
County House of Correction and is not open to visitors. From here
you'll enjoy a run along the ocean side of the peninsula and then
turn inland for a short distance back to the starting point.
    The long ride continues several miles north along the coast of
Revere, a congested and rather dreary suburb except for its four-

mile shorefront. The first mile is delightful as you pass between the ocean on your right and a steep hill on your left. Then the character of the shore changes as you pedal along Revere Beach, which is in the process of changing from a sleazy strip of pizza joints and pinball parlors to a gold coast of futuristic, high-rise condominiums. Beyond Revere Beach is Point of Pines, an attractive residential area at the beach's northern tip. You'll loop around the point and then head back along Revere Beach—there's no other road except suicidal Route 1A. At the end of the ride you'll cross back into East Boston and ascend Orient Heights, a 150-foot-high drumlin crowned by the Madonna Queen National Shrine, which provides an outstanding view of Boston and the waterways surrounding it. The Shrine, built in 1978, consists of a large square tower containing several chapels and an observation platform. The tower stands at the end of a brick terrace built into the steep hillside. The tower is open only on Sundays, but the view from the terrace, open all the time, is just as spectacular. Leaving the shrine, you'll enjoy the fast run back down the hill. From here it's less than a mile back to the start.

It's best not to do this ride on a beach day because of heavy traffic. Revere Beach has both parallel parking—which means car doors opening in front of you—and head-in parking, which means cars backing up without drivers' noticing you. On a cold, windy day the beach is actually pleasant.

One further note: The directions for the Winthrop section are complicated, with many turns only a block or two apart. I routed the ride this way to maximize views of the waterfront and to stay off the busy roads.

Directions for the ride: 19 miles

1. Turn left out of parking lot and go 4/10 mile to traffic light just after you cross the bridge into Winthrop (Pleasant Street, Route 145 turns right).

2. Turn right at light and go 4/10 mile to your first right, Court Road.

3. Turn right on Court Road and go 1/2 mile to fork where Circuit Road bears left.

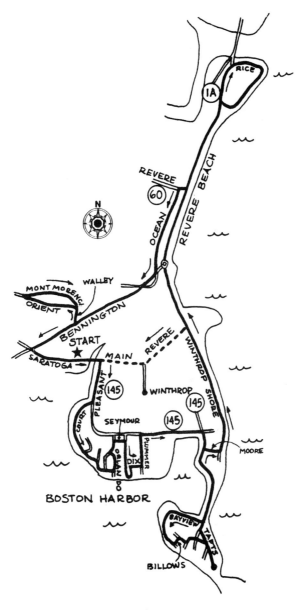

4. Bear slightly right at fork (still Court Road), following the harbor. Go 3/10 mile to end (Cottage Park Road).

5. Turn right on Cottage Park Road, which immediately curves left onto Bartlett Parkway. Go 1/10 mile to end (Orlando Avenue). The Cottage Park Yacht Club is on your right.

6. Turn left on Orlando Avenue and go 1/10 mile to end (Bartlett Road).

7. Turn right on Bartlett Road and go 100 yards to your first right, Seymour Street, which is one-way in the wrong direction.

8. Turn right and walk your bike one short block to end.

9. Turn right at end and go 2/10 mile to the water. Here the road makes a small counterclockwise loop.

10. Turn right at end of loop and go one short block to end (Plummer Avenue). You were just on Dix Street.

11. Turn left on Plummer Avenue and go 2/10 mile to cross-roads and stop sign (Route 145).

12. Turn right on Route 145 and go 7/10 mile to a busy inter-section where Route 145 turns left.

13. Turn right at this intersection and go 9/10 mile to Bay-view Avenue, your first right. It is just after house number 961.

14. Turn right on Bayview Avenue and go 1/2 mile to Billows Street on left at stop sign (Dead End and Private Way if you go straight).

15. Turn left on Billows Street and go one short block to end (Triton Avenue).

16. Turn right on Triton Avenue and go one short block to end.

17. Turn left at end and go 100 yards to crossroads.

18. Go straight at crossroads onto Elliott Street, bearing slightly right as you go through the intersection. (Don't turn 90 degrees right on Pebble Avenue.) Go 100 yards to end, at stop sign.

19. Bear right at stop sign on Tafts Avenue (don't turn sharp right on Otis Street). Go 2/10 mile to the gate of the Deer Island House of Correction.

20. Make a U-turn at the gate and go 3/10 mile to end (merge right at stop sign).

21. Bear right at stop sign and go 8/10 mile to Moore Street on right. It's just before blinking light, and just after house number 562.

22. Turn right on Moore Street and go 1/10 mile to end, at ocean.

23. Turn left at end along the shore and go 1.3 miles to a busy street that turns sharp left at blinking light, immediately after a little park on right. Here the short ride turns sharply left and the long ride goes straight.

24. Continue straight 1.3 miles to rotary.

25. Continue straight at rotary, following the ocean. Go 3.1 miles to where Route 1A bears left over a bridge across the channel to Lynn. • *CAUTION:* Heavy traffic along Revere Beach. Watch for cars backing up and car doors opening into your path.

26. Go straight where Route 1A bears left, following the water on your left. This is Rice Avenue. Go 9/10 mile to end.

27. Turn left at end and go 1.6 miles, back along Revere Beach, to a forced right turn (one-way in the wrong direction if you go straight).

28. Turn right and then immediately left (sign may say to Malden, Medford). Go 1.2 miles to second traffic light.

29. Bear right at light (sign may say to Beachmont, Sumner Tunnel). This is Bennington Street. Go 1.1 miles to Walley Street, which turns sharply right immediately after you go over a small railroad bridge. You'll pass Suffolk Downs on your right. Here the ride turns right to go to Orient Heights. If you want to omit the Heights, go straight 4/10 mile to traffic light (Saratoga Street), turn sharp left at light, and go 1/2 mile to drug store on left.

30. Turn sharp right on Walley Street and go 1/10 mile to fork where Orient Avenue bears left uphill.

31. Bear left on Orient Avenue and go 7/10 mile to Montmorenci Avenue, which turns sharply right. At the top of the hill is the Madonna Queen Shrine.

32. Turn sharp right on Montmorenci Avenue and go 8/10 mile to bottom of hill, where you'll merge to the right back onto Bennington Street.

33. Bear right on Bennington Street and go 4/10 mile to traffic light (Saratoga Street).

34. Turn sharply left on Saratoga Street. • *CAUTION:* Bad intersection—it's safest to walk your bike. Go 1/2 mile to Osco Drug on left.

Directions for the ride: 9 miles

    1. Follow directions for the long ride through number 23.

    2. Turn sharply left at this intersection. • *CAUTION:* Bad intersection—walk your bike. Go 1/2 mile to fork, at traffic light.

    3. Bear right at fork and go 9/10 mile to drug store on right.

3. The Close Northern Suburbs: Somerville–Cambridge–Medford–Malden–Everett–Chelsea

Number of miles: 19 (10 omitting Middlesex Fells Reservation, 24 with Malden–Everett–Chelsea extension)

Terrain: The 10-mile ride is flat, with two moderate hills. The 19-mile ride has an additional short, steep hill and a long, gradual one. The 24-mile ride has two additional short, steep climbs up drumlins.

Food: Numerous grocery stores and restaurants.

Start: Holiday Inn, Washington Street in Somerville, 3/10 mile east of McGrath Highway (Route 28).

How to get there: From the south, head north out of downtown Boston on Route 93 and go almost 2 miles to the Somerville-Everett exit. Bear left at bottom of ramp under the highway and immediately turn left. Go 9/10 mile, paralleling the highway on your left and following signs to Sullivan Square, until you come to a traffic light (Cambridge Street on right). Turn right on Cambridge Street and go 4/10 mile to Inn on left.

From the west, take the Massachusetts Turnpike all the way into downtown Boston and head north on Route 93. Follow directions above.

From the northeast, head south on Route 1, cross the Tobin Bridge, and bear right on Route 93 North. Follow directions above.

From the northwest, head south toward Boston on Route 93 and take the Sullivan Square-Charlestown exit. Go straight until you come to a traffic light (Cambridge Street on right). Turn right on Cambridge Street and go 4/10 mile to Inn on left.

This ride takes you exploring among the cluster of cities immediately north of Boston that are socially and geographically an extension of Boston itself. This is an urban ride rather than a suburban one, complete with heavy traffic and congested streets—in fact, Cambridge and Somerville have higher population densities than

Boston. The ride is a fascinating one, however, covering a wide variety of landscape ranging from the grace and elegance of Harvard Yard, the wooded hills and lakes of the Middlesex Fells Reservation, the humpbacked drumlins of Everett and Chelsea with dramatic views of the Boston skyline from their summits, to the otherworldly wasteland of storage tanks and refineries along the Mystic River in Everett.

You'll start from Somerville, a densely packed city of old wooden multifamily houses marching up a row of hillsides (which you won't climb). You'll quickly cross into Cambridge, a city of contrasts where dreary rows of tenements, spacious nineteenth-century homes, college campuses, and gleaming high-technology, boldly architectured industrial buildings fill the land close to each other. You'll go through Harvard University, the oldest in the country, passing through Harvard Yard, the elegant cluster of elm-shaded and ivy-covered buildings at its heart. Some of the buildings go back to the 1700s, others were designed by Charles Bulfinch and H. H. Richardson, and the broad-stepped Widener Library is almost intimidating in its grandeur. Across from the Yard is Memorial Hall, one of the finest Victorian buildings in the state, a soaring brick churchlike edifice built in 1871 as a Civil War memorial. Bordering the Yard is Harvard Square, the throbbing, traffic-clogged commercial center for the University community and the thousands of street people, hangers-on, weekend hippies, and tourists who gravitate to it.

From Harvard you'll cross back into Somerville and bike through dense middle-class neighborhoods to Tufts University, which boasts another impressive campus of dignified brick ivy-covered buildings just over the Medford line. From here it's a short trip along a parkway lined with fine homes to the Middlesex Fells Reservation, an extensive area of woods and lakes that forms a natural division between the urban areas to the south and the more spread-out suburbs to the north. The loop through the Reservation is a refreshing green interlude in this otherwise urban tour. You'll pass an observation tower with a splendid view of Boston, a zoo, and delightful Spot Pond.

From the Reservation you'll head into the compact center of Medford, another congested community indistinguishable from

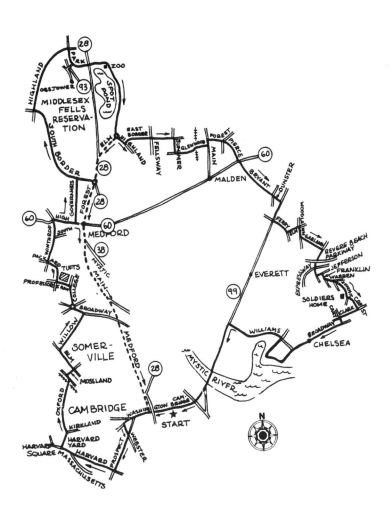

Somerville. You'll pass the endless fortress of Medford High School, a building intimidating enough to drive any high school kid to truancy, complete with the names of the major figures of Western civilization engraved at the top of its walls—even Raphael, whom I never heard of until college. From here it's a straight run back through Somerville to the starting point.

The long ride loops around the Middlesex Fells Reservation and then heads east through Malden and Everett, two more cities just like Somerville. At the Chelsea line you'll climb onto a drumlin with a dramatic view of Boston; then just ahead you'll top another drumlin crowned by the old brick Soldiers Home. From here you'll descend into downtown Chelsea, a city that for years was a decaying slum but is now enjoying a renaissance. The handsome brick Victorian business blocks downtown have had facelifts. The former Chelsea Naval Hospital, on a hilltop with a spectacular view of the Mystic River and the skyscrapers of Boston on the far side, is being transformed into a complex of apartments, stores, and restaurants. From Chelsea, the last lap brings you through a grimly fascinating landscape of oil and gas storage tanks, refineries, and old industrial buildings.

Directions for the ride: 24 miles

1. Turn left out of parking lot and immediately left on Washington Street. After 3/10 mile you'll go underneath the McGrath Highway. Continue 3/10 mile to traffic light at end of Union Square. Stay on the main road through the square. At the beginning of the square, the main road jogs 90 degrees left and then right.

Just off the square on your right is Prospect Hill Tower, which offers a fine view of Boston from its base (the tower itself is locked). Stone Avenue, on your right in the center of the square, leads 2/10 mile to the tower.

2. Turn left at traffic light on Webster Avenue (unmarked). Go 2/10 mile to Prospect Street, which bears right at traffic light. It's your second right.

3. Bear right on Prospect Street and go 7/10 mile to your fourth traffic light (Harvard Street).

4. Turn right on Harvard Street and go 7/10 mile to end (merge head-on into Massachusetts Avenue).

5. Go straight on Massachusetts Avenue. On your right is Harvard Yard, with Harvard Square just ahead. • *CAUTION:* If you explore the Square, do not under any circumstances leave your bike unattended. If your bike isn't stolen, everything that can possibly be removed from it probably will be.

6. Walk your bike into Harvard Yard. Go through the McKean Gate, which is opposite 1320 and 1324 Massachusetts Avenue, just before Harvard Square. Go clear through the yard to the far end. An additional assortment of elegant buildings, including the Widener Library, is in the next quadrangle to your right. Immediately after you leave the Yard, pass between the Science Center on your left and Memorial Hall, a magnificent red-brick churchlike building, on your right. You'll immediately come to a street with a 90-degree bend. At the bend, Oxford Street bears left and Kirkland Street bears right.

7. Bear left on Oxford Street and go 7/10 mile to end (Somerville Avenue), immediately after crossing railroad bridge.

8. Bear left on Somerville Avenue and immediately turn right on Mossland Street. Go one block to traffic light (Elm Street). Mossland Street is one-way in the wrong direction, and so walk your bike.

9. Turn left at light and go 3/10 mile to Willow Avenue, your fifth right.

10. Turn right on Willow Avenue and go 6/10 mile to end (Broadway).

11. Turn left on Broadway and go 2/10 mile to rotary.

12. Bear right at rotary, passing the Tufts University athletic fields on your left. Go 3/10 mile to Professors Row on left, at traffic island at top of hill. A sign in the island may say Tufts University.

13. Turn left on Professors Row and go 2/10 mile to crossroads and stop sign (Packard Avenue). Tufts University is on your right. • *CAUTION:* Professors Row is bumpy.

14. Turn right on Packard Avenue and go 3/10 mile to crossroads and stop sign (Winthrop Street).

15. Turn right at crossroads. After 1/2 mile South Street bears right, but bear left, crossing the Mystic River. Continue 2/10 mile to Route 60 (High Street), at top of hill.

16. Turn right on Route 60 and go 3/10 mile to Governors

Avenue, a divided parkway, on left. This is downtown Medford. Here the 10-mile ride goes straight and the 19- and 24-mile rides turn left.

17. Turn left on Governors Avenue and go 9/10 mile to end. You'll go up a short, sharp hill.

18. Turn left at end and go 1.8 miles to traffic light (Highland Avenue), passing through and alongside the Middlesex Fells Reservation.

19. Turn right at light and go 1.1 miles to stop sign at bottom of hill.

20. Bear right at stop sign and go 9/10 mile to traffic light (Park Street).

21. Turn right at light and go 7/10 mile to another light (Route 28). Midway along this stretch, an observation tower just off the road offers a fine view of the surrounding area and the Boston skyline, 8 miles to the south. To get to the tower, turn right after 4/10 mile, going underneath Route 93. Turn left immediately after the underpass. From the end follow the dirt road 100 yards and bear left up steep hill on a rutted foot trail for 2/10 mile to tower.

22. Cross Route 28 and go 2.2 miles to rotary. This is a delightful run along Spot Pond. You'll pass the Metropolitan District Commission Zoo on your right. At the rotary the 19-mile ride bears right and the 24-mile ride bears left.

23. Bear left at rotary on Highland Avenue and go 2/10 mile to East Border Road, your first left.

24. Turn left on East Border Road and go 1/2 mile to traffic light.

25. Go straight at light (do not bear right downhill). Go 3/10 mile to crossroads and stop sign (Summer Street).

26. Turn right on Summer Street and go 2/10 mile to end, at stop sign at bottom of hill (Glenwood Street).

27. Turn left on Glenwood Street and go 2/10 mile to traffic light.

28. Go straight at light over railroad bridge for 2/10 mile to end (Main Street).

29. Turn left on Main Street and immediately right on Forest Street. Go 3/10 mile to fork (Pierce Street bears slightly right at traffic island).

30. Bear slightly right on Pierce Street (don't turn 90 degrees

28

right uphill on Mount Vernon Street). Go 4/10 mile to end.

31. Jog left at end and immediate right on Bryant Street. Go 1 mile to the fourth traffic light, where Bryant Street becomes Dunster Road. You'll pass an unusual concrete synagogue that looks like a fortress on your left. Continue straight on Dunster Road (don't bear right) for one block to end.

32. Turn right at end and go 3/10 mile to traffic light (Ferry Street). Just before the light, notice the fine old red-brick library on your left.

33. Turn left on Ferry Street. • *CAUTION:* Bad intersection. Go 2/10 mile to traffic light (Elm Street), immediately after park.

34. Turn left on Elm Street and go 1/10 mile to Woodlawn Street, your first right.

35. Turn right on Woodlawn Street and go 2/10 mile to Garland Street, your third left, which bears up a steep hill.

36. Bear left on Garland Street and go 6/10 mile to end. • *CAUTION:* The end comes up suddenly at bottom of hill. From the top of the hill there's a great view of the Boston skyline. For an even better view, walk up to the roof of the garage across from Whidden Hospital.

37. Turn right at end. After 3 blocks bear left at little park, staying on the main road. Continue 1/10 mile to traffic light (Revere Beach Parkway, a six-lane highway).

38. Cross Revere Beach Parkway and immediately go over the Northeast Expressway. Immediately after the expressway bear left, then take your first left on Jefferson Avenue (sign may say to Soldiers Home), immediately turn right on Franklin Avenue, and then immediately bear left. Go 100 yards to a three-way fork.

39. Take the middle road 1/4 mile to another fork where one road (Summit Avenue) goes straight downhill, and the other road bears right uphill. There is a good view of the Boston skyline from the little park on your right. The Soldiers' Home is on top of the hill.

40. Bear right uphill and immediately curve left, passing between hospital buildings on both sides of street. Go 1/4 mile to end (Clark Avenue).

41. Turn right on Clark Avenue and go 3/10 mile to Cary Avenue, at stop sign and blinking light. It's one-way in the wrong direction if you go straight.

42. Turn left on Cary Avenue and go one short block to Broadway.

43. Turn right on Broadway and go 1.1 mile to end, at waterfront, in front of the Chelsea Yacht Club. You'll go through downtown Chelsea. The block in front of City Hall is one-way in the wrong direction, and so either walk your bike or detour to the right, passing City Hall on your left. • *CAUTION:* The last 1/4 mile is bumpy.

44. Turn right at end, following the water on your left, and go 8/10 mile to crossroads and stop sign (Williams Street). On your right are the Admiral's Hill Condominiums, one of the few condominium developments that are genuinely attractive. The area was formerly the Chelsea Naval Hospital. On your left is a waterfront park.

45. Turn left at crossroads and go 1.1 miles to end (Route 99). Turn left on Route 99 and go 8/10 mile to fork immediately after crossing the Mystic River.

46. Go straight at fork (don't bear left). Go 2/10 mile to traffic light just after you go underneath Route 93.

47. Bear slightly right at traffic light onto Cambridge Street and go 4/10 mile to Holiday Inn on left.

Directions for the ride: 19 miles

1. Follow directions for the 24-mile ride through number 22.

2. Bear right at rotary on Elm Street and go 6/10 mile to end (Route 28). Just off the road on the right is Wright's Pond, which has a beach. The entrance is 3/10 mile from the rotary, midway down sharp hill.

3. Turn left on Route 28 and go 1/2 mile to rotary.

4. Go one-third of the way around the rotary onto Forest Street. If you come to Route 28 South, you've gone one road too far. Follow Forest Street 8/10 mile to traffic light in center of Medford.

5. Go straight at light, crossing the Mystic River, for 2/10 mile to fork where Route 38 bears left.

6. Go straight at fork (do not bear left on Route 38), and go 9/10 mile to another fork with a little park in the middle.

7. Once again, go straight at fork (don't bear left). After 3/10 mile you'll cross Broadway, a wide, busy street, diagonally. Continue straight on Medford Street 1.1 miles until you merge head-on into a divided highway.

8. Go straight onto the highway and then immediately bear right onto an exit ramp, following the sign that says Washington Street, Union Square. At the bottom of the ramp there's a traffic light (Washington Street).

9. Turn left on Washington Street and go 3/10 mile to Holiday Inn on right.

Directions for the ride: 10 miles

1. Follow directions for the 24-mile ride through number 16.

2. Continue straight 1 block to traffic light.

3. Turn right at light and immediately cross the Mystic River. Continue 2/10 mile to fork where Route 38 bears left.

4. Follow directions for the 19-mile ride from number 6 to the end.

4. Nahant

Number of miles: 7
Terrain: Rolling, with several short, steep hills.
Food: Grocery and snack bar near center of town.
Start: Lynn Beach parking lot, on the east side of the causeway from Lynn to Nahant. On beach days get here early; the huge lot fills up by 10 o'clock. Do not park in Nahant itself; you'll get a ticket. If you wish you can park in Lynn just north of the rotary at the beginning of the causeway and bike along the beach on the bike path. This adds 3 miles to the ride. On beach days the bike path will be clogged with pedestrians.

This is a short ride that makes up in coastal scenery for what it lacks in distance. It's easy to spend half a day biking those seven miles if you take time to poke around the rocky ledges and remains of old forts along the shore, especially at the eastern tip of the island.

Nahant is an island two miles off the coast of Lynn and Revere, about two miles long and a half mile wide, connected to Lynn by a causeway. It contains some of the most pleasant and scenic bicycling close to Boston. Nahant is a wealthy community with fine homes and a number of mansions lining its rocky, convoluted coastline. For most of the ride you will be within sight of the ocean, and as you head along the southern shore you'll see the Boston skyline, ten miles away, rising up across the water. Traffic on Nahant is refreshingly light because it is an island, has a small population (only 4,000), and lacks public parking.

For a longer ride, the Nahant ride can easily be added to the Lynn-Swampscott-Marblehead ride, for a total of 29 miles, or the Saugus-Lynnfield-Lynn ride, for a total of 24 or 31 miles.

Directions for the ride

1. From the Nahant end of the parking lot, head along the main road, following the ocean on your right. Go 1/2 mile to fork at the Coast Guard station on your left.

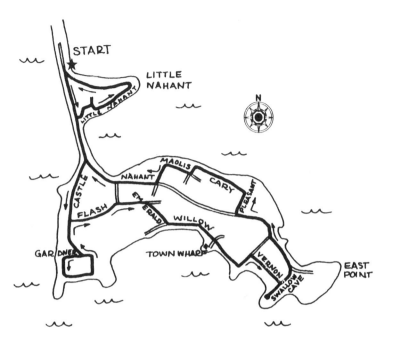

2. Bear right at fork on Castle Road and go 7/10 mile to Gardner Road, which turns sharp right. The main road curves left at the intersection. You will now do a small counterclockwise loop and return to this point after 6/10 mile.

3. Turn sharp right on Gardner Road and go 6/10 mile to this same intersection, making four 90-degree left turns. At the third turn is Fort Buckman, a park on a rocky outcropping with fine ocean views. It used to be a military installation. When you leave the park, you'll go up a short, steep hill. When you complete the loop, notice the square stone tower built into a house at the top of the hill.

4. When you complete the loop, turn right at crossroads and go 1/4 mile to Flash Road on right, just past the school.

5. Turn right on Flash Road and go 3/10 mile to fork.

6. Bear right at fork and go 2/10 mile to Emerald Road, which bears right.

7. Bear right on Emerald Road and go 2/10 mile to end (merge left into Willow Road at ocean).

8. Bear left on Willow Road, following the ocean on your right. After 4/10 mile you'll cross Wharf Street, which goes to the town wharf. Continue 3/10 mile to Vernon Street on right.

9. Turn right on Vernon Street and go 2/10 mile to end (Swallow Cave Road).

10. Turn right on Swallow Cave Road and go 1/10 mile to end, in front of a mansion. A path on the left side of the gate leads 100 yards to a small cave hollowed out by the sea. At high tide the ocean spills into the cave.

11. Head back on Swalllow Cave Road. After 2/10 mile you'll pass the Northeastern University Marine Science Institute on your right. This area encompasses East Point, the magnificent rockbound far tip of Nahant. Fascinating old bunkers are built into the rocky ledges. A road leads to the top of the bunkers, providing superb views.

12. From the Marine Science Institute, continue 1/2 mile to Pleasant Street on right. It passes between the library and town hall.

13. Turn right on Pleasant Street and go 1/10 mile to Cary Street, your second left.

14. Turn left on Cary Street and go 4/10 mile to Maolis Road at crossroads. It's just after you turn 90 degrees inland.

15. Turn right at crossroads onto a narrow lane. After 1/10 mile the road turns 90 degrees left (dead end if you go straight). Turn left and go 2/10 mile to crossroads and stop sign.

16. Turn right at crossroads and go 1.1 miles to Little Nahant Road on right (it goes up a steep hill). It's the first right after the Coast Guard station. You will now go around Little Nahant, a small island connected to the causeway just north of Nahant itself.

17. Go 2/10 mile to end of Little Nahant Road, at top of steep hill.

18. Turn right at end and immediately curve sharply to the left, staying on the main road. Go 7/10 mile to end. The entrance to the beach parking lot is on your right when you come to the end.

5. The Saugus Ironworks Ride: Stoneham–Wakefield–Saugus–Melrose

Number of miles: 18 (12 with shortcut omitting Saugus)
Terrain: Gently rolling, with several short, sharp hills.
Food: Groceries and restaurants in the towns.
Start: Redstone Shopping Center, Route 28 in Stoneham, 1/2
mile south of Route 128.

On this ride you explore four pleasant middle-class communities about ten miles directly north of Boston. The region is far enough from the city to be suburban rather than urban, with stretches of greenery, gracious residential neighborhoods, and roads that are not clogged with traffic. All four towns have attractive, well-defined centers with handsome churches, city halls, and other public buildings. The historical highlight of the ride is the Saugus Ironworks, one of the earliest industrial enterprises in America, dating from around 1650.

The ride starts near the Stoneham-Wakefield line and immediately heads into Wakefield, the most affluent of the four communities and one of the most visually pleasing suburbs inside the Route 128 semicircle. The center of town, a New England classic, could almost be from a rural town twenty miles farther from Boston. The large triangular green, at the southern end of Lake Quannapowitt, is framed by stately Colonial-style homes, a classic white church, and a handsome stone one. Across from the green lies a beautifully landscaped park stretching along the lakeshore, complete with a graceful old bandstand in the middle.

From Wakefield you'll head into Saugus, where the marvelous Victorian town hall will greet you as you pull into the center of town. Just outside of town is the Saugus Ironworks, a splendid example of historical reconstruction that is part of the National Park system. With meticulous attention to detail, the furnace, forge, massive water wheels, and the dam across the Saugus River have been rebuilt into working condition. And to top all this off, it's free.

From Saugus you'll head to the pleasant residential community of Melrose, where a cluster of fine old buildings—the town hall, two handsome churches with a school between them, and the graceful stone Soldiers and Sailors Memorial Hall, used as an auditorium, grace the main street. Adjoining the downtown area is delightful Ell Pond, with a park spreading along its northern shore. From here, go a short way across the Stoneham town line, where you'll go through a portion of the Middlesex Fells Reservation, a large expanse of wooded hills and ponds. You'll go along Spot Pond, which is completely surrounded by forest except for a zoo. From here you head into the center of town, with a compact business block and two distinctive white churches.

Directions for the ride: 18 miles

1. Turn left (north) out of parking lot onto Route 28 and go 3/10 mile to North Street, which bears right at traffic light.

2. Bear right on North Street and go 1.5 miles to Common Street, which bears right at the Wakefield town green, opposite the fine stone church. As you're coming down the hill into town, a little red schoolhouse is on the left, built in 1847.

3. Bear right on Common Street. Just ahead on the right is the magnificent First Baptist Church. Continue 1 mile to Green Street, which bears left uphill. Just before Green Street on the left is J. J. Rounds Park, a rocky outcropping providing a fine view of Crystal Lake. A lookout tower on the top has been torn down, another victim of vandalism and neglect.

4. Bear left on Green Street and go 1/2 mile to Oak Avenue on left. If you come to a fork you've gone one block too far.

5. Turn left on Oak Avenue and go 9/10 mile to end (Old Nahant Road).

6. Turn right on Old Nahant Road and go 1/4 mile to end.

7. Turn right at end and go 1.3 miles to the second of two traffic lights in quick succession. Here the short ride turns right and the long ride goes straight.

8. Continue straight. After 8/10 mile you'll cross Route 1 on an overpass • *CAUTION:* Watch for traffic bearing right onto Route 1. Continue 8/10 mile to a rotary with a monument in the center of

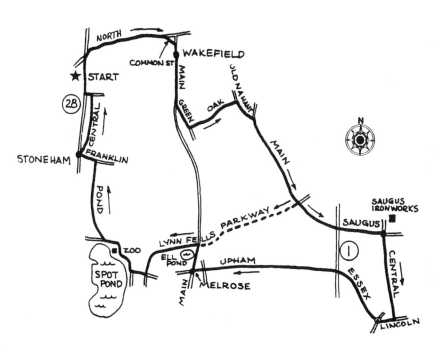

Saugus. The Victorian town hall is on the far side of the intersection.

9. Turn left at rotary and go 2/10 mile to the Saugus Ironworks on right.

10. Leaving the Ironworks, backtrack to the rotary in the center of town. Continue straight on Central Street 1.1 miles to end
(Lincoln Avenue). Turn right on Lincoln Avenue and go 1/4 mile to
another rotary.

11. Bear slightly right (almost straight) at rotary onto Essex
Street. After 1 mile you'll go across Route 1 on another overpass.
Once again, watch for traffic bearing right onto Route 1. Continue
2.1 miles to traffic light (Lebanon Street).

12. Go straight at light 2/10 mile to another traffic light (Main
Street). This is the center of Melrose. Notice the fine stone church
at the intersection.

13. Turn right on Main Street and go 4/10 mile to fork where
Green Street bears right, opposite Ell Pond on left.

14. Continue straight ahead on Main Street. Just ahead is a
traffic light.

15. Turn left at traffic light and go 1.3 miles to the third traffic
light, where a sign may point right to MDC Zoo and Route 28.

16. Turn right at light and go 3/10 mile to end, at top of hill.

17. Turn right at end, going along Spot Pond on your left.
After 4/10 mile the zoo will be on the left. Continue 2/10 mile to
Pond Street, which bears right.

18. Bear right on Pond Street and go 1 mile to end.

19. Turn left at end and go 3/10 mile to end, in the center of
Stoneham.

20. Turn 90 degrees right at end, passing fire station on right.
(Don't bear right on Route 28, a wide, busy road.) Go 9/10 mile to
end, passing through three traffic lights. This road runs parallel to
Route 28, 1 block east of it.

21. Turn left at end and go 1 block to end (Route 28).

22. Turn right on Route 28 and go 1/4 mile to shopping center on left.

Directions for the ride: 12 miles

1. Follow directions for the long ride through number 7.

Saugus Iron Works.

2. Turn right at second light and go 1.5 miles to another light (Green Street). Continue straight 1 block to a second traffic light (Main Street).

3. Cross Main Street and go 1.3 miles to third traffic light, where a sign may point right to MDC Zoo and Route 28.

4. Follow directions for the long ride from number 16 to the end.

6. Saugus–Lynnfield–Lynn

Number of miles: 15 (22 with Lynn loop)
Terrain: Flat, with one short hill.
Food: Numerous grocery stores and restaurants.
Start: Saugus Plaza, junction of Routes 1 and 129 in Saugus. If
you're heading north on Route 1, look for the Walnut Street
exit. Just ahead, as soon as you go under the bridge, take the
Route 129 West exit (a sign says to Wakefield). If you're
heading south on Route 1, you can enter the plaza directly
from the highway just beyond the Route 129 West exit.

This is a tour of pleasant residential areas north of Boston, going
by several delightful ponds, the elegant town center of Lynnfield,
the large, wooded Lynn Woods Reservation, and an attractive
stretch of coastline. The landscape is suburban but pleasant for
biking. The Saugus Ironworks, a restoration of a seventeenth-cen-
tury industrial enterprise and a National Historic Site, is a mile off
the route.

Starting in Saugus, you'll head north past Hawkes Pond and
Pillings Pond to the classic town center of Lynnfield, the most affluent of the three communities on the ride. The large, triangular
green is framed by a stately white church, and on the green itself
stands a meetinghouse built in 1714. Just out of town you'll again
go along Pillings Pond, this time on the opposite shore. From here
you'll head south into Lynn, passing the entrance to the massive
Lynn Woods Reservation, 2,000 acres of wooded hills and ponds
laced with miles of dirt paths. A half mile into the park, a graceful
stone observation tower stands on top of 285-foot Burrill Hill, providing a great view of the Boston skyline and surrounding area.

Lynn is primarily a congested, drab old industrial city with
some pleasant surprises. The half-mile-long common is beautiful,
lined on both sides with several graceful churches, some classic
brick schools, the old fortresslike armory, and the impressive public
library. A mile away is Lynn's best feature, the delightful span of
coastline along Lynn Shore Drive, with gracious older apartment
buildings on one side of the street and a well-maintained and land-

scaped shorefront park on the other. At the Swampscott line you'll head inland through attractive middle-class residential neighborhoods. The return to Saugus includes pleasant runs along Breeds Pond and Birch Pond, both bounded primarily by the Lynn Woods and undeveloped.

Directions for the ride: 22 miles

1. Turn left out of parking lot onto Route 129 and go 3/10 mile to fork where Route 129 bears left.

2. Bear right at fork and go 1.4 miles to traffic light. You'll go along Hawkes Pond.

3. Go straight at light 7/10 mile to Thomas Road on right. It goes up a short hill.

4. Turn right on Thomas Road and go 4/10 mile to end.

5. Turn left at end and go 1.5 miles to end, in the center of Lynnfield. You'll pass Pillings Pond.

6. Turn right at end and go 3/10 mile to Essex Street, your first right.

7. Turn right on Essex Street and go 9/10 mile to Pillings Pond Road on right, after high school.

8. Turn right on Pillings Pond Road and go 6/10 mile to fork.

9. Bear left at fork onto a narrow lane, following the shore of the pond on your right. Go 3/10 mile to crossroads (Walsh Road on left, Edgemere Road on right).

10. Turn right at crossroads, still following the pond, and go 1/2 mile to end (merge right).

11. Bear right at end and go 4/10 mile to end (merge right again).

12. Bear right at end and go 1/10 mile to crossroads and stop sign.

13. Turn left at crossroads and go 1/2 mile to end (Salem Street), just after you go underneath Route 128.

14. Turn left at end and go 4/10 mile to traffic light at Route 1.

15. Go straight at light, crossing the overpass over Route 1. Go 6/10 mile to rotary.

16. Bear right at rotary onto Route 129 East. After 2 miles the main road curves sharply to the left and a smaller road, Great Woods Road, turns sharp right. Here the ride stays on the main

LYNNFIELD MAIN ESSEX
SUMMER PILLINGS POND
PILLINGS POND
THOMAS
SUMMER
(128)
(1)
SALEM
LYNNFIELD
WALNUT
HAWKES POND
(129)
GREAT WOODS RD.
WALDEN POND
BROADWAY
EUCLID
START SAUGUS
TOWER
LYNN WOODS
BIRCH POND
BREEDS POND
PARKLAND
(1)
WALNUT
BOSTON
107
EASTERN
N
SAUGUS IRONWORKS
WESTERN
LYNN
MARION
COMMON
BROAD
LYNN SHORE
MT. VERNON ST.

43

road, but if you'd like to visit Lynn Woods, turn sharp right and go 1/4 mile. At the entrance to the reservation, Walden Pond is on your right and the road becomes dirt. To visit the observation tower, follow the dirt road 3/10 mile to fork. You'll have to walk your bike. Bear left at fork up steep hill 3/10 mile to tower.

17. Stay on the main road 7/10 mile to Parkland Avenue on right, at traffic light. Here the short ride turns right and the long ride goes straight.

18. Continue straight 4/10 mile to Boston Street on right, at traffic light.

19. Turn right on Boston Street and go 1.2 miles to Marion Street on left. There's an old factory on your left on the far side of the intersection.

20. Turn left on Marion Street and immediately curve right. Go 100 yards and turn left again (it's one-way in the wrong direction if you go straight). Go 2/10 mile to busy crossroads and blinking light (Western Avenue).

21. Cross Western Avenue and go 100 yards to end. This is Market Square.

22. Turn left at end, going along the Lynn Common on your left. Go 6/10 mile to Market Street, which bears right at end of the common. At the intersection, City Hall is on your left.

23. Bear right on Market Street and go 3/10 mile to traffic light just beyond railroad underpass (Broad Street, Route 1A).

24. Turn left on Broad Street and go 4/10 mile to Nahant Street, which bears right at grassy traffic island. When you first turn onto Broad Street, the area on your right used to consist of hulking brick factories that burned in the terrible fire of November 1981.

25. Bear right on Nahant Street and go 4/10 mile to end, at ocean. Here the ride turns left, but if you'd like to visit Nahant you can turn right, and just ahead pick up the bike path along the beach on the left side of the causeway. If you make the loop around Nahant you'll add 9 miles to the ride.

26. Turn left at end, following the ocean on your right, and go 9/10 mile to Eastern Avenue on left, at the Swampscott town line. There's a little green on your left at the intersection.

27. Turn left on Eastern Avenue and go 1.6 miles to end (Route 107).

28. At end jog left and then immediately right on Stanwood Street. Go 1/10 mile to stop sign at a small traffic island.

29. Bear right at stop sign up steep hill. Go 2/10 mile to another stop sign, while going down a little hill.

30. Continue straight at stop sign 8/10 mile to end (Broadway).

31. Turn left on Broadway and go less than 2/10 mile to traffic light, at busy intersection.

32. Bear left at traffic light and immediately turn right on Parkland Avenue. Go 1.4 miles to traffic light at bottom of hill (Walnut Street). You'll pass Breeds Pond.

33. Turn sharply right at bottom of hill and go 2.6 miles to shopping center on left. If you'd like to visit the Saugus Ironworks, turn left after 2 miles at traffic light on Central Street. Go 6/10 mile to fork, bear right, and go 1/2 mile to Ironworks on left.

Directions for the ride: 15 miles

1. Follow directions for the long ride through number 17.

2. Turn right on Parkland Avenue and go 1.4 miles to traffic light at bottom of hill (Walnut Street). You'll pass Breeds Pond.

3. Turn sharply right at bottom of hill and go 2.6 miles to shopping center on right. If you'd like to visit the Saugus Ironworks, see the final direction for the long ride.

7. Woburn–Winchester–Arlington–Belmont

Number of miles: 16 (20 with Belmont extension)
Terrain: The short ride is gently rolling, with two short, sharp hills. The long ride has two additional hills, one a real monster.
Food: Grocery stores and restaurants in the towns.
Start: Shopping center on Route 38 in Woburn, immediately north of Route 128. If you live in Boston and don't have a car, you can start from the center of Arlington or Belmont.

Just northwest of Cambridge, the older, fairly well-to-do suburbs stretching out to Route 128 provide surprisingly pleasant biking. The area is suburban in the gracious sense of the word, with well-spaced older homes on well-landscaped lots and tree-lined streets. A series of rolling hills across Winchester, Arlington, and Belmont add effort to biking but also heighten the attractiveness of the area. Adding variety to the landscape are Horn Pond in Woburn and the long, slender Mystic Lakes two miles south.

The ride starts from the pleasant, fairly affluent community of Woburn. Across the street from the starting point is a reconstructed section of the Middlesex Canal (see the Middlesex Canal ride for more detail) and the Federal-style mansion of its chief engineer, Loammi Baldwin. The building is currently a restaurant. During the summer, boat rides are available on a replica of the original towboats.

You'll go through the compact downtown area of Woburn and then pass the pride of the town, the magnificent Gothic-style stone library designed by H. H. Richardson and built in 1878. It's one of the finest in the state, and it's worth going inside to see its high vaulted ceilings and wooden alcoves. Just outside of town you'll bike along Horn Pond. The Middlesex Canal passed next to it, and during the canal's heyday boatloads of Bostonians would visit the pond for a day's outing. From here it's a short ride to Winchester, another pleasant residential community with two delightful duck-ponds adjoining the center of town. Just outside of Winchester is a relaxing run along the shore of the Mystic Lakes, two ponds con-

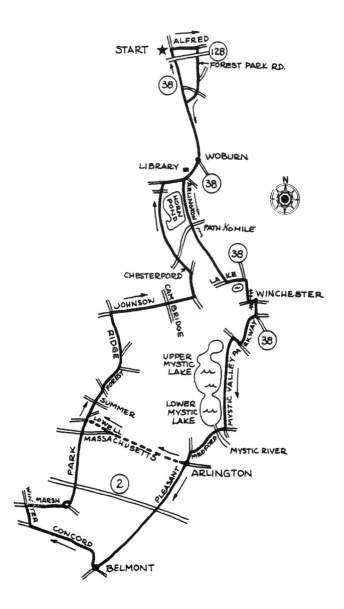

START ★ ALFRED
(128)
FOREST PARK RD.
(38)

WOBURN
LIBRARY ■ (38)
ARLINGTON
HORN POND
PATH ⅒ MILE

CHESTERFORD
(38)
LAKE
① WINCHESTER
JOHNSON CAMBRIDGE
(38)
RIDGE
UPPER MYSTIC LAKE
MYSTIC VALLEY PARKWAY
FOREST
SUMMER
LOWER MYSTIC LAKE
LOWELL
MASSACHUSETTS MEDFORD
MYSTIC RIVER
PARK ② ARLINGTON
W. MARSH PLEASANT
WINTER
CONCORD
BELMONT

N

47

nected like sausages by a narrow neck of land. The Mystic River flows as a small stream from the southern end of the lakes, dramatically increasing in size until it enters Boston Harbor.

From the end of the Mystic Lakes it's only a half mile to downtown Arlington, largest of the towns on this ride. The downtown area has a number of handsome public buildings and the historic Jason Russell House, with furnishings from the Revolutionary period. A mile out of town you'll pass the Old Schwamb Mill, a wooden building that was a mill during the 1800s and is now an arts and crafts center. From here you'll pass through gracious older residential neighborhoods to the western edge of Winchester and then back into Woburn, where you'll bike along the other side of Horn Pond through a large lakefront park.

The longer ride heads farther south into Belmont, wealthiest of the communities on the ride. It has a fair amount of greenspace and open fields in the western edge of the town, including the Rock Meadow Reservation, the Habitat Institute for the Environment (a wildlife sanctuary with nature trails), and an Audubon sanctuary. Any one of these spots is a good place to relax after the steep climb out of town. You'll then cross back into Arlington, where you'll climb more gradually to the highest point in the area, a 375-foot hill crowned by a stately concrete water tower. Two blocks off the route there's a superb view of Boston from a playground sloping along the hillside. After a fast downhill plunge you'll rejoin the short ride just in time to check out the Old Schwamb Mill.

Directions for the ride: 20 miles

1. Leaving the shopping center, cross Route 38 at traffic light onto Alfred Street. You'll immediately cross the Middlesex Canal and pass the Baldwin mansion, now a restaurant. You might want to explore the path leading alongside the canal. Follow Alfred Street 1/2 mile to a road on your right at a traffic island (sign may say Lutheran Church).

2. Turn right on this road. After 1/10 mile you'll go underneath Route 128. Continue 4/10 mile to end (merge to your right at stop sign).

3. Bear right at stop sign and go 3/10 mile to stop sign and blinking light. Continue straight at light 2/10 mile to end (Route 38).

48

your second traffic light (Concord Avenue). This is the center of Belmont. Notice the old brick town hall on your left at the intersection.

16. Turn right on Concord Avenue up a very steep hill and go 1.2 miles to Winter Street, which bears right.

17. Bear right on Winter Street and go 2/10 mile to crossroads (Marsh Street).

18. Turn right on Marsh Street and go 9/10 mile to rotary.

19. Bear left at rotary onto Park Avenue and go 1.2 miles to traffic light at bottom of steep hill (Massachusetts Avenue). • *CAUTION:* This intersection comes up suddenly while you're going downhill. At the top of the hill is the big water tower. If you head a couple of blocks downhill at the back of the tower on Eastern Avenue, which runs perpendicular to the route, you'll come to a playground with a splendid view of Boston.

20. Cross Massachusetts Avenue and go 1/10 mile to a six-way intersection. Here the ride bears slightly left uphill, but if you turn right for 2/10 mile and then take your first left on Mill Lane, you'll see the old red wooden Schwamb Mill.

21. At the six-way intersection, continue straight uphill on Park Avenue Extension. Go 3/10 mile to traffic light (Summer Street).

22. Cross Summer Street and go 1/10 mile to stop sign (merge left).

23. Bear left at stop sign and then immediately bear right uphill on Forest Street. Go 4/10 mile to fork at top of hill where the main road (Ridge Street) bears left.

24. Bear left on Ridge Street. After 1/4 mile Lockeland Road bears right, but continue straight 1/2 mile to crossroads and stop sign (Johnson Road).

25. Turn right on Johnson Road and go 1 mile to traffic light (Cambridge Street). Continue straight at light 4/10 mile to where the main road curves 90 degrees right and Woodside Road turns left.

26. Turn left on Woodside Road and go 2/10 mile to Chesterford Road, which bears left.

27. Bear left on Chesterford Road and go 2/10 mile to end.

28. At end, go straight ahead onto a blocked-off lane that

V

runs along the west shore of Horn Pond. After 7/10 mile you'll come to a parking lot. At the far end of the lot curve right, following the pond, and go 4/10 mile to the end of the blocked-off section.
• *CAUTION:* Watch for glass, joggers, and pedestrians.

29. At end of blocked-off section, continue straight 2/10 mile to end.

30. Turn right at end and go 1/2 mile to Route 38, back in the center of Woburn.

31. Turn left on Route 38 and go 1.5 miles to shopping center on left.

Directions for the ride: 16 miles

1. Follow directions for the long ride through number 14.

2. Turn right on Massachusetts Avenue and go 1.4 miles to Lowell Street, which bears right as Massachusetts Avenue curves left uphill. There is a Dunkin Donuts on the left just beyond the intersection. Just after you turn right, you'll pass the city hall on your left. Just ahead, you'll pass the Jason Russell House at the corner of Jason Street, also on left.

3. Bear right on Lowell Street and go 1/4 mile to six-way intersection and stop sign. To see the Old Schwamb Mill, turn onto Mill Lane, your second right. This mill is just ahead.

4. Turn 90 degrees right at stop sign, uphill (don't turn sharply right on Bow Street). Go 3/10 mile to traffic light (Summer Street).

5. Follow directions for the long ride from number 22 to end.

8. Newton–Brookline

Number of miles: 16 (24 with Brookline–Arnold Arboretum–Jamaica Pond extension).

Terrain: Gently rolling, with several hills, including two steep ones.

Food: Numerous groceries and restaurants.

Start: Parking lot at the corner of Auburn Street and Woodland Avenue, alongside the Massachusetts Turnpike, in the Auburndale section of Newton. From Route 128, get off at Route 30 (exit 24). Turn right (east) at end of ramp and go 2/10 mile to Auburn Street, which bears right at traffic light. Bear right and go 3/10 mile to parking lot on right, just after Woodland Road on right. If you're heading west on Commonwealth Avenue, turn left on Lexington Street (the first traffic light after the bridge over the Massachusetts Turnpike). Go 100 yards to your first right, Auburn Street. Turn right and go 1/4 mile to parking lot on left.

An alternate starting point, closer to Boston, is one of the side streets just off the Jamaicaway opposite Jamaica Pond. If you start the ride here, begin by heading counterclockwise on the bike path around the pond. Go to direction number 28 for the long ride.

This ride takes you exploring in two affluent suburbs immediately west of Boston filled with large, gracious homes from the nineteenth century and the early twentieth. The long ride heads across the Boston line to the Arnold Arboretum, a large, beautifully landscaped park with rolling, grassy hillsides and 6,000 varieties of trees, shrubs, and flowers from all over the world.

The ride starts from Newton, a classic "streetcar suburb" that evolved with public rail transportation during the second half of the nineteenth century. This sparked the construction of residential areas, generally aimed at a well-to-do market, beyond the confines of Boston itself yet easily accessible to the city for daily commuting. Newton is pleasant to bicycle through, with tree-lined, curving streets and spacious older wooden or brick homes surrounded by attractively landscaped yards. You'll bike past Boston College, with its dignified stone Gothic-style buildings, and return along broad, gracefully curving Commonwealth Avenue, with a grassy island in the middle for its entire length.

The long ride heads farther east across Brookline, which geographically should be part of Boston because it is surrounded by the city along three-quarters of its perimeter. The southern half of Brookline is even more elegant than Newton, with a broad belt of mansions and estates just south of Route 9. You'll explore this idyllic area, where it's hard to believe that you're only four miles from downtown Boston, and then head to the Arnold Arboretum. The most spectacular time to visit it is around Mother's Day, when thousands of lilacs and other flowers bathe the hillsides in a pink and purple haze. Just up the road from the Arboretum is Jamaica Pond, ringed by a bike path, with the built-up Boston neighborhood of Jamaica Plain on one side and estates just across the Brookline border on the other. You'll angle back across Brookline through more estates and gracious residential areas and then enjoy a relaxing run along the Chestnut Hill Reservoir, which is framed by two ornate Victorian stone pumping stations. Just beyond the reservoir you'll join the route of the short ride past Boston College and along Commonwealth Avenue to the end.

Directions for the ride: 24 miles

1. Turn left out of parking lot and immediately turn left on Woodland Road, crossing the bridge over the Massachusetts Turnpike. Go 1/4 mile to crossroads and blinking light (Grove Street).

2. Turn right on Grove Street. After 2/10 mile the main road curves sharply left. Continue 1.1 mile to end. You will pass the Riverside MBTA Station, a convenient spot for taking public transportation into Boston.

3. Turn left at end and go 2/10 mile, to end (Route 16).

4. Turn left on Route 16 and go 3/10 mile to the entrance road to Route 128 South, at traffic light. On this stretch you'll parallel the Charles River on your right. This area is called Newton Lower Falls.

5. Turn 90 degrees right at traffic light, passing the Pillar House on your left. (Don't turn sharply right onto Wales Street–

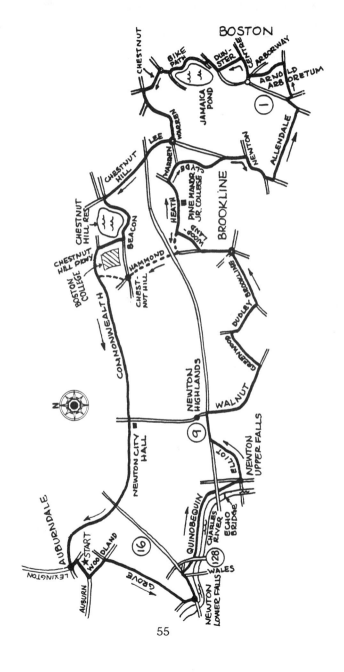

Walnut Street). Just ahead, go underneath the highway onto Quino-bequin Road. This is a great winding road with the Charles River on your right. After 1.5 miles you'll go underneath Route 9. Just beyond Route 9 is another bridge, a graceful, slender concrete span called Echo Bridge. To verify the accuracy of the name, walk to the bank of the Charles directly beneath the bridge and holler. A walkway runs along the top of the bridge providing a fine overview of the river, which flows between two hills with a dam just upstream.

6. From Echo Bridge, continue up a short, steep hill to stop sign at the top. Bear right at stop sign and go 1/10 mile to traffic light (Elliot Street). This area is called Newton Upper Falls.

7. Turn left on Elliot Street and go 9/10 mile to traffic light (Route 9).

8. Bear right on Route 9 and go 4/10 mile to Walnut Street on right, at far end of overpass and just before traffic light. • *CAUTION:* Route 9 is extremely busy. Please walk along the side of the road where there is no shoulder or breakdown lane.

9. Turn right on Walnut Street. After 6/10 mile the main road curves sharply left. Continue 7/10 mile to Greenwood Street on left, just past top of hill and house number 600.

10. Turn left on Greewood Street and go 7/10 mile to end (Dudley Road).

11. Turn right on Dudley Road and go 1/2 mile to end (Brookline Street).

12. Turn left on Brookline Street and go 7/10 mile to rotary.

13. Go two-thirds of the way around the rotary to Hammond Street, which comes after a divided parkway. If you come to Hammond Pond Parkway you've gone too far around. Follow Hammond Street 4/10 mile to Woodland Road, which bears right.

14. Bear right on Woodland Road and go 1/2 mile to end, at yield sign. Here the short ride turns left and the long ride turns right.

15. Turn right at end and go 7/10 mile to Warren Street, which turns right at traffic island at bottom of hill. You'll pass the gracious wooded campus of Pine Manor Junior College.

16. Turn right on Warren Street and go 2/10 mile to fork where Clyde Street bears right. You'll pass a Carmelite monastery on the right.

17. Bear right on Clyde Street and go 1/2 mile to end. You'll pass the entrance to The Country Club, oldest golf course in the nation, established in 1882.

18. Bear right at end onto divided parkway (still Clyde Street) and go 3/10 mile to end (Newton Street).

19. Turn right on Newton Street. After 3/10 mile there's a fork where the main road bears left, at blinking light. Bear left and go 1/10 mile to Allendale Road on left.

20. Turn left on Allendale Road and go 1.1 miles to end. The second half of this road is in Boston but the area is so undeveloped you'd never know it.

21. Turn left at end and go 2/10 mile to the entrance to Arnold Arboretum on right. It comes up suddenly as you're going downhill—don't whizz past it.

22. Turn right into the Arboretum. Just beyond the gate there's a road on your left. Turn left and go 4/10 mile to a road on left at bottom of hill. • *CAUTION:* Watch for pedestrians and joggers.

23. Turn left on this road and go 1/2 mile to end (Arborway). The visitors center is on your left just before the end.

24. Turn left on Arborway, using service road on the far side. (To cross the Arborway, use the crosswalk just to the right of the exit gate.) Just ahead is Centre Street.

25. Turn right on Centre Street and go 200 yards to Dunster Road, your third left.

26. Turn left on Dunster Road and go 3/10 mile to end (Jamaicaway).

27. Turn right on the Jamaicaway, being sure to use the sidewalk. Go 2/10 mile to traffic light. This is one of the busiest roads in the state, and if you don't use the sidewalk, you'll get killed.

28. Cross the Jamaicaway at traffic light and turn right onto the bike path that goes around Jamaica Pond, following the water on your left. After 2/10 mile there's a fork. Bear left, still following the water, and go 3/10 mile until you come to a road directly in front of you, at a water fountain. • *CAUTION:* The path is heavily used by joggers and pedestrians. Dismount if necessary.

29. Go straight ahead downhill 100 yards to rotary.

30. Bear left at rotary. Just ahead you'll pass the Brookline Hospital on your left. Continue 2/10 mile to fork where Kendall

Road bears right and Chestnut Street bears left.

31. Bear left on Chestnut Street and go 2/10 mile to crossroads and stop sign (Walnut Street).

32. Turn left on Walnut Street and go 2/10 mile to fork at top of hill. Notice the handsome stone church on your left at the fork.

33. Bear left at fork and immediately bear left again on Warren Street. Go 7/10 mile to end, at rotary (Lee Street). Just beyond the fork you'll pass the Frederick Law Olmsted National Historic Site on your right. This rambling old building was for many years the home and office of the country's foremost landscape architect of the nineteenth century. Olmsted is most famous for designing Central Park in New York City. He also designed an elaborate, linear park system for Boston, including Franklin Park, Jamaica Pond, the Muddy River between Brookline and Jamaica Plain, and the Back Bay Fens. Some of his original plans are on display at the Site, which is currently open afternoons from Friday through Sunday.

34. Bear right on Lee Street and go 4/10 mile to Route 9 at traffic light at top of hill.

35. Cross Route 9 diagonally onto Chestnut Hill Ave. • *CAUTION:* Bad intersection. Go 8/10 mile to traffic light at bottom of hill, immediately after trolley tracks (Beacon Street). • *CAUTION:* These are bad tracks. Walk your bike.

36. Turn left at light and go 8/10 mile to Chestnut Hill Parkway on right, at end of pond. You'll go along the Chestnut Hill Reservoir, passing two imposing Victorian waterworks buildings on your left.

37. Turn right on Chestnut Hill Parkway and go 1/2 mile to traffic light (Commonwealth Avenue). You curve sharply right just before the light. Boston College is on your left.

38. Turn left on Commonwealth Avenue. • *CAUTION:* There are more dangerous trolley tracks at the intersection; walk your bike. Follow Commonwealth Avenue 4.8 miles to Lexington Street, the first traffic light after the bridge over the Massachusetts Turnpike (sign may point left to Auburndale Center). Whenever possible, use the service road to the right of the center island. There is a tough hill at the beginning, followed by a long downhill, which is the infamous "Heartbreak Hill" on the Boston Marathon route. The marathoners, of course, are going in the opposite direction. Farther on you'll pass the ornate red-brick city hall on your left.

39. Turn left on Lexington Street and go 100 yards to your first right, Auburn Street. This is the center of Auburndale.

40. Turn right and go 1/4 mile to parking lot on left.

Directions for the ride: 16 miles

1. Follow directions for the long ride through number 14.

2. Turn left at end of Woodland Road and go 3/10 mile back to Hammond Street, at crossroads and stop sign.

3. Turn right on Hammond Street and immediately cross Route 9 at traffic light.(• *CAUTION:* Busy intersection.) Go 8/10 mile to Beacon Street, at traffic light.

4. Cross Beacon Street, bearing right on the far side of the intersection (it's one-way in the wrong direction if you go directly across). Go 3/10 mile to end (Commonwealth Avenue). Boston College is on your right.

5. Turn left on Commonwealth Avenue and go 4.4 miles to Lexington Street, the first traffic light after the bridge over the Massachusetts Turnpike (sign may point left to Auburndale Center). You'll go down "Heartbreak Hill" of Boston Marathon fame and then pass the ornate City Hall on your left.

6. Turn left on Lexington Street and go 100 yards to your first right, Auburn Street. This is the center of Auburndale.

7. Turn right and go 1/4 mile to parking lot on left.

9. The Blue Hills Ride: Milton–Quincy

Number of miles: 18 (11 with shortcut)
Terrain: Rolling, with one long, tough hill and several short ones.
Food: Howard Johnson's near end.
Start: Trailside Museum, Route 138, Milton, 1 mile north of Route 128.

Directly south of Boston is an area that's a pleasant surprise. Instead of dreary suburbs or industrial barrens, there are old mansions and gracious estates, a long, stately parkway with a broad, grassy island down the middle, and the elegant town center of Milton. Surrounding all this is the wonderful Blue Hills Reservation, the largest protected expanse of greenspace in the metropolitan area, yet very close to Boston. Five miles long, the reservation contains one of the most prominent natural features in the Boston area, the range of rugged wooded hills rising to a height of 630 feet at its western end on top of Great Blue Hill. Foot trails hop from hill to hill, providing some superb views; horseback riders and cross-country skiers can enjoy 65 miles of bridle paths. Also on the grounds are a natural history museum, an Audubon Society educational center, and two ponds.

The ride starts at the Trailside Museum, a natural history museum run by the Massachusetts Audubon Society at the foot of Great Blue Hill. It contains both live and stuffed animals and birds native to Massachusetts. Larger animals are exhibited outdoors. From behind the museum a trail leads a half mile to the summit, where an observation tower affords one of the best views to be found of Boston and vicinity. You'll head past estates and rolling hillsides to the center of Milton, a New England jewel with a large green framed by the town hall and two classic white churches.

From here you'll parallel the Neponset River estuary along a hillside with magnificent views. Sloping down the hill to the water's edge is Hutchinson Field, a lush, grassy meadow with a vista of the river and the Boston skyline. The field is one of the properties of the Trustees of Reservations, whose main office is next door. Across the street is the Museum of the China Trade, housed in the imposing mansion of Robert Bennett Forbes, who made his fortune that way.

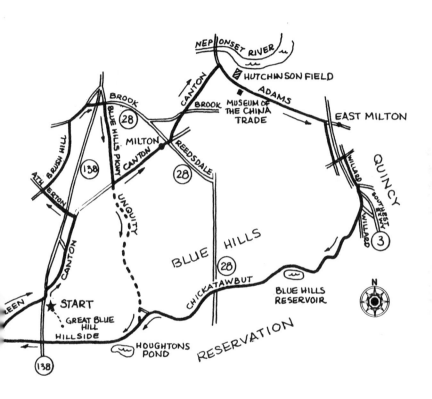

NEPONSET RIVER

HUTCHINSON FIELD

CANTON

BROOK

ADAMS

BROOK

MUSEUM OF THE CHINA TRADE

EAST MILTON

BRUSH HILL

BLUE HILLS PKWY

(28)

MILTON

REEDSDALE

QUINCY

ATHERTON

(138)

CANTON

(28)

WILLARD

SOUTHEAST EXP'WY

UNQUITY

(3)

WILLARD

BLUE HILLS

CANTON

(28)

CHICKATAWBUT

BLUE HILLS RESERVOIR

N

GREEN

★ START

GREAT BLUE HILL

HILLSIDE

HOUGHTONS POND

RESERVATION

(138)

Just ahead you'll enter the Blue Hills Reservation and traverse its entire length on smooth roads winding through the woods, passing Houghtons Pond, which has a beach. At the end you'll go by more estates along a tiny lane just over the Canton town line.

Directions for the ride: 18 miles

1. Turn right (north) out of parking lot and go 1/4 mile to Canton Avenue, which bears right (sign may say to Hyde Park).

2. Bear right on Canton Avenue. After 8/10 mile, Dollar Lane bears left and the main road curves right. Stay on main road 1/2 mile to Atherton Street on left. There's a graceful stone gatehouse on the right shortly before the intersection.

3. Turn left on Atherton Street. Just ahead is a traffic light (Route 138). Cross Route 138 and go 4/10 mile to crossroads and stop sign (Brush Hill Road).

4. Turn right at crossroads and go 1.2 miles to end.

5. Bear right at end onto divided highway and go 2/10 mile to Brook Road, which bears right.

6. Bear right on Brook Road and go 1/10 mile to traffic light (Route 138). Continue straight 1/10 mile to stop sign and a divided parkway.

7. Turn right on parkway (Blue Hills Parkway) and go 1.2 miles to stop sign where the divided road ends (Canton Avenue). Here the short ride goes straight and the long ride turns left.

8. Turn left on Canton Avenue and go 1 mile to traffic light at five-way intersection. The Milton town green is on your left just before the light.

9. Bear left at light, staying on Canton Avenue (don't turn 90 degrees left on Reedsdale Road). Go 4/10 mile to diagonal crossroads and stop sign (Brook Road).

10. Cross Brook Road and go 7/10 mile to end (Adams Street). Get in lowest gear at end.

11. Turn 90 degrees right on Adams Street. After 2/10 mile you'll pass Hutchinson Field on your left and the Museum of the China Trade on your right. Continue 8/10 mile to end, where you merge left at yield sign. Bear left (still Adams Street) and go 1/2 mile to traffic light immediately before the bridge over the Southeast Expressway (sign says to Route 93 South).

12. Bear right at light, paralleling expressway on left, and go 6/10 mile to crossroads (Robertson Street—sign may say to East Milton, West Quincy).

13. Turn left at crossroads and go 1/10 mile to traffic light (Willard Street).

14. Turn right at light and go 1/2 mile to fork where Willard Street bears right, under the expressway.

15. Bear right at fork and go 3/10 mile to another fork where Willard Street bears right and the ramp onto Route 93 (the Southeast Expressway) bears left.

16. Bear right at fork. Just ahead is another fork. Bear right again, following sign that may say to Milton, Canton, Blue Hills. After 1.3 miles you will merge to your right at stop sign. Bear right and go 1.6 miles to traffic light (Route 28). There's a long, steady hill to the Blue Hills Reservoir on your left. A half mile ahead is a small parking area with a fine view of Boston. From here it's all downhill to Route 28.

17. Cross Route 28 onto Chickatawbut Road and go 1.3 miles to fork.

18. Bear slightly left at fork (sign may say to Canton) and go 1.7 miles to traffic light (Route 138). You'll pass Houghtons Pond on your left at the far end of a large parking lot.

19. Go straight at light 7/10 mile to a small crossroads just beyond the Blue Hills Office Park on left.

20. Turn right at crossroads and go 1.2 miles to end (Route 138).

21. Turn right on Route 138. The Museum is just ahead on your left.

Directions for the ride: 11 miles.

1. Follow directions for the long ride through number 7.

2. Go straight at crossroads onto Uniquity Road. After 2 miles a road bears left, but continue straight for 1.8 miles to traffic light (Route 138). You'll pass Houghtons Pond on your left at the far end of a large parking lot.

3. Follow the directions for the long ride from number 19 to the end.

10. Quincy

Number of miles: 17 (14 omitting Squantum, 10 omitting
    Houghs Neck)
Terrain: Flat, with one short, steep hill.
Food: Several groceries and snack bars.
Start: Burger King, Adams Street in Quincy, 4/10 mile east of
    Southeast Expressway.
How to get there: From the south, take the Adams Street exit
    (exit 9). Turn right at end of ramp on Adams Street and go
    4/10 mile to start. From the north, take the Squantum Street
    exit (exit 10). Just ahead go straight, following sign to Adams
    Street. Turn left at end on Adams Street (sign says to East
    Milton Square) and go 7/10 mile to start.

Quincy, just southeast of Boston, is built on and between two peninsulas. This ride follows the perimeter of the southern one,
Houghs Neck, goes along the shore to the northern one, Squantum,
and then heads to the tip of Squantum, where you'll find a delightful oceanfront park. Either of the two peninsulas may be omitted if
you'd like to cut the ride short. A historical highlight of the ride is
the Adams National Historic Site, home of John Adams and succes-
sive generations until as recently as 1906. Also in the city are the
birthplaces of John Adams and John Quincy Adams (133 and 141
Franklin Street), about a mile off the route.

    The ride starts near the Milton line and heads to the Adams
National Historic Site, which is worth visiting. The splendid mansion contains a large array of furnishings, a flower garden, and an
elegant stone library in its own building. Just beyond the mansion
you'll go through Quincy Square—busy and congested, but impressive, with the imposing granite City Hall, built in 1844 in Greek
Revival style, an old cemetery next to it, and a handsome stone
church across the street. From here you'll head out onto Houghs
Neck, which is a middle-class residential area with some salt
marshes, a couple of marinas, and splendid views of Boston Harbor
and the Boston skyline. At the very tip, Nut Island, is a sewage

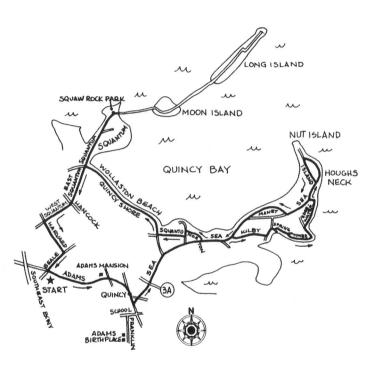

LONG ISLAND

SQUAW ROCK PARK

MOON ISLAND

NUT ISLAND

SQUANTUM

HOUGHS NECK

QUINCY BAY

EAST SQUANTUM

WOLLASTON BEACH

QUINCY SHORE

ISLAND

WEST SQUANTUM

HANCOCK

SEA

CASTLE

HARVARD

SQUANTO

MANET

SEA

INGSTON

KILBY

SPRING

TOWER

BEALE

ADAMS MANSION

ADAMS

SEA

QUINCY

3A

SOUTHEAST EXPWY

★ START

SCHOOL

FRANKLIN

ADAMS BIRTHPLACE

N

65

treatment plant, which, if you can ignore that fact, is a dramatic spot with a nearly 360 degree panorama of ocean views.

Leaving Houghs Neck you'll go along Wollaston Beach, which comprises the shoreline between Houghs Neck and Squantum, the northerly of Quincy's two peninsulas. Wollaston is one of the beaches near Boston where you don't want to swim—it's too close to the city, and too hemmed in by other land areas to be very clean. It's pleasant to bike along, however, especially if it's not a beach day, when there won't be much traffic. From Wollaston you'll head out to Squantum, where Squaw Rock, a craggy headland, commands the northern tip. The area is now a park with paths, trees, and magnificent views of Boston across Dorchester Bay.

East of Squantum lies a tale of bureaucratic simplemindedness. A mile-long causeway connects Squantum with Moon Island, and a slender half-mile-long bridge connects Moon Island with Long Island, which angles northeastward two miles to form half the outer rim of Boston Harbor (Deer Island in Winthrop forms the other half). Until a few years ago this was one of the most spectacular runs in the Boston area, with no traffic because the islands are uninhabited except for a hospital. Then in 1976 a young girl was killed while riding her bike across the bridge. The response? Close off the islands to the public and put them under twenty-four-hour guard.

After you leave Squantum it's a short run back to the start through residential neighborhoods.

Directions for the rides

1. Turn right out of parking lot onto Adams Street. After 1.2 miles, the Adams National Historic Site is on your left, just before the traffic light at Newport Avenue.

2. Continue straight on Adams Street 4/10 mile into Quincy Center. Notice the Greek Revival city hall on the right and the handsome stone church across the street. If you'd like to visit the Adams birthplace, continue beyond the city hall 4/10 mile to School Street on right. Turn right on School Street and go 2/10 mile to Franklin Street on left, just before railroad bridge. Turn left on Franklin Street and go 3/10 mile to the houses, numbers 133 and 141.

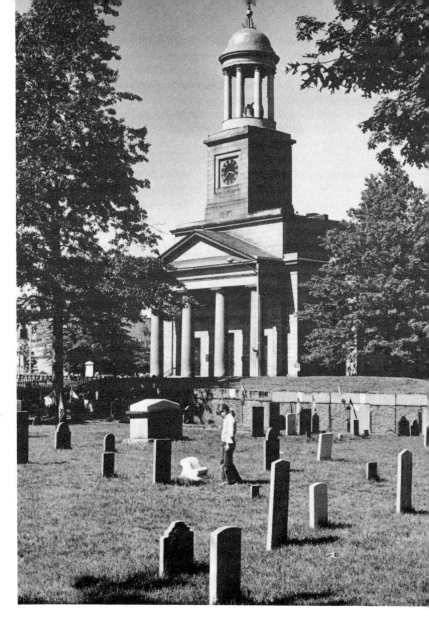

First Parish Church, Quincy.

3. Turn left immediately after the church across from City Hall. Just ahead, you'll pass the grim old high school on the left. Continue 3/10 mile to traffic light (Route 3A).

4. Cross Route 3A and go 3/10 mile to the next traffic light (sign pointing left may say Wollaston Beach, Boston). Here you can omit the Houghs Neck section of the ride by turning left. This cuts the ride down to 10 miles. To omit Houghs Neck, turn left and go 2.6 miles to traffic light (sign may say to Squantum). You'll go along Wollaston Beach—see direction number 20 for more information. Then resume with direction number 21.

5. Continue straight at light and go 9/10 mile to fork and traffic light (Sea Street bears left).

6. Bear left on Sea Street and go 3/10 mile to Kilby Street on right. It's after house number 655 on right.

7. Turn right on Kilby Street and go 7/10 mile to end.

8. Turn left at end and go 2/10 mile to Spring Street on right.

9. Turn right on Spring Street, following the water, and just ahead bear left uphill on Spring Terrace. Go 1/10 mile to Tower Street on right.

10. Turn right on Tower Street, following the bay on your right, and go 1/2 mile to Edgewater Drive on right.

11. Turn right on Edgewater Drive, following the water, and go 1/2 mile to end. • *CAUTION:* Edgewater Drive has several speed bumps, but you can bike around them at the edge of the road.

12. Turn right at end. After 3/10 mile you'll climb a short, steep hill. As you're coming down the other side of the hill, the road curves 90 degrees left onto Island Avenue. Here you can turn right onto the grounds of the Nut Island sewage treatment plant and go 1/4 mile to the tip of the peninsula for a great view.

13. Turn left on Island Avenue and go 3/10 mile to end (Sea Avenue). • *CAUTION:* The first hundred yards of Island Avenue are very narrow and bumpy—take it easy.

14. Turn right on Sea Avenue and go 1/2 mile to Manet Avenue on right (fire station on corner).

15. Turn right on Manet Avenue. Just ahead Babcock Street bears left, but go straight on Manet Avenue, following the ocean, 1/2 mile to end (merge with Sea Street at stop sign).

16. Go straight onto Sea Street 1.1 miles to Norton Road on right, at traffic light.

17. Turn right on Norton Road and go 3/10 mile to end (Chicatabot Road).

18. Turn left on Chicatabot Road and go 1 block to Squanto Road, which is your first right.

19. Turn right on Squanto Road and go 3/10 mile to traffic light and busy crossroads.

20. Turn right at light. Just ahead you'll cross a small bridge and follow the shore of Quincy Bay along Wollaston Beach. Go 2.2 miles to busy crossroads with traffic light (Squantum Street). • *CAUTION:* The road along the bay is a busy, four-lane road. If it is not a beach day, it's safest to ride on the sidewalk or along the parking area. If the parking area is busy, ride on the extreme right-hand edge of the road, keeping alert for cars backing up. When you get to the light the ride turns right, but if you want to omit Squantum, chopping 2.5 miles off the ride, turn left, go 9/10 mile to another traffic light (Hancock Street), and resume with direction number 24.

21. Turn right at light and go 7/10 mile to fork. Bear left, following the water on your left, and continue 1/2 mile to Squaw Rock Park on left. Just beyond the park is the causeway to Moon and Long Islands, which is blocked by a gate and security guards.

22. Backtrack from the park 1.2 miles to the traffic light.

23. Go straight at light 9/10 mile to traffic light (Hancock Street).

24. Cross Hancock Street onto West Squantum Street and go 7/10 mile to Harvard Street on left. There's a church on the far left-hand corner and a golf course on the right beyond the intersection.

25. Turn left on Harvard Street and go 7/10 mile to end (Beale Street).

26. Turn right on Beale Street and go 4/10 mile to Adams Street, at traffic light. Burger King is on your left.

🚲 Chapter 2:

The North Shore

Numbers on this map refer to rides in this book.

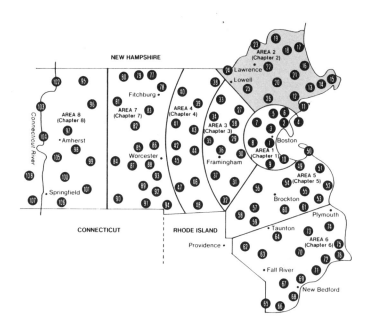

11. Lynn–Swampscott–Marblehead

Number of miles: 20
Terrain: Gently rolling.
Food: Numerous stores and restaurants on the route.
Start: Lynn Shore Drive in Lynn, just north of the causeway to Nahant. Head north on Route 1A into Lynn to fork. Bear right at fork, following sign to Nahant, and go 1/2 mile to rotary. Go three quarters of the way around the rotary. Park as soon as it's legal, or on the service road on the left (inland) side of road. If you're coming from the west on Route 128, exit onto Route 129 East (exit 44B). If you're coming from the north or the south on Route 1, exit onto Route 129 East, which is just south of Route 128. Instead of going under the two-lane underpass on Route 1, bear right alongside it to traffic light.

Follow Route 129 East about 3 miles to Route 107 (Western Avenue). Cross Route 107 onto Chestnut Street and follow it straight through 1.5 miles to the ocean. Turn right and go a couple of blocks. Park just after you pass Nahant Street.

This is a tour of the closest really nice coastline to Boston if you don't count Nahant. (You can do the Nahant ride too—from the starting point go along the bike path on the east side of the causeway to Nahant. Added distance is nine miles.) The area is similar to Cape Ann but only half the distance from Boston, with beautiful stretches of shoreline graced by elegant mansions and estates, some rocky headlands, and the maze of narrow streets lined with restored antique homes in the center of Marblehead. The town lies along a peninsula jutting northeastward into the Atlantic. Just east of it is Marblehead Neck, a bowling-pin-shaped island a mile long and a half mile wide, rimmed with elegant homes and connected to the mainland by a causeway. Between the two are the deep, sheltered waters of Marblehead Harbor, one of the yachting and sailing capitals of New England. The view of Marblehead across the harbor from the Neck, sloping up a low hillside crowned by Abbott Hall, the proud Victorian town hall that dominates the town, is inspiring.

You start the ride by heading up the Lynn shoreline, the best face of this otherwise drab industrial city, with a well-landscaped strip of parkland along the ocean on your right and gracious older homes and apartment buildings on your left. You then continue up the coast through Swampscott, an affluent community with attractive older homes, many quite elegant, lining the shore and the hillsides rising from it. Just off the route are two historic sites: the home of Mary Baker Eddy, founder of Christian Science, containing exhibits of her life and religion (23 Paradise Road), and the Humphrey House, which dates back to the 1600s and contains period furnishings (99 Paradise Road).

From Swampscott it's a short ride into Marblehead. First you'll go around the Neck. At its northern tip is Chandler Hovey Park, a beauty spot with a nearly 360 degree view of the sea and a tall old lighthouse. Then you'll go around Marblehead itself, where you're much better off on a bike than in a car as you weave along its narrow streets without worrying about finding a parking place. You'll pass Abbott Hall, the ornate town hall built in 1876, which contains an impressive painting, The Spirit of '76, commissioned for the American Centennial. Just ahead are two delightful waterfront parks, Chandler Park and Fort Sewell. The latter commands a small peninsula and contains the remains of a Revolutionary fort. Just north of town is Old Burial Hill, one of the state's outstanding historic cemeteries, with many slate headstones dating back to the 1700s and even earlier stretching up the terraced hillside.

Directions for the ride

1. Head north on Lynn Shore Drive, following the ocean on your right. After 1.1 miles you'll pass the Swampscott town green on your left, with the town hall a block inland. Just past the green on your right is Hawthorne-by-the-Sea, a well-known fancy restaurant. From the green, continue 1/2 mile to fork where Puritan Road bears right. If you'd like to visit the Mary Baker Eddy House or the Humphrey House, turn left at the Lynn-Swampscott line on Eastern Avenue, go 1 block to Route 1A, and turn right. The houses are just ahead.

2. Bear right on Puritan Road and go 1.2 miles to end (Atlantic Avenue, Route 129). Several dead-end lanes on the right lead to

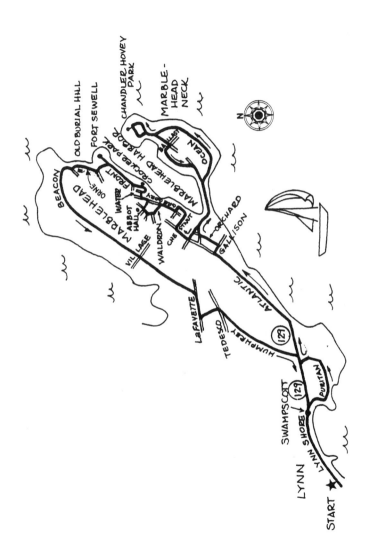

START

LYNN

LYNN SHORE

SWAMPSCOT 129

PURITAN

HUMPHREY 129

TEDESCO

LaFAYETTE

ATLANTIC

GALLISON

ORCHARD

CHURCH ST.

WALDRON

VILLAGE

ABBOT HALL

WATER

ORNE

FRONT

GLOVER SQUARE

STATE

CROCKER PARK

MARBLEHEAD

MARBLEHEAD HARBOR

BEACON

OLD BURIAL HILL

FORT SEWELL

CHANDLER HOVEY PARK

FORT

MARBLE-HEAD NECK

OCEAN

N

73

the rocky coastline past elegant homes and estates.

3. Turn right on Route 129 and go 2 miles to Gallison Avenue on right. It's the next street after Vassar Road.

4. Turn right on Gallison Avenue and go 1/10 mile to Orchard Street, your first left.

5. Turn left on Orchard Street and go 3/10 mile to your second crossroads, a one-way street.

6. Turn right at crossroads and go 1/10 mile to end (merge right).

7. Bear right at end and go 7/10 mile across the causeway to Marblehead Neck. There's a fork at the end of the causeway (Harbor Avenue bears left; Ocean Avenue bears right).

8. Bear right at fork and go 1.4 miles to a little traffic circle.

9. Bear right at traffic circle and go 3/10 mile to Chandler Hovey Park, at the northern tip of the neck.

10. Leaving the park, turn right on Kimball Street and go 3/10 mile to end.

11. Turn right at end and go 1/10 mile to the little traffic circle.

12. Bear right at traffic circle and go 1/4 mile to crossroads just beyond the crest of a little hill (Ballast Lane).

13. Turn right at crossroads, going along the shore of Marblehead Harbor on your right. Go 1/2 mile to end (merge to your right at stop sign).

14. Bear right at end and go 8/10 mile to traffic light, crossing the causeway in the opposite direction.

15. Turn right at traffic light and go 1/4 mile to Chestnut Street on right, just after church on left.

16. Turn right on Chestnut Street. After 2/10 mile the street turns 90 degrees left along the water, then left again. Continue 100 yards to Gregory Street on right.

17. Turn right on Gregory Street and go 2/10 mile to Waldron Street on left, at stop sign, at top of little hill.

18. Turn left on Waldron Street and go 1/10 mile to fork.

19. Bear right at fork. Just ahead, turn right at end and go 100 yards to your first right, Lee Street. At this intersection, the ornate brick building on the far-left corner is the town hall, Abbott Hall.

20. Turn right on Lee Street and go 100 yards to end (merge

Marblehead Harbor.

left at stop sign).

21. Bear left at end and go 100 yards to stop sign. Turn right downhill and immediately turn right again on Water Street to bottom of hill, where the main road curves 90 degrees left.

22. Curve left at bottom of hill. On your right is Crocker Park, a rocky outcropping with a magnificent view of the harbor. Continue straight, following the water on your right, for 6/10 mile to Fort Sewell at end.

23. Leaving Fort Sewell, backtrack 1/10 mile to a forced right turn (it's one-way in the wrong direction if you go straight). Turn right and go 1/10 mile to where the main road turns left and a smaller road, Orne Street, bears right (sign may say Lynn, Boston, Salem).

24. Bear right on Orne Street. After 1/4 mile the Old Burial Hill is on your left. It was founded in 1638 and is a great place to compare old gravestones. Across the road is still another waterfront park, Fountain Park. Just ahead, the main road curves left at bottom of hill. Continue 1/10 mile to end (Norman Street on left).

25. Turn right at end. Just ahead on your right is delightful Dolliber Cove. Continue 1.7 miles to traffic light (Village Street).

26. Go straight at light 8/10 mile to end (merge to your right onto Lafayette Street at another traffic light).

27. Bear right on Lafayette Street and go 1/4 mile to Maple Street, which turns sharp left at traffic island.

28. Turn sharp left on Maple Street and go 2/10 mile to traffic light.

29. Bear right at light on Humphrey Street. (Don't turn 90 degrees right on Tedesco Street.) Go 1.5 miles to end (merge into Route 129).

30. Bear right on Route 129 and go 2.5 miles back to start.

12. Witches and Waterfront: Peabody–Salem–Beverly–Danvers

Number of miles: 13 (18 with Historic Danvers extension)
Terrain: Flat
Food: Numerous groceries and restaurants on route.
Start: Northshore Shopping Center, Route 114 in Peabody, just north of Route 128. Take exit 25W.

• *CAUTION:* This ride contains several metal-grate bridges, which are extremely slippery when wet. If the road is wet, please walk your bike across. Also, the ride is primarily urban, so traffic will probably be heavy.

This is a fascinating ride through an urban but historic area, passing the landmarks of old Salem, running along the oceanfront in Beverly, visiting the stately town of Danvers, and crossing and recrossing the Danvers River estuary. If you're an American history buff or like early houses, you can easily stretch this ride over an entire day by visiting enough landmarks.

The ride starts from Peabody, an older middle-class North Shore suburb with a fine brick Victorian town hall and an old library in Greek Revival style. From here it's a stone's throw to Salem, among the oldest cities in the state, with its unique history as both a major seaport for the China trade during the late 1700s and the center of witch hysteria a century earlier, as well as the home of Nathaniel Hawthorne. You'll bike down Chestnut Street, the finest street in Salem and one of the finest in America, lined on both sides with graceful and dignified Federal-era mansions. Just ahead is the beautifully restored waterfront area, now the Salem Maritime National Historic Site, containing quarter-mile-long Derby Wharf, the heart of the old seaport, along with the handsome Custom House and the elegant home of Elias Derby, richest of the early Salem merchants. Within two or three blocks of the waterfront are most of the city's other attractions, including the outstanding Peabody Museum, focusing primarily on maritime history, the Witch Museum, a cluster of six elegant historic houses comprising the Essex Institute, the stately Old Town Hall, and the carefully restored brick commercial area, Derby Square. Just past Derby Wharf is the most famous landmark of all, the House of Seven Gables, built in 1668 and the setting for Hawthorne's immortal novel. A few blocks farther you'll pass Salem Common, a large, well-maintained, classic New England green with a bandstand in the middle and bordered by fine brick homes.

From Salem you'll cross the broad mouth of the Danvers River into Beverly, Salem's twin city, with its own share of historic houses and even a Historic District known as Fish Flake Hill. You'll bike along the handsome oceanfront area, with gracious old homes on the inland side of the road, and then recross the Danvers River over an old trussed drawbridge. Danvers is an attractive and historic city in its own right, overshadowed by its more famous neighbor. For starters you'll go by the Fowler House, a dignified Federal-style mansion maintained by the Society for the Preservation of New England Antiquities. In the center of town is the handsome town hall and the library, called the Peabody Institute, a magnificent Greek Revival building constructed in 1890. Just beyond is a pretty little millpond and then the Rebecca Nurse House, built in 1678, with its own story of witchcraft. As you head farther north, the landscape becomes more pleasantly suburban. You'll pass the Glen Magna estate, designed by Frederick Law Olmsted, and then return south through Danvers Center, with a graceful row of old houses from the early 1800s. From here it's a short pedal back to the starting point.

Directions for the ride: 18 miles

1. Turn right out of parking lot onto Route 114. Just ahead you'll cross Route 128 on an overpass. • *CAUTION:* Watch traffic entering and leaving Route 128. Continue 7/10 mile to crossroads and traffic light where Route 114 turns left.

2. Go straight at traffic light, bearing right as you go across the intersection. Go 6/10 mile into the center of Peabody. Notice the Victorian city hall a little to your right when you get to the center of town.

3. Bear left in the center of town onto Main Street and go 1.3 miles to end. Just past the center of town, notice the Greek Revival library on your left. There's an equestrian statue at the end.

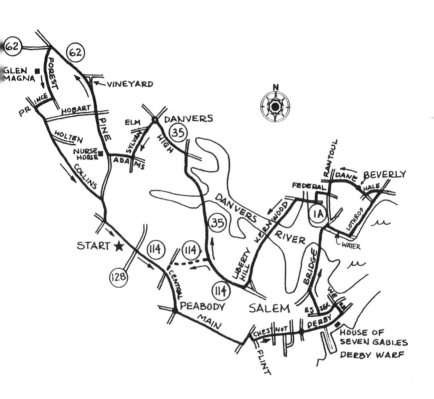

GLEN MAGNA

FOREST

62

62

VINEYARD

PRINCE

HOBART

PINE

ELM

DANVERS

35

HOLTEN

SYLVAN

HIGH

NURSE HOUSE

ADAMS

COLLINS

N

DANVERS

RANTOUL

DANE

BEVERLY

FEDERAL

KERNWOOD

HALE

1A

LOTHROP

START ★

35

RIVER

WATER

114

114

128

LIBERTY HILL

BRIDGE

WEBB

114

CENTRAL

SALEM

ESSEX

PEABODY

MAIN

CHESTNUT

DERBY

HOUSE OF SEVEN GABLES

FLINT

DERBY WARF

4. Turn left at end and go 1/10 mile to your second right (Flint Street), at traffic light.

5. Turn right on Flint Street and immediately left on Chestnut Street. Go 3/10 mile to stop sign (Summer Street). This is the gracious historic district of Salem.

6. Cross Summer Street. Just ahead it's one-way in the wrong direction; however, the ride goes straight and ends up on New Derby Street. Either walk your bike along the one-way section (it's only 100 feet) or bike counterclockwise around the parking lot until you come to New Derby Street on your right, at traffic light.

7. Follow New Derby street 1 block to the intersection with Lafayette Street, at traffic light. Here the ride goes straight, but it's worth a detour left for a couple of blocks to see the handsome Old Town Hall and Derby Square, the old market district that has recently been restored as a pedestrian mall with shops, restaurants, and summer fairs and concerts.

8. Cross Lafayette Street onto Derby Street. A half mile ahead is the old waterfront area and the House of Seven Gables. Continue beyond the House of Seven Gables, 1/4 mile to Webb Street on left, just after house number 40. Here the ride turns left, but if you wish you can go straight 1 mile to Salem Willows, an old-fashioned amusement park overlooking the harbor at the tip of a peninsula. Just before the park a road bears right and leads to the derelict, littered remains of Fort Pickering, a former Coast Guard air station.

9. Turn left on Webb Street. Just ahead is a stop sign. Continue 1 block to crossroads (Essex Street).

10. Turn left on Essex Street and go 1/4 mile to your first right (Washington Square East).

11. Turn right and go 4/10 mile to end (merge into Bridge Street). You'll go along Salem Common on your left.

12. Bear right on Bridge Street (Route 1A) and go 9/10 mile to the far side of the bridge, where you will see McDonald's on your right. • *CAUTION:* Metal grate bridge—walk if the road is wet.

13. Just after McDonalds, the main road bears left and Water Street bears right along the harbor.

14. Bear right on Water Street and go 2/10 mile to Lothrop Street on left, opposite the condominiums.

House of the Seven Gables, Salem.

15. Turn left on Lothrop Street and go 8/10 mile to traffic light (Hale Street), following the ocean on your right.

16. Turn sharply left at traffic light onto Hale Street (Route 62) • *CAUTION:* This is a bad corner—it's safest to walk your bike. Go 1/4 mile to crossroads (Dane Street). Route 62 turns to the right here.

17. Turn right at traffic light onto Dane Street (still Route 62). Go straight 1/2 mile through two traffic lights and a stop sign (Cabot Street) until you come to Rantoul Street, a wide, busy street at bottom of hill.

18. Turn left on Rantoul Street and go 1/10 mile to traffic light (Federal Street).

19. Turn right on Federal Street. Just past the railroad bridge the road turns 90 degrees left. Continue 1 block to end.

20. Turn right at end and cross the bridge. Continue 2/10 mile to Kernwood Avenue, which bears left just beyond steep part of hill • *CAUTION:* Metal-grate bridge; walk if road is wet. You will encounter another metal-grate bridge in direction number 21.

21. Bear left on Kernwood Avenue and go 1.5 miles to fork (Liberty Hill Avenue bears right). This road is a refreshing contrast to the dense urban landscape you've been passing through. You'll cross the Danvers River over an old metal drawbridge and pass a couple of golf courses.

22. Bear right on Liberty Hill Avenue and go 1/10 mile to a wide road, at stop sign (Route 114).

23. Turn right on Route 114 and go 6/10 mile to where Route 114 turns left onto a divided road. Here the short ride turns left and the long ride bears slightly right on Route 35.

24. Bear slightly right on Route 35 and go 1.4 miles to traffic light, where Route 35 turns left onto High Street.

25. Turn left at light (still Route 35) and go 9/10 mile to busy crossroads in the center of Danvers (Conant Street on right, Elm Street on left).

26. Turn left on Elm Street and go 2/10 mile to fork with the town hall and a granite monument in the middle.

27. Bear left at fork and go 4/10 mile to traffic light (Adams Street). The magnificent Greek Revival building on your right is the Peabody Institute, which is the town library.

28. Turn right on Adams Street and go 2/10 mile to end. At the end a long dirt driveway leads straight ahead to the Nurse House.

29. Turn right at end and go 9/10 mile to fork where one road bears left and the other (Vineyard Street) goes straight. On this stretch you'll go straight through two stop signs.

30. Bear left at fork and go 1/10 mile to stop sign (merge into Route 62).

31. Bear slightly left on Route 62 and go 1/2 mile to Forest Street on left at blinking light.

32. Turn left on Forest Street and go 7/10 mile to Prince Place on right, shortly after a modern church on left. You'll pass the Glen Magna estate on your right.

33. Turn right on Prince Place and go 2/10 mile to end.

34. Turn left at end and go 1/2 mile to fork, passing old historic homes and an unusual church on your left.

35. Bear slightly right at fork (almost straight) and go 9/10 mile to end, at traffic light.

36. Bear right at end and go 4/10 mile to second traffic light (Route 114, Andover Street).

37. Turn left on Route 114 (● *CAUTION:* Bad intersection) and go 3/10 mile to shopping center on right.

Directions for the ride: 13 miles

1. Follow the directions for the long ride through number 23.

2. Turn left on Route 114 and follow it 1.4 miles to the shopping center on left. Midway along this stretch, Route 114 turns left and then right just ahead.

13. Estates and Estuaries: Beverly–Manchester–
   Wenham–Essex–Hamilton

Number of miles: 16 (26 with Manchester–Essex–Hamilton
   extension)
Terrain: Gently rolling, with one short, sharp hill.
Food: Grocery in Beverly. Groceries and restaurants in
   Manchester. Grocery and restaurant in Essex. The local
   specialty here is clams.
Start: Hamilton Shopping Center, corner of Route 1A and Walnut
   Road, Hamilton, at the Wenham town line. It's three miles
   north of Route 128.

The region northeast of Beverly is the North Shore at some of its
finest: a magnificent landscape of rocky coastline with mansions
perched above it, the broad, gently rolling fields of gentleman farms
and old-moneyed estates, and gracious horse farms partitioned by
white wooden fences. The town centers are classic New England
gems. A fine network of smooth, little-traveled secondary roads
weaving across the landscape provides bicycling at its best.

The ride starts off by heading a few miles along winding lanes
to the ocean in Beverly. Like others across the state, Beverly is a
two-faced community. The negative face, which you won't come
anywhere near, is a congested, unattractive commercial area surrounded by factories and closely stacked houses. The positive face
is the eastern half of the city and the northernmost section along
the Wenham line, consisting primarily of woods, some gracious
residential neighborhoods, and the magnificent Atlantic shore. The
two eastern-most communities of Pride's Crossing and Beverly
Farms have been havens for Boston's landed gentry since the railroad was built in the 1800s. In the wedge of land between Route
127 and the ocean, dozens of mansions rise in isolated splendor at
the end of quarter-mile-long driveways.

Your first encounter with the shore comes at Lynch Park, commanding a promontory jutting into the ocean. As city parks go it is
a pleasure—clean, well landscaped, and well maintained. Just east
of the park on the next point stands a handsome lighthouse built in

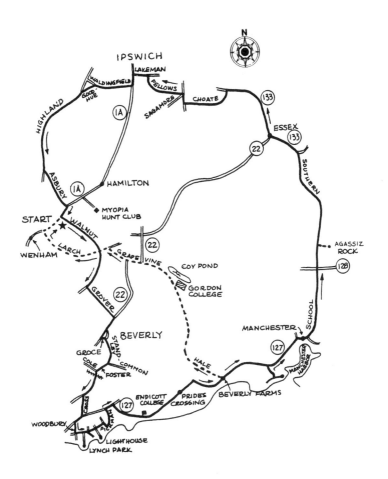

1871. A mile up the coast is Endicott College, a women's school and one of the most spectacularly located in the state. Several of its buildings are elegant mansions perched directly on the rocky shoreline.

From here it's a short ride through Pride's Crossing, with its touristy country store at the railroad crossing, and then Beverly Farms and on into Manchester, where you'll loop along the water on a little lane before coming into town.

Manchester is a gracious seaside town with more oceanfront estates belonging to Boston's bluebloods; fine old homes on the streets adjacent to the center of town; and beautiful Singing Beach, one of the North Shore's nicest. In the town center is the handsome town hall and a graceful white church dated 1809.

Leaving Manchester, you'll pass Agassiz Rock at the Essex town line. This is a large glacial boulder on top of a hill with a fine view of Massachusetts Bay. The area is maintained by the Trustees of Reservations. From here you'll have a smooth run into Essex, another delightful town with a cluster of antique shops along the main street. If you like clams you're in the right place—all the restaurants serve clams that were on the ocean floor only hours before. The best-known spot is Woodman's, on the left as you're heading down Route 133. The remainder of the town consists of vast salt marshes extending along the estuaries of the Essex and Castle Neck rivers, wooded hills, and some broad farms.

After you leave Essex, the remainder of the ride goes through a little bit of Ipswich and then across Hamilton, passing through magnificent horse-farm and estate country. Hamilton is another gracious, well-to-do-community where many of the residents are likely to feed the family horse in the morning. Its best-known landmark is the Myopia Hunt Club, an extensive estate founded in 1875 that is the major center for polo in the state. Polo matches are held on Sunday afternoons at 3 o'clock and are fascinating to watch. If you'd like to go to them after the ride, the Club is on Route 1A a half mile north of the starting point.

The short ride bypasses Manchester, Essex, and Hamilton by taking a direct route from Beverly Farms back to the start. You'll pass through a long slice of Wenham, going by Gordon College, beautifully situated on an unspoiled lake, and then past horse farms and country estates.

Directions for the ride: 26 miles

1. Turn right out of parking lot onto Walnut Road and go 1.1 miles to crossroads and stop sign (Larch Row).

2. Go straight at crossroads. You'll immediately pass an unusual Gothic-style church on your right. Go 7/10 mile to Grover Street on left.

3. Turn left on Grover Street and go 1.1 miles to end (Essex Street, Route 22). • *CAUTION:* Grover Street may be bumpy from recent sewer construction.

4. Turn right at end and go 2/10 mile to Groce Street, which turns sharply left just before a gas station.

5. Turn sharp left on Groce Street and immediately right on Standley Street. Go 7/10 mile to fork where Common Lane bears left and Foster Street bears right.

6. Bear right on Foster Street and go 3/10 mile to another fork, where Cole Street bears right and the main road bears left across railroad tracks.

7. Bear left across tracks and go 7/10 mile to Cross Street, which bears left immediately after traffic island.

8. Bear left on Cross Street and go 3/10 mile to end (Route 22).

9. Turn right on Route 22 and go 1/10 mile to Woodbury Street, which bears left. It's your second left.

10. Bear left on Woodbury Street and go 2/10 mile to crossroads and stop sign.

11. Turn left at crossroads. Just ahead is the entrance to Lynch Park. The view from the point is impressive.

12. Immediately past the park entrance, bear slightly left on Neptune Street (don't turn 90 degrees left on Evergreen Drive) and go 3/10 mile to end. If you want to visit the lighthouse, turn right at first crossroads on Bayview Avenue.

13. Turn right at end and go 3/10 mile to end (Route 127).

14. Turn right on Route 127. Just ahead Route 127 curves sharply right. Continue along Route 127 for 3 miles to Hale Street, which turns left immediately after the third railroad crossing. Here the short ride turns left and the long ride goes straight. • *CAUTION:* These are dangerous diagonal railroad crossings with frequent train traffic. Walk your bike over them.

15. Continue along Route 127 for 1.1 miles to Harbor Street, which bears to the right at a traffic island. The Old Corner Inn is on the far side of the intersection.

16. Bear right on this road and go 2/10 mile to end, immediately after a little railroad bridge.

17. Turn right at end and go 2/10 mile to where the road becomes private, just beyond the beautiful rockbound inlet called Black Cove. Make a U-turn here and backtrack to Route 127. If you wish you can bear right when you come to the road that crosses the railroad bridge and go 1/4 mile to the end at Tucks Point, a small peninsula at the mouth of Manchester Harbor. Here you'll find a yacht club and a small waterfront park with a gazebo.

18. Turn right on Route 127 and go 8/10 mile to School Street (unmarked), which bears left in the center of Manchester opposite the town hall/police station and the classical white church. A sign at the intersection points left to Essex.

19. Bear left on School Street and go 4.1 miles to end (Route 133). After 1.7 miles you'll see a dirt turnoff on the right. It's 6/10 mile beyond the Route 128 bridge, just after dirt road on the left merges into the main road. From here a path leads 1/4 mile to Agassiz Rock, a large boulder with a fine view of the bay.

20. Bear left on Route 133 and go 1/2 mile to fork where Route 133 bears right and Route 22 bears left. You'll go through the center of Essex. At the fork the ride bears right, but if you bear left for 2/10 mile you'll come to the town hall, a portly wooden Victorian monstrosity with the fattest clock tower in Massachusetts.

21. Bear right on Route 133 and go 1.9 miles to Choate Street on left, just before top of hill.

22. Turn left on Choate Street and go 1.3 miles to end.

23. Turn right at end and go 1/10 mile to your first left.

24. Bear left, and immediately go straight at crossroads onto Fellows Road. Continue 1.2 miles to end.

25. Turn left at end and go 3/10 mile to end (Route 1A).

26. Turn left on Route 1A and go 2/10 mile to Waldingfield Road on right.

27. Turn right on Waldingfield Road and go 8/10 mile to your first left. It comes up while you're going downhill.

28. Turn left and go 1/2 mile to end (merge head-on into Highland Street).

29. Go straight on Highland Street for 2.3 miles to Asbury Street, which bears left at blinking light.

30. Bear left on Asbury Street and go 1 mile to end (Route 1A).

31. Turn right on Route 1A and go 2/10 mile to shopping center on left.

Directions for the ride: 16 miles

1. Follow directions for the long ride through number 14.

2. Turn left immediately after railroad tracks on Hale Street and go 4.4 miles to end (Larch Row). Hale Street becomes Hart Street, which in turn becomes Grapevine Road. The lane along the lake behind Gordon College is delightful.

3. Turn left on Larch Row and go 1/10 mile to crossroads. Notice the unusual Gothic-style church on your left.

4. Go straight at crossroads 1.6 miles to end (Route 1A). Here the ride turns right, but if you turn left for 3/10 mile you'll come to the lovely town center of Wenham. On the left is the Claflin-Richards House, built in 1664, and an adjoining museum of nineteenth-century dolls, toys, and games.

5. Turn right on Route 1A and go 7/10 mile to shopping center on right.

14. Gateway to Cape Ann: West Gloucester–Essex–Manchester–Magnolia

Number of miles: 23

Terrain: Gently rolling, with two short hills.

Food: Grocery stores and restaurants in the towns. The regional favorite dish is clams, especially in Essex.

Start: West Gloucester T station, on Route 133, 1.1 miles east of Route 128 (take exit 14). It's on your left, immediately after you go under the railroad bridge.

The area just west of Cape Ann has the glorious seascape scenery of the Cape itself without the tourists and the traffic. Like Cape Ann, the region is characterized by gracious old towns; the rocky coastline with mansions and estates perched above it in baronial splendor; little sandy beaches tucked between craggy headlands; and lonely, unspoiled salt marshes along the northern shore.

The ride starts from West Gloucester, the less urban portion of the city on the western side of the canal that separates Cape Ann from the mainland. You will head westward along the rural, unspoiled northern shore past woods, small farms, and salt marshes to Essex, another picturesque community. In the center of town, just off the route, are several antique shops, snack bars serving clams dredged up from the ocean floor only hours before, and the mouth of the Essex River, filled with small fishing boats. From Essex it's a smooth run to Manchester. At the town line you'll pass Agassiz Rock, a large glacial boulder on top of a hill, from which there's a superb view of Massachusetts Bay. The area is maintained by the Trustees of Reservations.

Manchester is a stately seaside community with a graceful white church, built in 1809, dominating the center of town. Also in town are the Trask House, an elegant Federal-period mansion, and an old cemetery filled with weathered slate gravestones dating back to 1800 and before. Just outside of town is Smith Point, a rockbound, steep-spined peninsula just south of town rimmed with mansions of Boston Brahmins and landed gentry. The northern shore of the neck offers fine views of boat-filled Manchester Har-

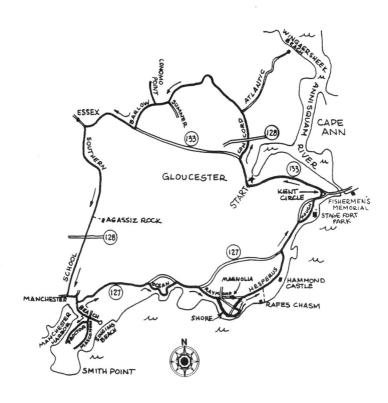

CONOMO POINT

ESSEX

BARLOW

SUMNER

ATLANTIC

WINGAERSHEEK BEACH

ANNISQUAM

CAPE ANN

SOUTHERN

133

CONCORD

128

133

RIVER

GLOUCESTER

START

KENT CIRCLE

FISHERMEN'S MEMORIAL

STAGE FORT PARK

AGASSIZ ROCK

128

SCHOOL

127

OCEAN

MAGNOLIA

RAYMOND

HESPERUS

HAMMOND CASTLE

MANCHESTER

127

RAFES CHASM

BEACH

PROCTOR

MANCHESTER HARBOR

MASONIC

SINGING BEACH

SHORE

N

SMITH POINT

bor. As you leave Smith Point you visit Singing Beach, one of the North Shore's finest, a wide, graceful curve of smooth but squeaky (singing) sand with rocky headlands at each end and a succession of mansions gracing the water's edge.

From Manchester you'll follow the coast across the Gloucester town line into Magnolia, a gracious nineteenth-century resort community with a row of smart shops and a delightful lane hugging the shore of the small peninsula on which the village is located. Just up the road a short trail leads to the shore, where you'll get a view of Rafe's Chasm, a spectacular narrow defile in the cliffs rising from the sea about 75 feet deep. A little further on is one of the North Shore's most distinctive landmarks, the Hammond Museum, often called the Hammond Castle. It is a medieval-style castle, complete with moat and drawbridge, spectacularly located on the oceanfront cliffs. It was built in 1928 by John Hays Hammond, inventor of systems to control the movement of vehicles from a distance by radio and an avid collector of medieval artifacts. Until legislation prohibited the practice, it was fashionable for the wealthy to plunder the European landscape for bits and pieces of old castles and palaces, which is exactly what Hammond did to construct his own. Inside is a fascinating collection of medieval furniture, tapestries, armor, and other relics. The centerpiece of the castle is a magnificent organ with more than 8,000 pipes, on which concerts are given during the summer. From behind the building you can see Normans Woe, the offshore rocks made famous by Longfellow's "The Wreck of the Hesperus."

From the Castle it's about two miles to the canal separating Cape Ann from the mainland. Just before the canal is Stage Fort Park, a dramatic oceanfront expanse that's worth exploring. From the canal, it's only a couple of miles back to the starting point.

Directions for the ride

1. Turn right (west) out of parking lot onto Route 133 and go 7/10 mile to Concord Street on right (sign may say to Wingaersheek Motel and Beach).

2. Turn right on Concord Street. After 1/2 mile you'll go underneath Route 128. Continue 7/10 mile to Atlantic Street on right. Here the ride goes straight, but if you turn right and go 2 miles

Annisquam River in Gloucester, separating Cape Ann from the mainland.

you'll come to Wingaersheek Beach. Atlantic Street is a pleasant, narrow road winding along salt marshes.

3. Continue straight on Concord Street 2.1 miles to fork where the right-hand road goes over a little bridge, and Summer Street bears left.

4. Bear right at fork. After 4/10 mile Conomo Point Road bears right, but curve left on main road and go 6/10 mile to end (Route 133).

5. Turn right on Route 133 and go 1.3 miles to Southern Avenue on left (there's a flower pot at the intersection). It's shortly after Grove Street, also on left. You'll pass Farnham's on your right; this is a well-known restaurant specializing in clams. When you get to Southern Avenue, the ride turns left, but if you go straight for 1/2 mile you'll come to the center of Essex, where you can browse through several antique shops.

6. Turn left on Southern Avenue and go 4.1 miles to end (Route 127), in the center of Manchester. After 2.4 miles, you'll see a small dirt turnoff on the left (it's just before a dirt road bears right). From here a path leads 3/10 mile to Agassiz Rock, a large boulder on a hilltop.

7. Turn left on Route 127. Just ahead it jogs right and immediately left.

8. Where Route 127 turns left, go straight ahead across the railroad tracks onto Beach Street. Go 4/10 mile to crossroads (Masconomo Street). Just past the tracks on your right is a little park overlooking Manchester Harbor.

9. Turn right on Masconomo Street. Just ahead is a fork. Bike along each branch until the road becomes private, then backtrack to Beach Street. The righthand branch leads 1/2 mile to a fine view of Manchester Harbor, and the lefthand branch winds 6/10 mile to Lobster Cove, a small inlet bounded by rocky headlands.

10. Turn right on Beach Street and go 2/10 mile to end. This is Singing Beach.

11. Make a U-turn and go 7/10 mile back to Route 127.

12. Turn right on Route 127 and go 1.6 miles to Ocean Street, which bears right.

13. Bear right on Ocean Street and go 9/10 mile to end (Route 127). You'll go along two little coves—the first one is called

White Beach, the second one Black Beach.

14. Turn right on Route 127 and go 4/10 mile to Raymond Street, which bears right.

15. Bear right on Raymond Street and go 1/2 mile to crossroads. This is Magnolia.

16. Turn 90 degrees right at crossroads onto Shore Road, following the ocean on your right and go 7/10 mile to end (merge to the right onto a wider road). • *CAUTION:* This second half of Shore Road is very bumpy, so slow way down and enjoy the scenery.

17. Turn sharply left at end and go 1/10 mile to crossroads at top of hill (Lexington Avenue).

18. Turn right on Lexington Avenue and go 2/10 mile to end (Hesperus Avenue).

19. Turn right at end. After 1/2 mile you'll see a small dirt parking lot and metal fence on your right. From here a path leads 1/4 mile to the ocean for the view of Rafe's Chasm.

20. Continue on Hesperus Avenue 1.2 miles to end (Route 127). The Hammond Castle will be on your right after 1/2 mile.

21. Turn right on Route 127 and go 7/10 mile to Hough Avenue on right (sign says Stage Fort Park).

22. Turn right on Hough Avenue and go 1/2 mile to end (merge into Route 127). You'll go through Stage Fort Park, a large oceanfront park.

23. Bear right on Route 127 and then immediately bear left on Kent Circle. Just ahead, Kent Circle merges into Route 133. (If you continue straight on Route 127 for 2/10 mile you'll come to the bridge over the Blynman Canal to Cape Ann. Just beyond the bridge is the famous statue of the weathered fisherman at the helm of his boat.)

24. Bear left on Route 133 and go 1.8 miles to T station on right, just before railroad bridge.

15. Cape Ann: Gloucester–Rockport

Number of miles: 27 (11 with East Gloucester area only, 20
    with shortcut from Rockport)
Terrain: Gently rolling, with a few short hills.
Food: Numerous groceries and snack bars along the way.
Start: Junction of Routes 127 and 133 in Gloucester, just west of
    the bridge over the Blynman Canal. Park on Route 127 on
    the ocean side of the road.

• *CAUTION:* On good weekend days Cape Ann is crowded with
people and traffic. It's not much of a hazard because it won't be
moving much faster than you. The main hazards are car doors
opening into your path, drivers pulling out in front of you without
looking, and getting your bike stolen. Don't leave it unlocked, and if
you leave it, take your accessories with you (pump, handlebar bag,
tools, and the rest).

You've probably been to Cape Ann. If you haven't, everything
you've heard about it is true. It's one of the most popular places to
visit in the state, and with good reason. Nowhere else on the coast
do four distinct elements—a working fishing port, historic communities filled with graceful, well-maintained old buildings, a glorious coastline with dozens of picturesque coves and rocky
headlands and curving beaches, and a major artists' colony and
crafts center—blend into a thoroughly appealing and satisfying
composite. And the only way to fully experience it—to smell the
sweet, freshly caught fish, to feel the power of surf crashing against
rocks, to let the impression of each mansion and each little cove
and beach imprint itself on your mind—is to tour it on a bicycle.

Much of Cape Ann's unique charm stems from its refreshingly
unspoiled condition despite the annual onslaught of millions of visitors. Except for a couple of ugly motels on the East Gloucester
shore and the cutesy-fake strip of shops on Bearskin Neck in Rockport, you will see none of the unsightly commercial development
and ripoff tourist traps that mar so many other naturally beautiful

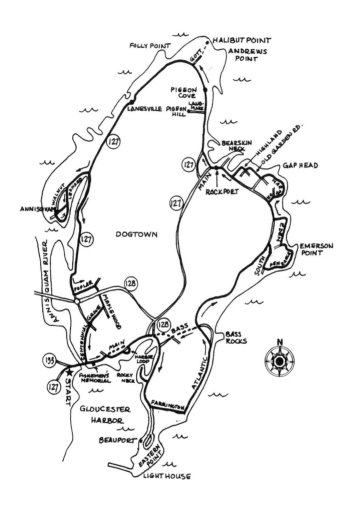

FOLLY POINT
HALIBUT POINT
ANDREWS POINT
GOTT
PIGEON COVE
LANESVILLE PIGEON HILL
LAND-MARK
127
BEARSKIN NECK
HIGHLAND
OLD GARDEN RD.
GAP HEAD
127
MAIN
ROCKPORT
WALNUT
LEONARD
ANNISQUAM
127
DOGTOWN
127
EDEN
SOUTH
EMERSON POINT
PEN LANCE
ANNISQUAM RIVER
POPLAR
128
MAPLEWOOD
128
BASS
BASS ROCKS
N
133
MAIN
FENTONHALL GROVE
HARBOR LOOP
ATLANTIC
127
START
FISHERMEN'S MEMORIAL
ROCKY NECK
FARRINGTON
GLOUCESTER HARBOR
BEAUPORT
EASTERN POINT
LIGHTHOUSE

97

areas across the country. No sleazy fast-food joints or shabby rows of beach cottages despoil the shore; instead you'll find gracious older homes, delightful old villages gracing the inlets and hillsides along the Cape's northern shore, and sometimes nothing man-made at all.

To fully enjoy the trip, pick a comfortable day, ideally not on a weekend, and take the whole day to explore what Cape Ann has to offer. Explore the historic old center of Gloucester, visit the forty-room Beauport mansion, poke around the art galleries on Rocky Neck, walk out to tips of land like the breakwater at the end of Eastern Point or rock-bound Halibut Point at the northern extremity of the Cape. When you get back to Gloucester, step onto the old wharves and watch the day's catch being unloaded. Don't try to rush—Cape Ann is too special for that.

You'll circle the Cape in a counterclockwise direction, heading first by the famous Fishermen's Memorial, a statue of the hardy fisherman gripping the helm of his boat. It was erected in 1923 during Gloucester's tricentennial. You'll go along the wharves and by fish-processing plants lining the inner harbor. A couple of blocks inland from the harbor is the old center of town, which is worth a look. The graceful Victorian town hall, built in 1871, and the hand-some library are New England classics. Also gracing downtown are several fine churches and elegant old homes.

You'll now head down to Eastern Point, the estate-lined penin-sula forming the southern tip of Cape Ann. First you'll visit Rocky Neck, center of the artist colony. A mile farther down is Beauport, one of the state's most impressive mansions. Its forty rooms over-flow with antiques and decorative artwork from every period of American history. It was the home of Henry Davis Sleeper, a promi-nent interior designer and antique collector early in the century. Maintained by the Society for the Preservation of New England Antiquities, it is unfortunately not open weekends except in Sep-tember and October, and then only in the afternoon. It's open weekdays all day from May through October.

At the southern end of Eastern Point is an Audubon sanctuary, a Coast Guard Station, a graceful old lighthouse, and a half-mile-long breakwater extending nearly halfway across the entrance to Gloucester Harbor. You'll now head up the eastern shore of the

Rockport Harbor with the peak-roofed building that is referred to as Motif Number One.

Cape, hugging the ocean on one of the finest coastal runs in the state. As you proceed to Rockport you'll go inland just a bit, then hug the shore again on little lanes.

Rockport is visually a delight, with the tiny boat-clogged harbor, complete with Motif Number One, looking just as it does in the ubiquitous pictures. Even the cutesy gift shops look properly old and weathered from the back. The gently curving beach, with the graceful churches and old white houses of the town stretching behind it, is delightful. A mile north of Rockport you can climb 200-foot-high Pigeon Hill for a magnificent view of the town. Just ahead is Halibut Point, the northern tip of Cape Ann, an impressive spot where the surf washes onto broad, flat rocks. It's maintained by our old friends, the Trustees of Reservations.

Beyond Halibut Point you'll cross the town line back into Gloucester and go through a string of unspoiled little villages—Lanesville, Bay View, Annisquam, and Riverdale. From here it's a short distance back to the starting point with the best downhill run of the ride.

Directions for the ride: 27 miles

1. Head east on Route 127 over the bridge. Just ahead on the right is the Fishermen's Memorial statue.

2. Just 2/10 mile beyond the Fishermen's Memorial, Route 127 jogs right and immediately left. Continue 1/4 mile to Harbor Loop on right.

3. Turn right on Harbor Loop and go 3/10 mile to end (Route 127). This is a small loop closer to the harbor.

4. Turn right on Route 127 and go 1/2 mile to fork where Route 127 bears left.

5. Bear right at fork and go 1/10 mile to another fork, at traffic light.

6. Bear right uphill at traffic light (sign may say to East Gloucester) and go 1.1 miles along the water to Rocky Neck Avenue on right (sign may say to Rocky Neck).

7. Turn right on Rocky Neck Avenue. Go 4/10 mile to end, then backtrack. The small Rocky Neck peninsula is the center of the Gloucester art colony.

Lobsterman's cottage in Rockport.

8. Leaving Rocky Neck, turn right and go 1/2 mile to a smaller road that bears right along the water through a pair of stone pillars. Here the ride bears left, but if you bear right and go 6/10 mile, the Beauport mansion is on your right. Just past the mansion, the road makes a small one-way loop; follow the "turn left" sign where a private road goes straight.

9. Bear left on main road and go 2.7 miles to crossroads and stop sign (Bass Avenue). This is a spectacular run along the ocean. At Bass Avenue the short ride turns left and the long ride goes straight.

10. Go straight at crossroads for 1 mile to fork where the main road bears left.

11. Bear left and go 1.8 miles to South Street, which turns sharply right at traffic island. It's at the top of a long, gradual hill.

12. Turn sharp right on South Street and go 4/10 mile to Penzance Road (unmarked) on left, just before ocean.

13. Turn left on Penzance Road and go 8/10 mile to Eden Road on right.

14. Turn right on Eden Road, following the ocean on your right, and go 8/10 mile to end (Route 127A). Eden Road is very bumpy; slow down and enjoy the scenery.

15. Turn right on Route 127A and go 3/10 mile to Marmion Way on right.

16. Turn right on Marmion Way. Just ahead is a fork. Bear right at fork, staying on the main road, and go 8/10 mile to small crossroads (Old Garden Road). You'll pass an old metal radio tower on your right.

17. Turn right on Old Garden Road and go 4/10 mile to another crossroads (Highland Avenue).

18. Turn right on Highland Avenue and go 3/10 mile to end. • *CAUTION:* Highland Avenue is bumpy. On your right is tiny Rockport Harbor. The small red wooden building on the opposite shore with the peaked roof is Motif Number One, one of the most frequently painted places in the country.

19. Turn right at end of Highland Avenue. After 2/10 mile the road widens into Dock Square and a narrow lane bears right onto Bearskin Neck. This is the heart of Rockport. On a nice day you'll have to walk your bike through the throngs of tourists swarming amid the clutter of crafts shops, boutiques, and ice cream stands.

20. From Bearskin Neck, continue on the main road 2/10 mile to fork. Here the ride bears right, but you can cut it short by bearing left and then going straight on Route 127 back to Gloucester.

21. Bear right at fork, following the ocean. Go 4/10 mile to end (merge to your right into Route 127).

22. Bear right at end. After 6/10 mile you'll see Landmark Lane on your left. This road climbs a steep hill with a broad, grassy park at the top and a magnificent view of Rockport and the surrounding coastline. Continue on Route 127 for 1.2 miles to Gott Avenue on right (Route 127 curves left at the intersection). If you turn right on Gott Avenue, just ahead a path leads 4/10 mile to Halibut Point.

23. Leaving Halibut Point, continue along Route 127 for 2.9 miles to Leonard Street on right (sign may say to Annisquam Village). There's a church on the far corner.

24. Turn right on this road and go 4/10 mile to fork (Walnut Street bears right uphill). You are now entering Annisquam.

25. Bear left downhill at fork and go 2/10 mile to Bridgewater Street on left.

26. Turn left on Bridgewater Street and immediately turn right, following Lobster Cove on your left. Go 3/10 mile to end (Leonard Street).

27. Turn right on Leonard Street. Just ahead is a fork. Bear right and go 7/10 mile to end (Route 127).

28. Turn right on Route 127 and go 2.9 miles to Poplar Street on left, immediately before rotary.

29. Turn left on Poplar Street and go 4/10 mile to Maplewood Avenue on right. There's a garage on the far corner. If you're adventurous, you can visit Dogtown, the wooded, uninhabited interior of Cape Ann, which is dotted with cellar holes of eighteenth-century dwellings. To get there, turn left on Cherry Street just before Maplewood Avenue. Go 7/10 mile to a lane bearing right up a steep hill, and follow the lane until it becomes dirt. A mazework of paths weaves through the scrubby, rolling landscape. It's very easy to get lost.

30. Turn right on Maplewood Avenue and go 2/10 mile to Grove Street, a crossroads just before an old factory on left.

31. Turn right on Grove Street. You'll immediately see a large cemetery on your left. Parallel the cemetery for 3/10 mile to end.

32. At end of Grove Street jog left and immediately right. Go 6/10 mile to end (Route 127).

33. Turn right on Route 127 and cross the bridge back to starting point.

Directions for the ride: 11 miles

1. Follow directions for the long ride through number 9.

2. Turn left on Bass Avenue and go 1/2 mile to traffic light where Route 128 turns right.

3. Go straight at light 3/10 mile to fork at top of hill.

4. Bear right at fork on Main Street (sign may say Business District). Go 6/10 mile through downtown Gloucester until you rejoin Route 127. If you wish, you can turn right on Pleasant Street and then take your next left on Middle Street, which goes past the Victorian city hall and other old buildings.

5. Go straight on Route 127 for 4/10 mile across the bridge back to starting point.

16. Ipswich Ride

Number of miles: 21 (11 with Crane's Beach section only, 11 with Great Neck section only).

Terrain: Flat, with a tough climb to the Crane estate on Castle Hill, and a couple of short, steep hills on Great Neck.

Food: Numerous stores and restaurants in the center of Ipswich. Here too the local specialty is clams.

Start: Free municipal parking lot behind the business block at the corner of Route 1A and Topsfield Road in downtown Ipswich. Entrance to the lot is on Hammatt Street, which is off Route 1A one block north of Topsfield Road.

Ipswich ranks high as one of the most beautiful towns in the state, both architecturally and geographically. If you're a historic-house enthusiast, you'll exult: the town has more pre-Revolutionary homes—some going back to the 1600s—than any other locale north of Williamsburg, Virginia. Beyond the center of town is an unspoiled mixture of wooded hills, broad, gently rolling horse farms and gracious country estates, vast salt marshes stretching to the horizon, the Great Neck peninsula rising steeply from the bay, and magnificent four-mile-long Crane's Beach, New England's finest beach north of Cape Cod.

The ride starts from the center of Ipswich, lying between a North Green and a South Green and surrounded by a marvelous variety of buildings, all painstakingly restored and maintained, spanning every architectural style from early Colonial days to the turn of the century. You'll head first to Crane's Beach through an idyllic landscape of salt marshes, horse paddocks, and estates. A quarter mile from the beach, the majestic Crane mansion, resembling a palace from the Italian Renaissance, crowns Castle Hill. The wide beach is unique in that it is almost completely unspoiled—no hot dog stands, no cottages, no anything except sand, dunes, and lots of people on a hot day. The beach, along with the Castle Hill estate, is owned by our friends the Trustees of Reservations.

From Crane's Beach you'll return to the center of town and then head through an endless expanse of salt marshes to the Great Neck peninsula, just north of Crane's Beach. Rising steeply from the bay in a succession of four round drumlins, it is surrounded by salt marshes on the west, the broad Plum Island Sound on the north, the southern tip of Plum Island on the east, and Crane's Beach on the south. The roads rimming the peninsula offer spectacular views of this varied and beautiful seascape. From Great Neck you return through the salt marshes to Ipswich.

Directions for the ride: 21 miles

1. Turn right out of lot onto Hammatt Street and go to end (Route 1A).

2. Turn right on Route 1A. After 1/10 mile you will cross the Ipswich River over the Choate Bridge, built in 1764. This graceful stone arch is one of the oldest original bridges in the country. A quarter mile beyond the bridge, the road curves sharply to the right. At the curve the John Whipple House is on your right. It is a fine example of Colonial architecture. Built in 1640, it has numerous period furnishings and an herb garden. Across the road is the Thomas Franklin Waters Memorial, a Federal-era mansion with articles from the China trade and a carriage collection. Both buildings are open to visitors.

3. A hundred yards beyond the John Whipple House, turn left on Argilla Road (sign may say to Castle Hill, Crane's Beach) and go 1/2 mile to Heartbreak Road on right.

4. Turn right on Heartbreak Road and go 7/10 mile to end (Route 133).

5. Turn left on Route 133 and go 1.1 miles to Northgate Road on left (sign says to Castle Hill, Crane's Beach).

6. Turn left on Northgate Road and go 7/10 mile to end.

7. Turn right at end (you're back on Argilla Road) and go 2.4 miles to the entrance to Crane's Beach. During the summer, there is unfortunately a fee for bicycles that is more than nominal. If you plan to spend some time here the fee is worth it, considering the beauty of the area and the fact that your money is supporting the Trustees of Reservations, without whom the place would probably be another Hampton Beach. During the off-season the fee is nominal and the attendant may wave you through.

8. Leaving Crane's Beach, backtrack on Argilla Road 1/4 mile to the entrance to Castle Hill on right. The climb to the top is un-

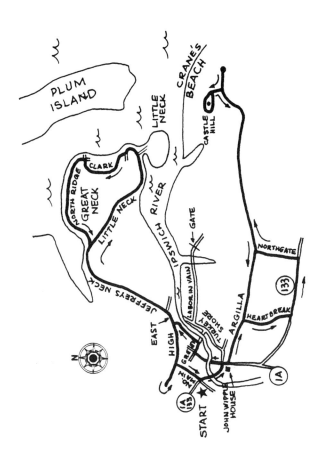

PLUM ISLAND

LITTLE NECK

CRANE'S BEACH

CASTLE HILL

CLARK

NORTH RIDGE

GREAT NECK

LITTLE NECK

IPSWICH RIVER

GATE

NORTHGATE

133

JEFFREY'S NECK

LABOR IN VAIN

TURKEY SHORE

ARGILLA

HEARTBREAK

EAST

HIGH

GREEN

NO. MAIN

1A

START

JOHN WHIPPLE HOUSE

1A 133

N

107

questionably worth the effort. You'll be rewarded by the view of the mansion along the smooth lawn undulating between two groves of trees in a rippling green ribbon for nearly half a mile between the mansion and the cliff overlooking the ocean. From the edge of the cliff a panorama of sea, marsh, and dune spreads before you. At the far end of the lawn, a path on the right leads down to accurately named Steep Beach.

9. Leaving Castle Hill, turn right on Argilla Road and go four miles to end (Routes 1A and 133).

10. Turn right on Routes 1A and 133. Just ahead the main road curves 90 degrees left, but go straight 3/10 mile to crossroads (Green Street, unmarked). If you wish you can take a side trip (1.5 miles out and 1.5 miles back) along the south bank of the Ipswich River on a narrow lane through idyllic landscape out of Tennyson's poetry. Turn right where Routes 1A and 133 curve left and go 1 block to your first left, Turkey Shore Road. Turn left and go 4/10 mile to Labor in Vain Road on right (dead end if you go straight). Turn right on Labor in Vain Road and go 1 mile to a gate across the road. Shortly before the gate is a delightful little wooden bridge. At the gate, backtrack to Routes 1A and 133, turn 90 degrees right and go 3/10 mile to crossroads (Green Street).

11. Turn right on Green Street and go 1/10 mile to your first left, immediately before a little bridge over the Ipswich River.

12. Turn left on this road, following the river, and go 4/10 mile to the far end of the town wharf parking lot.

13. At the end of the lot jog left and then immediately right onto the main road. Go 1/10 mile to fork (main road bears left).

14. Bear left on the main road and go 1.7 miles to another fork (North Ridge Road bears left).

15. Bear right at fork and follow the main road 1.4 miles to another fork where the right-hand branch goes over a causeway. On the far side of the causeway is Little Neck, a small ellipse about 1/4 mile across and filled with attractive older summer homes. This area is private.

16. Bear left at fork onto Bay View Road, following the ocean on your right, and go 2/10 mile to fork. The land across the bay is the southern tip of Plum Island.

17. Bear right at fork on Clark Road, following the water, and go 8/10 mile to crossroads (Colby Road). The large concrete building on top of hill is an Air Force installation.

18. Turn left on Colby Road. After 1 mile, you will merge right at yield sign, at bottom of hill. Continue 2.1 miles to a fork that is 1/4 mile beyond the town wharf. A sign may say East Street, which you were just on.

19. Bear right at fork and go 1/2 mile until you come to a cemetery on your right, rising in terraces up a steep hillside. This is High Street, the heart of Old Ipswich, with most of the houses predating 1800.

20. At the cemetery make a U-turn and backtrack 3/10 mile to North Main Street on right.

21. Turn right on North Main Street and go 3/10 mile to crossroads at bottom of hill (Routes 1A and 133). Notice the varied old buildings lining both sides of the green. The modern church in the center of the green, clashing with all the architecture surrounding it, comes as a surprise. It was built to replace a classic New England church that burned to the ground in 1965 after being struck by lightning.

22. Turn right on Routes 1A and 133. Go 1/10 mile to Hammatt Street on left.

23. Turn left on Hammatt Street. Parking lot is just ahead on left.

Directions for the ride: 11 miles (Crane's Beach section)

1. Follow directions for the 21-mile ride through number 9.

2. Turn right on Routes 1A and 133. Go 4/10 mile to crossroads immediately after the Choate Bridge. You may also want to take the side trip in direction number 10.

3. Continue straight at crossroads for 1/10 mile to Hammatt Street on left.

4. Turn left on Hammatt Street. Parking lot is just ahead on left.

Directions for the ride: 11 miles (Great Neck section)

1. Follow directions number 1 and 2 for the 21-mile ride.

2. At the John Whipple House, Routes 1A and 133 curve 90 degrees right, but turn left instead. Go 3/10 mile to crossroads

(Green Street).

3. Follow directions for the 21-mile ride from number 11 to the end.

17. Newburyport–Newbury–Rowley

Number of miles 17 (22 with western loop)
Terrain: Gently rolling, with one hill
Food: Grocery and snack bar in Rowley.
Start: Rupert A. Nock School, corner of Low and Johnson streets in Newburyport. If you're coming from the south on Route 95, take the Scotland Road exit. Turn right on Scotland Road and go 3 miles to end (Low Street). Turn left on Low Street and go 2/10 mile to school on right. If you're coming from the north, exit east from Route 95 onto Route 113. Go 3/10 mile to Low Street on right, just before Friendly. Turn right on Low Street and go 1.3 miles to school on left.

This ride takes you exploring among the broad salt marshes, prosperous farmland, and gracious estates just inland from the coast south of Newburyport. You'll pass imposing mansions built by sea captains and merchants in Newburyport and also Governor Dummer Academy, one of the oldest preparatory schools in the country. The area abounds with country roads that promise relaxed and delightful biking.

Situated at the mouth of the Merrimack River, Newburyport became a thriving shipbuilding community during the 1700s and then evolved as a commercial center. The most successful sea captains and merchants built elegant mansions along a two-mile stretch of High Street, which you'll go along at the beginning of the ride.

The downtown and waterfront areas, lying just off the route between High Street and the river, have recently been restored and are worth exploring. Gracious brick buildings from the Federal era line State Street, the main downtown street. At the base of State Street, next to the river, is Market Square, where the old brick mercantile buildings have been recycled into a mini-mall of antique shops, galleries, and craft shops. The result is tasteful rather than touristy. The library, built in 1771, is an especially fine building, as is also the stately granite Custom House, built in 1835 and now a maritime museum. Adjoining the downtown are narrow streets lined with old wooden homes.

Just south of Newburyport is Newbury, a small town consisting mainly of salt marshes and farmland. In the village center are several historic homes from the 1600s and 1700s. Just outside of town you'll pass Old Town Hill, a small glacial drumlin rising 170 feet above the Parker River. Maintained by the Trustees of Reservations, it offers an outstanding view of the Parker River, Plum Island, and the broad estuary separating it from the mainland.

From Newbury you'll head along Route 1A past broad salt marshes and well-kept farms to Rowley, an attractive small town. As numbered routes go, Route 1A is one of the best in the state for bicycling—smooth, flat, not heavily traveled, and with a good shoulder. In Rowley you'll head inland and then you'll pass the Daniels Wagon Factory, built in 1868. Its chief product is wooden wheels for vending wagons and pushcarts like those at Quincy Market. It turns out a few wagons and carriages also. The manufacturing is handcrafted by traditional methods, using primarily original tools and equipment. For maximum strength and resiliency, the wheels are made of hickory with elm hubs. Feel free to stop in; you'll get a tour if they're not too busy.

A few miles farther along you'll go through the gracious campus of the Governor Dummer Academy, founded in 1763 and one of the oldest preparatory schools in the country. The return to Newburyport leads along country lanes as you follow the Parker River a short distance, cross it, and proceed past stately old farmhouses and immaculate fields.

Directions for the ride: 22 miles

1. Turn right onto Low Street and go 2/10 mile to crossroads (Toppans Lane on right).

2. Turn right at crossroads and go 4/10 mile to end (Route 113).

3. Turn right on Route 113. After 1/2 mile, at the Route 1 overpass, Route 113 becomes Route 1A. Continue straight on Route 1A for 1.2 miles to Green Street, which bears right at the Newbury town green. As you're going along, notice the numerous mansions built by the sea captains and merchants. Cushing House,

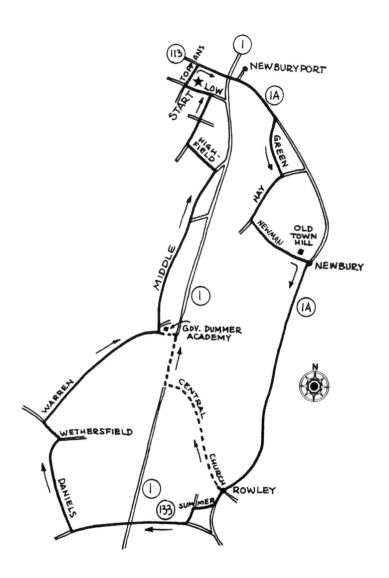

at 98 High Street, is open to the public. Just beyond Route 1 you'll pass the stately Bulfinch-designed courthouse and the old granite jail. A few blocks to your left are the downtown and waterfront.

4. Bear right on Green Street and go 2/10 mile to crossroads and stop sign. As you start down Green Street, notice the town hall on the left side of the green.

5. Go straight at crossroads 9/10 mile to end, at stop sign.

6. Turn right at end and go 8/10 mile to Newman Road (unmarked) on left, just after small bridge.

7. Turn left on Newman Road, crossing a salt marsh, and go 1.1 miles to Route 1A. Just before Route 1A you'll come to Old Town Hill on the left, maintained by the Trustees of Reservations. The view from the top is the scenic highlight of the ride.

8. Turn right on Route 1A and go 4.1 miles to traffic light and crossroads in the center of Rowley (Church Street on right). Here the short ride turns right and the long ride goes straight. You'll cross the Parker River just after you start down Route 1A.

9. Continue straight 2/10 mile to Summer Street, which bears right at the town green.

10. Bear right on this road and go 4/10 mile to end.

11. Turn left at end and go 2/10 mile to end (merge into Route 133).

12. Bear right on Route 133 and go 1.1 miles to traffic light (Route 1).

13. Cross Route 1 and go 8/10 mile to Daniels Road on right.

14. Turn right on Daniels Road and go 1.5 miles to Wethersfield Street on left, at traffic island. You'll pass the wagon factory on your right.

15. Turn left on Wethersfield Street and go 4/10 mile to Warren Street on right. It's your second right, after a housing tract.

16. Turn right on Warren Street and go 2.8 miles to Middle Road on left, just before a footbridge across the road.

17. Turn left just before the bridge and go 100 yards to traffic island. On your right is the Governor Dummer Academy.

18. Bear left at traffic island, staying on the main road. After 2 miles Boston Road bears right, but go straight 8/10 mile to an unmarked road on your left. • *CAUTION:* The first mile of Middle Road is bumpy, with potholes.

Old commercial buildings of Newburyport recycled into a pedestrian mall.

19. Turn left on this road (Highfield Road) and go 7/10 mile to end (Scotland Road).

20. Turn right at end and go 1.1 miles to end.

21. Turn left at end and go 2/10 mile to school on left.

Directions for the ride: 17 miles

1. Follow directions for the long ride through number 8.

2. Turn right at traffic light on Church Street and go 2 miles to crossroads and stop sign (Route 1).

3. Turn right on Route 1 and go 6/10 mile to your first left (sign may say Governor Dummer Academy).

4. Turn left on this road and go 2/10 mile to Middle Road on right, just beyond the footbridge. The buildings of the Governor Dummer Academy are on both sides of the road.

5. Turn right just beyond footbridge and go 100 yards to traffic island.

6. Follow directions for the long ride from number 18 to the end.

18. Newburyport–Byfield–Georgetown– Groveland–West Newbury

Number of miles: 18 (26 with Byfield–Georgetown–Groveland
   extension)
Terrain: Rolling, with one tough hill.
Food: Grocery in Byfield. Grocery and snack bar in Georgetown.
   Grocery in West Newbury.
Start: Port Plaza, Route 113 in Newburyport, 1/4 mile east of
   Route 95.

This is a tour of the delightfully rolling, prosperous farm country on
the southern side of the Merrimack Valley along the river's lower
reaches. The area has a succession of gently rounded hills with
broad fields sweeping up and over them. Near the end you'll parallel
the wide Merrimack River, curving between the hillsides with farms
and estates on its banks, along a narrow rural lane. You will pass
Maudslay State Park, one of the state's newest and most glorious. It
was formerly the 476-acre estate of financial baron F. S. Moseley
(Maudslay is the ancestral English spelling). The river is refreshingly undeveloped along its easternmost section between Haverhill
and Newburyport. The long ride dips farther south into a more
wooded area to the old town of Georgetown, and then back north
into rolling farm country.

The ride starts from the elegant and historic small city of Newburyport, which became a prosperous shipbuilding and commercial
center during Colonial times. During the first half of the 1800s, the
most successful merchants and sea captains built mansions along
High Street. The waterfront area and the graceful brick commercial
buildings in the downtown section have been restored and are
worth visiting after the ride.

Leaving Newburyport, you'll quickly get into open countryside
where large farms expand toward the horizon, and go along the
undeveloped Upper Artichoke Reservoir. The run from here to West
Newbury passes through inspiring rolling farmland reminiscent of
Grant Wood's paintings. West Newbury is a handsome town on a
hilltop overlooking the river, with two fine churches facing each

other at the summit. From here you'll descend to the riverbank and enjoy a delightful run along its shore on a country lane. The return leg to Newburyport passes farms and estates. You'll pass a large school, formerly the Cardinal Cushing Academy, perched on a hilltop 200 feet above the river. The view from behind the building is outstanding.

The long ride heads farther south through woodland and small farms to the small village of Byfield and then on to the handsome crossroads town of Georgetown. Several antique stores are in or just outside the center of town. Off the route 3/10 mile is the Samuel Brocklebank House, built in 1670 and open to visitors. Beyond Georgetown you'll head back into beautiful rolling farm country and pick up the short ride in West Newbury.

Directions for the ride: 26 miles

1. Turn right out of parking lot on Route 113, heading east, and go 1.3 miles to Toppans Lane (unmarked) on right. It is immediately before the red-brick high school on right, and just after house number 249 on right.

2. Turn right on Toppans Lane. After 4/10 mile you'll come to a crossroads. Continue straight 1.8 miles to another crossroads (Turkey Hill Road), shortly after you cross over Route 95.

3. Turn left on Turkey Hill Road and go 2 miles to end (South Street). You'll pass the Upper Artichoke Reservoir.

4. Turn right on South Street and go 2/10 mile to Indian Hill Street on right. Here the short ride turns right and the long ride continues straight.

5. Continue straight on South Street 6/10 mile to fork where the main road bears left and Moulton Street bears right.

6. Bear left (still South Street) and go 4.8 miles to traffic light (Route 97) in the center of Georgetown. You will pass through Byfield. In Georgetown the ride turns right, but if you'd like to see the Samuel Brocklebank House, turn left for 3/10 mile. The house will be on your left.

7. Turn right on Route 97 and go 1.1 miles to King Street (unmarked), which bears right.

8. Bear right on King Street and go 1.3 miles to crossroads and stop sign.

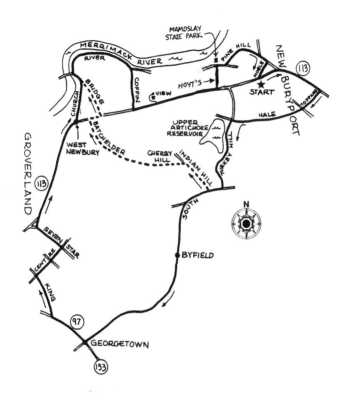

MERRIMACK RIVER

RIVER

MAMDSLAY STATE PARK

PINE HILL

NEW BURYPORT

113

COFFIN

BRIDGE

CHURCH

BATCHELDER

VIEW

HOYT'S

NOBLE

★ START

HALE

TOTTING

UPPER ARTICHOKE RESERVOIR

WEST NEWBURY

CHERRY HILL

INDIAN HILL

TURKEY HILL

GROVERLAND

113

N

SEVEN STAR

CENT RD

SOUTH

BYFIELD

KING

97

GEORGETOWN

133

119

9. Turn right at crossroads and go 1/2 mile to another cross-roads and stop sign. • *CAUTION:* Bumpy road.

10. Go straight at crossroads 1/2 mile to another crossroads.

11. Turn left at crossroads and go 1 mile to end, at traffic island.

12. Bear right at end. Just ahead you'll merge head-on into Route 113. Continue straight on Route 113 for 2.1 miles to Church Street, which bears left at top of hill just beyond traffic light. Notice the two churches at the intersection, one on each corner. This is West Newbury.

13. Bear left on Church Street. After 1 mile, merge left at stop sign onto Bridge Street. Go 1/10 mile to River Road on right, just before the bridge over the Merrimack. River Road goes up a sharp hill, so shift into low gear as you approach it.

14. Turn right on River Road and go 2.1 miles to fork.

15. Bear right at fork, heading away from the river, and go 9/10 mile to end (Route 113).

16. Turn left on Route 113. After 6/10 mile, at top of hill, you'll see the John C. Page Elementary School and a water tower on your left. From behind the school there's a superb view of the valley that you shouldn't miss.

17. From the school, continue on Route 113 for 1.7 miles to Hoyt's Lane or Gypsy Lane on left (the sign says both names), just before top of hill.

18. Turn left on Hoyt's Lane and go 6/10 mile to end. At the end, Maudslay State Park is in front of you. It's legal to ride on the network of dirt paths that wind through the park, but it's safer and more relaxing to walk.

19. Turn right at end of Hoyt's Lane and go 3/10 mile to fork.

20. Bear left at fork and go 1.2 miles to Noble Street on right. There's a little traffic island at the intersection.

21. Turn right on Noble Street and go 3/10 mile to end (Route 113). Port Plaza is on the far side of the intersection.

Directions for the ride: 18 miles

1. Follow directions for the long ride through number 4.

2. Turn right on Indian Hill Street. After 1 mile, the main road bears slightly left and an unmarked road turns right. Stay on the

Horse farm in Groveland.

main road for 1/10 mile to Cherry Hill Road, which bears left.

3. Bear left on Cherry Hill Road and go 2.4 miles to end (Route 113). This is a beautiful run through rolling farmland.

4. Turn right on Route 113 and go 2/10 mile to Bridge Street on left. This is West Newbury.

5. Turn left on Bridge Street and go 9/10 mile to River Road on right, immediately before the bridge over the Merrimack. This road goes up a sharp hill—shift into low gear as you approach it.

6. Follow directions for the long ride from number 14 to the end.

19. Whittier Country: Amesbury–Merrimac–Newton, New Hampshire–Plaistow, New Hampshire–Haverhill

Number of miles: 18 (29 with Newton–Plaistow–Haverhill extension)

Terrain: Rolling, with several moderate hills.

Food: Grocery and restaurant in Merrimac. Grocery in Newton, New Hampshire, Farm stand in Haverhill.

Start: Cross Roads Plaza, Route 110 in Salisbury, just east of Route 95 at the Amesbury town line.

This is a tour of the rolling countryside along the north bank of the Merrimack River at the northern tip of the state, and extending several miles into New Hampshire. At the end of the ride you'll parallel the river, a broad ribbon winding between gentle green hills, farms, estates, and gracious old homes overlooking its waters. The region is rural and excellent for biking, with a wealth of lightly traveled country roads. Unlike the stretch west of Haverhill, the river is surprisingly undeveloped along its lower reaches, paralleled by very pleasant secondary roads.

The ride starts by going through the lovely old town of Amesbury, with an unusual mixture of old mills and gracious, well-kept residential areas. The handsome nineteenth-century commercial area clusters around a central square. Amesbury is most famous as the longtime home of poet John Greenleaf Whittier, author of "Snowbound" and "Barefoot Boy." You'll bike past his house, which contains his original furnishings and is open to the public. Just outside of town is another historic landmark, the Rocky Hill Meetinghouse, a graceful yet simple wooden structure built in 1785. It is maintained by the Society for the Preservation of New England Antiquities and is open by appointment.

Leaving Amesbury, you'll crisscross the Massachusetts–New Hampshire border as you head on to Merrimac, passing between two ponds and then climbing onto an open ridge with a glorious view of the valley. Merrimac is another pleasant town with an ornate brick Victorian town hall, complete with clock tower. From here you'll parallel the river for five miles back to Amesbury in a beautiful, relaxing run.

The long, ride heads farther west to the pretty little town of Newton, New Hampshire, typical of the many graceful small communities dotting the southernmost section of the state. A classic white church and ornate old town hall grace the center of town. Beyond Newton you'll wind through forested hills, small farms, and over a ridge with a fine view of the valley. You'll go by Whittier's birthplace in Haverhill and finally arrive at the Merrimack River. For the rest of the ride you'll parallel the river. At first the road is inland just a bit, rolling up and down past gracious estates and gentleman farms, with views of the river from the crest of the hills. After a while the road converges with the riverbank and follows it all the way back to Amesbury, passing through the attractive waterfront villages of Rocks Village and Merrimacport.

Directions for the ride: 29 miles.

1. Turn left out of parking lot onto Route 110, heading west, and go 4/10 mile to traffic light just after the Route 95 interchange (Elm Street on right).

2. Turn right on Elm Street and go 1.7 miles to end, at small rotary at top of short hill in the center of Amesbury. Near the beginning of Elm Street you'll pass the Flanders House, built in 1665, on your right. Just ahead, immediately before the Route 495 overpass, the Rocky Hill Meetinghouse is on your right.

3. Turn left at rotary and go 100 yards to Friend Street, which bears right. There's a small park called the Millyard behind the buildings on your right, with a stream tumbling beneath a footbridge.

4. Bear right on Friend Street and go 3/10 mile to Whitehall Road, which bears right. You'll pass the Whittier home on your left on the corner of Pickard Street.

5. Bear right on Whitehall Road and go 1.7 miles to end. You'll pass Lake Gardner on the right, with Powwow Hill rising sharply on the opposite shore.

6. Turn left at end, crossing a small stream, and go 1.1 miles to your first paved right. It is after West Whitehall Road, a dirt road on right.

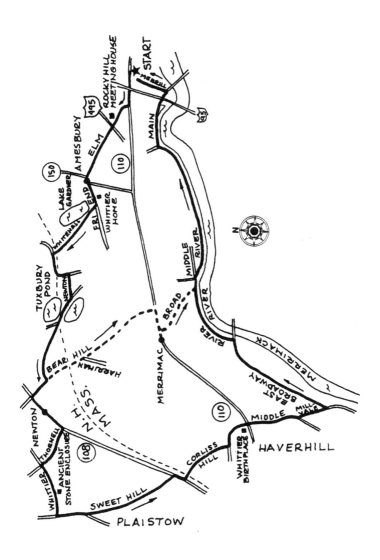

START

ROCKY HILL MEETINGHOUSE

MERRILL

495

93

AMESBURY

ELM

150

MAIN

110

LAKE GARDNER

FRI END

WHITTIER HOME

WHITTIER

TUXBURY POND

NEWTON

MIDDLE RIVER

BROAD

BEAR HILL

HARRIMAN

MERRIMAC

RIVER

MERRIMACK

N

MASS.

N.H.

EAST BROADWAY

NEWTON

THORNELL

ANCIENT STONE ENCLOSURE

108

MIDDLE

110

MILL VALE

HAVERHILL

WHITTIER BIRTHPLACE

CORLISS HILL

WHITTIER

SWEET HILL

PLAISTOW

7. Turn right on this road (Newton Road) and go 7/10 mile to end (merge right). Just before the end, there's a fine dam and mill-pond on your right.

8. Bear right at end and go 2.1 miles to end (Bear Hill Road on left). Here the short ride turns left and the long ride turns right.

9. Turn right and go 3/10 mile to crossroads and blinking light (Route 108 on left). This is Newton, New Hampshire. There's a grocery just beyond the intersection.

10. Turn left on Route 108 and go 1.3 miles to Thornell Road on right. Notice the old town hall on your left in the center of town.

11. Turn right on Thornell Road. After 1 mile, Peaslee Crossing Road bears left, but bear right on the main road 4/10 mile to crossroads (Whittier Street). An old church is at the intersection.

12. Turn left on Whittier Street and go 1.8 miles to end. Shortly after the railroad tracks, watch for a small stone shelter built into an earthen mound on your left. The origin of this structure, which predates the earliest white settlers, remains a mystery. It is probably related to the Mystery Hill site in nearby Salem, New Hampshire (see the America's Stonehenge ride for more detail).

13. Turn left at end and go 8/10 mile to fork just beyond railroad bridge.

14. Bear left at fork onto smaller road and go 3/10 mile to crossroads and stop sign.

15. Go straight at crossroads 1.7 miles to end (Route 108).

16. Bear right on Route 108 and go less than 2/10 mile to your first left, a narrow lane that goes up a steep hill.

17. Turn left on this road and go 1.1 miles to end. Notice the granite marker at the state line after 100 yards. • *CAUTION:* Watch for bumps and potholes while going downhill.

18. Turn left at end and go 4/10 mile to Route 110. Just before the intersection you'll pass the Whittier birthplace on the right. This old farmhouse is the locale for "Snowbound."

19. Cross Route 110 and go 1.5 miles to fork (Millvale Road bears left). You'll pass a Jewish cemetery on your left, and then a fine old church, dated 1744, on your right.

20. Bear left (almost straight) on Millvale Road and go 7/10 mile to end (merge right at stop sign).

21. Turn sharp left at end. • *CAUTION:* Watch for sand. Stay on the main road 2.7 miles to River Road on left, immediately before the bridge over the Merrimack. There's an old restored fire station on the corner. This is Rocks Village.

22. Turn left on River Road, paralleling the river on your right, and go 1.8 miles to fork where Middle Road goes straight and River Road bears right.

23. Bear right at fork (still River Road), following the water, and go 3.5 miles to a road that turns right at stop sign. It's 1/2 mile beyond a Victorian mill on the riverbank, built in 1877.

24. Turn right on this road, still following the river, and go 1.1 miles to a road that turns sharply left just after you go underneath Route 95.

25. Turn sharply left and go 6/10 mile to shopping center on right.

Directions for the ride: 18 miles.

1. Follow directions for the long ride through number 8.

2. Turn left on Bear Hill Road. After 1.1 miles Harriman Road bears right, but continue straight on the main road 1.9 miles to end. (Route 110). At the state line, 7/10 mile from where you turned onto Bear Hill Road, is a granite marker dated 1890. There's a glorious view from the top of the ridge, with glimpses of the Merrimack in the distance.

3. Bear right on Route 110 and go 1/2 mile to Broad Street on left, at bottom of hill. At the corner, on your right, is the Landing School, a one-room schoolhouse built in 1857. Here the ride turns left, but if you continue straight 1/10 mile you'll come to the center of Merrimac. There's a grocery and a snack bar in town.

4. Turn left on Broad Street and go 1 mile to end.

5. Turn left at end, paralleling the river on your right. Go 1/10 mile to fork.

6. Follow directions for the long ride from number 23 to the end.

20. Middleton–North Andover–Boxford–Topsfield

Number of miles: 18 (26 with Middleton–North Andover extension)

Terrain: Gently rolling, with a couple of short hills.

Road surface: 6/10 mile of dirt road in Middleton on the longer ride. An alternate route avoids the dirt section.

Food: Grocery and restaurant in Middleton. Country store in Boxford. Grocery and restaurant in Topsfield.

Start: Masconomet Regional High School, Endicott Road in Topsfield, just east of Route 95. Park at the tennis courts on the east side of the school.

This is a tour of the gently rolling, wooded, and well-to-do communities on the northern edge of the Boston metropolitan area, midway between the city and the New Hampshire border. The region is rural rather than suburban, with development limited to large, expensive homes on spacious wooded lots. The town centers of Boxford and Topsfield are New England classics.

At the beginning of the ride you'll bike through Middleton, a relatively undeveloped town consisting primarily of forest and small farms, many with horse paddocks. You'll head along lovely Middleton Pond, completely surrounded by pine groves, and then go through the Harold Parker State Forest, which comprises a large slice of the southern part of North Andover. You'll bike past two forest-rimmed ponds and then a pleasant mixture of small farms and attractive newer homes set back from the winding roads on large wooded lots. From North Andover you'll cross into Boxford, a gracious rural community that is one of the North Shore's most affluent suburbs, and a paradise for bicycling. The town center is delightful, with a proud old church, a country store, and appealing, rambling wooden homes.

At the end of the ride you'll pedal through Topsfield, another gracious, moneyed community where biking is a pleasure. The large green, with a stately white church and a marvelous Victorian town hall built in 1873, is one of the finest in the state. Just off the green is the Parson Capen House, built in 1681 and open to visitors.

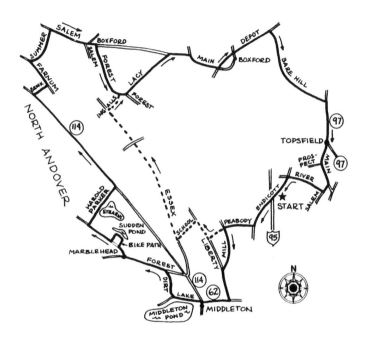

Just outside of town you'll go along the Ipswich River and then through majestic estates with broad fields sloping down to the riverbank.

Directions for the ride: 26 miles.

   1. Turn left out of parking lot onto Endicott Road and go 1.1 miles to Peabody Street on right. You'll cross the Ipswich River shortly before the intersection.

   2. Turn right on Peabody Street and go 8/10 mile to crossroads at top of short hill (Mill Street).

   3. Turn left on Mill Street and go 1 mile to end (Liberty Street). You'll pass another little dam and millpond on your right.

   4. Turn left on Liberty Street and go 6/10 mile to end (Route 62).

   5. Turn right on Route 62 and go 7/10 mile to end, at stop sign. This is the center of Middleton.

   6. At end, jog right and immediately left onto Lake Street. Go 7/10 mile to fork where both branches are dirt. (The left branch may be blocked by a gate). • *CAUTION:* The last quarter mile of Lake Street is bumpy with potholes. This is a great run along Middleton Pond. If you want to avoid the dirt stretch and miss Middleton Pond, turn right in the center of Middleton but don't jog left onto Lake Street. Go 4/10 mile to Forest Street, which bears left. Bear left on Forest Street and go 1.9 miles to a smaller road that turns right just after the North Reading town line (sign may say State Forest). Resume with direction number 9.

   7. Bear right at fork onto dirt road. After 4/10 mile the road curves sharply left and becomes paved. Continue 2/10 mile to end.

   8. Turn left at end and go 1.3 miles to a smaller road that turns right just after the North Reading town line (sign may say State Forest).

   9. Turn right on this road and go 2/10 mile to a bicycle path on your right. It comes up while you're going down a small hill. The path is probably blocked off to cars.

   10. Turn right on the bike path and go 1/2 mile to end. The path makes a little loop past Sudden Pond and comes back out on the main road. If you miss the path, or it doesn't look bikable, it's no problem—just stay on the main road 1 mile and resume with direction number 12.

11. Turn right at end of bike path and go 8/10 mile to a road on your right after the headquarters for the Harold Parker State Forest.

12. Turn right after forest headquarters and go 1.1 miles to Route 114.

13. Turn left on Route 114 and go 1.7 miles to Brook Street on right.

14. Turn right on Brook Street and go 3/10 mile to end (Farnum Street).

15. Turn left on Farnum Street and go 6/10 mile to Summer Street, which turns sharply right at yield sign.

16. Make a sharp right on Summer Street and go 1.1 miles to end (Salem Street).

17. Turn right on Salem Street. After 6/10 mile there's a cross-roads. Continue straight onto Boxford Street 2/10 mile to Forest Street on right.

18. Turn right on Forest Street and go 1.6 miles to fork (Lacy Street bears left).

19. Bear left on Lacy Street and go 1.7 miles to end (merge right).

20. Bear right at end and go 4/10 mile to end (merge to the right at a little traffic island).

21. Bear right at end and go 9/10 mile to crossroads.

22. Turn left at crossroads and go 4/10 mile to crossroads and stop sign. This is the center of Boxford. Here the ride goes straight, but if you turn right a country store is just ahead on your right.

23. Go straight at crossroads 1.2 miles to Bare Hill Road (un-marked) on right. It is immediately past a small pond on left.

24. Turn right on Bare Hill Road and go 2.4 miles to end (Haverhill Road, Route 97).

25. Turn right on Route 97 and go 8/10 mile to the Topsfield town green. The Parson Capen House is to your left just around the corner.

26. At the green go straight on Main Street (don't bear left on Route 97). Go 3/10 mile to fork just beyond the railroad tracks (the main road bears left).

27. Bear left on the main road and go 6/10 mile to Salem Road, which turns right just before Route 1.

28. Turn right on Salem Road and go 1/10 mile to River Road on right.

29. Turn right on River Road and go 1.3 miles to crossroads and stop sign. This is a magnificent run along the Ipswich River and then past broad fields and estates.

30. Turn left at crossroads and go 1/2 mile to school on left.

Directions for the ride: 18 miles

1. Follow directions number 1 and 2 for the long ride.

2. Continue straight on Peabody Street 4/10 mile to end.

3. Turn right at end and go 4/10 mile to School Street on left.

4. Turn left on School Street and go 8/10 mile to end (Essex Street).

5. Turn right on Essex Street and go 1.9 miles to crossroads and stop sign (Sharpner's Pond Road).

6. Go straight at crossroads 1.2 miles to Ingalls Street on right. There's a traffic island with a rock in the middle at the intersection.

7. Turn right on Ingalls Street and go 4/10 mile to end (Forest Street).

8. Turn right on Forest Street and go 2/10 mile to fork (Lacy Street bears left).

9. Follow directions for the long ride from number 19 to the end.

21. Topsfield–Ipswich–Wenham

Number of miles: 12 (24 with Ipswich extension)
Terrain: Gently rolling, with one tough hill.
Food: Groceries and snack bars in the towns. The local specialty in Ipswich is clams.
Start: Topsfield Village shopping center, Main Street in Topsfield, just south of the green.

This is a tour exploring three elegant old North Shore communities connected by delightful secondary roads winding past horse farms, country estates, ponds, and along the Ipswich River. You start from Topsfield, a handsome town with one of the finest traditional New England centers in the state. The large green is framed by an exceptionally fine classic white church and a marvelous Victorian town hall built in 1873. Adjoining the green is the Parson Capen House, built in 1681 and open to visitors. Topsfield is best known for its two giant annual fairs, the American Crafts Exposition in July and the Topsfield Fair in October. The latter is one of the country's oldest agricultural fairs, running since 1818. Surrounding the town are gentleman farms and estates spreading up rolling hills, and the marshes of the Ipswich River, along which is the state's largest Audubon sanctuary.

From Topsfield you'll head through gently rolling farmland to Ipswich, a jewel of a town both geographically and architecturally. It boasts more pre-Revolutionary houses, some going back to the 1600s, than any other place in America north of Colonial Williamsburg. With the continuing efforts of a preservation-conscious citizenry, these buildings have been painstakingly restored and maintained. The center of town lies between a North Green and a South Green, and contains a wonderful mixture of buildings of every architectural style from the early Colonial period to the turn of the century. Many of these houses are open to visitors; if you're a historic-house enthusiast you can spend the entire day in town. If you want to see just one house, the one to visit is the John Whipple House, built in 1640. It has an herb garden and period furnishings. The Ipswich River courses through town and passes underneath the graceful stone-arched Choate Bridge, built in 1764 and one of the oldest original bridges in the country. East of town are vast expanses of salt marsh, the steep-ridged Great Neck Peninsula, and magnificent Crane's Beach and Castle Hill, all of which you can explore on the Ipswich ride.

A couple of miles out of town is another splendid North Shore landmark, the LaSallette Shrine and Seminary. Formerly an estate, it is everything that a shrine should be, complete with spreading, elaborately landscaped grounds, sunken gardens with squared-off hedges and trees pruned into parabolas, an ornate red-brick mansion, and Stations of the Cross with a flight of stairs to be climbed on your knees. Beyond the Shrine, you'll parallel the Ipswich River and wind through carefully maintained horse farms and estates to Wenham, another gracious and moneyed town with a stately white church and old town hall. Next to the town hall is the Claflin-Richards House, built in 1664. It adjoins the Wenham Historical Association and Museum, which maintains a fascinating display of dolls, toys, and games from the 1800s. It's open afternoons every day except Saturday. From Wenham it's a short ride back to Topsfield, passing Wenham Lake and rolling, open hillsides.

Directions for the ride: 24 miles

1. Turn left (north) out of parking lot onto Main Street. Just ahead you'll merge head-on into Route 97 at the green. The Parson Capen House is on Howlett Street, the side street on your right running parallel to Route 97, just north of the green. It's a small building with a steeply pitched roof.

2. Go straight on Route 97 for 4/10 mile to fork where Route 97 bears left and Ipswich Road bears right. Here the short ride bears right and the long ride bears left.

3. Bear left on Route 97 and go 1.7 miles to Pond Street, a narrow lane that bears right. It comes up 8/10 mile beyond Rowley Road, which also bears right.

4. Bear right on Pond Street and go 2/10 mile to end (Boxford Road). Hood Pond is on your right.

5. Turn right at end and go 1.3 miles to fork. There's a cemetery on your left at the fork.

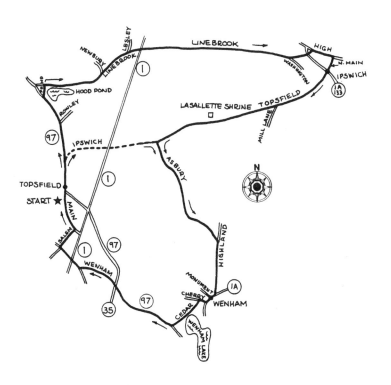

NEWBURY
LESLEY
LINE BROOK
LINEBROOK →
HIGH
N. MAIN
WASHINGTON
IPSWICH
1
HOOD POND
1A
133
ROWLEY
LASALLETTE SHRINE
TOPSFIELD
97
IPSWICH
MILL LANE
ASBURY
TOPSFIELD
N
1
START ★
MAIN
SALEM
HIGHLAND
97
1
WENHAM
MONUMENT
1A
CHERRY
WENHAM
35
97
CEDAR
WENHAM LAKE

6. Bear right at fork and go 8/10 mile to another fork where the main road bears right and Lesley Road bears left.

7. Bear right on main road and go 4/10 mile to traffic light (Route 1).

8. Cross Route 1 and go 3.6 miles to a large church on right. Continue past the church 2/10 mile to fork.

9. Bear left (almost straight) at fork and go 2/10 mile to stop sign. Continue straight at stop sign 100 yards to end, opposite cemetery. (Don't get on Route 133 or 1A at stop sign.)

10. Turn right at end, passing the cemetery on your left. Notice how it rises up the steep hillside in terraces. Go 4/10 mile to North Main Street on right (it's your third right). You're on High Street, the heart of old Ipswich, with most of the houses dating back to the 1700s.

11. Turn right on North Main Street and go 3/10 mile to Routes 1A and 133, at bottom of hill. This is Meeting House Green. The modern church in the center, clashing with the early buildings surrounding it, was built to replace the splendid traditional church that burned to the ground in 1965 after it was struck by lightning. It's surprising that this preservation-minded and history-conscious town did not rebuild the church to resemble the old one.

12. Cross Routes 1A and 133. After 1.4 miles, Mill Road bears left, but continue straight on the main road 3 miles to Asbury Street on left. You'll pass the LaSallette Shrine and Seminary, which is worth visiting, on your right. Beyond the Shrine you'll parallel the Ipswich River on your left. There's a fine dam 1 mile beyond the Shrine.

13. Turn left on Asbury Street and go 2.7 miles to end (merge to right at stop sign).

14. Bear right at stop sign and go 1.4 miles to end (Route 1A, in the center of Wenham).

15. Bear right on Route 1A and go 1/10 mile to Cherry Street, your second right. On your left you'll pass the town hall and the doll museum.

16. Turn right on Cherry Street and go 2/10 mile to Cedar Street on left.

17. Turn left on Cedar Street and go 9/10 mile to end (Route 97). You'll pass Wenham Lake on your left.

18. Turn right on Route 97 and go 1.8 miles to diagonal cross-roads where Route 97 bears right and Route 37 turns sharply left.

19. Go straight at crossroads onto Wenham Road 1 mile to end. You'll climb a steep hill.

20. Bear right at end and go 2/10 mile to Route 1. There's a great view from the far side of the intersection.

21. Cross Route 1 and go 2/10 mile to grassy traffic island at bottom of hill.

22. Bear right at traffic island and go 4/10 mile to end.

23. Turn left at end and go 8/10 mile to shopping center on left.

Direction for the ride: 12 miles

1. Follow directions number 1 and 2 for the long ride.

2. Bear right at fork on Ipswich Road and go 8/10 mile to traffic light (Route 1).

3. Cross Route 1 and go 1.2 miles to Asbury Street on right.

4. Turn right on Asbury Street and go 2.7 miles to end (merge to your right at stop sign). This is a pleasant run past horse farms and estates.

5. Follow directions for the long ride from number 14 to the end.

22. Pedaler's Paradise: North Andover–Boxford

Number of miles: 16 (32 with Boxford extension)
Terrain: Delightfully rolling, with lots of little ups and downs.
There's one hill on the long ride.
Food: Country store in South Groveland. Country store in
Boxford. Country store in West Boxford.
Start: Salem Street, Andover, just east of Route 28, adjacent to
Phillips Academy. It's 1 mile south of the center of town.
How to get there: If you're heading north on Route 93, exit
north onto Route 125, and then exit north onto route 28. Go
about 3 miles to Salem Street on right, at traffic light. There's
a tall brick tower at the intersection.

If someone asked you to describe the ideal bike ride, with the limitation that it be in the eastern half of Massachusetts, you'd probably end up describing a ride like this one. Just southeast of Lawrence, on the wealthy, woodsy fringe of Boston suburbia, is a bicyclist's paradise of untraveled and well-paved country lanes, gentleman farms, lakeside runs with manicured estates sloping down to the shore, and a couple of graceful, unspoiled New England town centers with stately old homes and picket fences. You might also have mentioned oceanfront runs with crashing surf, but, sorry—you can't have everything.

The ride starts next to Phillips Academy, the classic New England preparatory school. Its large, impressive campus equals that of any college for elegance. You'll quickly cross the town line into North Andover, a two- faced town. The section closest to Lawrence is a congested area of housing developments and industrial parks; everything else is a beautiful mixture of estates, woods, and large, well-landscaped newer homes on good-sized wooded lots. The old center of town is a gem, with a stately old church and green framed by gracious Colonial-style homes. The centerpiece of the town is Lake Cochichewick, a large, refreshingly unspoiled lake surrounded by estates and wooded hills. You'll parallel the shore and then bike past the Brooks School, another preparatory school with a magnificent campus of graceful white wooden buildings and broad fields

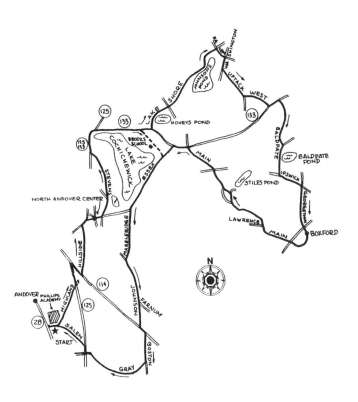

125

133

LAKE SHORE

JOHNSONS POND

WASHINGTON

UPTACK

WEST

133

BALDPATE

BALDPATE POND

HOVEYS POND

125
133

BROOKS SCHOOL

LAKE COCHICHEWICK

ESSEX

MAIN

STILES POND

IPSWICH

GEORGETOWN

STEVENS

NORTH ANDOVER CENTER

LAWRENCE

MAIN

BOXFORD

MARBLEHEAD

HILLSIDE

N

114

ANDOVER

PHILLIPS ACADEMY

JOHNSON

FARNUM

HIGHLAND

125

28

BOSTON

★

SALEM

START

GRAY

139

sweeping down to the lakefront. The rest of the ride brings you through the better of the town's two faces back to Phillips Academy.

The long ride makes a long loop through, Boxford, which is even nicer than North Andover. Boxford epitomizes the gracious, well-to-do suburb that is rural rather than suburban, like the setting for the movie, *Ordinary People*. (Funny how those ordinary people didn't have ordinary incomes.) Silk-smooth roads curve past wood-lots, horse farms with pastures crisscrossed by rustic white wooden fences, rambling old homes, and impressive new ones har-moniously integrated with the landscape on two- and three-acre forested lots. The center of town is another New England classic, with a fine old church, a country store, and stately old homes. After looping through Boxford you'll pick up the route of the short ride back in North Andover in time to bike along the estate-lined south-ern shore of Lake Cochichewick.

Direction for the ride: 32 miles

    1. Head east on Salem Street and go 1/10 mile to crossroads, (Highland Road).

    2. Turn left on Highland Road and go 1.3 miles to diagonal crossroads and stop sign (Route 125).

    3. Turn left on Route 125 and go 2/10 mile to Route 114. Turn sharply right on Route 114 and go 1/10 mile to your first left (Hill-side Road, unmarked).

    4. Turn left on Hillside Road and go 1.2 miles to end (merge right).

    5. Bear right at end and go 1/10 mile to fork.

    6. Bear right at fork and go 2/10 mile to stop sign, at a five-way intersection. This is the lovely village of North Andover Center.

    7. Go straight at stop sign, passing the church on left, and go one block to crossroads (Stevens Street bears left).

    8. Bear left on Stevens Street and go 4/10 mile to fork.

    9. Bear right at fork, passing a picturesque pond on your right and hideous condominiums on your left, and go 1/2 mile to stop sign. Continue straight 1/2 mile to end (merge into Routes 125 and 133).

    10. Bear right on Routes 125 and 133 and go 6/10 mile to fork where Route 133 bears right and Route 125 goes straight.

11. Bear right on Route 133, going along Lake Cochichewick, and go 1.4 miles to Great Pond Road, a smaller road that bears right. Here the short ride bears right and the long ride goes straight.

12. Continue straight 3/10 mile to a road that turns left at a traffic island. Route 133 curves to the right at the intersection.

13. Turn left on this road and go 9/10 mile to crossroads and stop sign. You'll pass Hovey's Pond on your right.

14. Go straight at crossroads 2.1 miles to Salem Street, at another crossroads and stop sign. Toward the end of this stretch you'll go along Johnson's Pond.

15. Turn right on Salem Street and go 3/10 mile to crossroads (Washington Street). This is the village of South Groveland.

16. Turn right on Washington Street and go 3/10 mile to a smaller road that bears left.

17. Bear left on this road and go 1.3 miles to fork. You'll climb a tough hill, the only one on the ride. • *CAUTION:* The road is bumpy near the end.

18. Bear left at fork and go 1 mile to end (Route 133).

19. Turn left on Route 133 and go 4/10 mile to your first right (sign may say Baldpate).

20. Turn right on this road (Baldpate Road) and go 1.4 miles to end. Shortly before the end, at top of hill, you'll see a rambling Victorian mansion on the right. This is Baldpate, a private psychiatric hospital.

21. Turn right at end (still Baldpate Road) and go 1 mile to end.

22. Turn left at end and go 8/10 mile to crossroads, just after a small pond on right.

23. Bear right at crossroads and go 1.5 miles to another crossroads (Middleton Road on right, Depot Road on left). This is the center of Boxford.

24. Go straight at crossroads. Just ahead there's a country store on the right. Continue 1.4 miles to fork. Bear slightly right for 2 miles to another fork (Maple Avenue bears left).

25. Bear right at fork and go 3/10 mile to another fork. Here the ride bears left, but if you bear right you'll come to the town beach on Stiles Pond after 2/10 mile.

26. Bear left at fork and go 9/10 mile to crossroads and stop sign.

27. Go straight at stop sign 1 mile to another crossroads and stop sign (Washington Street). This is the village of West Boxford.

28. Turn left on Washington Street and go 4/10 mile to Essex Street (unmarked), on left at traffic island. There is a good ice cream spot on the right as soon as you turn onto Washington Street.

29. Turn left on Essex Street. After 4/10 mile, merge left at bottom of hill (• *CAUTION* here; there are no stop signs for any of the roads). Bear left and go 1.6 miles to fork (Marbleridge Road bears left). You'll catch glimpses of Lake Cochichewick on your right.

30. Bear left on Marbleridge Road and go 1.1 miles to end, going straight at three crossroads.

31. Turn left at end and go 1 mile to fork where Johnson Street bears right and Farnum Street bears left.

32. Bear right on Johnson Street and go 6/10 mile to end (merge into Salem Turnpike, Route 114).

33. Bear left on Salem Turnpike and go 3/10 mile to Boston Street, which bears right.

34. Bear right on Boston Street and go 1/2 mile to fork (Gray Street bears right).

35. Bear right on Gray Street. After 1.5 miles you will merge to your right on Salem Street, at yield sign. Bear right for 4/10 mile to crossroads and stop sign (Route 125).

36. Turn right on Route 125 for 100 yards, and turn left on Salem Street. Go 1 mile back to starting point.

Directions for the ride: 16 miles

1. Follow directions for the long ride through number 11.

2. Bear right on Great Pond Road and go 1 mile to end (merge right at traffic island). You'll pass the Brooks School on your right.

3. Bear right at end and go 1.6 miles to fork where Marbleridge Road bears left.

4. Follow directions for the long ride from number 30 to the end.

23. America's Stonehenge Ride: Haverhill–Salem, New Hampshire–Hampstead, New Hampshire– Atkinson, New Hampshire

Number of miles: 12 (27 with America's Stonehenge extension)
Terrain: Rolling, with one tough hill near the beginning.
Food: None en route for the short ride. Grocery and snack bar in Hampstead. Country store in Atkinson.
Start: Haverhill High School, at the corner of Monument Street and North Broadway. If you're coming from the south on Route 495, take the Route 97–Broadway exit (exit 50). At end of exit ramp, go straight onto Monument Street and go 4/10 mile to school on right. If you're coming from the north on Route 495, get off at the same exit, turn left at end of ramp, cross over highway, and take your first left on Monument Street. The school is 4/10 mile ahead on right.

Just northwest of Haverhill, extending several miles into New Hampshire, is a delightful area for bicycling with gentle wooded hills, several lakes, some open hillsides with fine views, and unspoiled small towns. The long ride is highlighted by a visit to America's Stonehenge, formerly called Mystery Hill, a complex of prehistoric stone ruins and monoliths of unknown origin. It is one of the major archaeological sites in the Northeast.

The ride starts on the outskirts of Haverhill, a congested nineteenth-century mill city sloping up the hills on both sides of the Merrimack River. You quickly get into rural countryside as you head into Salem, New Hampshire, and ride along the twisting shore of Arlington Mill Reservoir, lined with older summer cottages nestled among pine groves. In the last twenty years, Salem has become a bedroom suburb of Boston, only forty-five minutes away along Route 93, which rams through the middle of the town. The ride sticks to the section farthest from the highway, still mostly undeveloped.

Shortly beyond the reservoir you'll come to America's Stonehenge. The complex consists of an elaborate pattern of walls, tomblike buildings, wells, drains, remains of buildings, and rocks carved with mysterious inscriptions. Radiocarbon dating has shown the site to be more than 2,000 years old, eliminating the possibility that Indians, colonists, or early European explorers could have constructed it. Around the perimeter of the site, various stones are placed to serve as a giant astronomical calendar, lining up with the North Star, the cycles of the moon, sunrise and sunset on the longest and shortest days of the year, and other celestial phenomena. Some of the inscriptions match those of ancient Celtic tribes, raising the possibility that Europeans may have visited North America even before the Vikings. The most distinctive artifact in the site is a massive grooved stone slab supported on legs, most likely to have been used for sacrifices. America's Stonehenge is privately owned and is the scene of continuing research.

From America's Stonehenge you'll head to Hampstead and Atkinson, two unspoiled little New England towns. At the village crossroads in Hampstead stand the handsome Victorian town hall and a classic white church. Atkinson boasts the Atkinson Academy, a graceful schoolhouse dated 1803. Leaving Atkinson, you'll enjoy a soaring downhill run. The homestretch back to Haverhill leads along broad, open ridges with sweeping views of the valley.

Directions for the ride: 27 miles

1. Turn left out of parking lot on Monument Street. Just ahead is a crossroads and blinking light. Continue straight 3/10 mile to Route 97, at stop sign.

2. Turn right on Route 97 and go 6/10 mile to Forest Street on left. There's a grassy traffic island at the intersection.

3. Turn left on Forest Street and go 1/2 mile to crossroads and stop sign midway down sharp hill.

4. Turn right at crossroads. After 4/10 mile you'll come to a little traffic island. Bear right, staying on the main road, and go 6/10 mile up a long, steep hill to fork. This is the toughest hill of the ride—don't get discouraged.

5. Bear left at fork and go 3/10 mile to another fork where a smaller road bears right.

6. Bear right at fork and go 1.2 miles to crossroads and stop sign. • *CAUTION:* The first half mile has bumps and potholes.

HAMPSTEAD

121

111

ISLAND POND

AMERICA'S
STONEHENGE

ERMER

KLEIN

HAVERHILL

WESTSIDE

ATKINSON

ACADEMY

MAPLE

121

121

ATKINSON

ARLINGTON MILL
RES.

DAM

SAWYER

N.H.
MASS.

SHORE

COVE DAM

WHEELER

HOOKER FARM

TOWN
FARM

CAPTAIN POND

N. BROADWAY

GREENWAY

97

SALEM

MONUMENT

97

N

NORTH

LAKE

FOREST

START

WEST LOWELL

145

7. Turn right at crossroads and go 1.2 miles to traffic light (Route 97, Ayers Village Road).

8. Cross Route 97 onto Hampstead Road and go 6/10 mile to another crossroads (Town Farm Road on left, Liberty Street on right). Here the short ride goes straight and the long ride turns left.

9. Turn left at crossroads. After 6/10 mile a road bears left, but curve right on main road 2/10 mile to crossroads and stop sign.

10. Turn right at crossroads and go 6/10 mile to Wheeler Dam Road, which bears left.

11. Bear left on Wheeler Dam Road and go 3/10 mile to fork (Cove Road bears left). • *CAUTION:* Bumpy road. Here the ride bears left, but if you bear right 200 yards you'll come to Wheeler Dam at the end of the Arlington Mill Reservoir. It's a great spot for a picnic and worth looking over.

12. Bear left on Cove Road and go 1/10 mile to another fork at top of hill (Shore Drive bears left).

13. Bear left on Shore Drive and go 2.6 miles to end. This is a delightful run winding along the shore of the Arlington Mill Reservoir. • *CAUTION:* This road is very curvy with a few bumpy spots; take it easy. At the end, there is a snack bar on left.

14. Turn sharp right at end and go 2/10 mile to fork. This is the village of North Salem, New Hampshire.

15. Bear left at fork and go 6/10 mile to another fork where the main road curves right and Ermer Road bears left.

16. Stay on main road for 4/10 mile to end, at stop sign.

17. Turn right at end and go 2/10 mile to fork where Klein Drive bears left and Haverhill Road bears right.

18. Bear right on Haverhill Road. After 3/10 mile, America's Stonehenge is on your right. Continue 1 mile to crossroads (Atkinson Road on right, West Side Road on left).

19. Turn left at crossroads and go 1.5 miles to end.

20. Turn left at end and go 8/10 mile to wide crossroads (Route 111).

21. Cross Route 111 and go 1.6 miles to crossroads and blinking light (Main Street, Route 121) in the center of Hampstead. There's a grocery and snack bar 100 yards to your left on Route 121. The graceful Victorian town hall is across the road.

22. Turn right on Route 121 and go 1.1 miles to Route 111, at traffic light.

23. Cross Route 111 and go 2.1 miles to Academy Avenue, which bears left at top of hill. There's a country store on the far side of the intersection. This is the village of Atkinson.

24. Bear left on Academy Avenue and go 1/2 mile to crossroads (Maple Avenue on right). You'll pass the graceful Atkinson Academy on your left.

25. Turn right at crossroads and go 1.5 miles to end (merge into Route 121 at bottom of little hill). There's a splendid downhill run on this stretch—enjoy it!

26. Turn sharp right on Route 121 and go 1/2 mile to fork where Sawyer Avenue bears left downhill.

27. Bear left on Sawyer Avenue and go 1.1 miles to a road that turns left at a grassy traffic island (North Broadway, unmarked).

28. Turn left on this road and go 3.5 miles to crossroads and blinking light (Monument Street). • *CAUTION:* Watch for occasional cracks and potholes.

29. Turn left on Monument Street. The school is just ahead on right.

Directions for the ride: 12 miles

1. Follow directions for the long ride through number 8.

2. Go straight at crossroads 3/10 mile to Hooker Farm Road on right.

3. Turn right on Hooker Farm Road and go 1.8 miles to end. You'll pass Captain Pond on your right.

4. Turn right at end and go 3/10 mile to fork.

5. Bear right at fork and go 3.5 miles to crossroads and blinking light (Monument Street).

6. Turn left on Monument Street. The school is just ahead on right.

24. Dracut–Pelham, New Hampshire–Hudson, New Hampshire–Tyngsborough–Lowell

Number of miles: 14 (28 with Hudson–Tyngsborough–Lowell extension)
Terrain: Rolling. The long ride is hilly.
Food: Grocery and snack bar in Pelham. Grocery just off the route in Tyngsborough.
Start: Dracut High School, Lakeview Avenue, Dracut. From the junction of Routes 38 and 113, go west on Route 113 for 1 mile to Lakeview Avenue, at traffic light. Turn right on Lakeview Avenue and go 1 mile to school on left.

Directly north of Lowell is a rural region of rolling hills and open farmland, crisscrossed by a network of winding country lanes and secondary roads. The long ride parallels the Merrimack River for several miles and offers a view of the impressive rapids that sparked the birth of Lowell as an industrial center during the 1820s. The ride starts in Dracut, a residential suburb immediately north of Lowell, and heads across broad hilltop farms with fine views to the graceful town of Pelham, New Hampshire. The center of town is another New England gem, with a well-kept green, stately white church, and a handsome brick turn-of-the-century library. From Pelham it's a straight run along a smooth secondary road through farmland back to Dracut. Just before the end you'll go through the little mill village of Collinsville, with a fine dam tucked between two hulking brick mills.

The long ride heads farther west into rugged, wooded hill country. About a mile off the route is a fire tower on top of Jeremy Hill. Just ahead you'll cross the town line into Hudson, New Hampshire. Its main claim to fame for many years was Benson's Animal Park, an expensive tourist trap that was part zoo and part children's amusement park. Mercifully, it went out of business in 1987.

After winding up and down on narrow lanes, you'll work your way to the Merrimack River in Tyngsborough and parallel it for most of the remainder of the ride into Lowell. One of America's outstanding examples of a nineteenth century industrial city, Low-

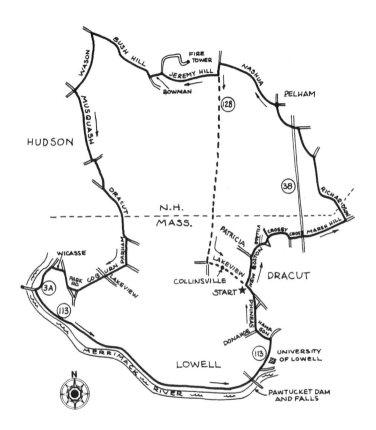

FIRE TOWER

BUSH HILL

MASON

JEREMY HILL

BOWMAN

NASHUA

PELHAM

MUSQUASH

HUDSON

128

DRACUT

38

RICHARDSON

N.H.
MASS.

PATRICIA

CROSBY

CROS

MARSH HILL

WICASSE

PARHAM

AUBURN

PARK RD.

COG

LAKEVIEW

LAKEVIEW

NEW BOSTON

DRACUT

3A

COLLINSVILLE

START ★

113

PHINEAS

DONAHOE

HAMPSON

113

UNIVERSITY
OF LOWELL

MERRIMACK

RIVER

LOWELL

N

PAWTUCKET DAM
AND FALLS

ell is enjoying a renaissance. The old mill district, laced with an elaborate network of canals to divert the descending waters of the Merrimack into the mills, is now a National Historic Park. I did not put this area on the ride because Lowell is not very pleasant to bike through, and you would have no safe place to put your bike while touring the historic district. It's worth spending a few hours exploring the city after the ride, or even making a separate trip to do so.

Directions for the ride: 28 miles

1. From opposite the south end of the school, head north on New Boston Road and go 8/10 mile to fork (Patricia Lane bears left, and the main road bears right).

2. Bear right at fork, staying on main road, and go 3/10 mile to another fork, where Village Drive bears left.

3. Bear right at fork, again staying on main road. You'll immediately come to a traffic island. Bear left at traffic island and go 100 yards to another fork (Crosby Road bears right).

4. Bear right on Crosby Road. After 6/10 mile the road curves sharply right. Immediately ahead. Cross Road is on your left.

5. Turn left on Cross Road and go 1/2 mile to crossroads and stop sign (Route 38).

6. Cross Route 38 onto Marsh Hill Road and go 1.4 miles to Richardson Road on left, at top of hill. At top of ridge, notice the old windmill on your left and the newer one behind it.

7. Turn left on Richardson Road. After 1.3 miles a road turns left, but bear slightly right on the main road. Continue 9/10 mile to fork where Island Pond Road bears right.

8. Bear left at fork and immediately ahead bear right, staying on the main road. Go 8/10 mile to end.

9. Turn left at end and go 100 yards to Route 38.

10. Cross Route 38 and go 6/10 mile to crossroads and blinking light in the center of Pelham.

11. Turn left at crossroads and go 1.4 miles to end (Route 128).

12. Turn left on Route 128 and go 1/10 mile to Jeremy Hill Road on right. Here the short ride goes straight and the long ride turns left.

13. Turn right on Jeremy Hill Road, up a tough hill, and go 1.3

miles to fork (Bowman Lane bears left). If you'd like to visit the fire tower on Jeremy Hill, bear right at fork and go 6/10 mile to a narrow, rutted road that bears right at top of hill. Bear right downhill on this road, which immediately turns to dirt. After 2/10 mile, turn 90 degrees left and go 2/10 mile to tower.

14. Bear left on Bowman Lane and go 2/10 mile to end.

15. Turn right at end and go 1.7 miles to Wason Road, which turns sharply left midway down a steep hill.

16. Turn sharply left on Wason Road and go 1.5 miles to crossroads at bottom of hill (Musquash Road on left).

17. Turn left on Musquash Road and go 1.7 miles to end, at stop sign.

18. At stop sign, jog left and immediately right (still Musquash Road). Go 1/2 mile to end (merge left).

19. Turn left at end and go 1 mile to fork where Long Pond Road bears left and Parham Road bears right.

20. Bear right on Parham Road and go 1/2 mile to another fork, where Coburn Road bears right.

21. Bear right on Coburn Road and go 1/2 mile to crossroads and stop sign (Lakeview Avenue).

22. Cross Lakeview Avenue and go 6/10 mile to fork (Park Road bears right).

23. Bear right on Park Road, which immediately merges to the right into Lawndale Road. Bear right and go 3/10 mile to Wicasse Avenue, which bears left. It's your second left.

24. Bear left on Wicasse Avenue and go 2/10 mile to end (Route 3A). The Merrimack River is in front of you.

25. Turn left on Route 3A and go 6/10 mile to Route 113 on left, immediately before the bridge over the Merrimack. Just across the bridge is the center of Tyngsborough

26. Turn left on Route 113, following the river, and go 6 miles to the second bridge over the river. You'll see spectacular rapids just before the bridge.

27. Continue beyond the bridge 1/10 mile to fork, where the main road curves right and Route 113 bears slightly left, diverging from the riverbank.

28. Bear slightly left, staying on Route 113, and go 8/10 mile to Hampson Street on left, just after the Dracut line. You'll pass the

University of Lowell on your right. At the intersection the main road curves right.

29. Turn left on Hampson Street and go 3/10 mile to fork where Phineas Street bears right and Donahoe Road bears left.

30. Bear right on Phineas Street. After 3/10 mile, just past bridge, a road bears right, but bear slightly left 3/10 mile to end (merge left). The bridge is currently blocked off to cars, but you can walk your bike across.

31. Bear left at end and go 2/10 mile to school on left.

Directions for the ride: 14 miles

1. Follow directions for the long ride through number 12.

2. Continue straight on Route 128 for 4.4 miles to crossroads and traffic light. (Lakeview Avenue). It's about 1 mile beyond the Massachusetts line.

3. Turn left on Lakeview Avenue and go 1.1 miles to school on right. Notice the dam on your left between the two mills at the bottom of the first hill.

25. Middlesex Canal Ride: Burlington–Billerica–Wilmington

Number of miles: 16 (24 with Billerica extension)
Terrain: Rolling, with several short hills and one tough one.
Food: Groceries and snack bars in the towns.
Start: Burlington Mall, Middlesex Turnpike in Burlington, just
      north of Route 128. Take exit 32B. Start from the northern
      end of the mall near Sears Auto Center.

On this ride you'll explore three pleasant middle-class communities midway between Boston and Lowell. The region is primarily suburban, interspersed with some wooded stretches and a few small farms. Biking in this area is pleasant if you stick to the secondary roads. A fascinating feature of the ride are traces of the Middlesex Canal, which was completed in 1803, connecting Boston with the Merrimack River in Lowell. The canal was the first in the country and sparked the growth of Lowell as an early industrial center. A massive feat of civil engineering for its time, the canal had twenty locks, eight aqueducts, and forty-eight bridges. Today only traces remain, most notably the Shawsheen River Aqueduct, which you'll see on the longer ride. The canal suffered an early death with the completion of the Boston and Lowell Railroad in 1835. It took all day for the small-capacity, horse-drawn towboats to run the length of the waterway, but the railroad could carry a much larger payload from Lowell to Boston in an hour. By 1850 the canal was virtually unused.

You'll head north from Burlington Mall, the Boston area's largest shopping center. Every week the Burlington police receive reports of stolen cars from shoppers who can't locate their car when they emerge from the stores because it's surrounded by 10,000 others. You'll go along the ramrod-straight Middlesex Turnpike, sprouting with new, boldly architectured high-technology firms. After crossing Nutting Lake you'll come to the center of Billerica, which is surprisingly attractive for a populous bedroom suburb. The large, well-landscaped green, with a monument in the middle, is framed by a traditional white New England church and an ornate brick Victorian library. A couple of miles ahead is North Billerica, an old mill village with a row of identical houses, two grim but ornate Victorian mills, and a fine dam spanning the Concord River.

From here you'll parallel the remains of the Middlesex Canal, which is noticeable only as a slight depression running in a straight line across the land. When you cross the Shawsheen River into Wilmington, the three stone abutments of the aqueduct, one on each bank of the river and one in the middle, remain intact. The canal was built across the top of the river, fitting into the U-shaped slot visible in the center abutment. The canal couldn't have simply been built at ground level or its waters would have been diverted by the river. The only solution was to build an aqueduct above the river. These aqueducts severely limited the size of the boats that the canal could accommodate.

From the aqueduct, the return trip to Burlington leads through some surprisingly rural stretches.

Directions for the ride: 24 miles

1. Turn right from the mall onto Middlesex Turnpike, heading north, and go 1.2 miles to Route 62 (Bedford Street), at traffic light. Here the short ride turns right and the long ride goes straight.

2. Continue straight for 4.2 miles to end (Concord Road). You'll cross Nutting Lane 1 mile before the end.

3. Turn right at end. After 7/10 mile the main road curves left and Charnstaffe Lane, a smaller road, goes straight. Stay on main road for 3/10 mile to end (Route 3A). You'll go alongside the Billerica town green on your left. Notice the fine white church and Victorian library on the far side of the green.

4. Turn left on Route 3A. Just ahead a road turns right, but go straight for 9/10 mile to where Route 129 turns 90 degrees right and another road (Pollard Street) bears slightly right.

5. Bear slightly right on Pollard Street (sign may say to North Billerica). Go 1.2 miles to a three-way fork immediately after you cross the Concord River.

6. At the three-way fork, take the middle road, passing the church on your left. Go 3/10 mile to fork, at a grassy, triangular traffic island. This is North Billerica, also called Talbot Mills.

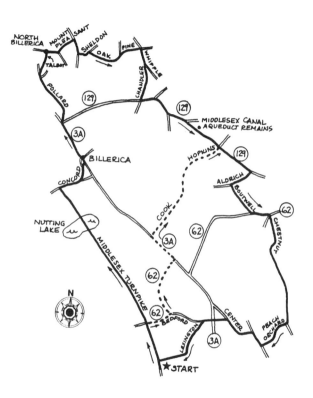

NORTH
BILLERICA
MOUNT
PLEASANT
SHELDON
OAK
PINE
TALBOT
WHIPPLE
POLLARD
CHANDLER
129
121
MIDDLESEX CANAL
& AQUEDUCT REMAINS
3A
HOPKINS
129
BILLERICA
ALDRICH
CONCORD
BOUTWELL
62
NUTTING
LAKE
COOK
CHESTNUT
3A
62
MIDDLESEX TURNPIKE
62
N
62
BEDFORD
LEXINGTON
CENTER
PEACH
ORCHARD
3A
★ START

7. Bear right at fork, passing factory on left, and go 4/10 mile to another fork where Mount Pleasant Street bears left. The dam spanning the Concord River on your right is impressive. Here the Middlesex Canal crossed the river at water level. To enable the horsemen pulling the towboats to get across the river, the engineers built a floating bridge. The bridge could be opened to allow traffic on the river itself to pass through.

8. Bear left at fork, going under railroad bridge, and go 4/10 mile to end.

9. Turn right at end and go 2/10 mile to fork (High Street bears right, Sheldon Street bears left).

10. Bear left at fork and go 3/10 mile to your second right, which bears right up a tiny hill.

11. Bear right on this road (Oak Street). After 8/10 mile you will merge head-on at stop sign. Continue straight for 1/10 mile to fork.

12. Bear right at fork and go 3/10 mile to crossroads and stop sign (Whipple Road).

13. Turn right on Whipple Road and go 4/10 mile to fork just after stop sign (Chandler Street bears right).

14. Bear right on Chandler Street and go 1.1 miles to crossroads and stop sign (Route 129).

15. Turn left on Route 129. Just ahead merge left at stop sign. Bear left and go 3/10 mile to fork.

16. Bear right at fork (still Route 129) and go 1/2 mile to another fork.

17. Bear left at fork (still Route 129). After 7/10 mile, the remains of the Shawsheen River aqueduct of the Middlesex Canal are on your left. Continue on Route 129 for 8/10 mile to traffic light (Hopkins Street on right).

18. Continue straight at light 8/10 mile to Aldrich Road on right. There is a little red schoolhouse, built in 1875, on your left at the intersection.

19. Turn right on Aldrich Road and go 1/2 mile on Boutwell Street on left. It is just after Mozart Street on left.

20. Turn left on Boutwell Street and go 8/10 mile to end (merge into Route 62 at stop sign).

21. Bear left on Route 62 and go 4/10 mile to Chestnut Street on right, at blinking light.

22. Turn 90 degrees right on Chestnut Street (don't turn sharply right on Marion Street) and go 2.7 miles to Peach Orchard Road on right. It goes up a steep hill, and the main road curves left at the intersection.

23. Turn right on Peach Orchard Road and go 9/10 mile to end.

24. Turn right at end and go 2/10 mile to fork at far end of school (Center Street bears left uphill).

25. Bear left at fork and go 6/10 mile to Bedford Street which bears left at the Burlington green. There's a tough hill at the beginning of this stretch.

26. Bear left at the green and go 2/10 mile to Route 3A, at traffic light.

27. Cross Route 3A (• *CAUTION:* busy intersection). Go 1/10 mile to fork where Lexington Street bears left.

28. Bear left on Lexington Street and go 1.4 miles to end. The mall is on the far side of the intersection, and Sears Auto Center is to your right.

Directions for the ride: 16 miles

1. Turn right from the mall onto Middlesex Turnpike and go 1.2 miles to Route 62 (Bedford Street), at traffic light.

2. Turn right on Route 62 and go 6/10 mile to where Route 62 (Francis Wyman Road) turns left.

3. Turn left on Route 62 and go 1.5 miles to end (Route 3A). There's a tough hill at the end.

4. Turn left on Route 3A and go 9/10 mile to Cook Street on right, at the third traffic light.

5. Turn right on Cook Street. After 1.2 miles the main road curves left at a large school on the left. Stay on the main road 1.4 miles to traffic light (Shawsheen Avenue, Route 129). Here the ride turns right, but if you turn left and go 8/10 mile, you'll come to the Shawsheen River aqueduct of the Middlesex Canal on your right.

6. Turn right on Route 129 and go 8/10 mile to Aldrich Road on right. At the intersection, on the left, you will see a little red schoolhouse, built in 1875.

7. Follow directions for the long ride from number 19 to the end.

26. Reading–Wilmington–North Reading–Lynnfield–Wakefield

Number of miles: 16 (26 with Wilmington–North Reading extension)
Terrain: Gently rolling, with a couple of moderate hills.
Food: Groceries and snack bars in the towns.
Start: Lord Wakefield Motor Hotel, North Avenue, Wakefield, just south of Route 128. Take exit 39.

This ride loops through a cluster of attractive middle-class to affluent communities midway between Boston and Lawrence. The region is semisuburban and semirural, with large expanses of greenspace in the northern sections of the ride as you head through the Harold Parker State Forest. The town centers are New England classics, with well-tended greens framed by old churches and town halls, unspoiled even though there may be residential and commercial development close by.

At the beginning of the ride you'll pass through the graceful town center of Reading, where six roads radiate symmetrically from the green and a stately white church stands proudly above the town. From here you'll proceed to Wilmington, with an old cemetery and church marking the original center of town, and then head north into more wooded, less-developed landscape. You'll pass unspoiled Fosters Pond and Field Pond as you wind through the Harold Parker State Forest. From here it's a smooth run to North Reading, a charming town with a large triangular green, an old clock-towered grange hall, and a striking white Victorian town hall. From North Reading you'll parallel the upper reaches of the Ipswich River for a couple of miles and then turn south to Lynnfield, the most affluent of the five communities along the route. The town center is a New England classic, with a handsome white church and a slender triangle of a green surrounding a meetinghouse built in 1715. From here it's not far to Wakefield, one of the most visually appealing of the suburbs inside the Route 128 semicircle. The focal point of the community is Lake Quannapowitt, with the center of town at its southern end. You'll enjoy a mile-long run along the

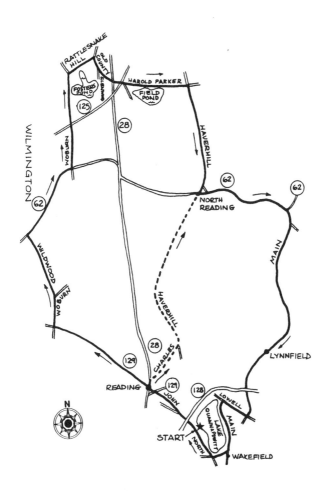

RATTLESNAKE HILL

OLD COUNTY

HAROLD PARKER

FOSTERS POND

FIELD POND

125

28

WILMINGTON

WOBURN

HAVERHILL

62

62

62

NORTH READING

WILDWOOD

WOBURN

HAVERHILL

MAIN

28

CHARLES

LYNNFIELD

129

129

128

READING

JOHN

LOWELL

MAIN

LAKE QUANNAPOWITT

N

START

NORTH

WAKEFIELD

159

lakefront. At the far end of the lake is a beautifully landscaped park with an old bandstand overlooking the water. Across from the park is the town green, framed by a classic white church, an impressive stone church, and fine old homes. From here, take a short run up the other side of the lake back to the start.

Directions for the ride: 26 miles

1. Turn right onto North Avenue and go underneath Route 128. Continue 4/10 mile to fork where John Street, a smaller road, bears right.

2. Bear right on John Street and go 1/2 mile to end. Here the short ride turns left and then right on Route 28, and the long ride turns left but stays on Route 129.

3. Turn left at end and then immediately bear right on Route 129, passing the Reading town green on your left and the fine white church on your right. Follow Route 129 for 2.6 miles to traffic light (Woburn Street). It is the second traffic light after the Route 93 interchange.

4. Turn right on Woburn Street and go 1/2 mile to fork, where Wildwood Street bears left.

5. Bear left on Wildwood Street and go 1.1 miles to end (Route 62).

6. Turn right on Route 62 and go 1.8 miles to crossroads shortly after you cross the bridge over Route 93 (Woburn Street; sign may also say Andover Street).

7. Turn left on Woburn Street and go 9/10 mile to crossroads and blinking light (Route 125).

8. Cross Route 125 and go 1.4 miles to fork, at traffic island (Rattlesnake Hill Road bears right).

9. Bear right at fork and go 8/10 mile to end (Old County Road). You'll pass a little dam on the right at bottom of hill.

10. Turn right at end and go 1/10 mile to fork where Glenwood Road, a newer road, bears right.

11. Bear left at fork. After 1/2 mile you'll come to Route 28. Cross Route 28 and go 3/10 mile to Route 125.

12. Cross Route 125, continuing straight ahead through a pair of stone pillars into the Harold Parker State Forest (don't bear right past police station). Go 1.5 miles to crossroads and stop sign

(Jenkins Road). You'll pass Field Pond.

13. Turn right at crossroads and go 2.7 miles to fork at the North Reading town green. There's an old clock-towered grange hall in the middle of the fork.

14. Bear right at fork and go 1/10 mile to crossroads and stop sign (Route 62).

15. Turn left on Route 62. As soon as you turn, notice the Victorian town hall. Go 2.8 miles to grassy traffic island where Route 62 turns left and another road bears right. This stretch parallels the Ipswich River, visible from a few spots on your right.

16. Bear right at this intersection and go 2/10 mile to fork immediately after you cross the river (Russell Street bears left).

17. Bear right at fork and go 4.5 miles to crossroads and stop sign (Lowell Street). It's 6/10 mile after you go underneath Route 128. You'll just nick a corner of Peabody for about 50 feet, 4/10 mile from the fork. At the second town line sign, if you follow the stone wall to your right about 50 feet, you'll see an old granite marker indicating the point where Peabody, Lynnfield, and Middleton meet. Two miles farther on you'll go through the center of Lynnfield.

18. Turn right on Lowell Street and go 7/10 mile to Main Street on left, at Lake Quannapowitt.

19. Turn left on Main Street, going along the lake on your right, and go 1.1 miles to your first right at the Wakefield town green (Church Street). Notice the fine church at far end of green.

20. Bear right at the green and go 4/10 mile to traffic light (North Avenue).

21. Bear right on North Avenue and go 7/10 mile to motel on right.

Directions for the ride: 16 miles

1. Follow directions 1 and 2 for the long ride.

2. Turn left at end and immediately bear right on Route 129. Then immediately turn right on Route 28 at traffic light. Go 1/10 mile to Charles Street, which bears right.

3. Bear right on Charles Street and go 1.2 miles to end, staying on the main road. At end, merge left onto Haverhill Street.

4. Bear left on Haverhill Street and go 2.4 miles to crossroads and stop sign (Route 62) in the center of North Reading.

5. Turn right on Route 62 and go 2.8 miles to grassy traffic island where Route 62 turns left and another road bears right. The Ipswich River is visible in a few spots on your right.

6. Follow the directions for the long ride from number 16 to the end.

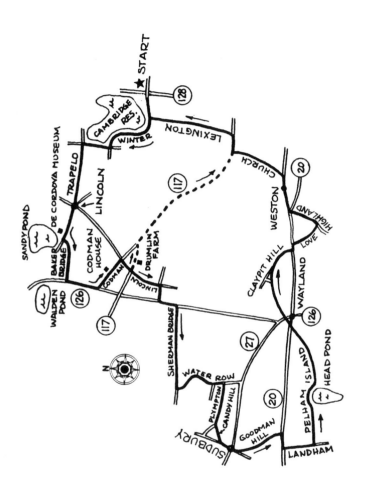

The long ride heads farther west across the Sudbury River into the beautiful rural town of Sudbury. In the center of town are two fine old churches facing each other across the road and a handsome, pillared town hall. Sudbury is best known for the Wayside Inn, celebrated in Longfellow's "Tales of a Wayside Inn." It is in the southwestern corner of the town, several miles off the route. You can visit it on the Wayside Inn Ride. After you leave Sudbury, you'll head past unspoiled Heard Pond on country lanes to Wayland, another attractive town with a large, graceful white church and an old country store housed in a distinctive, pillared building. From Wayland it's a short ride to Weston, a community as affluent as Lincoln, with a similar landscape of estates on spacious grounds and large homes nestled amid five-acre wooded lots. The center of town is elegant, with an attractive row of shops, two handsome stone churches, and a large, football-shaped green with the impressive, pillared town hall standing over it.

Directions for the ride: 27 miles

1. Turn right (west) onto Totten Pond Road and cross the bridge over Route 128. Just ahead, bear right on Winter Street, the main road. Continue 1.4 miles to fork where Winter Street bears left uphill and Old County Road bears right. • *CAUTION:* Watch for potholes.

2. Bear right on Old County Road and go 7/10 mile to crossroads and stop sign (Trapelo Road).

3. Turn left on Trapelo Road and go 1.7 miles to a crossroads where five roads come together. This is the center of Lincoln. Notice the library on your right and the church just up the hill from the library.

4. Go straight at crossroads onto Sandy Pond Road. After 6/10 mile the entrance to the DeCordova Museum is on your right. Continue 2/10 mile to Baker Bridge Road on left. Here the ride turns left, but if you go straight 1/10 mile you'll come to unspoiled Sandy Pond.

5. Turn left on Baker Bridge Road and go 1.2 miles to end (Route 126). You will pass a stark, square house on the left designed by Walter Gropius in 1938. When you come to Route 126 the ride turns left, but if you turn right and go 6/10 mile you will come

Sudbury.

to famed Walden Pond in Concord, where Thoreau built his cabin. There's a beach and a footpath circles the pond.

6. Turn left on Route 126 and go 8/10 mile to first left, Codman Road (sign may say to Lincoln Center).

7. Turn left on Codman Road and go 6/10 mile to crossroads and stop sign (Lincoln Road). You'll pass the Codman House on left.

8. Turn right at crossroads and go 3/10 mile to another crossroads and stop sign (Route 117). Immediately before the intersection is a traffic island; bear left when you come to it. Here the short ride turns left and the long ride goes straight. If you turn left you'll come to Drumlin Farm just ahead on your right.

9. Cross Route 117 and go 7/10 mile to another crossroads.

10. Turn right at crossroads and go 2/10 mile to end (Route 126).

11. Turn left on Route 126 and go 1/2 mile to Sherman Bridge Road on right.

12. Turn right on Sherman Bridge Road and go 1.9 miles to Water Row Road on left, at traffic island with a stone milepost on it. You will see several similar mileposts further along the ride. A half mile beyond the Sudbury River bridge, a lane on the right leads to a state wildlife refuge.

13. Turn left on Water Row Road and go 1.4 miles to Plympton Road, your second right.

14. Turn right on Plympton Road and go 8/10 mile to fork (Candy Hill Road bears left).

15. Bear left on Candy Hill Road and go 1/4 mile to end. This is the toughest hill of the ride.

16. Turn left at end and go 3/10 mile to traffic light (Route 27), in the center of Sudbury.

17. Cross Route 27 and go 1/10 mile to Goodman Hill Road, which bears left.

18. Bear left on Goodman Hill Road and go 1.6 miles to end (Route 20).

19. Turn right on Route 20 and go 2/10 mile to Landham Road on left (sign may say to Framingham).

20. Turn left on Landham Road and go 6/10 mile to Pelham Island Road on left immediately after church on left.

21. Turn left on Pelham Island Road and go 2.5 miles to Route 20. You'll pass Heard Pond on your right and cross the Sudbury River.

22. Cross Route 20 diagonally and go 100 yards to Route 126. This is the center of Wayland. Notice the church at the corner of Routes 20 and 126, and the pillared country store on your left.

23. Cross Route 126 and go 9/10 mile to a little green, where the main road bears right. • *CAUTION:* Bumpy road.

24. Bear right at green and immediately merge to your right into Claypit Hill Road. Go 9/10 mile to end (Route 20). • *CAUTION:* This section is also bumpy.

25. Turn left on Route 20 and go 3/10 mile to fourth right, Love Lane. (The second and third rights are both Buckskin Drive.)

26. Turn right on Love Lane and go 7/10 mile to end. This is a steady climb, but a fast descent follows.

27. Turn left at end and go 6/10 mile to crossroads and stop sign (Route 20).

28. Cross Route 20 onto Boston Post Road and go 9/10 mile, through the center of Weston, to a fork with a stone church in the middle. At the fork, notice the pillared town hall on your left on the far side of the green.

29. Bear left at fork. After 1/10 mile Conant Road turns left, but curve right on the main road. Continue 1.1 miles to end (Route 117).

30. Turn right on Route 117 and go 2/10 mile to Lexington Street on left.

31. Turn left on Lexington Street and go 1.4 miles to end.

32. Turn right at end and go 1/2 mile to hotel on left.

Directions for the ride: 14 miles

1. Follow directions for the long ride through number 8.

2. Turn left on Route 117 and go 4 miles to Lexington Street on left. It comes up 2/10 mile after you pass Church Street on your right. Just after you turn onto Route 117 you'll come to Drumlin Farm on the right.

3. Turn left on Lexington Street and go 1.4 miles to end.

4. Turn right at end and go 1/2 mile to hotel on left.

29. Weston–Wellesley–Wayland

Number of miles: 22 (31 with Wellesley extension)
Terrain: Gently rolling.
Food: Grocery stores and restaurants in the towns.
Start: M.D.C. Duck Feeding Area parking lot on the Charles River, immediately north of Route 30 and immediately east of Route 128.
How to get there: Getting there by car is a little tricky, because the access road is on the *west* side of Route 128.

If you're heading south on Route 128, take the Route 30 exit (exit 24). At the end of the ramp, cross Route 30 at traffic light. Go 1/10 mile to the first right after the entrance to the Massachusetts Turnpike. Turn right, and just ahead turn right again into parking lot.

If you're heading north on Route 128, take the Route 30 exit (exit 24). Turn left (west) at end of ramp on Route 30 and go to traffic light on the far side of Route 128. Turn right and go 1/10 mile to your first right after the entrance ramp to the Massachusetts Turnpike. Turn right, and just ahead turn right again into parking lot.

From the Massachusetts Turnpike, follow the signs to Route 128 North and Route 30. Turn left (west) at end of ramp onto Route 30 and follow directions for heading north on Route 128.

If you're coming from Newton on Commonwealth Avenue, turn right onto the entrance ramp to Route 128 North. Just ahead, bear right (don't get on Route 128) and then turn right into parking lot.

This is a tour of three wealthy, gracious communities west of Boston just outside the Route 128 semicircle. The region is a pleasure for bicycling, with smooth roads winding past seminaries, colleges, and stately older brick and wooden homes. Highlights of the ride are two colleges in Wellesley—Babson College, where you'll visit the largest revolving globe in the world and a giant relief map of the country, and Wellesley College, which has one of the most

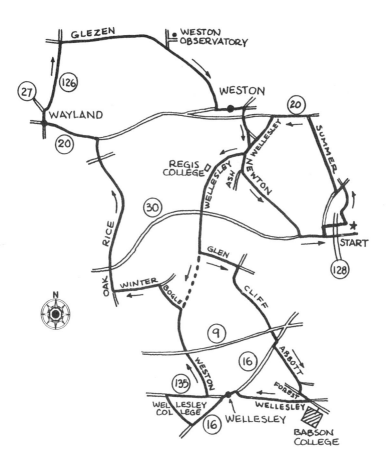

GLEZEN

WESTON
OBSERVATORY

WESTON

27

126

20

WAYLAND

20

SUMMER

WELLESLEY

NEWTON

REGIS
COLLEGE

WELLESLEY

ASH

30

START

128

RICE

GLEN

N

OAK

WINTER

BOGLE

CLIFF

9

16

ABBOTT

WESTON

135

FOREST

WELLESLEY

WEL LESLEY
COL LEGE

16   WELLESLEY

BABSON
COLLEGE

179

beautiful campuses in the state.

You'll start by going through Weston, one of Boston's most affluent suburbs, with estates on spacious grounds and large homes, each surrounded by five acres of trees and lawn. You'll pass Regis College, a Catholic women's school with a handsome stone and brick main building, a tall stone tower on a hilltop, and a postal museum on the campus. The town center is a New England jewel, with an attractive row of shops, two handsome stone churches, and an impressive, pillared town hall standing over the large elliptical green. From Weston you'll ride through Wayland, the next town to the west. Wayland is a little more rural, with some extensive sections of woods and rolling pastureland. The center of town boasts a dignified white church, a country store housed in an unusual pillared building, and a fine brick library. The return trip brings you back through another section of Weston, passing the Weston Observatory, where there are rocks containing the imprint of fossils and dinosaur footprints.

The long ride heads south into Wellesley, a more densely populated but equally elegant suburb. You'll visit Babson College, a top-rated business school with one of the state's most fascinating attractions—a relief map of the United States, 65 feet long and 40 feet wide, which you view from a balcony above. The map was built from 1937 to 1940 with painstaking attention to detail, including the curvature of the earth. Outside the building where the map is housed is the largest revolving globe in the world, 28 feet in diameter. There is no admission charge. From Babson you'll go through the center of Wellesley, with its ornate, clock-towered, Gothic-style town hall and an attractive row of smart shops. Just ahead is the centerpiece of the town, Wellesley College. The rolling, elm-shaded campus, bordering the shore of Lake Waban, is a delight to bike through as you pass its dignified ivy-covered buildings in a wide variety of architectural styles. After leaving the college you'll join the route of the short ride, going through Wayland and then back through Weston.

Directions for the ride: 31 miles

1. Head out of the parking lot, following the Charles River on your right, and go 7/10 mile to crossroads and stop sign.

Wellesley College.

2. Turn left at crossroads and go 2/10 mile to Summer Street on right, immediately after the bridge over Route 128.

3. Turn sharply right on Summer Street and go 1.4 miles to end (Route 20).

4. Turn left on Route 20 and go 8/10 mile to Wellesley Street on left, at traffic island (sign may say to Regis College, Wellesley).

5. Turn left on Wellesley Street and go 1/2 mile to fork where Newton Street bears left and Wellesley Street bears right. At the fork, notice the mansion of the Weston school administrative offices.

6. Bear right at fork on Wellesley Street and go 1.5 miles to traffic light (Route 30). You'll pass the Case Estate of Arnold Arboretum, 112 acres of nurseries and cultivated plants, on your right. Then you'll pass Regis College. Unfortunately, its hilltop tower is locked. The postal museum is open Tuesdays and Thursdays from 10 to 4, and Sundays from 2 to 5.

7. Cross Route 30 and go 8/10 mile on Glen Road on left. It is the first left after you go underneath the Massachusetts Turnpike. Here the short ride goes straight and the long ride turns left.

8. Turn left on Glen Road and go 1 mile to crossroads (Cliff Road on right, Oak Street on left). You'll pass the Norumbega Reservoir on your left.

9. Turn right on Cliff Road and go 1.7 miles to end.

10. At end, turn right and then immediate left on Abbot Road (sign may say to Babson College). Go 7/10 mile to fork where Inverness Road bears left.

11. Bear right uphill at fork (still Abbot Road) and go 100 yards to end (Forest Street).

12. Turn left on Forest Street and go 2/10 mile to diagonal crossroads (Wellesley Avenue). Here the ride turns sharply right, but if you would like to visit the map at Babson College, continue straight for 2/10 mile to the college entrance on right. The map is in Coleman Hall. Turn right into the college and take second left to end.

13. Turn sharp right on Wellesley Avenue (bear left if you visited the map), and go 8/10 mile to stop sign at bottom of hill. Continue straight for 6/10 mile to end (Routes 16 and 135).

14. Turn left on Routes 16 and 135. Just ahead on right, set back a little from the road, is the town hall. The front of the building has an ornate clock tower that is worth looking at. Immediately after the town hall is a fork where Route 16 bears left and Route 135 bears right.

15. Bear left on Route 16 and go 6/10 mile to the entrance to Wellesley College on right, at traffic light.

16. Turn right into the College and go 8/10 mile to end (Route 135). You'll see Lake Waban on your left as soon as you enter the college. Side roads on the left lead down to the lakeshore.

17. Turn right on Route 135 and go 6/10 mile to traffic light (Weston Road).

18. Turn left on Weston Road. After 1 mile you'll go underneath Route 9. Continue 8/10 mile to Bogle Street on left (sign may say Rivers School). • *CAUTION:* Weston Road is narrow and very busy. Keep to far right.

19. Turn left on Bogle Street and go 6/10 mile to end.

20. Turn left at end. After 6/10 mile Frost Street is on your right and Winter Street, the main road, curves left. Stay on Winter Street 4/10 mile to end (Oak Street).

21. Turn right on Oak Street and go 1/2 mile to crossroads and stop sign (Route 30).

22. Cross Route 30 onto Rice Road and go 2.5 miles to crossroads and stop sign. • *CAUTION:* Watch for bumpy spots.

23. Go straight at crossroads onto Pine Brook Road. Go 3/10 mile to end (Route 20).

24. Turn left on Route 20 and go 1 mile to traffic light (Routes 27 and 126) in the center of Wayland.

25. Turn right on Routes 126 and 27. Just ahead is a fork where Route 27 bears left and Route 126 bears right. Notice the white, pillared country store on your left and the library on your right.

26. Bear right on Route 126 and go 1.3 miles to Glezen Lane, which is your second crossroads.

27. Turn right on Glezen Lane and go 3.6 miles to end. • *CAUTION:* The first 1.2 miles of Glezen Lane is bumpy. After 2 miles you'll pass the Campion Center, an impressive domed building, on your left. Just north of the main building is the Weston Observatory, in front of which are rocks with fossils and dinosaur footprints. To get there, turn sharp left on Concord Street just before the main building and then immediate right.

28. Turn left at end and go 4/10 mile, through the center of Weston, to School Street on right. Notice the pillared town hall to the left on the far side of the green.

29. Turn right on School Street. Just ahead, cross Route 30 at traffic light and go 1/2 mile to fork (Wellesley Street bears right, Newton Street bears left).

30. Bear left on Newton Street and go 1/10 mile to another fork, where Ash Street bears right.

31. Bear left at fork (still Newton Street) and go 1.7 miles to end (South Avenue, Route 30).

32. Turn left on Route 30 and go 4/10 mile to traffic light just before Route 128.

33. Turn left at light and go 1/10 mile to your first right after the entrance to the Massachusetts Turnpike.

34. Turn right, go 1/10 mile to end, and turn right into parking lot.

Directions for the ride: 22 miles

1. Follow directions for the long ride through number 7.

2. Continue straight 1.1 miles to Bogle Street on right, at bottom of hill (sign may say Rivers School).

3. Turn right on Bogle Street and go 6/10 mile to end.

4. Follow directions for the long ride from number 20 to end.

30. Charles River Tour: Westwood–Dover– South Natick–Needham–Dedham

Number of miles: 20 (31 with South Natick extension, 14 with shortcut bypassing Dover)
Terrain: Gently rolling.
Food: None on two shorter rides until near end. Grocery store in South Natick.
Start: Holiday Inn, Route 1 in Dedham, just north of Route 128. Park at west side of the lot near Route 1A.

The valley of the Charles River upstream from Newton provides relaxed and scenic cycling. The river flows peacefully past landed estates with broad meadows sloping gently to its banks and graceful old communities as it follows a west-to-east course from South Natick to Dedham. A fine network of country roads crisscrosses the region, winding past country estates, gentleman farms where horses graze in pastures set off by stone walls and white wooden fences, and stately old homes.

The ride starts off by heading through Westwood, an affluent estate-dotted community, and then into Dover, one of Boston's most heavily old-moneyed enclaves. Dover is the closest really rural and undeveloped town to Boston and a paradise for biking. After paralleling the Charles through Dover, you'll cross the river into Needham. Most of Needham is a bedroom suburb, but the southern rim of the town along the river has the same gracious landscape you rode through on the south bank. From Needham you'll go into Dedham, a handsome town with a distinguished cluster of public buildings gracing its center. Approaching downtown you'll pass fine old Colonial-style homes and two graceful white churches facing each other across the road. Just ahead are a trio of stately granite courthouses and the handsome stone public library, a New England classic built in 1873. After passing one more impressive, Gothic-style stone church, it's a short ride back to the starting point.

The long ride heads farther upriver through more elegantly rural countryside to the delightful old community of South Natick. Like Needham, most of Natick is an uninspiring bedroom community along the dreadful Route 9 commercial strip, but the southern part of the town near the Charles is beautiful and quite rural. Gracing the village of South Natick are a pair of handsome churches, an ornate Victorian library, and a dam across the Charles.

Directions for the ride: 31 miles

1. Turn left out of the west side of the parking lot onto Route 1A, heading south, and go 3/10 mile to Gay Street on right, at the Westwood town line.

2. Turn right on Gay Street. After 1 mile Milk Street turns left, but bear slightly right on the main road. Go 6/10 mile to Fox Hill Street, which bears right up a gradual hill.

3. Bear right on Fox Hill Street and go 9/10 mile to end (Route 109).

4. Turn right on Route 109 and go 4/10 mile to Summer Street on left (sign may say to Dover, 4 miles).

5. Turn left on Summer Street and go 1.2 miles to end (Westfield Street).

6. Turn left on Westfield Street and go 2/10 mile to a narrow lane that bears left.

7. Bear left on the lane and go 1.2 miles to end. Here the main road turns right and a dead end, private road is on the left.

8. Turn right at end and go 4/10 mile to end.

9 Turn left at end and go 4/10 mile to Mill Street on right, at top of little hill.

10. Turn right on Mill Street and go 4/10 mile to end, where you'll merge to the right. The road runs along the Charles River on your right.

11. Bear right at end. Immediately ahead on your right is a beautiful little dam, and then a bridge over the Charles River. Immediately after the bridge, Fisher Street is on your left. Here the 14-mile ride goes straight and the two longer rides turn left.

12. Turn left on Fisher Street and go 4/10 mile to end. (• *CAUTION:* Bad diagonal railroad tracks.)

13. Turn left at end and go 3/10 mile to Claybrook Road on right, just after recrossing the Charles. You are now in Dover.

14. Turn right on Claybrook Road and go 1.6 miles to cross-

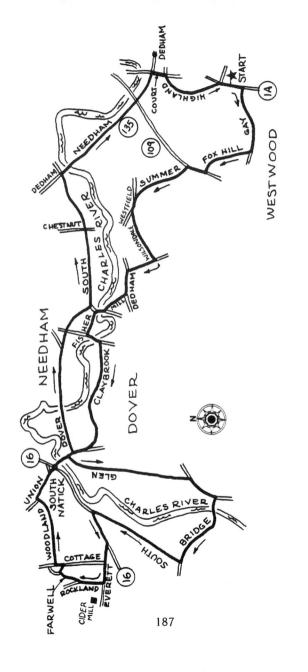

DEDHAM

START

1A

HIGHLAND

GAY

COURT

FOX HILL

135

109

WESTWOOD

SUMMER

WESTFIELD

DEDHAM

CHESTNUT

CHARLES RIVER

WILSONDALE

SOUTH

DEDHAM

MILL

NEEDHAM

FISHER

CLAYBROOK

DOVER

DOVER

N

16

UNION

GLEN

SOUTH NATICK

WOODLAND

CHARLES RIVER

COTTAGE

BRIDGE

ROCKLAND

SOUTH

FARWELL

CIDER MILL

EVERETT

16

187

roads and stop sign. You can catch glimpses of the Charles on your right.

15. Go straight at crossroads and go 4/10 mile to end (merge to your right on Pleasant Street).

16. Bear right on Pleasant Street and go 1/2 mile to Dover Road on right. Here the 20-mile ride turns right and the long ride goes straight. You'll pass Lookout Farms, an excellent fruit and vegetable stand, on your left.

17. Continue straight for 1/10 mile to Glen Street on left.

18. Turn left on Glen Street and go 2.4 miles to end (merge to your right at bottom of hill).

19. Bear right at end and go 1/2 mile to fork where Bridge Street bears right.

20. Bear right on Bridge Street (sign may say to Sherborn, Framingham) and go 1.3 miles to South Street on right, at top of hill. You will cross the Charles into Sherborn, and pass a magnificent old dairy farm on the right shortly before the intersection.

21. Turn right on South Street and go 1.7 miles to end (merge into Route 16).

22. Turn sharp left on Route 16 and go 1/2 mile to Everett Street, which bears right uphill.

23. Bear right on Everett Street and go 8/10 mile to Rockland Street on right, just past the condominiums on right at top of hill.

24. Turn right on Rockland Street and go 6/10 mile to fork (Farwell Street bears right). Just after you turn onto Rockland Street you'll see a cider mill on your left. It's a great rest stop during apple season.

25. Bear right on Farwell Street and go 1/2 mile to end.

26. Turn right at end and go 50 yards to end.

27. Turn left at end and then immediately right on Woodland Street. Go 1.3 miles to end. • *CAUTION:* The end comes up suddenly at bottom of sharp hill. Toward the end of this section you'll pass the Oblate Center, an impressive brick building set back from the road.

28. Turn right at end and go 1/2 mile to fork with a church in the middle. This is South Natick.

29. Bear right at fork and immediately cross Route 16 at blinking light onto Pleasant Street. Notice the ornate Victorian library on

Horse farm in Dover.

the far right-hand corner. Just ahead you'll cross the Charles, with a little dam on your right. Continue 3/10 mile to Dover Road on left.

30. Turn left on Dover Road and go 2.3 miles to crossroads and stop sign (Central Avenue). After 6/10 mile you'll cross the Charles again into Needham.

31. Go straight at crossroads 6/10 mile to end (merge left onto South Street).

32. Bear left on South Street and go 1.3 miles to stop sign and blinking light (Chestnut Street).

33. Cross Chestnut Street and go 1 mile to another stop sign and blinking light (Dedham Avenue, Route 135).

34. Turn right on Dedham Avenue and go 2.3 miles to traffic light (Route 109). At the beginning of this section, you will cross the Charles once more, into Dedham.

35. Cross Route 109 and go 4/10 mile to another light (Court Street). This is the center of Dedham. The granite buildings on the far side of the intersection are courthouses.

36. Turn right on Court Street and go 2/10 mile to crossroads where Highland Street bears right. It's your second right. Notice the classical white church on your right just after you turn right, and the magnificent stone church just before Highland Street.

37. Bear right on Highland Street. After 7/10 mile the main road bears left at fork. Stay on main road 4/10 mile to end (merge into Route 1A).

38. Bear right on Route 1A. The Holiday Inn is 2/10 mile ahead on left, just before the Route 128 overpass.

Directions for the ride: 20 miles

1. Follow directions for the 31-mile ride through number 16 to Dover Road. Here the ride turns right, but if you go straight 3/10 mile you'll come to the dam in South Natick.

2. Turn right on Dover Road and go 2.3 miles to crossroads and stop sign (Central Avenue). After 6/10 mile you'll cross the Charles into Needham.

3. Follow directions for the 31-mile ride from number 31 to the end.

Directions for the ride: 14 miles

1. Follow directions for the 31-mile ride through number 11.

2. Continue straight 1/10 mile, then bear slightly right on South Street. Go 1.3 miles to stop sign and blinking light (Chestnut Street).

3. Follow directions for the 31-mile ride from number 33 to the end.

31. The Upper Charles River: Walpole–Millis– Medfield–Sherborn–Dover

Number of miles: 16 (28 with Millis–Sherborn–Dover extension)
Terrain: Delightfully rolling, with lots of little ups and downs.
Food: Grocery store and restaurants in Medfield. Lunch counter in Dover.
Start: Main Street Shopping Center, Route 1A in Walpole, immediately north of Route 27.

The wealthy, woodsy suburbs southwest of Boston, halfway between the city and the northeastern corner of Rhode Island, provide ideal cycling on an impressive network of well-maintained, winding country lanes. The region is far enough from Boston to be rural rather than suburban. The landscape has a trim, prosperous look to it, with stone walls, old, well-maintained farmhouses framed by shade trees, spacious homes nestled on five-acre, pine-studded lots, and some estates in Dover. Coursing through the region are the upper reaches of the Charles River, a favorite canoeing run.

You'll start from Walpole, an attractive residential community with a brick Victorian town hall framing its green. You'll quickly head into undeveloped countryside as you cross the Charles into Millis and recross it into Medfield, both well-scrubbed, upper-middle-class communities. The return leg to Walpole brings you through forests with a few well-designed, spacious homes set back from the road among the trees.

The long ride heads farther north into Sherborn, one of Boston's most unspoiled suburbs and a paradise for bicycling. You'll ride beside pretty Farm Pond, pass a sweeping dairy farm, and cross the Charles again into Dover, the closest truly rural and unspoiled town to Boston, and one of the city's most upper-crust, old-moneyed suburbs. You'll pass several estates with mansions surrounded by acres of rolling meadows. The return run to Walpole brings you through a large stretch of open farmland and then along beautiful Willett Pond.

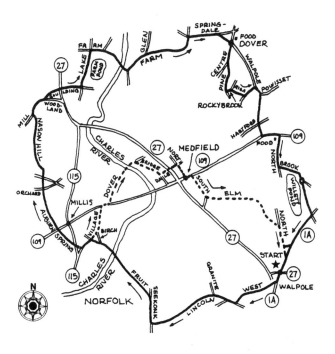

Directions for the ride: 28 miles

1. Turn right out of parking lot onto Route 1A. You'll immediately cross Route 27. Go 1/10 mile to fork, at the green (there is a traffic light here). Notice the Victorian town hall on the left just before the fork.

2. Bear right at fork. After 2/10 mile, the main road bears right under railroad bridge and a dead-end road bears left. Stay on main road for 9/10 mile to end.

3. Turn right at end and go 2/10 mile to fork where Lincoln Road, a smaller road, bears right.

4. Bear right on Lincoln Road. After 3/10 mile Granite Street turns right, but curve left, staying on the main road. Go 1.9 miles to end.

5. Turn right at end and go 6/10 mile to Fruit Street, which bears left up a little hill.

6. Bear left on Fruit Street and go 1/4 mile to crossroads and stop sign.

7. Go straight at crossroads. After 2.3 miles, Birch Street bears right, but curve left on the main road 2/10 mile to crossroads and stop sign. Here the short ride turns right and the long ride turns left.

8. Turn left at crossroads and go 2/10 mile to your first right, Spring Street.

9. Turn right. Just ahead is a crossroads and stop sign. Continue straight for 7/10 mile to crossroads and stop sign (Route 109).

10. Cross Route 109 onto Auburn Road. After 4/10 mile, Curve Street bears right, but go straight for 1/2 mile to stop sign (merge head-on into Ridge Street). Continue straight at stop sign 6/10 mile to crossroads and stop sign (Orchard Street).

11. Cross Orchard Street and go 3/10 mile to another crossroads and stop sign (Middlesex Street). Continue straight 2.1 miles to end (merge to right into Mill Street).

12. Bear right on Mill Street and go 6/10 mile to fork where Woodland Street bears right and West Goulding Street bears left.

13. Bear left at fork and go 1/2 mile to crossroads (Route 27).

14. Cross Route 27 onto East Goulding Street and go 6/10 mile to Lake Street, which turns sharp left at top of hill.

15. Turn sharp left on Lake Street and go 1.1 miles to crossroads and stop sign (Farm Road). You'll pass Farm Pond.

16. Turn right on Farm Road and go 1.7 miles to end (Farm Street). You'll cross the Charles near the end.

17. Turn left on Farm Street. After 1/2 mile, Glen Street bears left, but continue straight 1.5 miles to Springdale Avenue on right (sign may say to Dover, Needham).

18. Turn right on Springdale Avenue and go 8/10 mile to fork just before railroad tracks.

19. Bear right at fork and go 2/10 mile to traffic light in the center of Dover. There's a lunch counter at the Dover Pharmacy, on the far side of the intersection.

20. Turn right at light on Centre Street and go 4/10 mile to Pine Street, a smaller road that bears left.

21. Bear left on Pine Street and go 1.1 miles to Rockybrook Road on left. Just before the intersection, a dirt road on the right leads 1/2 mile to a fire tower, from which you can see Boston on a clear day.

22. Turn left on Rockybrook Road and go 1/10 mile to fork (Riga Road bears right).

23. Bear right on Riga Road and go 3/10 mile to end.

24. Turn left at end and go 4/10 mile to end.

25. Turn right at end. After 3/10 mile Powisset Street bears left, but curve right, staying on the main road. Go 7/10 mile to crossroads (Hartford Street).

26. Cross Hartford Street and go 1/2 mile to end (County Street, Route 109).

27. Turn left on Route 109 and go 1/2 mile to North Street on right. The Bubbling Brook, a great spot for ice cream, is on your right.

28. Turn right on North Street and go 1 mile to Brook Street on left. The farmland on your right belongs to the Norfolk County Agricultural Laboratory.

29. Turn left downhill on Brook Street and go 8/10 mile to rotary. You will go along Willett Pond on your right.

30. Bear slightly right at rotary, following the shore of Willett Pond, and go 1.1 miles to Route 1A, at crossroads and stop sign.

31. Turn right on Route 1A and go 1.8 miles to shopping center on right. • *CAUTION:* Route 1A is very busy.

Directions for the ride: 16 miles

1. Follow directions for the long ride through number 7.

2. Turn right at crossroads and go 8/10 mile to end (merge into Route 109).

3. Bear right on Route 109 and go 3/10 mile to Dover Road on left.

4. Turn left on Dover Road and go 1.2 miles to Bridge Street on right, just after you cross the Charles River. (Ignore another Bridge Street before you cross the river.)

5. Turn right on Bridge Street and go 6/10 mile to Dale Street (unmarked) on left. It's your fourth left, opposite house number 20 on right.

6. Turn left on Dale Street and go 4/10 mile to traffic light (Route 27, North Meadow Road).

7. Go straight at light 3/10 mile to end (North Street).

8. Turn right on North Street and go 4/10 mile to end (Route 109), in the center of Medfield. For a side trip you can visit the Medfield Rhododendrons, a 200-acre preserve with one of the few remaining stands of native rhododendron in the state, maintained by the Trustees of Reservations. The flowers bloom in early July. It's on Route 27 1/2 mile south of Route 109, on right. Paths lead from the parking lot of Saint Edward's Church.

9. Turn left on Route 109 and go 100 yards to South Street on right, at traffic light. Notice the small church on right with unusual Gothic architecture.

10. Turn right on South Street and go 8/10 mile to Elm Street on left, just before railroad tracks.

11. Turn left on Elm Street and go 2.9 miles to end (merge right.).

12. Bear right at end and go 4/10 mile to fork where Gile Street bears left and the main road bears right.

13. Bear right on the main road and go 2/10 mile to end (Route 1A).

14. Turn right on Route 1A and go 4/10 mile to shopping center on right.

32. South Attleboro–Cumberland, Rhode Island– Wrentham–North Attleboro

Number of miles: 17 (28 with Wrentham extension)
Terrain: Gently rolling, with one tough hill climbing up from the reservoir. The long ride is rolling.
Food: Grocery on Route 114 opposite Reservoir Road. Big Apple fruit stand and cider mill, Wrentham. Country store on corner of Route 121 and Hancock Street, Wrentham. Pizza at end.
Start: Washington Plaza, junction of Routes 1 and 123 in South Attleboro, Massachusetts.
How to get there: From the south, exit north from I-95 onto Route 1A (the first exit in Massachusetts). Go 1 mile to Route 123 and turn left. The parking lot is just ahead on your right on the far side of Route 1. From the northeast, exit west from I-95 onto Route 123. The parking lot is 2 miles ahead on your right. From the west, exit south from Route 295 onto Route 1. Parking lot is 2 miles ahead on your right.

The region straddling the Rhode Island–Massachusetts border is surprisingly rural considering that it's sandwiched between Pawtucket and North Attleboro. Its many quiet country roads are ideal for bicycling.

The ride begins in the suburban community of South Attleboro, just north of Pawtucket. The route angles northwestward into Cumberland, Rhode Island, on Mendon Road which turns into Abbott Run Valley Road. This long road is predominantly rural, but new homes keep springing up along it. You pass an open hillside which is now a housing tract, but around the next curve is open country again. This part of Cumberland, called the Arnold Mills section, is considered a desirable place to live.

When you reach Route 120, the village of Arnold Mills itself lies a half mile off the route to your right. It boasts a rickety old antique shop, a small dam, and an excellent Fourth of July parade. Continue north along the Diamond Hill Reservoir that provides Pawtucket's water supply. Parking was recently banned from this road, so you can pedal in peace without worrying about car doors opening in your face.

Just past the reservoir, the short ride crosses back into Massachusetts in North Attleboro. After a steep climb leading out of the watershed, the remainder of the ride in a delight—passing large, prosperous dairy farms. Then you come down from the ridge on a long, lazy descent. Near the end of the ride is the Abbott Run, a stream flowing between two old stone embankments from the Diamond Hill Reservoir through Arnold Mills to the Blackstone River. Just before the parking lot is Fuller Memorial Hospital, a private psychiatric facility with a campuslike setting.

The long ride makes a loop through the rural, rolling countryside of Wrentham, Massachusetts. This is a gracious community on the outer fringe of the Boston metropolitan area, far enough from the city to be nearly undeveloped. The last mile of Williams Street crosses into Franklin, which in contrast to Wrentham is courting suburban growth. But soon you pedal past Wrentham's horse pastures and barns once again. Union Street ascends gradually onto a ridge with fine views; then you descend past the Big Apple, a large orchard featuring hot and cold cider, doughnuts and freshly-picked apples in season. It's a refreshing rest stop on a nippy fall day. Just ahead you nick the northeast corner of Rhode Island on Burnt Swamp Road, passing small farms bordered by forest, before rejoining the short ride.

Direction for the ride: 28 miles

1. Turn right out of south side of parking lot on Route 123 and go 7/10 mile to Adamsdale Road on right.

2. Turn right on Adamsdale Road and go 7/10 mile to end, at stop sign.

3. Bear left for 1.8 miles to fork (Bear Hill Road bears left).

4. Bear right, staying on the main road, and go 2.2 miles to end (Route 120).

5. Turn left on Route 120 and go 2/10 mile to traffic light (Route 114).

6. Turn right on Route 114 and go 6/10 mile to Reservoir Road on right.

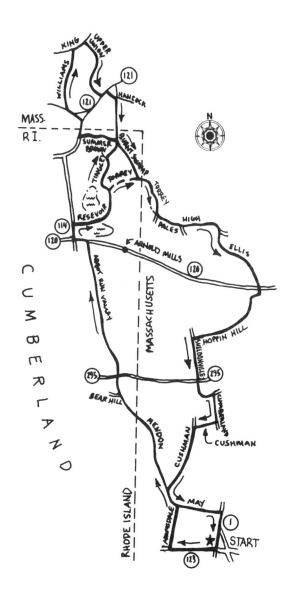

7. Turn right on Reservoir Road and go 1.6 miles to fork where Torry Road bears right and Tingley Road bears left. Here the short ride bears right and the long ride bears left.

8. Bear left for 9/10 mile to another fork (Burnt Swamp Road on right). • *CAUTION:* This stretch is bumpy, with gravel patches.

9. Curve left on main road and go 3/10 mile to Sumner Brown Road on left. • *CAUTION:* Bumpy.

10. Turn left on Sumner Brown Road and go 1.6 miles to end (Route 121).

11. Turn right on Route 121 and go 6/10 mile to one-way road on left.

12. Turn left and go 2/10 mile to end (merge left).

13. Bear left and go 2/10 mile to Williams Street on right.

14. Turn right on Williams Street and go 2.4 miles to end.

15. Bear right and go 2/10 mile to Upper Union Street on right, just before Route 495.

16. Turn right on Upper Union Street and go 2.8 miles to end (Route 121). After about 2 miles, while going downhill, you'll pass the Big Apple, an excellent fruit and cider stand in an old barn.

17. Turn left on Route 121 and go 2/10 mile to Hancock Street on right.

18. Turn right on Hancock Street and go 2/10 mile to diagonal crossroads (Burnt Swamp Road).

19. Turn right on Burnt Swamp Road and go 1.3 miles to where Burnt Swamp Road turns left and the main road curves right. • *CAUTION:* The last quarter mile is bumpy.

20. Turn left (still Burnt Swamp Road) and go 8/10 mile to crossroads (Torry Road).

21. Turn left at crossroads and go 1.1 miles to second left (dirt road on right).

22. Turn left and go 4/10 mile to fork.

23. Bear slightly left and go 7/10 mile to another fork (Ellis Road bears right).

24. Bear right on Ellis Road and go 1.4 miles to crossroads (Route 120).

25. Continue straight for 1.3 miles to end.

26. Turn left and go 1.1 miles to Cumberland Avenue on right, after the Route 295 underpass.

27. Turn right and go 3/10 mile to first right (Cushman Road, unmarked).

28. Turn right and go 2/10 mile to end.

29. Turn left (still Cushman Road) and go 1 mile to end (Mendon Road).

30. Turn left and go 2/10 mile to fork (May Street bears left).

31. Bear left on May Street and go 7/10 mile to traffic light (Route 1).

32. Turn right on Route 1 and go 3/10 mile to shopping center on right.

Directions for the ride: 17 miles

1. Follow directions for the long ride through number 7.

2. Bear right on Torry Road and go 6/10 mile to crossroads.

3. Go straight for 1.1 miles to second left (dirt road on right).

4. Follow directions for the long ride from number 22 to the end.

33. Chelmsford–Carlisle–Westford

Number of miles: 14 (25 with Westford extension)
Terrain: Rolling, with a few moderate hills and one tough one.
Food: Grocery in Carlisle, Grocery and pizza parlor in Westford.
  Friendly Ice Cream at end.
Start: Friendly Ice Cream, Route 4, Chelmsford, just south of the
  center of town. If you're coming from the south on Route 3,
  exit west onto Route 129 and go into the center of
  Chelmsford. Turn left on Route 4 and make a U-turn to your
  left at the first opportunity (a sign says Route 4 North).
  Friendly is on your right.

This ride takes you exploring three attractive towns on the outer
edge of suburban Boston. You start from Chelmsford, a pleasant,
middle-class suburb of Lowell with an attractive town center. Several churches, an old cemetery with slate tombstones from the
early 1800s, and the Victorian town hall frame the green with a
monument in the middle. The first few miles go through residential
areas and pass several industrial parks, but fortunately the landscape changes 100 percent as you cross the town line into Carlisle.
Carlisle is the closest truly unspoiled town to Boston, with a strict
no-growth policy. Narrow lanes weaving past farms, estates, and
woodland provide a paradise for biking. The center of town is a
jewel, with a magnificent old church fronting the green, a fine brick
Victorian library, and an old wooden schoolhouse on top of a hill.
From Carlisle to Westford the rural landscape of gentleman farms,
woodland, and an occasional orchard continues. Westford is an
unspoiled hilltop town with a large green framed by a classic white
church, a fine turn-of-the-century library, and gracious old homes.
The return to Chelmsford passes farms and orchards, and then becomes more residential but still pleasant after you cross the
Chelmsford town line.

  The short ride bypasses Westford, taking a more direct route
from Carlisle back to Chelmsford along a rolling secondary road.

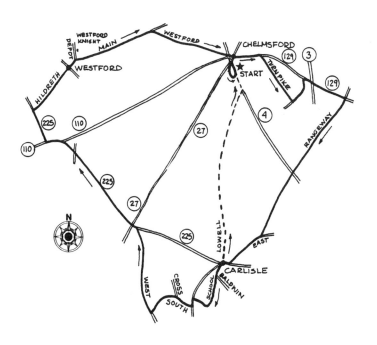

WESTFORD
KNIGHT
DEPOT
MAIN
WESTFORD
WESTFORD
CHELMSFORD
129
3
HILDRETH
START
TURNPIKE
129
225
110
4
27
RANGEWAY
110
225
27
225
LOWELL
EAST
CARLISLE
N
WEST
CROSS
SCHOOL
BALDWIN
SOUTH

Directions for the ride: 25 miles

1. Turn right out of the parking lot and go 2/10 mile to Route 129, in the center of town.

2. Turn right on Route 129. As soon as you turn, notice the splendid stone church on your left. Continue 1/2 mile to Turnpike Road, a smaller road that bears right.

3. Bear right on Turnpike Road and go 1.6 miles to end, at bottom of steep hill (• *CAUTION:* here). Unfortunately, the land on your left is being despoiled by the construction of industrial parks. Fifteen years ago it was woods and orchards.

4. Turn left at end and go 7/10 mile to end (Route 129).

5. Turn right on Route 129 and go 1.1 miles to crossroads (Rangeway Road).

6. Turn right on Rangeway Road and go 2.1 miles to crossroads and stop sign (Route 4).

7. Cross Route 4 and go 1.6 miles to end, at stop sign.

8. Bear right at stop sign and go 1.1 miles to end (merge into Route 225).

9. Bear right on Route 225 and go 1/10 mile to rotary in the center of Carlisle. Notice the handsome brick library on your left, built in 1895. At the rotary there's a country store serving sandwiches on your right. When you get to the rotary, the short ride turns right and the long ride goes straight and then left.

10. Go straight at rotary and then immediately bear left uphill on School Street, passing the magnificent white church on your left, built in 1811. At the top of the hill there's a fine old wooden school on your left. Then 3/10 mile beyond the school, Baldwin Road bears left at the bottom of the hill, but continue straight 1.5 miles to end.

11. Turn left at end and go 1/10 mile to South Street on right.

12. Turn right on South Street and go 3/10 mile to fork (Cross Street bears right).

13. Bear left at fork (still South Street) and go 1 mile to end (merge left into West Street).

14. Turn sharp right on West Street. After 1.5 miles you'll come to a diagonal crossroads (Acton Street). Continue straight 7/10 mile to end (merge into Route 225). • *CAUTION:* West Street has bumpy spots. Take it easy.

Farm in Carlisle.

15. Bear left on Route 225. Immediately ahead is a traffic light (Route 27). Stay on Route 225 for 2.5 miles to a diagonal cross-roads and stop sign.

16. Continue straight on Route 225 for 3/10 mile to where you merge into Route 110 at stop sign.

17. Bear left on Routes 110 and 225. Go 3/10 mile to where Route 225 (Concord Road) turns right and Route 110 goes straight. Here the ride turns right, but if you go straight 1/2 mile you'll come to a terrific ice cream place, Kimball's, on your left.

18. Turn right on Route 225 and go 7/10 mile on Hildreth Street (unmarked) on right, at small traffic island.

19. Turn right on Hildreth Street and go 1.6 miles to the traffic island with a monument in the middle at the top of the hill, in the center of Westford.

20. Bear right at traffic island and immediately go straight at crossroads onto Lincoln Street, passing the green on your left. Go 3/10 mile to fork where Depot Street bears left and Main Street bears right. Notice the elegant white church and the handsome beige-brick library on the far side of the green. Just beyond the green on your right is the town hall and a wooden Victorian schoolhouse, now a community center. When you get to the fork the ride bears right on Main Street, but if you bear left and go 2/10 mile you'll come to the Westford Knight, one of New England's unsolved mysteries. It is an outline of a medieval knight, complete with shield and sword, drawn on a rock. It was noticed by the earliest settlers and its origin remains unknown. The Knight will be on your right just as you start to go downhill—watch for a stone marker and four small stone pillars connected by chains. If you come to Abbott Middle School you've gone 1/10 mile too far.

21. Bear right on Main Street and go 2.9 miles to Westford Street, which bears right just beyond a ball field and fire station. There's a fast downhill run out of Westford. At the bottom of the hill there's a grocery and pizza parlor on your right.

22. Bear right on Westford Street and go 2.1 miles to stop sign in the center of Chelmsford. Two smaller roads bear left on this stretch, but stay on the main road. Just before the green you'll pass an unusual Gothic church on your left, and then an old cemetery with weathered slate tombstones on your right. Notice the fine Victorian town hall and the monument in the center of the green.

23. Bear slightly right at the stop sign onto Route 4. • *CAUTION:* Busy intersection. Just ahead you'll pass the back of the red-brick library on your left. Make a U-turn around the library (sign may say Route 4 North), and Friendly is on your right. Take a look at the library as you pull into the parking lot—it's a handsome building.

Directions for the ride: 14 miles

1. Follow the long ride through direction number 9.

2. Turn right at rotary onto Lowell Street and go 3.9 miles to end (merge left on Route 4). As soon as you turn onto Lowell Street there's a country store serving sandwiches on your right.

3. Bear left on Route 4 and go 9/10 mile to Friendly on right.

34. Nashoba Valley Tour: Littleton–Boxboro–Harvard–Bolton–Stow–Acton

Number of miles: 18 miles (33 with Harvard–Bolton–Stow extension)

Terrain: Very rolling, with one long, gradual hill and several shorter ones on the longer ride.

Food: Groceries or restaurants in all the towns except Boxboro.

Start: Acton Mall, Route 119 in Acton at the Littleton town line. It's between Routes 27 and 110.

The Nashoba Valley is the nickname for the rolling, rural, apple-growing country northwest of Boston near Route 495. The Nashua Valley would be a more accurate name, because the Nashua River flows along the region's western edge. The area is just far enough away from Boston to be rural rather than suburban, and is dotted with graceful, unspoiled New England towns. Abounding with narrow lanes twisting past orchards and old farmhouses, the Nashoba Valley provides superb biking that is a bit challenging because of the numerous ups and downs in the landscape. On the longer ride, a scenic and historic highlight are the Fruitlands Museums, set on a broad hillside with an outstanding view.

At the start of the ride you'll immediately head into Littleton along the shore of undeveloped Nagog Pond and then get into rolling orchard country. After going through the tiny center of Littleton, you'll ascend onto a long, high ridge capped with orchards into Harvard. At the highest point is an astronomical observatory belonging to Harvard University (the names of the town and the University are coincidental and confusing to newcomers) and a fire tower.

Harvard is one of the most graceful and classically elegant of the outer Boston suburbs, and strict zoning laws will keep it that way for the foreseeable future. No tract housing mars the landscape; instead you'll find only gentleman farms with broad fields, orchards, weathered barns, and widely spaced newer homes tastefully integrated with the wooded landscape on large lots. The town center is a jewel, with a fine old brick library, a general store, a large

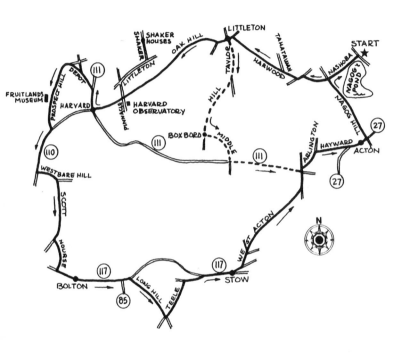

SHAKER HOUSES
SHAKER
OAK HILL
LITTLETON
TAHATAWAN
START
HARWOOD
FRUITLANDS MUSEUM
PROSPECT HILL
DEPOT
111
LITTLETON
TAYLOR HILL
NASHOBA
NAGOG POND
HARVARD
HAYWARD
HARVARD OBSERVATORY
NAGOG HILL
BOXBORO
MIDDLE
27
110
111
ARLINGTON
HAYWARD
ACTON
WESTBARE HILL
111
27
SCOTT
N
NOURSE
WEST ACTON
117
117
BOLTON
LONG HILL
STOW
85
TEELE

sloping green, and a classic white church on a little hill at the head of the green.

Just outside of town you'll ascend Prospect Hill, a magnificent open ridge with a spectacular view to the west. On a clear day you can see Mount Wachusett and even Mount Monadnock, forty miles away. At the top of the ridge are the Fruitlands Museums, a group of buildings with an eighteenth-century farmhouse, a Shaker house, a museum of American Indian relics, and a gallery of early American portraits and landscape paintings. The farmhouse contains a museum of the Transcendentalist movement, with memorabilia of the Alcott family, Emerson, Thoreau, and its other leaders, along with period furnishings and early farm implements. The Shaker house was moved several miles from a small Shaker village built during the 1790s. The rest of the village is two miles off the route.

From Harvard you'll proceed on winding lanes to Bolton, another delightful rural town with a cluster of antique shops and an ornate stone library, and then east to Stow, another unspoiled community consisting mainly of orchards, wooded hills, and farms along the Assabet River, a favorite of canoeists. From Stow you'll return to the start through the length of Acton, the most populous of the towns on the ride, but still essentially rural. The center of town is another New England classic, with a fine, white, clock-towered town hall, graceful old church, and a small green with a tall obelisk honoring the leader of the Acton Minutemen. The homestretch takes you through woods, old farms, and back along the shore of Nagog Pond.

The short ride bypasses Harvard, Bolton, and Stow by cutting across Boxboro, which was circled by the long ride but never actually touched. Boxboro, a rural wooded town like Bolton and Stow, is unique in that it has no town center, just a small town hall at a backroads intersection.

Directions for the ride: 33 miles

1. Turn right out of parking lot and immediately left onto Nashoba Road. Go 1.2 miles to crossroads and stop sign. You'll go along Nagog Pond.

2. Go straight at crossroads 6/10 mile to end (merge left at stop sign).

3. Bear left at end and go 1/10 mile to Harwood Avenue, which bears right.

4. Bear right on Harwood Avenue. After 6/10 mile, Tahatawan Road bears right, but continue straight 9/10 mile to crossroads and stop sign (Foster Street).

5. Cross Foster Street and go 1.2 miles to end. This is Littleton. The commercial center of town, Littleton Common, is 2 miles east at the junction of Routes 110 and 27.

6. Turn left at end, crossing railroad tracks, and go 2/10 mile to fork where Oak Hill Road bears right. The short ride turns left immediately after the tracks instead of going straight.

7. Bear right on Oak Hill Road, which climbs gradually up a long hill. After 2.9 miles, shortly beyond the top, Old Schoolhouse Road bears left, but bear right, staying on the main road. Go 4/10 mile to crossroads and stop sign (Pinnacle Road). Here the ride goes straight, but if you turn left for 1/4 mile, you'll come to the Harvard Observatory. If you'd like to visit Shaker Village, which is 2.3 miles away, turn right on Pinnacle Road, go 1/2 mile to cross-roads at bottom of steep hill, turn right at crossroads for 1 mile to Shaker Road on left just after you go over Route 495, and turn left for 8/10 mile to village. On the return trip, backtrack to the base of the hill and avoid the climb back up by continuing straight 1.6 miles to the center of Harvard and resuming with direction number 9.

8. Cross Pinnacle Road and go 1.4 miles to Route 111, at blinking light, in the center of Harvard. Notice the stately brick library on right.

9. Turn right on Route 111 and go 4/10 mile to Depot Road, which bears left while you're going downhill.

10. Bear left on Depot Road and go 7/10 mile to fork where the main road bears left.

11. Bear left at fork (still Depot Road) and go 1/2 mile to end (merge left into Prospect Hill Road; Old Shirley Road is on right).

12. Bear left on Prospect Hill Road and go 1.9 miles to end (Route 110). Fruitlands is on your right just past the top of the hill.

13. Turn right on Route 110 and go 1.3 miles to West Bare Hill

Road on left. There's a big old weathered barn on the right as soon as you turn onto this road.

14. Turn left on this road and go 4/10 mile to fork (West Bare Hill Road bears left, Scott Road bears right).

15. Bear right on Scott Road. After 1.3 miles you merge to your right at stop sign. Bear right and go 3/10 mile to Nourse Road on left.

16. Turn left on Nourse Road and go 1 mile to end (Route 117).

17. Turn left on Route 117 and go 2.1 miles to Long Hill Road, which bears right just after you pass Route 85 on your right. You'll go through the center of Bolton. Notice the ornate stone library on your right.

18. Bear right on Long Hill Road. After 3/10 mile Meadow Road bears left, but curve right uphill, staying on the main road. Go 1.1 miles to diagonal crossroads (Teele Road).

19. Turn sharply left on Teele Road and go 1.5 miles to end.

20. Turn right at end and go 4/10 mile to end (merge into Route 117).

21. Bear right on Route 117 and go 1.7 miles to a road that bears left at the Stow town hall (sign may say to Acton).

22. Bear left here and go 3/10 mile to fork where West Acton Road bears left. As soon as you leave Route 117, notice the fine church and library on your right.

23. Bear left on West Acton Road (sign may say to Route 2, Acton) and go 2/10 mile to a three-way fork.

24. Continue straight 2.3 miles to end (merge left at stop sign).

25. Bear left at end and go 2/10 mile to Route 111, in the center of West Acton.

26. Cross Route 111 and immediately turn right on Arlington Street. Go 1/2 mile to Hayward Road, which turns right uphill.

27. Turn right on Hayward Road. After 1.3 miles you'll merge head-on into Route 27. Continue straight on Route 27 for 7/10 mile to crossroads just beyond the center of Acton (Nagog Hill Road).

28. Turn left on Nagog Hill Road and go 2.4 miles to crossroads and stop sign at top of hill. There's a fast downhill to Nagog Pond. • *CAUTION:* The road becomes bumpy toward bottom of hill.

29. Turn right at crossroads and go 1.2 miles to end (Route 119). The shopping center is just to your right.

Directions for the ride: 18 miles

1. Follow directions for the long ride through number 5.

2. Turn left at end across railroad tracks, and then immediately turn left again at crossroads onto Taylor Street. Go 1.9 miles to Hill Road, which bears right at a small green.

3. Bear right on Hill Road and go 1.8 miles to Middle Road (unmarked) on left, just before you go downhill. Believe it or not, this intersection is the center of Boxboro.

4. Turn left on Middle Road and go 1.1 miles to crossroads and stop sign (Route 111). Just before the intersection, the town hall is on your left.

5. Turn left on Route 111 and go 2.1 miles to crossroads at bottom of hill (Central Street). This is West Acton.

6. Turn left on Central Street and immediate right on Arlington Street. Go 1/2 mile to Hayward Road, which turns right uphill.

7. Follow directions for the long ride from number 27 to the end.

35. Assabet Valley Tour: Maynard–Stow–Marlboro–Hudson

Number of miles: 13 (28 with Marlboro–Hudson extension)
Terrain: Rolling.
Food: Grocery stores and snack bars in the towns. McDonald's at
end.
Start: Junction of Routes 62 and 27, in the center of Maynard. It's
best to park on Douglas Avenue, which runs off Route 62
one block east of Route 27. If you're coming from the east
on Route 62, turn left on Douglas Avenue; if you're coming
from the west, turn right.

On this ride you'll explore a fascinating mixture of old mill towns
and delightful, rolling orchard country with some fine views from
open hillsides. Meandering through the region is the Assabet River,
a favorite for canoeists, which eventually joins the Concord River in
that town. The area is midway between Boston and Worcester, and
a little north of both.

The ride starts from Maynard, a compact, visually striking nineteenth-century mill town on the Assabet River, with hulking, grim
textile factories that could have served as models for the dark,
satanic mills in William Blake's famous poem. But within a mile
you'll be in green and pleasant land heading toward Stow, a delightful rural town consisting primarily of wooded hills, orchards, and
farms along the river. In the center of town is a classic white
church and a handsome brick library. Just outside of Stow you'll
bike along the convoluted shoreline of Boons Pond, an attractive
lake lined with cozy pine-shaded summer cottages, and then head
past rolling horse farms and orchards to Marlboro, a rather nonde-
script industrial town except for an ornate brick Victorian town hall
with a graceful bell tower and some nineteenth-century commercial buildings along the main street. Unlike the gracious, unspoiled
New England towns surrounding it. Marlboro is courting industrial
development with the recent growth of unsightly industrial parks
raping the land along Route 495.

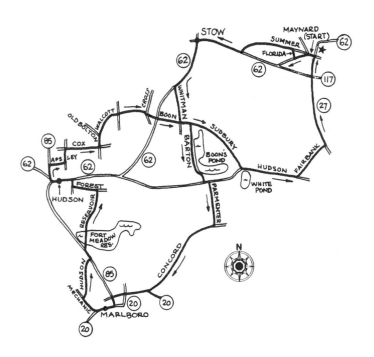

From Marlboro it's a short run across the delightful Fort Meadow Reservoir to Hudson, an attractive mill town on the Assabet River. The downtown area is classic late nineteenth century, with a compact business block of stately brick buildings and a portly Victorian town hall. The return to Maynard brings you through a varied landscape of woods and open farmland, with a spin along White Pond. Near the end of the ride you'll pass the headquarters of Digital Corporation, the giant computer company whose plants are sprinkled over a wide area northwest of Boston.

Directions for the ride: 28 miles

1. Turn left (west) onto Route 62, which immediately turns right at traffic light and then left, passing McDonald's on your left. Continue on Route 62 through downtown Maynard for 3/10 mile to Florida Road on right, just past the small bridge over the Assabet River. There's a striking view from the left side of the bridge of the river flowing between the mills.

2. Turn right on Florida Road and go 2/10 mile to end (Summer Street).

3. Turn left on Summer Street and go 1.6 miles to end (Route 62).

4. Turn right on Route 62 and go 1.1 miles to crossroads and traffic light where Route 62 turns left. This is the center of Stow. Notice the graceful church and library on your right at the intersection.

5. Turn left at crossroads, staying on Route 62, and go 1.1 miles to Whitman Street, which bears left. It's just beyond Treaty Elm Lane, which also bears left.

6. Bear left on Whitman Street and go 8/10 mile to crossroads and stop sign (Boon Road).

7. Turn left on Boon Road and go 3/10 mile to Barton Road on right, just past the bridge over the Assabet River. Here the short ride goes straight and the long ride turns right.

8. Turn right on Barton Road. After 1.2 miles a road bears right, but bear left on main road, following Boons Pond on your left. Go 4/10 mile to end. • *CAUTION:* Watch out for bumps, potholes, and sand patches. This road needs repaving.

216

9. At end jog left and immediate right onto Parmenter Road. Go 1.1 miles to end, at top of short hill. • *CAUTION:* Bad railroad tracks on this stretch.

10. Bear right at end and go 2.7 miles to end (Route 20).

11. Bear right on Route 20. After 1/2 mile, Route 20 turns right at traffic light, but continue straight 3/10 mile to another light (Bolton Street, Route 85).

12. Turn left on Bolton Street and go 2/10 mile to end (Route 20), in downtown Marlboro.

13. Turn right on Route 20 and go 4/10 mile to fork with a unique wooden church in the middle. You'll pass the Victorian city hall on your left.

14. Bear right at fork. After 1/10 mile you'll cross Lincoln Street at traffic light. Continue straight 2/10 mile to Hudson Street, your third right.

15. Turn right on Hudson Street. After 2/10 mile, Union Street bears right uphill, but curve left, staying on Hudson Street. Go 7/10 mile to grassy traffic island. Bear right (still Hudson Street) for 1/10 mile to end (Route 85, Bolton Street).

16. Turn left at end and go 2/10 mile to Reservoir Street, which bears right.

17. Bear right on Reservoir Street and go 1.7 miles to end (Forest Avenue).

18. Turn left on Forest Avenue and go 6/10 mile to end.

19. Turn right at end and go 2/10 mile to Route 62, at stop sign.

20. Turn left on Route 62. Just ahead is a traffic light. At the light there's an old wooden mill on the left with a graceful, slender spire. Continue straight 3/10 mile through downtown Hudson to fork and small rotary where Route 62 bears right. Notice the Victorian town hall on right.

21. Bear right at fork. Just ahead is another fork where Route 62 bears left and Route 85 bears right.

22. Bear right on Route 85 (Lincoln Street) and go 2/10 mile to traffic light (Apsley Street).

23. Turn right on Apsley Street and go 4/10 mile to end. Just before the end you'll cross Bruces Pond.

24. Turn left at end and go 2/10 mile to traffic light (Cox Street).

25. Turn right on Cox Street and go 8/10 mile to crossroads (Old Bolton Road on left).

26. Turn left at crossroads and go 2/10 mile to Walcott Street, which bears right. It's your first right.

27. Bear right on Walcott Street and go 9/10 mile to crossroads and stop sign.

28. Go straight at crossroads onto Randall Road for 8/10 mile to fork where Cross Street turns left uphill and the main road bears right.

29. Bear right at fork, and then immediately bear left at another fork on Boon Road. Go 2/10 mile to crossroads and stop sign (Route 62).

30. Cross Route 62 and go 2.7 miles to end (merge left at stop sign).

31. Bear left at end, immediately passing White Pond on right, and go 1.9 miles to Fairbank Road on left, immediately after a large athletic field on left.

32. Turn left on Fairbank Road and go 8/10 mile to end (Route 27).

33. Turn left on Route 27. After 1.9 miles you'll come to Route 117. Continue straight on Route 27 for 7/10 mile to Route 62, at traffic light.

34. Go straight at light on Route 62. Douglas Avenue is just ahead on right.

Directions for the ride: 13 miles

1. Follow directions for the long ride through number 7.

2. Continue straight on Boon Road 2.1 miles to end (merge left at stop sign).

3. Follow directions for the long ride from number 31 to the end.

36. Wayside Inn Ride: Framingham–Southboro–Sudbury

Number of miles: 22

Terrain: Gently rolling.

Food: Grocery and pizza place just off the route in Southboro. Snack bars on Route 20 in Marlboro. Numerous stores and restaurants at end.

Start: Shopping center at corner of Franklin Street and Mount Wayte Avenue in Framingham, about a mile south of Route 9.

How to get there: From Route 9, if you're coming from the east, take the Route 30 West exit and turn left at light on Main Street. Go 2/10 mile to second right, Franklin Street. Turn right and go 6/10 mile to Mount Wayte Avenue, at traffic light. The shopping center is on right on the far side of intersection. If you're coming from the west on Route 9, take the Edgell Road-Main Street exit and turn right at traffic light on Main Street. Go 2/10 mile to second right, Franklin Street. Turn right and go 6/10 mile to Mount Wayte Avenue, at traffic light.

From the junction of Routes 135 and 126, go north on Route 126 and just ahead bear left on Union Avenue. Go 1 mile to Mount Wayte Avenue, at traffic light. Turn left, and just ahead is another light (Franklin Street). Shopping center is on left on the far side of the intersection.

Midway between Boston and Worcester, delightful bicycling abounds in the region surrounding the Sudbury Reservoirs, a long chain of lakes surrounded by rolling hills, orchards, and open farmland. The landscape is rural in a prosperous, well-scrubbed sort of way, with gentleman farms, horse paddocks, and rambling, well-maintained old New England farmhouses set off by spreading shade trees and stone walls. A network of smooth secondary roads, many going along the lakeshores, gets you away from the traffic. A historic highlight of the ride is the Wayside Inn in Sudbury, the oldest continually operating inn in the country, built around 1700 and visited by Longfellow during the mid-1800s. The poet was fascinated and celebrated it in his famed poems, "Tales of a Wayside Inn." Sixty years later another captivated visitor, Henry Ford, decided to construct elements of a New England village next to the Inn, and so he added an operating gristmill, a little red schoolhouse, and a classic white church.

The ride starts from Framingham, one of Boston's most populous suburbs, with 65,000 residents. Framingham is a city of three faces: partly an old industrial town with dreary rows of old wooden houses, partly a bedroom suburb with tract houses and modern apartment complexes, and partly a gracious rural town with lakes, horse farms, and a classic New England green. This ride goes through the third face. At the beginning you'll head along two ponds and pass Macomber Farm, formerly an estate and now an educational farm, with a variety of barnyard creatures, run by the Massachusetts Society for the Prevention of Cruelty to Animals (MSPCA). Its rather steep admission fee is, a staff member explained to me with blunt honesty, a forced contribution to the MSPCA. From here you'll head into Southboro, a gracious, well-to-do community with gentleman farms spreading across rolling hillsides, prestigious St. Mark's preparatory school, and a classic New England village center. The school and center of town are about a mile off the route. After two delightful runs along the lake it's not far to the Wayside Inn.

Approaching the Inn you first come to the gristmill, a masterpiece of historical reconstruction built for Henry Ford in 1929. It is an authentic, working reproduction of an eighteenth-century stone mill, with a massive water wheel 18 feet in diameter. Just past the mill is the Martha-Mary Chapel, a replica of a New England church that somehow looks more sterile than the real one. It is now used only for weddings. Next to the chapel is the Redstone School, an actual one-room little red schoolhouse that was moved in 1926 from Sterling, twenty miles to the west, and used as a public school until 1951. This is the school Mary and her little lamb went to. Just past the school is the Inn itself, a graceful gambrel-roofed building all but overshadowed by the attractions leading up to it.

The return to Framingham takes you back through the city's third face, passing horse farms and gracious old Colonial-style homes. At the end you'll go by the handsome green, framed by two

The gristmill next to the Wayside Inn, Sudbury.

stately brick churches facing each other across the road and an ornate, steep-gabled Victorian library.

Directions for the ride:

1. Turn left out of parking lot onto Mount Wayte Avenue and go 1.1 miles to end (Fountain Street). You'll pass Farm Pond on your left.

2. Turn right on Fountain Street and go 4/10 mile to traffic light (Winter Street). Continue straight at light 1/2 mile to Jodie Road on right, just after bridge.

3. Turn right on Jodie Road and go 2/10 mile to Singletary Lane, your first right, halfway up the hill.

4. Turn right on Singletary Lane and go 1.4 miles to end (Salem End Road). On your right is one of the several lakes comprising the Sudbury Reservoir system.

5. Turn left on Salem End Road and go 4/10 mile to fork where Gates Road bears right. You'll pass Macomber Farm on the left.

6. Bear right at fork on Gates Road and go 1/10 mile to another fork where Parker Road bears left.

7. Bear left on Parker Road and go 1.3 miles to end (merge to your right on Oregon Road).

8. Bear right on Oregon Road and go 6/10 mile to crossroads and stop sign.

9. Go straight at crossroads. You'll immediately come to a fork. Bear slightly left, staying on the main road, and go 1 mile to fork immediately after you pass underneath the Massachusetts Turnpike.

10. Bear left at fork on Breakneck Hill Road and go 9/10 mile to another fork. (Mount Vickery Road bears left.)

11. Bear right at fork (still Breakneck Hill Road) and go 1/10 mile to Route 9, at traffic light.

12. Cross Route 9 onto White Bagley Road and go 4/10 mile to fork, following the shore of the Sudbury Reservoir. • *CAUTION:* Be very careful crossing Route 9.

13. Bear right at fork, following the Reservoir, and go 1/2 mile to crossroads and stop sign (Route 30).

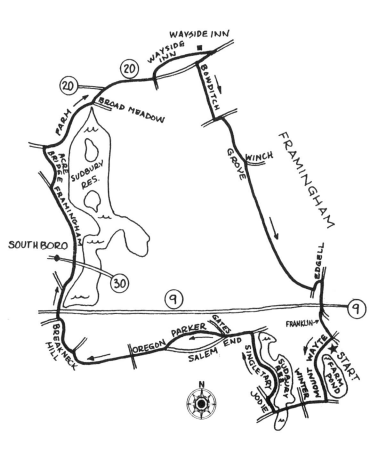

WAYSIDE INN

WAYSIDE
INN

20

20

FARM

BROAD MEADOW

BOWDITCH

FRAMINGHAM

WINCH

GROVE

ACRE BRIDGE FRAMINGHAM

SUDBURY RES.

SOUTHBORO

30

EDGELL

9

9

FRANKLIN→

BREAKNECK HILL

OREGON

PARKER

GATES

SALEM END

SINGLETARY

JOOIE

SUDBURY

WAYTE

MOUNT

WINTER

START (FARM POND)

N

14. Cross Route 30 and go 1.6 miles to Acre Bridge Road, which bears right.

15. Bear right on Acre Bridge Road and go 7/10 mile to end (Farm Road).

16. Turn right at end. After 1.5 miles, Broad Meadow Road bears right, but stay on the main road, which curves to the left. Continue 1/2 mile to end (merge head-on into Route 20).

17. Go straight onto Route 20 for 1.2 miles to Wayside Inn Road, at traffic light. Here you will turn left by making a jug-handle turn—you bear right just before the light and cross Route 20 at right angles. • *CAUTION:* Route 20 is very busy.

18. Make a jug-handle left turn at traffic light. After 7/10 mile you'll pass the gristmill, the chapel, the little red schoolhouse, and finally the Wayside Inn itself. From the Inn, continue 3/10 mile to end (Route 20).

19. Turn sharp right on Route 20 and go 4/10 mile to your second left, Bowditch Road.

20. Turn left on Bowditch Road. After 1/4 mile a smaller road bears right, but curve left on the main road. Go 1.1 miles to end.

21. Turn left at end, and then immediately bear right on Grove Street. Go 9/10 mile to fork where Winch Street bears left uphill.

22. Bear right at fork (still Grove Street) and go 2 miles to end, opposite the Framingham town green.

23. Turn left at end, going alongside the green on your right, and go 1/10 mile to end (Edgell Road). Notice the two impressive brick churches facing each other across the road at the head of the green.

24. Turn right on Edgell Road. After 2/10 mile you'll cross the overpass above Route 9. (• *CAUTION* here—busy intersections). Continue 2/10 mile to second right, Franklin Street.

25. Turn right on Franklin Street and go 6/10 mile to Mount Wayte Avenue, at traffic light. The shopping center is just past light on right.

37. Holliston–Hopkinton

Number of miles: 19 (32 with western loop, 14 if you do the western loop only)

Terrain: Rolling, with one tough hill on the Hopkinton loop and several shorter ones along both loops.

Food: Grocery store and restaurant in Hopkinton. Fast-food places at end.

Start: K-Mart, Route 109 in Milford, just west of Route 495 at exit 19. To do just the western loop, start at the junction of Routes 135 and 85 in the center of Hopkinton.

This ride will take you exploring two wooded, wealthy communities on the outer edge of Boston's suburbia, midway between Boston and Worcester and a little south of both. The landscape is rural rather than suburban, consisting mainly of wooded hills, some open farmland and orchards, and several unspoiled lakes. A wide-ranging network of narrow country roads provides superb bicycling if you're willing to tackle a few hills. The ride consists of a figure eight with Hopkinton at the center. You can do either loop or both.

The eastern loop heads through woods and past small farms to the center of Hopkinton, located on a broad hilltop. Hopkinton becomes known to the world on Patriot's Day, in April, when the Boston Marathon starts here at noon. In recent years the number of contestants has far surpassed that of the town's 6,000 residents. From Hopkinton you'll traverse larger expanses of farmland and pass the undeveloped Ashland Reservoir. Then you'll ascend onto a long ridge with orchards on the top and fine views of the surrounding hills and valleys. The return leg brings you through a rural landscape along winding lanes through woods, past old barns and farmhouses, and along Weston Pond.

The western loop passes through a similar landscape past three large, undeveloped lakes—North Pond; Whitehall Reservoir, protected by Whitehall State Park; and the Hopkinton Reservoir, adjoining Hopkinton State Park. All three lakes are surrounded by round, green hills.

Directions for the ride: 32 miles

1. Turn left out of the east side of the parking lot onto the side road paralleling Route 495. Go 4/10 mile to crossroads and stop sign (Route 16).

2. Turn right on Route 16 and go 1 mile to a small road that bears left.

3. Bear left on this road (Adams Street) and go 9/10 mile to fork where Marshall Street bears right. • *CAUTION:* This road has bumpy spots.

4. Go straight at fork (don't bear right on Marshall Street). Go 1 mile to end (Hanlon Road).

5. Turn left on Hanlon Road. Just ahead is a fork. Bear slightly left and go 8/10 mile to end (Route 85). • *CAUTION:* Hanlon Road is very narrow, twisting, and bumpy.

6. Turn right on Route 85. After 1.7 miles, Route 85 curves sharply to the left at blinking light. Continue on Route 85 for 6/10 mile to traffic light (Route 135). This is the center of Hopkinton. Here the 19-mile ride turns right and the 32-mile ride turns left.

7. Turn left on Route 135 and go 4/10 mile to fork where Route 135 bears right.

8. Bear left at fork (sign may say to Route 140, Upton) and go 2.8 miles to crossroads at top of long, tough hill (School Street). Before climbing the hill you'll pass North Pond on your left.

9. Turn right at top of hill on School Street and go 7/10 mile to fork.

10. Bear left at fork. • *CAUTION:* You are about to go down a steep, bumpy hill—go slow. After 4/10 mile, near the bottom of the hill, the main road curves sharply left at a traffic island, and you'll immediately see the Whitehall Reservoir on your right. Continue 1.5 miles to end (merge to your right into Spring Street). There is no stop sign at this intersection.

11. Bear right on Spring Street and go 1.4 miles to crossroads (Wood Street, Route 135). You'll go along the shore of the Whitehall Reservoir.

12. Cross Wood Street onto Cunningham Street. Go 3/10 mile to where the main road curves sharply right and Fruit Street turns left.

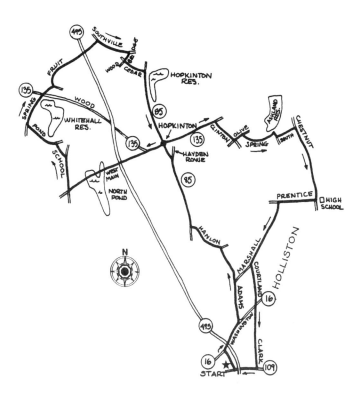

13. Turn left on Fruit Street and go 2.3 miles to end.

14. Turn right at end and go 8/10 mile to Bridge Street on right, opposite the church. This is the tiny village of Southville, a part of Southboro.

15. Turn right on Bridge Street and go 1/10 mile to crossroads.

16. Turn left at crossroads and go 6/10 mile to end (Cordaville Road, Route 85). • *CAUTION:* Bumpy road.

17. Turn right on Route 85 and go 2.3 miles to traffic light (Route 135), back in the center of Hopkinton. You'll pass the Hopkinton Reservoir on your left.

18. Turn left on Route 135 and go 1.7 miles to Clinton Street on right (sign may say Laborers Training Center).

19. Turn right on Clinton Street and go 6/10 mile to traffic island with a crossroads immediately after it.

20. Turn left at traffic island and go 2/10 mile to Spring Street on right.

21. Turn right on Spring Street. After 7/10 mile you'll pass the Ashland Reservoir on your left. Just ahead the road turns 90 degrees right up a steep hill. Go uphill 1/10 mile to a road on your left.

22. Turn left on this road and go 4/10 mile to end. • *CAUTION:* The first half of this road has bumps and potholes.

23. Turn right at end. After 1.9 miles Hollis Street turns left and the main road curves right. Stay on main road for 100 yards to Prentice Street on right.

24. Turn right on Prentice Street and go 1.6 miles to Marshall Street on left.

25. Turn left on Marshall Street and go 1.7 miles to fork where Courtland Street bears left.

26. Bear left on Courtland Street and go 7/10 mile to crossroads and stop sign (Route 16, Washington Street). Just before the intersection you'll pass Weston Pond on your left.

27. Cross Route 16 onto South Street and go 1.8 miles to end (Route 109).

28. Turn right on Route 109 and go 7/10 mile to K-Mart on right.

Directions for the ride: 19 miles

    1. Follow directions for the long ride through number 6.

    2. Turn right on Route 135 and go 1.7 miles to Clinton Street on right (sign may say Laborers Training Center).

    3. Follow directions for the long ride from number 19 to the end.

Directions for the ride: 14 miles (start from junction of Routes 135 and 85 in the center of Hopkinton)

    1. Head west on Route 135 and go 4/10 mile to fork where Route 135 bears right.

    2. Follow directions for the 32-mile ride from numbers 8 through 17.

Chapter 4

The Farther Western Suburbs

Numbers on this map refer to rides in this book.

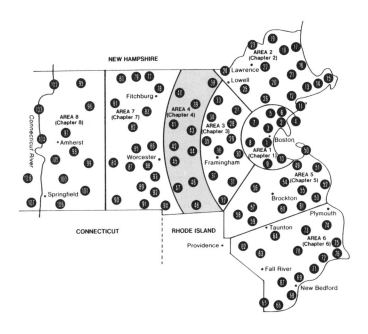

38. Westford–Dunstable–Tyngsborough

Number of miles: 12 (28 with Dunstable–Tyngsborough
  extension)
Terrain: Rolling with a tough hill at the beginning and another
  one in Dunstable.
Food: Groceries and snack bars in the towns.
Start: Shopping center on Route 110 in Westford, just northeast
  of Boston Road. From Route 495, take the Boston Road exit.
  Turn right at the end of the ramp if you were heading north
  on 495, or left if you were heading south. Route 110 is just
  ahead. Turn left on Route 110. The shopping center is just
  ahead on your left.

Just west of Lowell, along the west bank of the Merrimack River, is
a delightful biking area of gentle wooded hills, small farms, and
unspoiled small towns. As you head west of Lowell the countryside
quickly becomes rural, because you're just far enough from Boston
to make commuting impractical. Westford actually lies on the fringe
of the metropolitan area, but it is a well-to-do community with a
no-growth policy, and very much a small town.

The ride starts from Westford, one of the many gracious, still-
unspoiled towns that dot the countryside northwest of Boston
along Route 495. The hilltop village center is exceptionally appealing, with a large tree-studded green framed by a graceful white
church, the stately white wooden town hall, and a turn-of-the-century beige-brick library. Just beyond the green is an ornate wooden
Victorian schoolhouse, now a community center. On the edge of
town sits the Westford Knight, one of New England's unsolved mysteries. It is an outline of a medieval knight, complete with shield
and sword, drawn on a rock. It was noticed by the earliest settlers
and its origin remains unknown.

From Westford you'll enjoy a long downhill run, and then proceed on wooded backroads to Dunstable, a graceful picture post-
card town with a traditional old church, little village green, and a
fine brick library. From Dunstable you'll hug the Massachusetts–
New Hampshire border to Tyngsborough, a rather forlorn-looking

town in need of a facelift. Its major landmark is the graceful steel-arched bridge across the Merrimack. Until 1960, Tyngsborough sat on the main road from Boston to New Hampshire; then Route 3 was built, bypassing the town, and it became nearly forgotten.

From Tyngsborough you'll return to Westford along winding lanes through the handsome mill village of Graniteville, which is part of Westford. Graniteville is accurately named, with a handsome bell-towered granite mill standing above a delightful little millpond. At the end of the ride you'll return down the same hill that you struggled up at the beginning.

Directions for the ride: 28 miles

1. Turn right out of parking lot onto Route 110 and immediately turn right at traffic light on Boston Road. Go 1.2 miles to Lincoln Street, which bears right at the Westford town green at top of hill.

2. Bear right on Lincoln Street and go 3/10 mile to fork where Main Street bears right and Depot Street bears left.

3. Bear left on Depot Street and stay on the main road 1 mile to fork immediately after railroad tracks. The Westford Knight will be on your right after 2/10 mile, just as you start to go downhill. Watch for a stone marker and four small stone pillars connected by chains. If you come to Abbott Middle School, you've gone 1/10 mile too far. Beyond the Knight there's a magnificent downhill run.

4. Bear left at fork (still Depot Street). After 8/10 mile there'll be a small crossroads. Continue straight 3/10 mile to fork (Dunstable Road bears left).

5. Bear left on Dunstable Road and go 1/2 mile to crossroads and stop sign (Groton Road, Route 40).

6. Cross Route 40 and go 8/10 mile to crossroads at end of Long-Sought-for Pond on right.

7. Go straight at crossroads 3/10 mile to another crossroads (Tenney Road). Here the short ride turns left and the long ride goes straight.

8. Go straight at crossroads. After 1/2 mile Ingalls Road bears left at top of hill, but bear right, staying on the main road. Go 3.4 miles to end (Route 113).

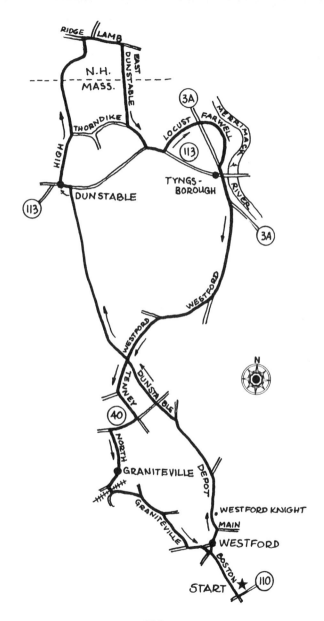

RIDGE LAMB

EAST DUNSTABLE

N.H.
MASS.

3A

THORNDIKE

LOCUST FARWELL

MERRIMACK

HIGH

113

TYNGS-
BOROUGH

113

DUNSTABLE

RIVER

3A

N

WESTFORD

WESTFORD

TENNEY

DUNSTABLE

40

NORTH

DEPOT

GRANITEVILLE

WESTFORD KNIGHT

GRANITEVILLE

MAIN

WESTFORD

BOSTON

START ★ 110

9. Turn left on Route 113 and go 2/10 mile to High Street on right, opposite the church in the center of Dunstable. Notice the fine brick library on your right. Here the ride turns right, but there's a country store just ahead on Route 113.

10. Turn right on High Street and go 8/10 mile to fork where Thorndike Street bears right.

11. Bear left at fork and go 1.8 miles to end (Ridge Road). You are now in Nashua, New Hampshire, a city promoting condominium development.

12. Turn right on Ridge Road and go 1 mile to East Dunstable Road on right. There's a tough hill midway along this stretch.

13. Turn right on East Dunstable Road and go 1.4 miles to end (merge left).

14. Bear left at end and go 6/10 mile to end (Route 113).

15. Turn left on Route 113 and go 1/2 mile to Locust Avenue on left, shortly before the Route 3 overpass.

16. Turn left on Locust Avenue. Just ahead a road bears right, but continue straight for 8/10 mile to crossroads and stop sign Route 3A (Middlesex Road). You'll pass Locust Pond on your right.

17. Cross Route 3A onto Farwell Road and go 1.4 miles to end (merge into Route 3A). Notice the fine brick library on the far side of the intersection.

18. Bear left on Route 3A. Just ahead, at the junction of Route 113, is the center of Tyngsborough. Continue on Route 3A for 3/10 mile to Westford Road, which bears right at traffic light.

19. Bear right on Westford Road and go 1.7 miles to fork (Westford Road bears right).

20. Bear right at fork (still Westford Road) and go 9/10 mile to another fork.

21. Bear left at fork (still Westford Road) and go 1.5 miles to crossroads (Dunstable Road).

22. Cross Dunstable Road onto Tenney Road and go 7/10 mile to fork (Keyes Road bears right).

23. Bear slightly left at fork and go 6/10 mile to Route 40. You'll pass Keyes Pond on your right.

24. Turn right on Route 40 and go 6/10 mile to North Street on left (sign may say to Forge Village).

25. Turn left on North Street and go 1.1 miles to a small road that bears left underneath a narrow railroad bridge. This is Graniteville, a village in Westford.

26. Bear left under the railroad bridge and then immediately bear left again on Bridge Street. Go 1/2 mile to end (merge to your right at stop sign).

27. Bear right at end and go 4/10 mile to fork. (Cold Spring Road bears left, Graniteville Road bears right.)

28. Bear right at fork and go 8/10 mile to end, at top of long hill.

29. Turn left at end and go 1/10 mile to fork, at the Westford green.

30. Bear right at fork and immediately go straight onto Boston Road. Go 1.2 miles to traffic light (Route 110).

31. Turn left on Route 110. Shopping center is just ahead on left.

Directions for the ride: 12 miles

1. Follow directions for the long ride through number 7.

2. Turn left on Tenney Road and go 7/10 mile to fork (Keyes Road bears right).

3. Follow directions for the long ride from number 23 to the end.

39. Covered-Bridge Ride: Groton–Pepperell–Hollis, New Hampshire–Ayer

Number of miles: 20 (30 with Hollis extension)
Terrain: Rolling
Food: Grocery stores and snack bars in the towns.
Start: Supermarket on Route 2A, Ayer, 8/10 mile north of the center of town. It's just north of the fork of Routes 2A and 111.

The valley of the Nashua River, midway between Fitchburg and Lowell, is a bicyclist's paradise of country roads traversing broad farms and orchards, and winding through rolling hills. The region is one of the major apple-growing areas of the state. Adding variety to this refreshingly rural landscape are the three gracious New England towns of Groton, Pepperell, and Hollis, New Hampshire. In Pepperell you'll bike over the only original (actually a reproduction of the original) covered bridge in the eastern half of the state.

The ride starts on the outskirts of Ayer and immediately heads through rolling orchards and farmland to the classic New England town of Groton, one of the most elegant in the state. Just over the town line is the stately, meticulously landscaped campus of the Groton School, one of the most prestigious boys' preparatory schools in the country. The most prominent landmark of the campus is the graceful Gothic-style stone chapel. A fine green, several graceful old churches, and the handsome brick buildings of Lawrence Academy, another prep school, dignify the center of town. Surrounding the town are broad acres of gentleman farms, estates, and orchards spreading over the rolling hills.

From Groton it's several miles along backroads to Pepperell, another classic town with a handsome old white church and town hall, and an ornate, pillared red-brick library. Just outside of town you'll cross the Nashua River over the covered bridge, a replica of the original rebuilt in 1962. The return trip loops back through Groton across more inspiring rolling estate and orchard country to the center of Ayer, which can be described only as a depressed mill town. When the main line of the Boston and Maine railroad be-

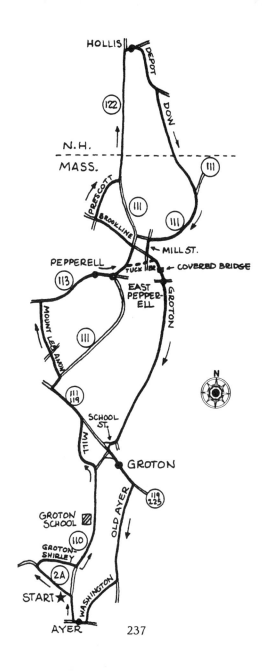

HOLLIS

DEPOT

DOW

122

N.H.

MASS.

111

PRESCOTT

111

BROOKLINE

111

MILL ST.

PEPPERELL

TUCKER BR.

COVERED BRIDGE

113

EAST
PEPPER-
ELL

GROTON

111

MOUNT LEA ANON

111
119

SCHOOL
ST.

MILL

N

GROTON

119
225

GROTON
SCHOOL

OLD AYER

110

GROTON-
SHIRLEY

2A

START ★

WASHINGTON

AYER

237

tween Boston, Fitchburg, and Albany declined, the town declined with it. Ayer is now primarily an extension of Fort Devens, the large military base just outside of town. Although shabby, the downtown area is still fascinating, with an ornate Victorian town hall and an old, arcaded commercial block.

The long ride heads north out of Pepperell along a broad, open ridge to Hollis, New Hampshire, just across the Massachusetts border. Hollis is a delightful old town with a classic New England church and green, and a handsome white, pillared library. From Hollis you'll head back toward Pepperell through broad farms and orchards and pick up the route of the short ride just in time to go over the covered bridge.

Directions for the ride: 30 miles

1. Turn left (north) out of the parking lot onto Route 2A and go 8/10 mile to Groton-Shirley Road on right, just before bridge and the Shirley town line. You'll pass the Fort Devens airport on your left.

2. Turn right on Groton-Shirley Road and go 9/10 mile to end (Route 111). You'll pass a state-run pheasant farm on your left. Visitors are welcome from 10 a.m. to 4 p.m.

3. Turn left on Route 111 and go 2 miles to where Route 225 turns left and Route 111 goes straight. You'll pass the Groton School on your left after 1 mile. It's worth making a loop around the grounds to catch the flavor of this gracious and distinguished school.

4. Continue straight 2/10 mile to fork where Routes 111 and 225 bear right and a smaller road bears left.

5. Bear left onto smaller road (Mill Street) and go 1.1 miles to end, where you'll merge into Routes 111 and 119.

6. Bear left on Routes 111 and 119. Go 8/10 mile to where Route 111 (River Road) turns right at blinking light.

7. Turn right on Route 111 and go 3/10 mile to Mount Lebanon Street on left. It's your first left.

8. Turn left on Mount Lebanon Street. After 6/10 mile you'll come to a crossroads and stop sign. Continue straight 1.3 miles to end (Townsend Street, Route 113). You'll climb a long hill and have a fine view from the top.

9. Turn right on Route 113 and go 1.4 miles on Route 111, at rotary. You'll go through the center of Pepperell.

10. Bear left on Route 111 and go 2/10 mile to fork where Tucker Street, a smaller road, bears right. Here the short ride bears right and the long ride bears left.

11. Bear left, staying on Route 111, and go 4/10 mile to crossroads (Groton Street on right, Brookline Street on left).

12. Turn left on Brookline Street and go 1.2 miles to crossroads (Prescott Street).

13. Turn right on Prescott Street and go 1.1 miles to end (Route 122).

14. Turn left on Route 122 and go 3 miles to a road that bears right immediately before the Hollis police station, a small white wooden building.

15. Bear right on this road and then immediately bear right again. This is the center of Hollis, New Hampshire. Go 8/10 mile to Dow Road, which bears right.

16. Bear right on Dow Road and go 2.6 miles to end (merge into Route 111).

17. Bear right on Route 111 and go 1.8 miles to crossroads and blinking light (Mill Street).

18. Turn left on Mill Street and go 2/10 mile to crossroads and stop sign (Groton Street).

19. Turn left on Groton Street. Just ahead you'll cross the covered bridge over the Nashua River. Continue 2/10 mile to stop sign where Route 113 turns right. This is East Pepperell. Here the ride goes straight, but there are stores and restaurants if you turn right.

20. Continue straight at stop sign. After 3.4 miles you'll merge to your right at yield sign. Bear right and go 1/2 mile to fork where School Street bears right.

21. Bear right on School Street and go 1/10 mile to another fork.

22. Bear left at fork and go 1/10 mile to crossroads and blinking light (Route 119).

23. Turn left on Route 119 and go 9/10 mile to Old Ayer Road, which bears right. You'll go through the center of Groton.

24. Bear right on Old Ayer Road and go 2.4 miles to fork (Washington Street bears right).

25. Bear right on Washington Street and go 1.1 miles to end (Main Street) in the center of Ayer.

26. Turn right on Main Street and go 1/10 mile to Routes 2A and 111 (Park Street) on right.

27. Turn right on Routes 2A and 111. Go 6/10 mile to fork where Route 2A bears left and Route 111 goes straight.

28. Bear left on Route 2A. The supermarket is just ahead on left.

Directions for the ride: 20 miles

1. Follow directions for the long ride through number 10.

2. Bear right on Tucker Street and go 4/10 mile to crossroads and stop sign (Mill Street). Continue straight 100 yards to end (merge right).

3. Bear right at end. Just ahead you'll cross the covered bridge over the Nashua River. Continue 2/10 mile to stop sign where Route 113 turns right. This is East Pepperell. Here the ride goes straight, but if you turn right there's a grocery store and snack bar.

4. Follow directions for the long ride from number 20 to the end.

40. Shirley–Townsend–Lunenburg

Number of miles: 18 (26 with Townsend extension)
Terrain: Rolling, with one long hill.
Food: Groceries and restaurants in the towns.
Start: Center of Shirley. From Route 2, take the Shirley exit and
go 2 miles to fork where Main Street bears right and Center
Road bears left, just after police station on left. Bear right,
and the center of town is just ahead. Main Street becomes
Front Street.

Just east of Fitchburg is a prime area for biking. It has rolling hills
and open ridges with fine views, crisscrossed by a network of
lightly traveled secondary roads and winding rural lanes. The unspoiled classic New England towns of Shirley Center, Townsend,
and Lunenburg are an attractive change of pace from the otherwise
rural landscape.

The ride starts from Shirley, a small, somewhat tired-looking
town that seems as though it's seen happier days. There's not much
keeping the town going except the nearby Fort Devens military
reservation. A couple of miles north is the town's better half, Shirley
Center, one of the finest traditional villages in central Massachusetts. The small green is framed by an elegant old white church,
pillared town hall, old cemetery, and gracious old wooden homes.

From Shirley Center you'll go through woods and farmland,
with a run along Hickory Hills Lake, to the stately hilltop town of
Lunenburg, another New England beauty with the traditional white
church and old wooden town hall facing each other across the
road, and a handsome, pillared library. The return leg to Shirley
leads through spectacular, rolling ridge country, with a run past
unspoiled Massapoag Pond.

The long ride heads farther north to Townsend, yet another
classic New England town. The handsome town green, highlighted
by a bandstand in the center, is framed by the Victorian town hall
and a magnificent church with a tall ornate steeple, dated 1770. On
the edge of town is an old cemetery; most of the gravestones are
nearly two hundred years old.

Directions for the ride: 26 miles

1. Head east on Front Street, paralleling the railroad tracks on your left, and go 2/10 mile to crossroads (Phoenix Street on right), after house number 43.

2. Turn left at crossroads. Cross the tracks and go straight ahead onto Benjamin Road. Go 1.3 miles to end (Hazen Road).

3. Turn right on Hazen Road and go 2/10 mile to Brown Road on left.

4. Turn left on Brown Road. After 1/2 mile you'll come to the graceful village of Shirley Center. Continue straight 9/10 mile to end (Route 2A).

5. Turn left on Route 2A and go 1/10 mile to your first right, Townsend Road.

6. Turn right on Townsend Road and go 9/10 mile to crossroads and stop sign (Route 225). Just before the intersection is a fork; bear left on the main road here.

7. Cross Route 225 and go 1.2 miles to Spaulding Road, a smaller road that bears left uphill.

8. Bear left on Spauling Road and go 9/10 mile to fork where Pierce Road bears slightly left and Turner Road bears right. • *CAUTION:* Watch for bumps and potholes.

9. Bear left on Pierce Road and go 7/10 mile to crossroads (Warren Road). Here the short ride turns left and the long ride turns right.

10. Turn right on Warren Road and go 2.1 miles to Route 119, at stop sign. Immediately before Route 119 notice the fine dam on your left.

11. Cross Route 119 and go 6/10 mile to end (merge left onto Wallace Hill Road)

12. Bear left on Wallace Hill Road and go 9/10 mile to Highland Street on left. This is a long, steady hill.

13. Turn left on Highland Street and go 1 mile to fork where the main road bears slightly left. Bear left and go 4/10 mile to end (merge head-on into Route 13).

14. Go straight on Route 13 for 2/10 mile to traffic light (Route 119), in the center of Townsend.

15. Cross Route 119 and go 1.3 miles to Emery Road on left.

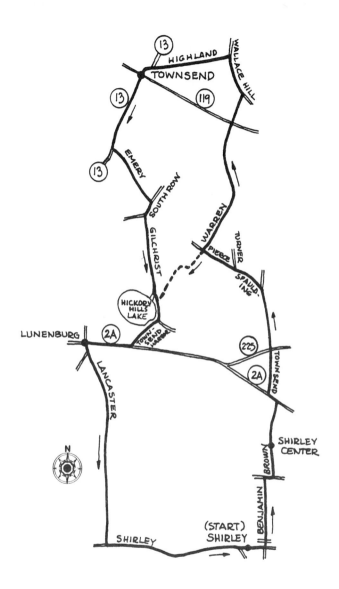

13
HIGHLAND
WALLACE HILL
TOWNSEND
13
119
13
EMERY
SOUTH ROW
GILCHRIST
WARREN
TURNER
PIERCE
SPAULDING
HICKORY HILLS LAKE
LUNENBURG
2A
TOWNSEND HARBOR
225
2A
TOWNSEND
LANCASTER
SHIRLEY CENTER
BENJAMIN
BROWN
N
SHIRLEY
(START) SHIRLEY

16. Turn left on Emery Road and go 1.3 miles to end (South Row Road).

17. Turn right on South Row Road and go 3/10 mile to fork (Gilchrist Road bears left).

18. Bear left on Gilchrist Road. After 1.2 miles the main road bears left and Peninsula Drive goes straight. Bear left on main road for 3/10 mile to stop sign. Continue straight 4/10 miles to fork, going along the shore of Hickory Hills Lake. At the fork, Mulpus Road bears left and Townsend Harbor Road bears right.

19. Bear right on Townsend Harbor Road and go 8/10 mile to end (merge into Route 2A, Massachusetts Avenue). You'll pass an attractive dam on your right.

20. Bear right on Route 2A and stay on it 9/10 mile to crossroads in the center of Lunenburg, at top of hill (Main Street on right, Lancaster Avenue on left).

21. Turn left at top of hill. You'll immediately come to a fork.

22. Go straight at fork on Lancaster Avenue (don't bear right) and go 4.2 miles to end (Shirley Road). This is a glorious run through rolling ridge country. You'll pass Massapoag Pond and a little dam on your right.

23. Turn left at end and stay on main road for 2.7 miles to fork at an old wooden mill on your left. Shortly before the mill there's a delightful little millpond on your right.

24. Bear left at fork and go 1/10 mile to another fork where Main Street bears right and Center Road bears left.

25. Bear right on Main Street. The center of town is just ahead.

Directions for the ride: 18 miles

1. Follow directions for the long ride through number 9.

2. Turn left on Warren Road and go 1.8 miles to fork where Mulpus Road bears left and Townsend Harbor Road bears right. At the fork, Hickory Hills Lake is on your right.

3. Follow directions for the long ride from number 19 to the end.

41. West Boylston–Sterling–Lancaster

Number of miles: 14 (28 with Lancaster extension)
Terrain: Rolling, with several hills, one a real monster.
Food: Grocery stores and snack bars in the towns.
Start: Picnic area at the fork of Route 12 and 140 in West
Boylston, just north of the bridge over the Wachusett
Reservoir. Park at side of road.

Just north of the Wachusett Reservoir, midway between Worcester
and Fitchburg, superb biking abounds on narrow roads winding
through woods and along broad, open hilltops with impressive
views. The area is very rural except for the two classic New England towns of Sterling and Lancaster.

You start from the western edge of the Wachusett Reservoir,
second largest lake in the state, and head north along its slender
western arm to the fine valley town of Sterling, best known as the
locale of "Mary Had a Little Lamb." The fabled schoolhouse was
reconstructed by Henry Ford fifteen miles away, next to the Wayside
Inn in Sudbury instead of in its original location. A small white
statue of a lamb on the green commemorates the nursery rhyme.
From Sterling you'll return to the start, traversing a broad, open
hillside through farms and orchards with fine views of the surrounding countryside.

The long ride heads farther north along country lanes and over
another open hilltop to the elegant town of Lancaster, oldest in
Worcester County. The town is on the Nashua River, surrounded by
broad expanses of farmland. The town green is uniquely impressive, flanked by the graceful brick First Unitarian Church, an ornate,
domed Victorian library dated 1867, and two fine old schools. The
church, designed by Charles Bulfinch, was built in 1816. Just past
the green you'll pass the handsome campus of Atlantic Union College, run by the Seventh-Day Adventists. Shortly beyond Lancaster
you'll join the short ride, traversing the hillside near the end.

Directions for the ride: 28 miles

1. Head north on Route 140, paralleling the western arm of the reservoir on your left. As soon as you start, notice the Old Stone Church, built in 1890, on your left. It was recently restored after years of neglect. Go 1.3 miles to where Route 140 curves sharply right, at yield sign. Continue 1/10 mile to Waushacum Street, which bears right (a sign may say to Sterling).

2. Bear right on Waushacum Street and go 1.4 miles to crossroads and stop sign.

3. Turn right at crossroads over a small bridge and go 1.1 miles to fork (Jewett Road, a smaller road, bears left). On your left you'll get a view of Mount Wachusett, 2,000 feet high. It's the tallest mountain in the state east of the Connecticut River.

4. Bear left on Jewett Road and go 9/10 mile to end (Route 62).

5. Turn right on Route 62 and go 4/10 mile to end (merge into Route 12).

6. Bear left on Route 12 • *CAUTION:* Busy intersection. Go 3/10 mile, through the center of Sterling, to fork where Route 12 bears left and Route 62 goes straight. Notice the fine, brick Victorian library, built in 1885, on your left.

7. Go straight onto Route 62 and go 1/10 mile to Redstone Hill Road, which bears right uphill.

8. Bear right on Redstone Hill Road and go 2.2 miles to end (Route 62). There's a tough climb to the top of the ridge, but you'll be rewarded with a long, lazy downhill through farms and orchards with views of distant hills.

9. Turn right on Route 62 and go 3/10 mile to crossroads (Chace Hill Road). Here the short ride turns right and the long ride turns left.

10. Turn left on Chace Hill Road and go 6/10 mile to fork at a small green.

11. Bear left at fork and then immediately bear right on George Hill Road. Go 1 mile to fork at bottom of hill, where one road bears right and Hill Top Road turns left. The large, wrought-iron gate on the far side of the intersection leads into the Maharishi Ayurveda Health Center.

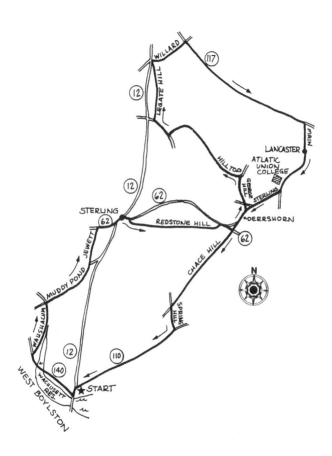

WILLARD
117
12
LEGATE HILL
MAIN
LANCASTER
ATLANTIC
UNION
COLLEGE
HILLTOP
12
GEORGE HILL
STERLING
62
STERLING
62
REDSTONE HILL
DEERSHORN
62
JEWETT
CHACE HILL
N
MUDDY POND
SPRING HILL
WAUSHACUM
12
110
WEST BOYLSTON
140
WACHUSETT RES.
★ START

247

12. Turn left on Hill Top Road. After 1.9 miles you'll go underneath Route 190. Continue 1/2 mile to end, opposite gravel pit.

13. Turn right at end (don't turn sharply right into gravel pit) and go 1/2 mile to Legate Hill Road on right, just before Route 12.

14. Turn right on Legate Hill Road and go 1.5 miles to end (merge into Route 12 at bottom of hill). You'll climb onto a ridge with fine views and then descend steeply. • *CAUTION:* The descent has bumpy spots; take it easy.

15. Bear right on Route 12 and then immediately turn right at blinking light on Willard Street. Go 1 mile to crossroads and stop sign (Route 117).

16. Turn right on Route 117 and go 3.7 miles to Main Street, which bears right (sign may say to Lancaster, 1 mile). It comes up 1/2 mile after you cross the Nashua River, and there's a school on the corner.

17. Bear right on Main Street. After 9/10 mile you'll pass the Lancaster town green on your left. Continue 1.2 miles to fork shortly beyond Atlantic Union College (Sterling Road bears right).

18. Bear right on Sterling Road and go 8/10 mile to another fork (Deershorn Road bears slightly left).

19. Bear left on Deershorn Road. After 4/10 mile, South Meadow Road bears left, but continue straight 1/10 mile to fork (Chace Hill Road bears left).

20. Bear left on Chace Hill Road and go 1/10 mile to crossroads (Route 62).

21. Cross Route 62 and go 2.1 miles to fork where the main road bears left. This is a delightful run through orchards and open fields.

22. Bear left at fork and go 7/10 mile to end (Route 110). Here the ride turns right, but if you turn left for 2/10 mile you'll get a sweeping view of the Wachusett Reservoir.

23. Turn right on Route 110 and go 2.7 miles to traffic light (Route 12).

24. Bear left on Route 12. The picnic area is immediately ahead.

Wachusett Reservoir, West Boylston.

Directions for the ride: 14 miles

1. Follow directions for the long ride through number 9.

2. Turn right on Chace Hill Road and go 2.1 miles to fork where the main road bears left. This is a beautiful run through orchards and broad fields.

3. Follow directions for the long ride from number 22 to the end.

42. Wachusett Reservoir Ride: West Boylston–Clinton–Boylston

Number of miles: 18
Terrain: Hilly, with two long, steady hills and one short, steep one.
Food: Groceries and restaurants in Clinton.
Start: Picnic area at the fork of Routes 12 and 140 in West Boylston, just north of the bridge over the Wachusett Reservoir. Park at side of road.

The area just northeast of Worcester is dominated by the Wachusett Reservoir, second largest lake in Massachusetts. It is about six miles long and averages a mile across. The lake was created in 1906 to augment the water supply for the Boston area by constructing a massive stone dam 1,000 feet long and 125 feet high.

You'll start the ride from West Boylston, a pleasant small town at the reservoir's western edge. Just outside of town the road curves downhill across a graceful stone bridge over the Thomas Basin, the small western arm of the reservoir. Next to the bridge is a graceful stone lakefront church, now restored after lying in ruins for many years. From here you'll parallel the western shore to Clinton. The road heads inland for a few miles, then dips down to the water's edge.

Clinton is a compact well-planned mill town, more attractive than most. It shone briefly in the national spotlight when President Carter had one of his "town meetings" here. For years Clinton was one of America's largest producers of carpets and gingham; now the formidable brick Victorian mills house diversified industries. You'll pass the graceful, bell-towered Bigelow Carpet mill, built in 1864, sloping up a hill. In the downtown area, long, well-maintained, brick nineteenth-century buildings line both sides of the main street. A block away is Central Park, an attractive square block of greenery framed by the handsome town hall and the courthouse, which was originally the main office of the Bigelow Carpet Company. Just beyond the center of town you'll come to the dam. Nestled beneath it is the old pumping station and the finely landscaped Lancaster Millpond, complete with fountains, which forms the beginning of the Nashua River. The river drains a large swath of north-central Massachusetts and eventually flows into the Merrimack in Nashua, New Hampshire.

There's a long climb to the top of the dam, but you can rest with a spectacular stroll along it, with the broad expanse of the lake on your left and a bird's-eye view of Clinton on your right. Beyond the dam you'll head inland from the reservoir for a short distance, passing through a landscape of orchards and rolling hills. A couple of miles ahead is Boylston, an unspoiled gem of a town, with a triangular green framed by a graceful white church, a small stone town hall, and an ornate fieldstone library. From here it's a relaxing few miles back to West Boylston with a long downhill run and a stretch along the water's edge.

Directions for the ride

1. Head north on Route 12 (away from the bridge) and go 1/10 mile to Route 110, which bears right.

2. Bear right on Route 110 and go 5.6 miles to Route 62 on right, at blinking light at bottom of hill. At the intersection, the Bigelow Carpet mill is on your left.

3. Turn right on Route 62 and go 2.2 miles to where Route 62 turns left and Route 70 continues straight. There's a long, steady climb to the top of the dam, but the magnificent view will reward your efforts. The small millpond and old pumping station at the base of the dam are worth a look.

4. Go straight on Route 70 for 3/10 mile to Mile Hill Road, which bears left uphill.

5. Bear left on Mile Hill Road for 1/2 mile to five-way intersection, at stop sign.

6. Bear right on Linden Street (don't turn sharply right on Duffy Road), and go 3.2 miles to end (Route 70).

7. Turn left on Route 70. After 3/10 mile you'll pass the lovely Boylston town green on your left. Notice the handsome library on your right opposite the green. Continue on Route 70 for 1.3 miles to Route 140, at traffic light.

8. Turn right on Route 140 and go 2.9 miles to traffic light where you merge into Route 12, in West Boylston.

9. Bear right at light (still Route 140) and go 9/10 mile to picnic area on far side of bridge. This is a fast downhill run.

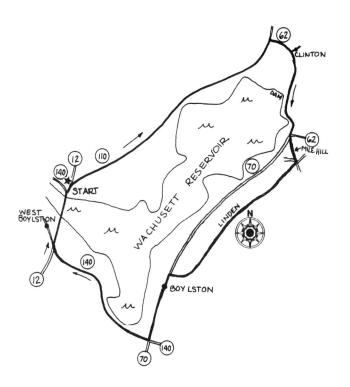

62
CLINTON
DAM
62
MILE HILL
WACHUSETT RESERVOIR
70
12
110
140
START
WEST
BOYLSTON
LINDEN
N
12
140
140
BOYLSTON
70
140

43. Apple Country Adventure: Northboro–Berlin–Bolton

Number of miles: 15 (23 with Bolton extension)
Terrain: Rolling, with a couple of good hills.
Food: Country store in Berlin. Grocery and snack bar in Bolton.
Start: Small shopping center at the junction of Routes 20 and 135 in the center of Northboro. It's on the north side of Route 20, at the corner of Church Street. From Route 290, take the Church Street exit if you're coming from the west, and the Solomon Pond Road exit if you're coming from the east. From either direction, turn right at the end of the exit ramp and go 2 miles into Northboro.

The rolling, refreshingly rural apple-orchard country along the western edge of Route 495 provides delightful bicycling on an elaborate network of winding country roads with no traffic. This is a region of classic New England scenery, with old barns, rambling wooden farmhouses, and stone walls crisscrossing the rolling pastureland. Berlin and Bolton are unspoiled towns with elegant village centers. The best time to take this ride is in mid-May, when the apple blossoms cover the orchards with a pink canopy, or in September and early October, when the foliage is peaking and you can stuff your saddlebag full of apples for pennies.

The ride starts in Northboro, an attractive town with a graceful old church and a couple of Victorian mills on the Assabet River, a small stream here. You'll head to Berlin (accented on the first syllable) on back roads winding through rolling hills crowned with orchards and open farmland. Berlin is a picture-postcard New England town with an exceptionally graceful church and green, a country store, and an old cemetery filled with weathered slate gravestones dating back to 1800. From Berlin you'll head north through the same type of countryside to Bolton, another gracious little town with a handsome stone library and a cluster of antique shops. The return leg to Northboro brings you along ridgetops with inspiring views and then down to the valley of the Assabet River through prosperous, well-landscaped farmland with grazing horses

Wachusett Aqueduct, Northboro.

and cows. Just before the end you'll go underneath the graceful stone arches of the Wachusett Aqueduct, which carries water from the Wachusett Reservoir to metropolitan Boston.

The short ride bypasses Bolton by taking a more direct route from Berlin back to Northboro.

Directions for the ride: 23 miles

1. Turn right (west) out of parking lot onto Route 20 and immediately bear right on Church Street. Go 1/10 mile to fork (Whitney Street bears right).

2. Bear left at fork, passing church on right. Immediately after the church turn right on Howard Street and go 9/10 mile to fork (Green Street bears left).

3. Bear left at fork and go 1/2 mile to crossroads just beyond the Route 290 overpass.

4. Go straight at crossroads (still Green Street) 2.5 miles to Mile Hill Road on right, at top of second hill. The first hill is a long, tough one; the second hill is short.

5. Turn right on Mile Hill Road and go 1.4 miles to crossroads and stop sign (Linden Street). Here the ride turns right, but if you go straight for 1/2 mile to the end you'll have a good view of the Wachusett Reservoir. It's a steep descent and then a tough climb back up to Linden Street.

6. Turn right on Linden Street and go 2.9 miles to end (merge right at stop sign). This is Berlin.

7. Bear right at stop sign and then immediately bear left on Woodward Avenue (sign may say to Bolton, 4 miles). Go 1/10 mile to stop sign, passing the church on your right. At the stop sign, the short ride bears slightly right and the long ride bears left.

8. Bear left at stop sign, passing the small brick library on right. After 3.7 miles, merge to your right at yield sign. Bear right for 3/10 mile to end (Route 117). Several roads bear off the main road, but go straight on the main road at all intersections.

9. Turn left on Route 117 and go 7/10 mile to Wilder Road, which bears left uphill. As soon as you get on Route 117, notice the fine stone library on your left.

10. Bear left on Wilder Road (sign may say Industrial School for Girls) and go 9/10 mile to fork where Ballville Road bears left.

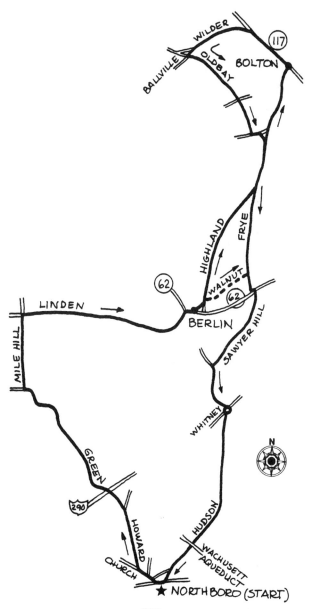

WILDER

117

BALLVILLE

OLDBAY

BOLTON

HIGHLAND

FRYE

62

WALNUT

62

LINDEN

BERLIN

SAWYER HILL

MILE HILL

WHITNEY

N

GREEN

290

HUDSON

HOWARD

CHURCH

WACHUSETT
AQUEDUCT

★ NORTHBORO (START)

11. Bear left on Ballville Road and immediately turn sharp left on Oldbay Road. Go 9/10 mile up a tough hill to crossroads and stop sign.

12. Go straight at crossroads 8/10 mile to end. • *CAUTION:* The end comes up suddenly at bottom of steep hill.

13. Turn left at end and go 1/10 mile to fork.

14. Bear right at fork, and just ahead bear right at end. Go 7/10 mile to fork (Frye Road bears left).

15. Bear left on Frye Road and go 1.5 miles to end (Route 62).

16. At end jog left and immediately right onto Sawyer Hill Road, up a steep hill. Go 1.7 miles to end (cemetery on left). At the top of the hill you'll be rewarded with a panoramic view and a relaxing downhill run.

17. Turn left at end. After 4/10 mile the main road curves sharply left. Stay on the main road 1/4 mile to rotary.

18. Bear slightly right at rotary, following sign to Northboro (don't turn 90 degrees right on Whitney Street). After 2 miles you'll go under the Wachusett Aqueduct. Just before the aqueduct is a narrow sluiceway on your left, followed by a little dam.

19. From the viaduct, continue 7/10 mile to fork where Pierce Street bears right.

20. Bear left at fork and go 2/10 mile to end (Route 20). The shopping center is 100 yards to your right.

Directions for the ride: 15 miles

1. Follow directions for the long ride through number 7.

2. Bear slightly right at stop sign onto Walnut Street, passing the library on your left. Go 1 mile to end.

3. Turn right at end and go 2/10 mile to end (Route 62).

4. Follow directions for the long ride from number 16 to the end.

44. Triboro Tour: Westboro–Shrewsbury–
Northboro–Southboro

Number of miles: 21 (29 with Shrewsbury extension)
Terrain: Rolling. Several moderate hills, but nothing bad.
Food: Groceries and snack bars in the towns.
Start: Friendly Ice Cream, junction of Routes 9 and 30 in Westboro.

On this ride you'll explore the rolling, well-groomed farm country and graceful small towns east of Worcester. The region is just far enough from both the Boston and Worcester metropolitan areas to be rural rather than suburban. Smooth, well-maintained back roads weave among the hillsides and rolling pastures, providing relaxed and scenic biking.

You start from Westboro, an attractive town with a compact, Victorian brick business block, several fine churches, and gracious Colonial-style homes on the outskirts of town. From Westboro it's a smooth run to Northboro, with a spin along the Assabet Reservoir. The reservoir is one of the state's newest, formed in 1969 by damming the Assabet River. Northboro is another attractive community with a graceful white church and a handsome stone Victorian library built in 1894. The stretch from Northboro to Southboro is a delight, heading across prosperous, open farmland with wooded hills rising in the background. You'll cross the Wachusett Aqueduct, which carries water from the Wachusett Reservoir to the Boston metropolitan area, and pass Saint Mark's School, one of the numerous prestigious preparatory schools scattered across the state. Its main building is an elegant, rambling hall with English Tudor architecture, surrounded by extensive lawns.

Saint Mark's is just outside the center of Southboro, the most graceful New England classic of the three "boro" towns. The sloping, half-moon-shaped green is a beauty, framed by two fine old churches on a small rise. The return to Westboro heads along Route 30, a winner for biking among numbered routes, lightly traveled and passing through sweeping expanses of open farmland. At the end of the ride you'll detour past unspoiled Chauncy Lake. The grounds of Westboro State Hospital, dominated by a massive, ornate Victorian building, crown a hilltop overlooking the lake in a hauntingly beautiful setting that seems more like an old, distinguished college campus than a mental institution.

The long ride heads farther west to Shrewsbury through magnificent rolling countryside with some sharp ups and downs. You'll pass the new Veterinary School of Tufts University, on the grounds of the former Grafton State Hospital, another mental institution. Massachusetts has dozens of state institutions for persons with mental and physical disabilities, most of them on large, gracious college-like campuses in attractive rural surroundings. Adjacent to the Veterinary School, just off the route, is the Willard House and Clockshop, an eighteenth-century saltbox house with an impressive collection of antique clocks.

Shrewsbury is another handsome old town on a hilltop, with a classic white church and a fine brick library. The community is a well-to-do suburb of both Worcester and Boston, with the look and feel of a smaller, rural town. Most people know Shrewsbury only from the ugly commercial strip along Route 9; the rest of the town is pleasant. From Shrewsbury you'll head through wooded hills and past an orchard to Northboro, where you'll pick up the route of the shorter ride.

Directions for the ride: 29 miles

1. Turn right out of parking lot onto Route 30, heading west, and go 1.4 miles to the center of Westboro. Continue straight on Route 30 for 9/10 mile to Mill Road on right. Here the short ride turns right and the long ride goes straight.

2. Continue straight on Route 30 for 3.3 miles to Pine Street on right, shortly after the Tufts Veterinary School. (Pine Street crosses a small railroad bridge at the beginning; you can see it from Route 30.) If you'd like to visit the clock museum, turn left on Willard Road, which leads into the grounds of the school, and go 6/10 mile to museum on right.

3. Turn right on Pine Street and go 2 miles to crossroads and stop sign (Route 20).

4. Cross Route 20 onto South Street. After 8/10 mile you'll come to Route 9 at a traffic light. Continue straight 1.3 miles to another light.

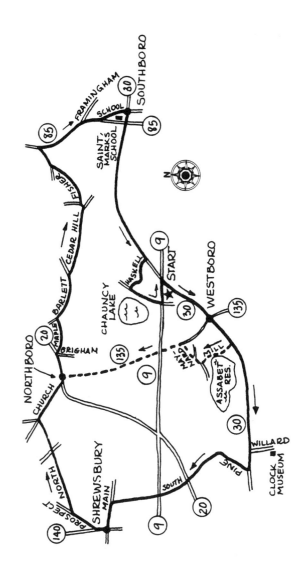

5. Turn left at light and go 1/2 mile to another light (Route 140) in the center of Shrewsbury. Notice the handsome brick library on your right, just before the intersection.

6. Turn right on Route 140 and go 1/10 mile to fork where Route 140 bears left and Prospect Street bears right.

7. Bear right on Prospect Street and go 8/10 mile to North Street, which bears right.

8. Bear right on North Street and go 1.8 miles to crossroads and stop sign.

9. Go straight at crossroads 7/10 mile to another crossroads and stop sign.

10. Turn right at stop sign and go 1.2 miles to end (merge into Route 20 in the center of Northboro). Shortly before the end there's a graceful church on your left.

11. Bear left on Route 20 and go 6/10 mile to Maple Street on right. You'll pass the Victorian library on your right and then a little dam at the bottom of the hill, also on the right. Just before Maple Street the White Cliffs Restaurant, an elegant, white Victorian mansion, is on the left.

12. Turn right on Maple Street (don't turn sharply right on Brigham Street). After 3/10 mile Bridge Street turns right, but curve left on the main road for 4/10 mile to end, opposite the entrance to the high school.

13. Turn right at end and go 1.2 miles to Cedar Hill Street, which bears right at bottom of hill.

14. Bear right on Cedar Hill Street and go 1.9 miles to Fisher Road on left, shortly after you go underneath Route 495.

15. Turn left on Fisher Road. Just ahead is a fork. Bear right at fork (still Fisher Road). After 1.3 miles you'll merge to the right at stop sign. Bear right and go 4/10 mile to end (Route 85), at busy intersection.

16. Turn right on Route 85 and go 9/10 mile to fork, where Route 85 bears right.

17. Bear right, staying on Route 85, and go 4/10 mile to School Street, which bears left. There's a garage at the intersection on left.

18. Bear left on School Street and go 7/10 mile to crossroads and stop sign (Route 30, Main Street). You'll pass Saint Mark's

School on right. The ride turns right on Route 30, but if you turn left for 100 yards there's a grocery and pizza place. This is Southboro.

19. Turn right on Route 30 and go 2/10 mile to traffic light (Route 85).

20. Go straight on Route 30 for 3.6 miles to Haskell Street on right, just as you start to go downhill. It's just after the Windsor Ridge apartments on left.

21. Turn right on Haskell Street and go 9/10 mile to end.

22. Turn left at end and go 8/10 mile to traffic light (Route 9). Just after you turn left you'll pass the entrance to Westboro State Hospital. Just beyond is Chauncy Lake.

23. Turn left on Route 9. • *CAUTION:* Bad intersection. Go 1/2 mile to Friendly on right.

Directions for the ride: 21 miles

1. Follow direction number 1 for the long ride.

2. Turn right on Mill Road and go 9/10 mile to end. You'll pass the Assabet Reservoir.

3. Turn right at end on Fisher Street. Just ahead is a fork where Maynard Street bears left.

4. Bear left on Maynard Street and go 6/10 mile to end (Route 135).

5. Turn left on Route 135 and go 3.3 miles to end (Route 20) in the center of Northboro.

6. Turn right on Route 20 and go 6/10 mile to Maple Street on right. Notice the Victorian library and then the little dam at bottom of hill, both on your right. Just before Maple Street on the left is a restaurant in an elegant Victorian mansion.

7. Follow directions for the long ride from number 12 to the end.

45. Around Lake Quinsigamond: Worcester–Shrewsbury

Number of miles: 11 (17 with Shrewsbury loop)
Terrain: Flat, with one short, steep hill. The longer ride has a long, steady hill coming into Shrewsbury.
Food: Numerous stores and restaurants along the way.
Start: White City shopping center on Route 9 at the corner of South Quinsigamond Avenue, Shrewsbury, just east of the bridge across Lake Quinsigamond and the Worcester-Shrewsbury line.

This ride goes around Lake Quinsigamond, a five-mile-long, slender lake, which forms the southeastern border of Worcester. The lake lies in a north-south direction along the Worcester-Shrewsbury town line. Although not rural, this ride is pleasant and relaxing, with glimpses of the lake around every bend. At the southern end of the lake, you'll bike around a small peninsula jutting into the water, and just ahead you'll pass Quinsigamond State Park, an attractively landscaped lakeside park with a beach, picnic area, and boat ramp.

The longer ride makes a small loop to the northeast into Shrewsbury, a well-to-do hilltop town with a classic New England center. Adjoining the small green is a magnificent white church predating 1800 with an equally old burying ground, and the handsome beige-brick library. Although adjacent to Worcester and within commuting range of Boston, Shrewsbury retains the look and feel of a small town, with no dreary housing tracts. Most people are familiar only with the town's worst face, the ugly Route 9 commercial strip, but the remainder of Shrewsbury is delightful.

Directions for the ride: 17 miles

1. Turn right out of the parking lot onto South Quinsigamond Avenue, heading south, and go 2.7 miles to end, at traffic light (Route 20). Lake Quinsigamond is on your right.

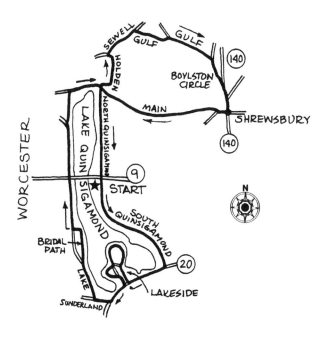

SEWELL

GULF

GULF

140

HOLDEN

BOYLSTON
CIRCLE

MAIN

SHREWSBURY

140

WORCESTER

LAKE QUIN SIGAMOND

NORTH QUINSIGAMOND

9

START

N

SOUTH
QUINSIGAMOND

BRIDAL
PATH

LAKE

20

SUNDERLAND

LAKESIDE

2. Turn right on Route 20 and go 6/10 mile to Lakeside Drive on right, just before a classic railroad-car diner. You'll now go around a small peninsula jutting into the lake north of Route 20.

3. Turn right on Lakeside Drive and go 8/10 mile to Bay View Drive, which bears right shortly after playground on left. (Don't bear right directly opposite the playground.)

4. Bear right on Bay View Drive and go 4/10 mile to end (merge to your right into Edgemere Boulevard).

5. Bear right on Edgemere Boulevard and go less than 2/10 mile to end (Route 20).

6. Turn right on Route 20 and go 3/10 mile to Sunderland Road, which bears right at a traffic light (sign may say Quinsigamond State Park).

7. Bear right at traffic light and go 2/10 mile to Lake Avenue on right.

8. Turn right on Lake Avenue and go 6/10 mile to Bridle Path, a smaller road that bears right along the shore of the lake.

9. Bear right on Bridle Path. After 4/10 mile the road turns 90 degrees left at a gate. Continue 100 yards to end. If in the future the gate is opened or removed, continue straight along the lakeshore until you end up back on Lake Avenue. Beyond the gate is Quinsigamond State Park.

10. Turn right at end, back on Lake Avenue, and go 1.3 miles to traffic light (Route 9). There's a small fee to visit the park.

11. Cross Route 9 and go 1 mile to fork where North Lake Avenue bears right uphill. You'll pass another section of the park.

12. Bear right at fork and go 7/10 mile to end, at top of steep hill.

13. Turn right at end and go 3/10 mile to crossroads just before Route 290 interchange (Holden Street on left, North Quinsigamond Avenue on right). Here the short ride turns right and the long ride turns left.

14. Turn left at crossroads and go 2/10 mile to end (main road turns left).

15. Turn left (still Holden Street) and go 4/10 mile to Sewell Street on right, at gravel pit. Holden Street curves left at the intersection.

16. Turn right on Sewell Street and go 9/10 mile to Gulf Street, which bears right at top of hill. It's shortly after Greenbrier Drive on right.

17. Bear right on Gulf Street and go 4/10 mile to end, where the main road bears right and Bannister Street turns left.

18. Bear right (still Gulf Street) and go 1.1 miles to end (merge right).

19. Bear right at end and go 3/10 mile to end (merge onto Route 140).

20. Bear right on Route 140 and go 3/10 mile to traffic light in the center of Shrewsbury (Main Street).

21. Turn right on Main Street. Just ahead is another light. Continue straight (don't bear left on Maple Street) and go 2.2 miles to crossroads just after the Route 290 interchange (Holden Street on right, North Quinsigamond Avenue on left). This is a relaxing descent.

22. Turn left on North Quinsigamond Avenue and go 1.7 miles to traffic light (Route 9). The shopping center is on your right at the far side of the intersection. • *CAUTION* turning left, and also crossing Route 9.

Directions for the ride: 11 miles

1. Follow directions for the long ride through number 13.

2. Turn right at crossroads on North Quinsigamond Avenue and go 1.7 miles to traffic light (Route 9). The shopping center is on your right at the far side of the intersection.

46. Upper Blackstone Valley Tour: Uxbridge–Whitinsville–Northbridge–Grafton

Number of miles: 17 (29 with Grafton extension)
Terrain: Rolling, with one tough hill. The long ride has an
 additional challenging climb.
Food: Groceries and snack bars in the towns. Pizza place at end.
Start: Rico's Supermarket, Route 122, Uxbridge, 6/10 mile north
 of Route 16.

Southeast of Worcester, between the city and the Rhode Island border, lies a fascinating and scenic area for bicycling dotted with
ridges, wooded hills, and unspoiled little mill towns right out of the
Industrial Revolution. Bisecting the region is the Blackstone River,
among the first New England rivers to become industrialized.
Traces of the old Blackstone Canal, which opened the valley to
commerce during the 1830s, can still be seen in Uxbridge and
Northbridge near Route 122. The river is currently being developed
by the state into a linear historical park, called the Blackstone River
and Canal Heritage State Park. In future years, the state plans to
renovate some of the old mills into museums and visitor centers,
and restore segments of the canal and its towpath. Rhode Island
has similar plans for its portion of the river. When the project is
completed in both states, the Blackstone River will be a "heritage
corridor" nearly forty miles long.
 The ride starts from Uxbridge, among the finest of the Blackstone Valley mill towns, with a compact old brick business block, a
graceful brick library built in 1893, the Victorian Uxbridge Inn, and
a distinctive Gothic-style church with a graceful turretlike steeple.
Several of the mills have retail outlets where you can get bargains
on clothing. Unlike many mill towns, Uxbridge has no congested
tenements or even rows of identical mill housing, just old wooden
homes that you'd expect to see in a more rural town.
 From Uxbridge it's a short ride to Whitinsville, passing the unusually graceful Linwood Mill and along Linwood Pond. Whitinsville is a fine example of a planned industrial community–a
miniature Lowell. The formidable brick mill slants uphill for a quar-

Grafton.

ter of a mile, and across the road are orderly rows of identical houses. As you climb the hill north of town you pass gracious old wooden homes and then enter inspiring, rolling farm country. You'll fly downhill into Farnumsville, another small mill town on the Blackstone River, and then climb onto a ridge through farms and orchards into the hilltop town of Grafton.

Grafton is my favorite town in the state. As you approach the center you'll climb gradually past handsome Victorian homes. Suddenly the large oval green lies before you, complete with a bandstand in the middle, and surrounded by several stately white churches, a handsome brick library, and the ornate brick Victorian town hall. From Grafton you'll return to Uxbridge along a succession of winding country lanes. At the end you'll pass the Stanley Mill, a handsome wooden building from the mid-nineteenth century, and a good place to pick up bargains on woolen goods. Just ahead is the John Farnum House, built in 1715.

Directions for the ride: 29 miles

1. Turn left (north) out of parking lot and go 4/10 mile to fork (Route 122 bears right).

2. Bear right, staying on Route 122, and go 3/10 mile to traffic light.

3. Go straight at light 4/10 mile to Linwood Avenue on left, immediately before railroad bridge (sign may say to Whitinsville).

4. Turn left on Linwood Avenue and go 1.4 miles to two traffic lights 50 yards apart, in the center of Whitinsville. As soon as you turn, notice the graceful Victorian mill on your left. Just past the mill, on your right, is a lovely Victorian mansion built in 1871. It is now a highly regarded country inn, called, appropriately enough, The Victorian.

5. Turn right at second traffic light on Hill Street, which lives up to its name. After 3.2 miles you'll cross Sutton Street at blinking light. Continue straight 1.2 miles to fork where Ferry Street bears left, and Depot Street (unmarked) turns right across railroad bridge.

6. Turn right and go 4/10 mile to end (Route 122). There's a fine dam across the Blackstone River on your left. It's hidden by the bridge abutment; dismount to get a look. At Route 122, the short ride turns right and the long ride turns left.

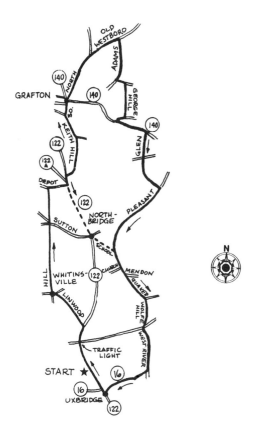

OLD WESTBORO

ADAMS

140 NORTH

GRAFTON 140

GEORGE HILL

140

SO.

KEITH HILL

GLEN

122

PLEASANT

122 A

DEPOT

122

NORTH-BRIDGE

SUTTON

SCHOOL

N

HILL

WHITINS-VILLE 122 CHURCH MENDON

LINWOOD QUAKER

WOLFE HILL

WEST RIVER

TRAFFIC LIGHT

START ★ 16

16

UXBRIDGE 122

271

7. Turn left on Route 122 and go 2/10 mile to fork where Route 122A bears left and Route 122 bears right.

8. Bear right on Route 122 and then immediately turn right on Keith Hill Road. Go 1.7 miles to stop sign (merge left).

9. Bear left at stop sign and go 8/10 mile to fork at very bottom of hill. At the fork, South Street bears right uphill.

10. Bear right on South Street and go 4/10 mile to stop sign (Route 140) in the center of Grafton.

11. Go straight at stop sign and then immediately bear right, passing the tall monument on your left. Go 8/10 mile to fork where the main road (Old Westboro Road) bears right, and a smaller road (North Street) goes straight.

12. Bear right on main road and go 2.4 miles to Adams Street on right. You'll come within 1/2 mile of the Willard House and Clockshop, an eighteenth-century saltbox house with an impressive collection of antique clocks. To visit it, turn left after 1.6 miles on Wesson Street. Go 4/10 mile to Willard Street on right. Turn right and go 1/10 mile to museum on left.

13. Turn right on Adams Street and go 1.8 miles to traffic island where the main road bears right uphill and another road turns left.

14. Turn left at traffic island and go 3/10 mile to George Hill Road on right.

15. Turn right on George Hill Road and go 1.9 miles to end (Leland Street). This is a pleasant narrow lane along a hillside. • *CAUTION:* The end comes up suddenly at bottom of hill.

16. Turn right on Leland Street and go 2/10 mile to end (Route 140).

17. Turn sharp left on Route 140 and go 1.7 miles to Glen Avenue on right. It comes up immediately after Williams Street, also on right.

18. Turn right on Glen Avenue and go 1/2 mile to crossroads and stop sign. Continue straight for 9/10 mile to end.

19. Turn right at end and go 2.5 miles to fork where Mendon Road bears left and Quaker Street goes straight ahead downhill. After 1.5 miles, Riverdale Street on right leads 1/10 mile to the Blackstone River and an old mill that may become part of the Blackstone Heritage State Park system. Church Street, the next right after Riverdale Street, also leads 1/10 mile to the river.

20. Continue straight on Quaker Street for 1.3 miles to fork (Wolfe Hill Road bears right).

21. Bear right on Wolfe Hill Road and go 1 mile to crossroads (Hartford Avenue). Here the ride goes straight, but if you bear right for 3/10 mile, you'll cross the Blackstone River, where you can see vestiges of the old Blackstone Canal and a lock.

22. Bear slightly left at crossroads onto West River Road (don't turn sharply left) and go 1.4 miles to crossroads (Route 16).

23. Bear right on Route 16 and go 1.2 miles to end (Route 122). Just before the end, there's a little dam on your right.

24. Turn right on Route 122 and go 6/10 mile to supermarket on left.

Directions for the ride: 17 miles

1. Follow directions for the long ride through number 6.

2. Turn right on Route 122 and go 2 miles to School Street, which bears left at blinking light. This is Northbridge, another mill town on the Blackstone River. Route 122 parallels the river closely; look for historic sites in the Blackstone Heritage State Park system.

3. Bear left on School Street and go 1.3 miles to end (Quaker Street). You'll pass a magnificent brick church on your right.

4. Bear right on Quaker Street and go 1.1 miles to fork where Mendon Road bears left and Quaker Street continues straight ahead downhill.

5. Follow directions for the long ride from number 20 to the end.

47. Purgatory Chasm Ride: Uxbridge–Whitinsville– Sutton–Douglas

Number of miles: 21 (27 with Singletary Pond extension)
Terrain: Hilly.
Food: Refreshment stand at Purgatory Chasm, open during the summer in good weather. Grocery and snack bar in East Douglas. Pizza place at end.
Start: Rico's Supermarket, Route 122, Uxbridge, 6/10 mile north of Route 16.

Southeast of Worcester, midway between the city and the Rhode Island border, is an area of ruggedly beautiful ridge-and-valley country dotted with picturesque small towns. Biking in this region is challenging but inspiring: there are several tough climbs, but each is balanced by a ridgetop run with sweeping views or a long, smooth downhill run. Highlighting this ride is a visit to Purgatory Chasm, a deep, boulder-strewn gorge between towering rocky cliffs.

The ride starts in Uxbridge, a beautiful old mill town on the upper Blackstone River, which slices diagonally from Worcester to Providence. In the center of town is a compact brick business block, the graceful brick library built in 1893, the Victorian Uxbridge Inn, and a distinctive Gothic-architectured church with a graceful turretlike steeple. From Uxbridge it's a short way to Whitinsville, one of the state's best examples of a planned, orderly mill village—a miniature Lowell or Holyoke. The original stone mill, a graceful bell-towered beauty, stands over a little dam in the center of town. Around the corner a more recent, massive brick mill extends along the road up a hillside for nearly a quarter of a mile. Across the road, ordered rows of identical long, wooden mill houses with broad porches march along the side streets.

From Whitinsville it's not far to Purgatory Chasm, where a rocky trail leads half a mile along the bottom of the ravine to its far end. Beyond the Chasm there's a steady two-mile climb, relieved by several flat spots, which more than one cyclist has spontaneously named the Stairway to Heaven. By the time you get to the top you'll feel like a lead zeppelin, but you'll get a lift from the inspiring views

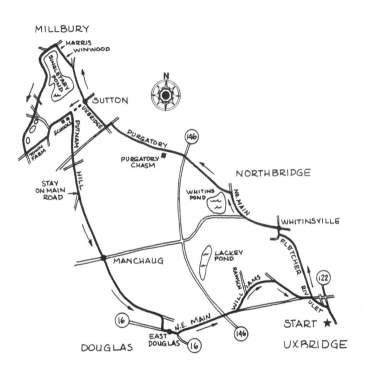

MILLBURY

HARRIS
WINWOOD
SINGLETARY POND
SUTTON
HARRIS
SCHOOL
UXBRIDGE
PURGATORY
146
DOWN FARM
PUTNAM
PURGATORY
CHASM
NORTHBRIDGE
STAY
ON MAIN
ROAD
HILL
WHITINS
POND
NO. MAIN
WHITINSVILLE
LACKEY
POND
FLETCHER
MANCHAUG
RANCH
WILLIAMS
RIVULET
122
16
N.E. MAIN
146
START ★
DOUGLAS
EAST
DOUGLAS
16
UXBRIDGE

and the screaming downhill plunge that awaits you around the corner. One more steep climb brings you to the classic New England village of Sutton, with a graceful church and green and an old wooden town hall.

Beyond Sutton the rest of the ride is easier, with only one more tough climb. Just ahead is a fine run along Singletary Pond and the three small Stockwell Ponds, followed by a long, lazy downhill run through the little mill village of Manchaug. Then you'll head to East Douglas, another attractive town with a pair of old churches and a handsome little red-brick library. Beyond here you'll have one more climb onto an open ridge with superb views, followed by a long, well-earned descent back to Uxbridge.

Directions for the ride: 27 miles

1. Turn left (north) out of parking lot and go 4/10 mile to fork where Rivulet Street bears left.

2. Bear left on Rivulet Street and immediately bear left at another fork, staying on the main road. Go 3/10 mile to crossroads and stop sign.

3. Go straight at crossroads 1.7 miles to end (Douglas Road), in Whitinsville.

4. Bear right on Douglas Road across a little bridge to traffic light. From the left side of the bridge there's a fascinating view of the Mumford River flowing beside the massive mills and over a little dam.

5. Turn left at traffic light and go 7/10 mile to fork (North Main Street bears right).

6. Bear right on North Main Street and go 6/10 mile to another fork, where the main road bears left (a sign may say to Route 146, Purgatory Chasm).

7. Bear left at fork, staying on main road. Just ahead is a lovely little pond and dam on your right. Continue 1.5 miles to Purgatory Chasm on left. A long, tough hill leads up to the Chasm.

8. Leaving the Chasm, continue uphill 1.8 miles to end. Just before the end there's a great view on your right.

9. Turn left at end and go 2/10 mile to crossroads and blinking light (Uxbridge Road).

10. Turn right on Uxbridge Road and go 1.2 miles to crossroads and stop sign in the center of Sutton. You'll have a flying downhill run followed by a hard climb. In Sutton the short ride turns left and the long ride goes straight.

11. Go straight at crossroads 9/10 mile to Winwood Road, a narrow lane that bears left.

12. Bear left on Winwood Road and go 8/10 mile to end. Singletary Pond is on your left.

13. Turn left at end and go 3/10 mile to fork.

14. Bear left at fork, following the water, and go 3.2 miles to your fourth crossroads (Town Farm Road). The first three come in quick succession, then it's 1.2 miles to the fourth where the right-hand road bears up a steep hill. You'll go along Singletary Pond and then the three small Stockwell Ponds.

15. Turn left on Town Farm Road and go 8/10 mile to end (merge left).

16. Bear left at end and go 2/10 mile to fork where the main road bears right.

17. Bear right, staying on main road, and go 1 mile to Putnam Hill Road on right, at stop sign, just past high school.

18. Turn right on Putnam Hill Road and go 2.1 miles to fork where the main road bears left, just beyond the top of long hill. (Lackey Road, a smaller road, goes straight.)

19. Bear left, staying on main road, and go 2 miles to cross-roads and blinking light in the small, somewhat depressed village of Manchaug.

20. Go straight at crossroads 2 miles to fork where one road bears right and the other goes straight. It's just after a red-brick church on left.

21. Bear right at fork, and after 1/10 mile bear right again on the main road across a little bridge. Go 1/10 mile to end (Route 16). This is East Douglas.

22. Turn left on Route 16. After 1/4 mile, North Street bears left, but continue straight on Route 16 for 1/4 mile to blinking light where Route 16 curves sharply right.

23. Immediately beyond the light, bear left down sharp hill on Northeast Main Street. • *CAUTION* here. Go 1.4 miles to Williams Street, which bears left shortly after the bridge over Route 146.

24. Bear left on Williams Street. After 8/10 mile, the main road curves right and Rawson Street bears left. Continue on main road for 6/10 mile to end.

25. Bear right at end and go 9/10 mile to stop sign at bottom of hill (merge left).

26. Bear left (almost straight) for 1/10 mile to crossroads.

27. Turn right at crossroads and go 4/10 mile to end (merge into Route 122).

28. Bear right on Route 122 and go 4/10 mile to parking lot on right.

Directions for the ride: 21 miles

1. Follow directions for the long ride through number 10.

2. Turn left at crossroads and go 1/2 mile to Putnam Hill Road on left, just before school (sign may say to Manchaug, East Douglas).

3. Turn left on Putnam Hill Road and go 2.1 miles to fork where the main road bears left, just beyond top of long hill. (Lackey Road, a smaller road, goes straight.)

4. Follow directions for the long ride from number 19 to the end.

48. The Rhode Island Connection: Mendon–Blackstone–Millville–Slatersville, Rhode Island–Uxbridge

Number of miles: 16 (28 with Rhode Island extension)
Terrain: Rolling, with several short hills and one tough one.
Food: Grocery in Millville. Supermarket and bakery in Slatersville. Lowell's at end—first-rate ice cream and fish and chips.
Start: Lowell's Restaurant, Route 16 in Mendon, three miles southwest of the center of Milford and just west of a traffic light.

This is a tour of the rolling hills and little valley towns midway between Worcester and Providence. Between the towns, the countryside is very rural, with a couple of open hillsides offering fine views. The long ride dips south into the northwestern corner of Rhode Island, where you'll visit the classic New England mill town of Slatersville.

The ride starts from Mendon, a stately hilltop town with a dignified white church and an old wooden town hall. Leaving Mendon you'll ascend a small ridge with fine views to the east, and then enjoy a long, lazy downhill run into Millville, a small mill town on the Blackstone River that has seen better days. You'll pass the Chestnut Hill Meeting House, a simple wooden church built in 1769. A couple of miles ahead, you'll come to Southwick Wild Animal Farm, a large collection of animals from all over the world. You'll return to Mendon along winding, narrow lanes.

The long ride heads south from Millville to Slatersville, Rhode Island, one of the finest mill villages in that state, with well-maintained old homes, an old Gothic-style grange hall, and a classic New England church and green. Just outside of town is a beautiful two-tiered dam. From here you'll head on remote wooded roads back to Millville, where you'll pick up the shorter ride.

Directions for the ride: 28 miles

1. Turn left from *back* of parking lot, immediately passing the church on your left. Just ahead is a traffic island where the main road curves right downhill. Stay on main road 1/10 mile to first right, Blackstone Street. It comes up while you're going downhill—don't whizz past it.

2. Turn right on Blackstone Street and go 5.5 miles to the second crossroads (Lincoln Street), staying on main road. There's a school on the left-hand corner.

3. Turn right on Lincoln Street and go 9/10 mile to fork (main road bears slightly left downhill).

4. Bear left and go 8/10 mile to Chestnut Hill Road on right, just before traffic light. Here the short ride turns right and the long ride goes straight.

5. Continue straight for 50 yards to traffic light (Route 122). Cross Route 122 and go 1.5 miles to end (merge left on Route 146A). • *CAUTION:* Metal-grate bridge over the Blackstone River is very slippery when wet. Please walk across.

6. Bear left on Route 146A and go 2/10 mile to traffic light (Route 102 on right).

7. Go straight at light for 4/10 mile to Ridge Road on left.

8. Turn left on Ridge Road for 1/10 mile to end.

9. Turn right and go one block to crossroads (church straight ahead). This is the center of Slatersville.

10. Turn right. Just ahead is a blinking light. Continue straight down the hill 1.1 miles to crossroads and stop sign (Route 102). Shortly before the intersection is a beautiful two-tiered dam on your left.

11. Cross Route 102 and go 9/10 mile to third left (Joslin Road, unmarked). If you take the second left, Inman Road, and go 1/2 mile, you'll come to Wright's Farm, a restaurant with excellent and reasonably priced fried chicken.

12. Turn left on Joslin Road and go 8/10 mile to crossroads and stop sign (Douglas Pike).

13. Turn right on Douglas Pike and go 8/10 mile to Ironmine Road, which bears right.

14. Bear right on Ironmine Road and go 1.8 miles to Elmwood Street on right.

15. Turn right on Elmwood Street and go 1.6 miles to five-way intersection (Chestnut Street on left). Continue straight for 3/10 mile to crossroads and stop sign.

16. Turn right and go 1/10 mile to Route 146A, at stop sign.

17. Cross Route 146A and go 1 mile to fork (smaller road

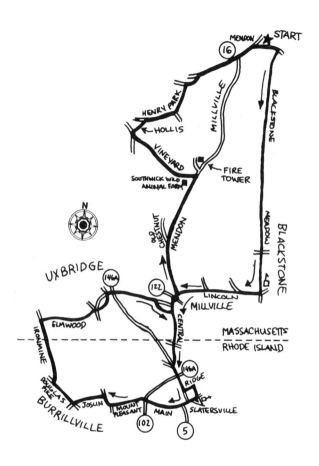

N

MENDON ★ START

16

HENRY PARK

HOLLIS

VINEYARD

MILLVILLE

BLACKSTONE

SOUTHWICK WILD ANIMAL FARM

FIRE TOWER

OLD CHESTNUT

MENDON

MEADOW

BLACKSTONE

UXBRIDGE

146A

122

LINCOLN

MILLVILLE

CENTRAL

ELMWOOD

IRONMINE

MASSACHUSETTS

RHODE ISLAND

146A

RIDGE

DOUGLAS PIKE

JOSLIN

MOUNT PLEASANT

MAIN

SLATERSVILLE

BURRILLVILLE

102

5

bears right). You'll follow the Blackstone River on your left. The river and the vestiges of the canal paralleling it are currently being developed into a Heritage State Park; there may be historic sites in the area in future years.

18. Bear right on smaller road and go 4/10 mile to end (Central Street), in Millville.

19. Go left for 3/10 mile to traffic light (Route 122). You'll cross the metal-grate bridge again at bottom of hill; • *CAUTION* here. The remains of an old mill on the right may become part of the Heritage State Park.

20. Cross Route 122 and immediately turn left on Chestnut Hill Road. Go 1.8 miles to fork. The Chestnut Hill Meeting House is on your right shortly before the fork.

21. Bear right at fork, staying on main road, and go 8/10 mile to Vineyard Street on left (sign may say Southwick Wild Animal Farm). Here the ride turns left, but if you go straight for 2/10 mile and then left on a narrow lane (Tower Road) for 1/4 mile, you'll come to a fire tower with a magnificent view.

22. Turn left on Vineyard Street and go 1.9 miles to end. The animal farm is on your left after 1/2 mile.

23. Turn right at end and go 100 yards to Hollis Street, which bears right.

24. Bear right on Hollis Street and go 3/10 mile to end (merge right).

25. Bear right at end and go 1.1 mile to fork. • *CAUTION:* The last quarter mile has bumps and potholes.

26. Bear left at fork up a short, steep hill and go 9/10 mile to end.

27. Turn right at end and go 1/10 mile to end (Route 16). Nipmuck Pond is on your right.

28. Bear right on Route 16 and go 1.2 miles to Lowell's restaurant on right.

Directions for the ride: 15 miles

1. Follow directions for the long ride through number 4.

2. Turn right on Chestnut Hill Road and go 1.8 miles to fork. The Chestnut Hill Meeting House is on your right shortly before the fork.

3. Follow directions for the long ride from number 21 to the end.

 **Chapter 5:**

The South Shore

Numbers on this map refer to rides in this book.

49. Weymouth–Hingham

Number of miles: 12 (26 with Hingham extension)
Terrain: Gently rolling, with a few short hills and one hard climb.
Food: Several grocery stores and restaurants in Weymouth and
   Hingham.
Start: Shaw's Plaza, Middle Street, Weymouth, just north of Route
   53.
How to get there: From Route 3, exit north onto Route 18 and
   go 3/10 mile to Winter Street, at traffic light. Turn right on
   Winter Street and go 1/2 mile to end (Middle Street). Turn
   left at end. The shopping center is just beyond the light on
   the right.

This ride brings us exploring two communities of contrasting character. Weymouth is a middle-class residential community, eastern-
most of the built-up suburbs southeast of Boston. It has a beautiful
stretch of waterfront along Hingham Bay, hemmed in by Houghs
Neck in Quincy on the west and by the Hull peninsula on the east.
Rising up from the shore is Great Hill, which provides a most spectacular view, among the best in the Boston area. Hingham is a
wealthy community filled with elegant wooden homes from the
early 1800s, horse farms, and country estates with gently rolling
meadows. It is the first town southeast of Boston that is more rural
than suburban.

   The ride starts from the center of Weymouth and passes the
handsome red-brick town hall, topped by a cupola. From here it's
not far to the run along boat-filled Weymouth Harbor. A small peninsula juts northeastward into Massachusetts Bay, with Webb Memorial State Park, one of the state's newest, at its tip. Dirt paths
wind along the shoreline, and a lookout platform on the highest
point provides a fine view of the harbor and offshore islands. A
missile base during the 1950s, the park is a wonderful example of
how land can be recycled for public enjoyment. It is relatively un-
discovered, and you'll probably have the place nearly to yourself.
Just beyond the park you'll scale 150-foot Great Hill for an even
better view of the harbor and the Boston skyline.

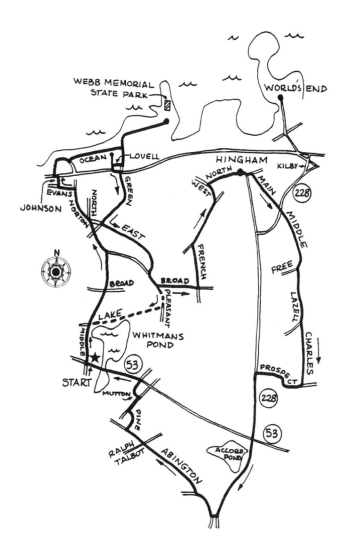

WEBB MEMORIAL STATE PARK

WORLD'S END

OCEAN LOVELL

HINGHAM KILBY

EVANS

JOHNSON

GREEN

NORTH

NORTH WEST

MAIN

228

EAST

N

FRENCH

MIDDLE

FREE

BROAD BROAD

PLEASANT

LAZELL

CHARLES

LAKE

MIDDLE

WHITMANS POND

PROSPECT

START

53

228

MUTTON

53

PINE

RALPH TALBOT

ABINGTON

ACCORD POND

285

The long ride heads east into the gracious community of Hingham, which is unique because it has two centers of town, Hingham and Hingham Center, a mile apart. Both are New England classics, with proud old churches and fine Colonial-style homes with peaked roofs and dormer windows. You'll go by the Old Ship Church, built in 1681 and the oldest church in America in continuous use. You can take a two-mile side trip to World's End, as idyllic a spot as any on the Massachusetts coast. It is a small peninsula originally designed by Frederick Law Olmsted and now maintained by the Trustees of Reservations. Its three drumlins are connected by a narrow neck between the first and second. Broad, grassy slopes, interspersed with a few stately trees, slant gently down to the shore and give views of the Boston skyline. Beyond the center of town you get into a pastoral landscape of meticulous gentleman farms with broad fields and gracious old farmhouses.

Directions for the ride: 26 miles

1. Turn right out of parking lot onto Middle Street and go 1/2 mile to traffic light (Lake Street).

2. Cross Lake Street and go 6/10 mile to another light (Broad Street).

3. Cross Broad Street and go 1/2 mile to end. You'll pass the Weymouth town hall on your left.

4. Turn left at end and go 1/2 mile to fork just after you go under a railroad bridge.

5. Bear left at fork and go 1/2 mile to a street on left immediately before a school on right.

6. Turn left on this street (Evans Street) and go 3/10 mile to Johnson Road on right.

7. Turn 90 degrees right on Johnson Road (don't turn sharply right on Standish Street) and go 1/10 mile to end.

8. Turn left at end and then immediately right on Birch Brow Avenue. After 3/10 mile the road turns 90 degrees right along the ocean. Continue 2/10 mile to Ocean Avenue on left.

9. Turn left on Ocean Avenue and go 2/10 mile to stop sign.

10. Bear left at stop sign, following the ocean, and go 4/10 mile to fork. Bear left, still following the ocean, and go 1/4 mile to end, at bottom of hill (• *CAUTION* here).

11. Turn left at end and go 8/10 mile to Webb Memorial State Park.

12. Leaving the park, you have to go back along the same road. Go 1.3 miles to Lovell Street on right, just before the traffic light at Route 3A.

13. Turn right on Lovell Street and go 1/10 mile to end (Bradley Road).

14. Turn right on Bradley Road and go 1/4 mile to the top of Great Hill.

15. Leaving Great Hill, go back down the hill 4/10 mile to end (Route 3A).

16. Turn left on Route 3A and go 1/10 mile to traffic light (Green Street). • *CAUTION:* Use sidewalk—Route 3A is too busy for safe riding on the roadway. There's a Burger King on the far side of the intersection.

17. Turn right on Green Street. After 6/10 mile the main road curves sharply right at blinking light. Stay on the main road 1/2 mile to traffic light.

18. Turn left at light. After 6/10 mile a road bears right across railroad tracks, but curve to the left, staying on the main road. Go 7/10 mile to end, at stop sign.

19. Turn left at end and go 1/4 mile to stop sign. Immediately after the stop sign is a square where Pleasant Street bears slightly right and Broad Street bears left. Here the short ride bears right and the long ride bears left.

20. Bear left on Broad Street and go 7/10 mile to French Street, at crossroads at top of hill.

21. Turn left on French Street and go 9/10 mile to end (merge right at stop sign).

22. Bear right at end and go 8/10 mile to West Street, which bears left at railroad tracks.

23. Bear left on West Street and go 2/10 mile to end, at stop sign (North Street on right).

24. Turn right on North Street and go 7/10 mile to fork with statue of Abraham Lincoln in middle. Bear right and go 1/10 mile to another fork, in the center of Hingham.

25. Bear left at fork and immediately turn right on Main Street opposite Saint Paul's Church on left. Go 9/10 mile until you merge into Route 228. Here the ride bears left on Middle Street but if you wish you can go 2 miles to World's End and then backtrack to this point. To get to World's End, turn sharply left on Route 228 and go 2/10 mile to fork. Bear left (still Route 228) and go 6/10 mile to Kilby Street, which bears left. Bear left on Kilby Street and just ahead bear left at crossroads on Summer Street. Just ahead, cross Route 3A at stop sign diagonally. Go 4/10 mile to traffic light. Go straight at light 7/10 mile to entrance.

26. When you merge into Route 228, bear left on Middle Street, passing the green on your left (don't bear right onto Route 228). Go 1.2 miles to fork where Lazell Street bears left and Free Street bears right. Just before the fork, a road on your left leads to Wompatuck State Park, a massive, 3,000-acre expanse of woodland with campsites and 6 miles of bicycle paths.

27. Bear left on Lazell Street and go 8/10 mile to another fork where the main road bears slightly left.

28. Bear slightly left at fork, staying on the main road, and go 1 mile to end.

29. Turn right at end. After 1/2 mile the main road curves sharply left at traffic island (Amber Road turns right and Hoover Road goes straight at the intersection). Continue on main road 3/10 mile to end (Main Street, Route 228).

30. Turn left on Route 228 and go 1.3 miles to traffic light (Route 53).

31. Go straight at light 1.8 miles to V.F.W. Cutoff, a very short road on your right.

32. Turn right on this road and go 100 yards to end.

33. Turn right at end and go 1/2 mile to Abington Street on right.

34. Turn right on Abington Street and go 1.5 miles to crossroads and blinking light.

35. Go straight at crossroads. After 2/10 mile bear left at stop sign. Go 2/10 mile to your first right, Pine Street.

36. Turn right on Pine Street and go 4/10 mile to end.

37. Turn right at end, going underneath Route 128, and go 1/2 mile to Mutton Lane on left.

38. Turn left on Mutton Lane and go 1/4 mile to traffic light (Route 53).

39. Turn left on Route 53 and go 8/10 mile to shopping center on right. You'll cross Whitmans Pond.

Directions for the ride: 12 miles

1. Follow directions for the long ride through number 19.

2. Bear slightly right on Pleasant Street and go 2/10 mile to your first right, Shawmut Street, just over the brow of a little hill.

3. Turn right on Shawmut Street. Just ahead, bear left at traffic island, staying on the main road. Go 9/10 mile to traffic light. You'll pass Whitmans Pond on your left.

4. Turn left at light and go 1/2 mile to shopping center on left.

50. Hull

Number of miles: 15
Terrain: Flat, with two short, steep hills.
Food: Several groceries and snack bars.
Start: Junction of Route 228, Jerusalem Road, and Rockland Road in North Cohasset, 1.5 miles north of Route 3A. Park on Route 228 or Rockland Road (where legal), or at the small row of stores if they're not busy. You can also get to Hull by boat from Boston. The boat lands at Nantasket Beach, near the start of the ride.

The town of Hull is a long, slender peninsula jutting north and then west into Massachusetts Bay, about six miles long and a half mile wide. Along its eastern shore is Nantasket Beach, the closest half-way decent beach to Boston. The peninsula contains several round drumlins about 100 feet high connected by narrow, flat strips of land. The ride around the perimeter is enjoyable, with views of the ocean, the numerous islands dotting Massachusetts Bay, and the Boston skyline in the distance around every bend. The vistas from the tops of the hills are dramatic.

For years one of Hull's fond landmarks was Paragon Park, old-est amusement park in New England, across the street from Nan-tasket Beach. It was built in 1868 by the New Haven Railroad and the Schlitz Beer Company to lure tourists to the luxurious Victorian hotels that once lined the shore. The big roller-coaster was a classic, along with the old merry-go-round and the Tunnel of Love. In 1984 the park's owners, seeing more money in condominiums than in cotton candy, sold the park to developers who promptly tore down the amusements and put up condominiums. You'll follow the beach to the northeastern shoulder, where a superb view of the entire beach unfolds before you from the top of the hill. From here you'll head to the western tip and then back along Hull Bay.

Today the giant resort hotels are gone, replaced by congested rows of houses and beach cottages, and an ever-increasing number of glossy new condominiums. Some of the homes are graceful Victorian structures; others, especially along the bay side of the peninsula, are run-down.

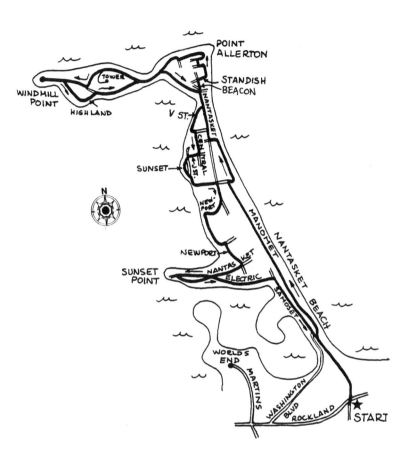

POINT
ALLERTON

STANDISH
BEACON

TOWER

WINDMILL
POINT

HIGHLAND

V ST.

NANTASKET

SUNSET

CENTRAL
ST.

NEW
PORT

N

NEWPORT

NANTASKET

MANOMET

NANTASKET BEACH

SUNSET
POINT

ELECTRIC

SAMOSET

WORLDS
END

MARTINS

WASHINGTON
BLVD

ROCKLAND

★ START

291

At the end of the ride you can go two miles in the opposite direction to a totally different landscape, World's End, a small peninsula just west of Hull. This is an idyllic spot, formerly an estate and now maintained by the Trustees of Reservations. It consists of two tall drumlins joined by a narrow neck. Tree-lined paths wind around the perimeter, and the broad, grassy slopes provide superb views of the bay.

Directions for the ride:

1. Head north on Route 228 and go 1.2 miles to where the main road bears right along the ocean at traffic light. After 8/10 mile you'll come to the beginning of Nantasket Beach, with the ocean on your right and a pleasantly sleazy strip of video arcades and junk-food stands on your left. If it's not a beach day, get on the sidewalk along the beach and stay on it until it ends; otherwise follow the road along the beach, watching out for entering and backing traffic.

2. Bear right along the ocean and go 3/10 mile to Hull Shore Drive Extension on right. Turn right, still following the ocean, and go 1.4 miles to end. • *CAUTION:* The beginning of this stretch has head-in parking on both sides; watch out for cars backing up.

3. Turn right at end and go 6/10 mile to traffic light (Nantasket Avenue).

4. Turn right at light. After 4/10 mile, watch for a pair of brick apartment buildings on your right. Just beyond, there's an intersection where two roads bear left and Beacon Road bears right up steep hill.

5. At this intersection, bear right up steep hill on Beacon Road. Go 1/10 mile to crossroads (Standish Avenue).

6. Turn right on Standish Avenue. Go 2/10 mile to your first right, which goes downhill one block. As soon as you turn onto Standish Avenue there's a dramatic view of the entire beach to your right. Just before you come to the road on your right, notice the unusual concrete watchtower at the top of the hill on your left. The tower is privately owned and is in someone's back yard.

7. Turn right and go one block downhill to end.

8. Turn right at end and go 1/2 mile to end (merge right).

9. Bear right at end on Nantasket Avenue and go 1/2 mile to fork at sewage treatment plant (it's after a small one-way road that bears right). If it's a clear day you can see Boston to your right. You'll also notice a pointed tower straight ahead. It's at Fort Revere Park and unfortunately is open during limited hours that seem to be reduced each year.

10. Bear right at fork and stay on the main road 6/10 mile to end, at bottom of hill. To visit the tower, bear left uphill after 4/10 mile on Farina Avenue.

11. Turn right at end and go 8/10 mile to end. This is Windmill Point, western tip of the peninsula. The channel in front of you is Hull Gut, with Peddocks Island on the far side.

12. From the point, backtrack 1/2 mile to Highland Avenue, which bears right up a steep hill.

13. Bear right on Highland Avenue and go 1/2 mile to end, at bottom of hill.

14. Bear right at end, following the water on your right, and go 8/10 mile to fork. The island on your right, connected to the mainland by a bridge, is Hog Island. It was formerly a Nike missile site and is now a luxury condominium development with the more appealing name of Spinnaker Island.

15. Bear right at fork, still following the water, and go 6/10 mile to V Street, which is just past a pair of brick apartment buildings on your left.

16. Turn right on V Street, following the bay. After 1/4 mile the road turns 90 degrees left. Immediately after, turn right on Central Avenue and go 3/10 mile to J Street.

17. Turn right on J Street and go 1/10 mile to end.

18. Bear left at end along the water on Sunset Avenue. After 4/10 mile the road curves 90 degrees left. Continue 2/10 mile to traffic light (Nantasket Avenue).

19. Turn right at light and go 2/10 mile to Newport Road, which bears right.

20. Bear right on Newport Road and go 7/10 mile to where Warfield Avenue goes straight and another road turns right along the water.

21. Turn right on this road, following the water, and go 4/10 mile to crossroads and stop sign (Nantasket Road).

22. Turn right on Nantasket Road and go 1/2 mile to Clifton

Avenue, a smaller road that bears right. You will now head out to the tip of Sunset Point.

23. Bear right on this road. After 3/10 mile, just before the point, turn sharply left and go 3/10 mile to a road that bears right.

24. Bear right, following the water on your right, and go 9/10 mile to end.

25. Turn right at end and go 1.7 miles back to start. If you'd like to visit World's End, turn right after 4/10 mile on Washington Boulevard (sign says to Boston, Quincy), following the water on your right. After 1.8 miles, merge to your right and go 3/10 mile to traffic light. Turn right at light on Martins Lane and go 7/10 mile to entrance. To return to the start, backtrack to where Washington Boulevard bears left toward Nantasket. Go straight ahead at this intersection on Rockland Road 1.3 miles to Route 228. • *CAUTION:* The 3/10 mile stretch between Washington Boulevard and Martins Lane is an undivided four-lane highway with no shoulder. If traffic is heavy, walk your bike along the side of the road.

51. Cohasset–Scituate

Number of miles: 17 (26 with Scituate extension)
Terrain: Gently rolling, with a couple of short hills.
Food: Grocery stores and restaurants in both Cohasset and Scituate.
Start: Cohasset High School on Pond Street, Cohasset, just north of Route 3A. There's a traffic light at the corner of Route 3A and Pond Street.

On this ride you explore the shoulder of land southeast of Boston where the coastline curves primarily from an east–west to a north–south direction. It is the first really nice stretch of coast heading southeast from the city, and the Cohasset section, just east of Hull, is among the most scenic in the state. A network of smooth secondary roads connecting these two affluent communities provides bicycling at its best.

The ride starts in Cohasset, an unspoiled community that is one of the finest of the Boston suburbs. Its splendid rocky coastline, rimmed by large, impressive homes hovering above the waves with the Boston skyline in the distance, rivals Cape Ann and Newport for elegance. The center of town is a New England jewel, with a long, stately green framed by a pair of graceful white churches, the town hall, and fine Colonial-style wooden homes. The church at the head of the green was built in 1747. Cohasset received a burst of publicity in 1986 when much of the movie *The Witches of Eastwick* was filmed here.

The long ride heads farther southeast into Scituate, another handsome community with a large green, a small, boat-filled harbor, and a compact row of shops along its shore. Just outside of town is the Lawson Tower, a handsome wooden-shingled landmark with a water tower inside. It was built in 1902 and given to the town by Thomas Lawson, a copper magnate. At the top is a set of bells that are played on special town occasions. The Scituate coast, not as elegant as the Cohasset section, is bordered by smaller homes and cottages. It is spectacular, however, especially on a windy day when the surf crashes against the seawalls, which are necessary to protect the shore from the brunt of northeasters. There's a graceful white lighthouse at the tip of Cedar Point, and the bridge over the tidal inlet that forms the border of the two towns is a great spot.

Directions for the ride: 26 miles

1. Turn right out of parking lot onto Pond Street and go 2/10 mile to Route 3A, at traffic light.

2. Cross Route 3A and go 2/10 mile to end (King Street).

3. Turn left on King Street and go 6/10 mile to end (merge to your right onto Beechwood Street). You'll pass Lily Pond on your right.

4. Bear right on Beechwood Street and go 1 mile to crossroads (Doane Street).

5. Turn left on Doane Street and go 7/10 mile to another crossroads (Clapp Road).

6. Turn left on Clapp Road and go 1.7 miles to a wide fork (Mann Lot Road bears left; Grove Street bears right).

7. Bear left on Mann Lot Road and go 4/10 mile to crossroads and stop sign (Route 3A).

8. Cross Route 3A and go 6/10 mile to end (Country Way). A fine white church built in 1869 is at the intersection.

9. Turn right at end and go 3/10 mile to Hollett Street, which turns sharply left. Here the short ride turns left and the long ride goes straight.

10. Continue straight 7/10 mile to fork where Country Way bears right and Branch Street goes straight.

11. Bear right on Country Way and go 1/2 mile to traffic light (First Parish Road).

12. Turn left at light and go 3/10 mile to fork at the Scituate town green (Beaver Dam Road bears left). There's a handsome Civil War monument on the green. Just before the green you'll pass the Lawson Tower on your left.

13. Bear left on Beaver Dam Road and go 9/10 mile to traffic light (Tilden Road).

14. Turn right on Tilden Road and go 8/10 mile to end.

15. Turn left at end and go 4/10 mile, through downtown Scituate, to Jericho Road on right. There's a traffic light at the intersection. Scituate Harbor is on your right.

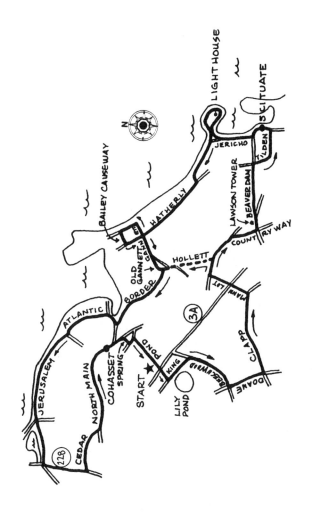

LIGHT HOUSE

SCITUATE

BAILEY CAUSEWAY

N

JERICHO

ALDEN

LAWSON TOWER

BEAVER DAM

HATHERLY

COUNTRY WAY

HOLLETT

OLD GANNETT

GREEN

MAIN LOT

BORDER

3A

ATLANTIC

CLAPP

JERUSALEM

COHASSET

SPRING

START

KING POND

BEECHWOOD

DOANE

NORTH MAIN

LILY POND

CEDAR

128

16. Turn right on Jericho Road and go 7/10 mile to traffic island. To your right is Cedar Point, a small peninsula with a lighthouse at the tip.

17. Bear right at traffic island, following the water on your right, and go 1/10 mile to fork (Lighthouse Road bears right).

18. Bear right on Lighthouse Road and go 7/10 mile around Cedar Point to fork at end of neck that connects the point to the mainland.

19. Bear right at fork, following the ocean on your right, and go 1.2 miles to end.

20. Turn right at end and go 1.8 miles to traffic light (Gannett Road).

21. Turn right on Gannett Road and go 6/10 mile to Bailey Causeway on left.

22. Turn left on Bailey Causeway and go 3/10 mile to end (Hatherly Road). There's a golf course to the right.

23. Turn left on Hatherly Road and go 4/10 mile to traffic light (Gannett Road).

24. Turn right on Gannett Road and go 4/10 mile to where the main road curves left and a smaller road, Old Gannett Road, goes straight.

25. Go straight onto smaller road 2/10 mile to Border Street on right, at traffic island.

26. Turn right on Border Street and go 1.6 miles to end (Margin Street). The little bridge near the end is worth stopping at. Beyond the bridge you'll follow the shore of tiny Cohasset Cove.

27. Turn right on Margin Street, following the water, and go 3/10 mile to fork where Atlantic Avenue bears left and Howard Gleason Road bears right.

28. Bear left on Atlantic Avenue and go 7/10 mile to another fork with a large flower pot in the middle. A sign may say Perry Johnson Square.

29. Bear right at fork and go 1.9 miles to crossroads. This is a magnificent run along the coast.

30. Go straight at crossroads onto Jerusalem Road (don't bear right along the ocean). Go 1 mile to stop sign (Hull Street, Route 228 on left). This is the starting point for the Hull ride, and if you're game for another 15 miles, you can give it a try.

Cohasset Harbor.

31. Turn 90 degrees left on Route 228 and go 8/10 mile to Cedar Street, a small lane that turns sharply left at bottom of little hill.

32. Make a sharp left on Cedar Street and go 1.1 miles to end (merge left).

33. Bear left at end and go 1.5 miles to fork in downtown Cohasset where Elm Street bears left and the main road bears slightly right through the business district. You'll go past the lovely town green just before the fork.

34. Bear right on the main road and go 2/10 mile to Spring Street, a small road that bears right opposite the library. Bear right on Spring Street and go 1/10 mile to end.

35. Turn left at end and go 100 yards to your first right, Pond Street, which goes up a short, steep hill.

36. Turn right on Pond Street and go 1/2 mile to school on right.

Directions for the ride: 17 miles

1. Follow directions for the long ride through number 9.

2. Turn sharply left on Hollett Street and go 8/10 mile to end, at stop sign (merge to your right at bottom of hill).

3. Bear right at end and go 1/10 mile to fork.

4. Bear left at fork and immediately bear left again on Border Street. Go 1.6 miles to end (Margin Street). At the end you'll follow the shore of tiny Cohasset Cove.

5. Follow directions for the long ride from number 27 to the end.

52. Scituate–Marshfield

Number of miles: 16 (27 with Marshfield extension)
Terrain: Gently rolling, with a couple of short hills and two long, gradual ones.
Food: Grocery store and restaurants in Scituate. Grocery store in Humarock.
Start: Scituate High School, Route 3A, just north of First Parish Road, next to the police station and town offices.

This ride takes you exploring the midsection of the South Shore, midway between Boston and Plymouth. This area, bisected by the marsh-lined North River, is more rural than suburban, with gentle wooded hills and some prosperous farms sloping down to the river. Paralleling the shore, you'll pass extensive salt marshes at the river's mouth and loop around three headlands standing guard above the ocean.

The ride starts from Scituate, an affluent community that boasts a large green with a Civil War monument in the middle, a graceful white church, and one of the state's more striking landmarks, the 150-foot-high Lawson Tower. This is a water tower covered on the outside by wooden shingles and donated to the town in 1902 by Thomas Lawson, a copper magnate. Atop the tower is a set of bells that are played on special town occasions.

From Scituate you'll head south to Marshfield, inland from the coast. Marshfield is primarily a gracious rural community that unfortunately is becoming suburban because of its proximity to Route 3. The ride sticks to the unspoiled sections, heading through wooded hills and then along the salt marshes bordering the South and North Rivers. A small detour brings you through the beach community of Humarock, attractively located on a long, narrow peninsula with the open sea on one side and the South River, a tidal estuary, on the other. Shortly after crossing the North River back into Scituate, you'll go by the Stockbridge Mill, built in the mid-1600s and occasionally open for demonstrations of grinding cornmeal in the same way it was done three hundred years ago. From here you'll pedal past broad salt marshes to the coast, where you'll go through two attractive oceanfront communities, River-moor and Second Cliff, both commanding headlands jutting into the ocean. From Second Cliff it's a short ride through the center of town back to your starting point.

Directions for the ride: 27 miles

1. Turn left from the school driveway onto Route 3A and immediately turn right at crossroads onto First Parish Road. Go 3/10 mile to Maple Street, which bears left.

2. Bear left on Maple Street and go 4/10 mile to end (merge left at stop sign).

3. Bear left at stop sign and go 3/10 mile to crossroads and stop sign (Old Oaken Bucket Road).

4. Go straight at crossroads 1.7 miles to end (Main Street, Route 123).

5. Turn left on Route 123 and go 3/10 mile to Bridge Street on right.

6. Turn right on Bridge Street and go 1.1 miles to fork where Highland Street bears left. You'll cross the North River and climb a long, gradual hill.

7. Bear left on Highland Street and go 6/10 mile to Spring Street on left, just past bottom of big hill. Here the short ride turns left and the long ride goes straight.

8. Continue straight on Highland Street and go 3 miles to crossroads and stop sign just after Marshfield High School on right (Furnace Street). It's your fourth crossroads.

9. Turn left on Furnace Street and go 4/10 mile to traffic light (Route 3A).

10. Turn right on Route 3A and go 1 mile to South River Street on left.

11. Turn left on South River Street. Just ahead on your right is the Marshfield town hall, a handsome wooden Victorian building dated 1895. Continue 1.5 miles to fork at traffic island (Grove Street bears left).

12. Bear right at fork (still South River Street) and go 1.2 miles to another fork. You'll climb a short, steep hill.

13. Bear right at fork and go 1/10 mile to stop sign (merge to your right into Ferry Street).

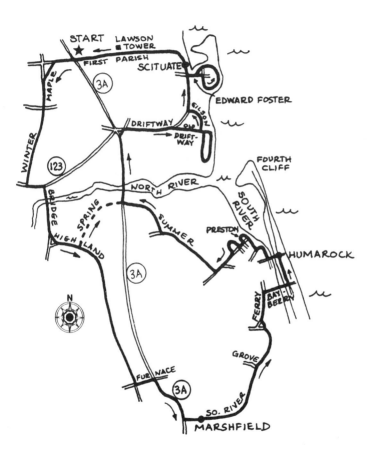

START LAWSON TOWER

FIRST PARISH

SCITUATE

EDWARD FOSTER

3A

MAPLE

WINTER

123

BRIDGE

HIGHLAND

SPRING

SUMMER

DRIFTWAY

GILSON

OLD DRIFT-WAY

NORTH RIVER

FOURTH CLIFF

SOUTH RIVER

PRESTON

HUMAROCK

3A

FERRY

BAY-BERRY

N

GROVE

FURNACE

3A

SO. RIVER

MARSHFIELD

14. Bear right on Ferry Street and go 6/10 mile to Bayberry Road on right. It's just after Blueberry Road, also on right.

15. Turn right on Bayberry Road and go 4/10 mile to crossroads and stop sign after bridge. This is Humarock. The ocean is 100 yards in front of you.

16. Turn left at crossroads and go 1/2 mile to another crossroads and stop sign (Marshfield Avenue).

17. Turn left on Marshfield Avenue and go 2/10 mile to crossroads immediately after bridge.

18. Turn right at crossroads, going along the harbor on your right. After 1/10 mile the main road turns 90 degrees left up a short, steep hill. Go 100 yards up the hill to Preston Terrace, which turns sharply right at the top of the hill.

19. Make a hairpin right turn on Preston Terrace and go 3/10 mile to crossroads (Pollard Street). There's a magnificent view of the South River and Humarock Beach to your right. You'll see another part of Pollard Street on your left before you come to the crossroads, but continue straight 1/10 mile to the crossroads.

20. Turn right on Pollard Street and go one short block to another crossroads.

21. Turn right at crossroads and go 4/10 mile to end (merge head-on into a larger road).

22. Go straight at end 3/10 mile to Summer Street, which bears right at traffic island.

23. Bear right on Summer Street and go 1.6 miles to where Summer Street bears right and Prospect Street goes straight. A little pond is on your right at the intersection.

24. Bear right on Summer Street and go 7/10 mile to Route 3A, at a traffic island. You'll climb a long, gradual hill.

25. Bear right at traffic island onto Route 3A and go 1.4 miles to a road that bears right just before traffic light (sign may say Scituate, 2 miles). Here the ride bears right, but you can go 3/10 mile off the route to visit the Old Oaken Bucket Homestead, the home where poet Samuel Woodworth, author of "The Old Oaken Bucket," was born in 1784. The farm is scheduled for restoration if a nationwide funding campaign is successful. To see it, continue straight 100 yards to traffic light, bear left on Old Oaken Bucket Road, and go 2/10 mile to farm on left.

26. Bear right just before light and go 100 feet to Driftway on

Lawson Tower, Scituate.

right. Here the ride turns right, but if you go straight 100 yards, the Stockbridge Grist Mill is on your right and the millpond on your left.

27. Turn right on Driftway and go 1.3 miles to Old Driftway, which bears right. It's just after the entrance to a water-pollution-control facility (a good euphemism for sewage treatment plant).

28. Bear right on Old Driftway. After 6/10 mile the road turns 90 degrees right along the ocean onto Collier Road. Continue 8/10 mile to end. You'll loop around the headland of Rivermoor.

29. At end turn left and then immediately right on Gilson Road. Go 7/10 mile to end.

30. Turn right at end and go 6/10 mile to crossroads and stop sign (Edward Foster Road).

31. Turn right on Edward Foster Road and go 3/10 mile to crossroads after little bridge. You will now loop around the Second Cliff headland.

32. Turn right at crossroads. After 7/10 mile, bear right across the same bridge and go 3/10 mile to crossroads.

33. Turn right at crossroads and go 1.8 miles to a five-way intersection where Branch Street bears right and Beaver Dam Road bears slightly left (almost straight). You'll go through downtown Scituate and then straight at two traffic lights.

34. Bear slightly left on Beaver Dam Road, passing the Scituate town green on your left, and go 4/10 mile to traffic light (Country Way). You'll see the Lawson Tower on your right just beyond the green.

35. Go straight at light for 1/2 mile to Route 3A, at stop sign.

36. Turn right on Route 3A. The high school is just ahead on right.

Directions for the ride: 16 miles

1. Follow directions for the long ride through number 7.

2. Turn left on Spring Street and go 1.3 miles to wide crossroads and stop sign (Route 3A). • *CAUTION:* Spring Street has bumpy spots.

3. Turn left on Route 3A and go 1.3 miles to a road that bears right just before traffic light (sign may say Scituate, 2 miles). To visit the Old Oaken Bucket Homestead, see direction number 25 for the long ride.

4. Follow directions for the long ride from number 26 to the end.

53. Duxbury–Marshfield

Number of miles: 19 (31 with Marshfield extension)
Terrain: Gently rolling.
Food: Grocery stores in Marshfield. McDonald's at end.
Start: Kingsbury Square shopping center, junction of Routes 3A and 53 in Kingston. It's just west of Route 3; take exit 10. If you're heading south on Route 3, turn right at the end of the exit ramp. If you're heading north on Route 3, turn left at end of ramp.

The South Shore coast just north of Plymouth provides superb bicycling. The protected waters of Kingston and Duxbury Bays are lined with graceful old homes from the 1800s and even earlier. The coast itself, consisting mainly of slender peninsulas with the sea on one side and salt marshes on the other, is beautiful; inland lies a pretty rural landscape of cranberry bogs, small ponds, and snug, cedar-shingled homes.

The ride starts from Duxbury, one of the most affluent and thoroughly unspoiled of the Boston suburbs. The town green, graced by the handsome, pillared town hall and a classic white church, is one of the most dignified in the state. First you'll parallel the shore of Kingston Bay to the Myles Standish monument, a graceful stone tower 100 feet high on top of a hill that rises 200 feet from the shore. The view from the top is as dramatic as any in the state. Unfortunately, like so many of the most interesting places in Massachusetts, it's open only during the summer. From here you'll follow Duxbury Bay to the picturesque Currier-and-Ives village of Snug Harbor, with a rambling wooden block of stores and gracious old homes just inland from the harbor full of boats. Just ahead is Powder Point, a peninsula lined with mansions and estates. One of them, the King Caesar House, is a Federal-era beauty open to the public on summer afternoons. It was built in 1807 by Ezra Weston, nicknamed King Caesar, one of the many post-Revolutionary merchant princes who made millions in shipbuilding and the China trade, and then flaunted their success by constructing a mansion on the Massachusetts coast.

From Powder Point you'll cross the bay over the Powder Point Bridge, a narrow, ramshackle wooden span nearly half a mile long. On the far side is Duxbury Beach, the South Shore's finest. Completely undeveloped, it extends southward four miles along a fragile sandy spit of land only a tenth of a mile wide. You'll head north along the ocean to Brant Rock, another peninsula with a road hugging the rocky coastline. Beyond Brant Rock you'll enter an area of beach cottages across the town line in Marshfield, which is more built-up and not as well-to-do as Duxbury. You'll now head inland and then return south into Duxbury through a peaceful rural area dotted with ponds and cranberry bogs. At the end of the ride you can visit the Duxbury Art Complex, a striking modern building opened in 1971. From here it's a short trip back to the start past the town green.

The short ride takes a more direct route back to the start after crossing the Powder Point Bridge. You'll pass the Governor Winslow House, built in 1699 and one of the finer historic houses on the South Shore, with a full complement of period furnishings. On the grounds are Daniel Webster's law office and a blacksmith shop. Across the street is a schoolhouse built in 1857, now headquarters of the Marshfield Historical Society.

Directions for the ride: 31 miles

1. When you leave the shopping center, go straight at traffic light onto Route 3A for 8/10 mile to crossroads (Park Street on right, Oak Street on left).

2. Turn right on Park Street and go 4/10 mile to fork.

3. Bear left at fork and go 2/10 mile to stop sign (Bay Road).

4. Turn left on Bay Road and go 2.1 miles to crossroads and stop sign in the village of South Duxbury. Some fine views of Kingston Bay lie to your right.

5. Turn right at stop sign on Standish Street and go 4/10 mile to Crescent Street, a smaller road that bears right.

6. Bear right on Crescent Street. After 4/10 mile, the road to the Myles Standish Monument bears left uphill. It's a steady grade, 3/10 mile to the top.

7. Continue 1 mile to stop sign (Marshall Street on right).
• *CAUTION:* Midway along this stretch the road curves sharply left

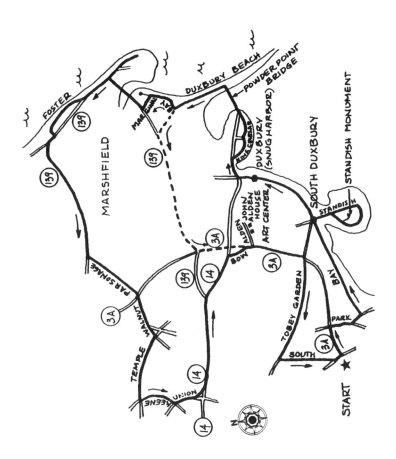

FOSTER

DUXBURY BEACH

POWDER POINT BRIDGE

139

MARSHFIELD

139

(139)

MARSHALL AVE

KING CAESAR

DUXBURY (SNUG HARBOR)

SOUTH DUXBURY

STANDISH MONUMENT

139

JOHN ALDEN HOUSE

ALDEN ART CENTER

STANDISH

3A

PARSONAGE

3A

BOW

3A

14

139

3A

TOBEY GARDEN

BAY

PARK

TEMPLE

WALNUT

14

SOUTH

3A

KEENE

UNION

14

N

START

309

at bottom of steep hill. At the stop sign, continue straight 1/2 mile to crossroads (Washington Street). You're back in South Duxbury.

8. Turn right at crossroads and go 1.9 miles to an intersection with a flagpole in the middle. (There's a fork just beyond the intersection.) A half mile before the intersection you'll go through Snug Harbor. It's worth taking one of the little lanes on the right to the bay.

9. Bear right at fork immediately beyond the flagpole, staying on the main road and following the harbor on your right. Go 2/10 mile to King Caesar Road, which bears right.

10. Bear right on King Caesar Road and go 1/2 mile to fork. You'll pass the King Caesar House.

11. Bear right at fork (still King Caesar Road) and go 7/10 mile to the beginning of the Powder Point Bridge.

12. Cross the bridge. During the summer a policeman is stationed at the entrance to the bridge to make sure that only Duxbury residents drive across, but you're perfectly okay on a bike. At the far end of the bridge, the ocean is 100 yards in front of you. Turn left into the Duxbury Beach parking lot.

13. At the far end of the parking lot, continue straight 1/4 mile along a dirt road. You should walk your bike. At the end of the dirt section, you'll enter another beach parking lot. Continue straight 1.2 miles to Bay Street on right, immediately after the Marshfield town line. Here the short ride goes straight and the long ride turns right.

14. Turn right on Bay Street and go 7/10 mile to dead end, where you have a fine view of Green Harbor. Backtrack 1/10 mile to your first right, at stop sign.

15. Turn right, crossing little bridge, and go 3/10 mile to end (Route 139).

16. Turn right on Route 139 and go 1 mile to end. At the end, notice the fine stone church on the left. You will now head out to the Brant Rock peninsula.

17. Turn right at end onto a wide divided road and go 2/10 mile to fork (Island Street bears right).

18. Bear left at fork, following the ocean on your left, and go 1/2 mile to end. Shortly after the fork you'll see Brant Rock jutting into the ocean.

Miles Standish Monument.

19. Make a U-turn at the end and backtrack 7/10 mile until you come back to Route 139. • *CAUTION:* Watch out for sewer grates.

20. Go straight onto Route 139, still following the ocean on your right, 6/10 mile to Foster Avenue, which bears right.

21. Bear right on Foster Avenue. • *CAUTION:* Bad sewer grate at intersection. After 7/10 mile, the road turns 90 degrees left. Continue 1/10 mile to end (Route 139).

22. Turn right on Route 139. After 2/10 mile there's a fork where Route 139 bears left. Stay on Route 139 for 1.8 miles to Parsonage Road on left, immediately after police station.

23. Turn left on Parsonage Road. After 1/2 mile you'll come to a crossroads and stop sign. Continue straight 7/10 mile to traffic island.

24. Bear right at traffic island and then immediately cross Route 3A at stop sign onto Walnut Street. Go 6/10 mile to end (merge left onto Acorn Street at stop sign).

25. Bear left on Acorn Street and go 2/10 mile to fork (Franklin Street bears right; Lincoln Street bears left).

26. Bear right on Franklin Street and go 2/10 mile to crossroads (Temple Street).

27. Turn right on Temple Street and go 1.6 miles to Keene Street (unmarked) on left. Another road bears right immediately after the intersection.

28. Turn left on Keene Street. As soon as you turn a little pond is on your right. Go 8/10 mile to crossroads and stop sign (Union Street).

29. Turn left on Union Street and go 6/10 mile to fork.

30. Bear left at fork and immediately merge onto Route 14. Go 2 miles to fork where Route 14 bears right and Route 139 bears left.

31. Bear right, staying on Route 14, and go 1.1 miles to Bow Street on right, at top of hill.

32. Turn right on Bow Street and go 1/4 mile to end (merge into Route 3A).

33. Bear right on Route 3A and go 1.6 miles to crossroads and blinking light (Tobey Garden Street). You'll go by the Duxbury town green. To visit the Duxbury Art Complex, turn left after 2/10 mile on Alden Street. The Complex is just ahead on your right. Just beyond it on the right is the John Alden House, built in 1653.

34. Turn right on Tobey Garden Street and go 1.9 miles to South Street, which turns left at a little green. It's 3/10 mile after bridge over Route 3. This is the Tree of Knowledge Corner. A tablet on the green explains why.

35. Turn left on South Street and go 1.2 miles to end (Route 53).

36. Bear left on Route 53. Shopping center is just ahead on right.

Directions for the ride: 19 miles

1. Follow directions for the long ride through number 13.

2. Continue straight 7/10 mile to end (Route 139).

3. Turn left on Route 139 and go 2 miles to Route 3A, at stop sign. You'll pass the Governor Winslow House on your right after 6/10 mile.

4. Turn left on Route 3A and go 8/10 mile to traffic light (Route 14).

5. Continue straight on Route 3A for 1.8 miles to crossroads and blinking light (Tobey Garden Street). To visit the Duxbury Art Complex, turn left after 4/10 mile on Alden Street. The Complex is just ahead on your right. Just beyond it on the right is the John Alden House, built in 1653. Beyond Alden Street you'll go by the Duxbury town green.

6. Follow directions for the long ride from number 34 to the end.

54. Braintree–Holbrook–Randolph

Number of miles: 15
Terrain: Gently rolling, with one hill.
Food: Grocery stores and restaurants in the towns.
Start: Small shopping center on Route 37 in Braintree, 1 mile south of Route 128 at a five-way intersection.

This ride takes you exploring an area of residential and older industrial suburbs between Boston and Brockton, and a little east of both. The Boston-Brockton axis, extending east through Weymouth, is fairly built-up without too many stretches of undeveloped country. The ride cannot really qualify as scenic, yet it is pleasant, sticking to less-busy roads, with several points of interest and old town centers along the way.

The ride starts in Braintree, a middle-class residential suburb best known for its massive shopping mall next to Route 128. The town is the birthplace of Sylvanus Thayer (786 Washington Street, off the route), founder of West Point. From Braintree you'll head along quiet residential roads to Holbrook, which has an ornate brick Victorian town hall built in 1878. From Holbrook it's a short ride to Randolph, another solidly residential community with a graceful, pillared town hall. The return leg from Randolph to Braintree is the most scenic, with a long run following the shore of the Great Pond Reservoir. Just ahead is the Blue Hill Cemetery, which is large enough to get lost in. It is beautifully landscaped; a stream of water cascades through a rock garden at the entrance.

Directions for the ride

1. Turn right out of parking lot onto Route 37, heading south, and go 1 mile to traffic light where Pond Street bears right. Curve left, staying on Route 37, and go 3/10 mile to traffic light where Route 37 bears right.

2. Bear left at light across Hancock Street onto Plain Street, immediately crossing railroad tracks. Go 1.2 miles to traffic light (Liberty Street).

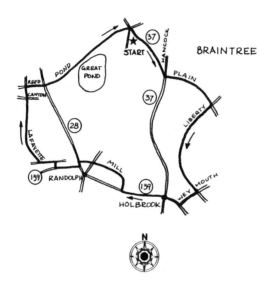

BRAINTREE

START

GREAT
POND

POND

REED

CANTON

LA FAYETTE

(28)

(139) RANDOLPH

MILL

HOLBROOK

(139)

(37)

(37)

HANCOCK

PLAIN

LIBERTY

WEYMOUTH

N

3. Turn right on Liberty Street and go 2.8 miles to crossroads and stop sign (Weymouth Street). There's a water tower just beyond the intersection.

4. Turn right at crossroads and go 1/2 mile to end (Route 139).

5. Turn right on Route 139 and go 1/2 mile to traffic light (Route 37), in center of Holbrook. Notice the Victorian town hall on right.

6. Cross Route 37 and go 1 mile to Mill Street on right, immediately after railroad tracks.

7. Turn right on Mill Street and go 1 mile to traffic light up a long, tough hill.

8. Go straight at light 3/10 mile to end (Route 28). This is the center of Randolph. To your left you can see the pillared town hall.

9. Turn left on Route 28 and then immediately turn right at traffic light on Route 139. Go 7/10 mile to a very short street on right (sign may say to West Street). It's just before a shopping center on your left.

10. Turn right and then immediate left at end. Go 1/4 mile to Lafayette Street, which bears right.

11. Bear right on Lafayette Street and go 1.6 miles to Canton Street, at blinking light and stop sign.

12. Continue straight 2/10 mile to Reed Street, at another blinking light.

13. Turn right on Reed Street and go 4/10 mile to Route 28, at traffic light.

14. Cross Route 28 onto Pond Street and go 2.7 miles to five-way intersection and shopping center on right. You'll go along Great Pond and then pass the Blue Hills Cemetery on left.

55. South-Shore Scenic Circuit: Norwell–Pembroke–Hanson–Hanover

Number of miles: 17 (31 with Pembroke–Hanson extension)
Terrain: Gently rolling, with one long but gradual hill.
Food: Groceries and restaurants in the towns. McDonald's at end.
Start: McDonald's, Route 53 in Hanover, 1/2 mile south of Route 3. It's just south of Hanover Mall on the opposite side of the road.

The pond-studded, largely rural landscape just inland from the shoulder of land jutting east between Boston and Plymouth offers delightful bicycling. The region is fairly affluent, with large, spacious homes nestled among pine groves; impeccable gentleman farms with rustic barns and rambling Colonial-style farmhouses; and trim, cedar-shingled houses with peaked roofs. The area is far enough from Boston to be more rural than suburban, although new homes keep springing up near Route 3 in Pembroke. The North River, a tidal stream meandering through salt marshes, flows through the area.

The ride starts through the gracious town of Norwell, an affluent but unpretentious community filled with homes dating back to the early 1800s and even the 1700s. The Jacobs Farm, a mid-eighteenth-century farmhouse maintained by the Society for the Preservation of New England Antiquities, is just off the route and open to visitors (June through September on Tuesday, Thursday, and Sunday afternoons). From Norwell you'll proceed to Hanover, another fine old town with a beautiful town hall topped by a cupola, built in 1863, and a handsome brick library next to it. Most people know Hanover by its hideous commercial strip on Route 53, where the ride starts, but when you get away from this road the rest of the town is delightful.

The long ride heads farther south across the North River into a more rural area of pines and ponds. In Pembroke you'll skirt the edge of the cranberry-growing region farther south and then weave past a pleasing cluster of ponds into Hanson. Hanson is another attractive town with a marvelous Victorian town hall built in 1872 commanding the head of Wampatuck Pond. From Hanson you'll head to Hanover, where you'll pick up the route of the short ride.

Directions for the ride: 31 miles

1. Turn right out of parking lot onto Route 53 and go 1/10 mile to Mill Street on left.

2. Turn left on Mill Street. • *CAUTION* making this turn. Go 4/10 mile to end.

3. Turn left at end and go 3/10 mile to fork just beyond the bridge over Route 3 (South Street bears left).

4. Bear left on South Street and go 8/10 mile to end (Route 123). Here the ride turns right, but if you'd like to visit Jacobs Farm, turn left and go 1/2 mile to Jacobs Lane on right. The farm is on the corner.

5. Turn right on Route 123 and go 1/2 mile to Bowker Street on left.

6. Turn left on Bowker Street and go 1.2 miles to end (Grove Street).

7. Turn left on Grove Street and go 4/10 mile to fork (School Street bears right).

8. Bear right on School Street and go 1/2 mile to end (Mount Blue Street).

9. Turn right on Mount Blue Street and go 6/10 mile to fork (Lincoln Street bears right).

10. Bear left at fork (still Mount Blue Street) and go 1.2 miles to end (Old Oaken Bucket Road).

11. Turn right at end and go 3/10 mile to end (Central Street on left, Norwell Avenue on right).

12. Turn left on Central Street and go 9/10 mile to crossroads and stop sign (Route 123). On the far side of the intersection is a little green and a fine, traditional white church. This is the center of Norwell. Here the short ride goes straight and the long ride turns left.

13. Turn left on Route 123 and go 9/10 mile to Bridge Street on right.

14. Turn right on Bridge Street. After 1.1 miles, Highland Street bears left, but continue straight on Union Street. Go 2.6 miles to end (Route 139). You'll cross the North River over a metal-grate

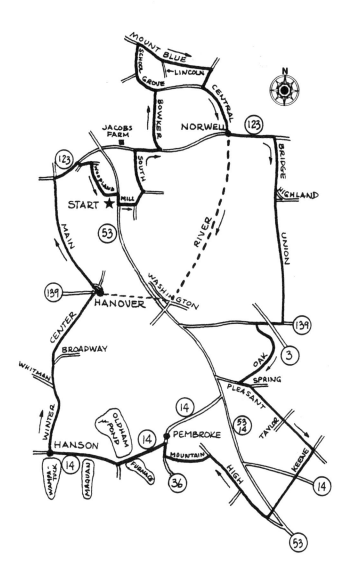

MOUNT BLUE

SCHOOL
GROVE

←LINCOLN

CENTRAL

BOWKER

JACOBS
FARM

NORWELL

(123)

123

SOUTH

HADLAND

MILL

START ★

53

BRIDGE

HIGHLAND

UNION

RIVER

MAIN

WASHINGTON

139

HANOVER

139

CENTER

BROADWAY

OAK

SPRING

3

WHITMAN

PLEASANT

WINTER

OLDHAM
POND

14

PEMBROKE

53
14

TAYLOR

HANSON

14

MAQUAN

FURNACE

MOUNTAIN

HIGH

KEENE

14

WAMPA-
TUCK

36

53

N

bridge shortly after turning on Bridge Street. • *CAUTION:* The bridge is extremely slippery when wet. If the road is wet, be sure to walk your bike across.

15. Turn right on Route 139 and go 4/10 mile to Oak Street on left, just after you go underneath Route 3. • *CAUTION:* Watch traffic bearing right onto Route 3.

16. Turn left on Oak Street and go 1.6 miles to end (merge right).

17. Turn sharply left at end and go 2/10 mile to fork where Spring Street bears left and Pleasant Street bears right.

18. Bear right on Pleasant Street. After 1 mile you'll come to a crossroads (Taylor Street). Continue straight 9/10 mile to another crossroads (Keene Street on right, Union Street on left).

19. Turn right on Keene Street and go 6/10 mile to crossroads and stop sign (Congress Street, Route 14).

20. Cross Route 14 and go 6/10 mile to another crossroads and stop sign (Route 53).

21. Cross Route 53 and go 1/10 mile to end (High Street).

22. Turn right on High Street and go 1.6 miles to Mountain Avenue on left, just after crossroads.

23. Turn left on Mountain Avenue and go 9/10 mile to end (Route 36).

24. Turn right on Route 36 and go 3/10 mile to Route 14 (Mattakeesett Street) on left.

25. Turn left on Route 14 and go 1.5 miles to fork where Route 14 bears right. You'll pass Furnace Pond on your left, and then Oldham Pond on your right. Just before the fork is a small beach on Oldham Pond. At the fork the ride bears right, but if you bear left and, within 100 yards, left again onto a small lane, you'll see an old brick pumping station where visitors are welcome.

26. Bear right on Route 14 and go 1.7 miles to Winter Street on the right, at bottom of hill opposite the Hanson town hall.

27. Turn right on Winter Street. After 1.2 miles Whitman Street bears left, but continue straight 3/10 mile to crossroads (East Washington Street).

28. Continue straight 6/10 mile to fork where Center Street bears left and Broadway bears right.

29. Bear left on Center Street. After 7/10 mile there's a crossroads and stop sign. Continue straight 1.1 miles to end (Route 139) in the center of Hanover.

30. Turn right on Route 139 and immediately left before the church on Center Street. Go 100 yards to stop sign. Notice the town hall and library across from the church.

31. Bear left at stop sign and go 2.4 miles to crossroads and stop sign (Webster Street, Route 123).

32. Turn right on Route 123 and go 6/10 mile to Woodland Drive on right.

33. Turn right on Woodland Drive. Just ahead the main road bears left. Bear left and go 1/10 mile to where the main road turns right; it's a dead end if you go straight.

34. Turn right. After 6/10 mile the main road curves sharply left. Continue on main road 1/4 mile to end (Route 53).

35. Turn right on Route 53. McDonald's is just ahead on right.

Directions for the ride: 17 miles

1. Follow directions for the long ride through number 12.

2. Cross Route 123 and go 3.6 miles to Washington Street, at crossroads and stop sign.

3. Turn right on Washington Street and go 1/10 mile to fork (Rockland Street bears left).

4. Bear left on Rockland Street and go 1/4 mile to traffic light (Route 53).

5. Cross Route 53 onto Route 139. • *CAUTION:* Busy intersection. Go 1.3 miles to Center Street on right, immediately after church. This is the center of Hanover. Notice the town hall opposite the church and the brick library next to the town hall.

6. Turn right on Center Street and go 100 yards to stop sign.

7. Follow directions for the long ride from number 31 to the end.

56. Canton–Stoughton–North Easton–Sharon

Number of miles: 16 (26 with North Easton extension)
Terrain: Gently rolling.
Food: Grocery stores and snack bars in the towns. Ground
    Round Restaurant at end.
Start: Ground Round, junction of Routes 1 and 27 in Walpole,
    just north of the Sharon line.

This ride takes you exploring a cluster of four pleasant suburban communities about twenty miles south of Boston and just northwest of Brockton. The landscape is semirural and semisuburban. The long ride goes through North Easton, a classic, nineteenth-century planned industrial community with a collection of magnificent stone buildings.

The ride heads first through a rural stretch of Sharon into Canton, where you'll see the Canton Viaduct, a graceful stone-arched railroad abutment crossing a small valley. It was built in 1834 and is a landmark of early railroad engineering. Built to accommodate the small, slow-moving early trains, it now supports the continuous traffic of the Boston to New York main line. Beyond the viaduct you'll bike past Reservoir Pond and head into Stoughton, a middle-class residential community, and then into Easton.

Shortly after you cross the town line you'll come to North Easton, a village of impressive elegance bearing the stamp of one man, Oliver Ames. Ames was a nineteenth-century industrialist who amassed his fortune making shovels, of all things, including most of the shovels used to build the railroads and mine the earth of the developing West. After making his millions, he decided to donate money to construct a village that his workers could be proud of, and so he hired the foremost architect of the day, H. H. Richardson, and the foremost landscape designer, Frederick Law Olmsted, to do the job. Coming into town, you'll pass the handsome stone railroad station with its graceful arched entryway. Then you'll see the Ames Memorial Hall, an imposing Victorian building. Next to this is the Ames Free Library, one of the most beautiful in the state, a fine stone edifice with a clock tower and an ornate, wood-paneled inte-

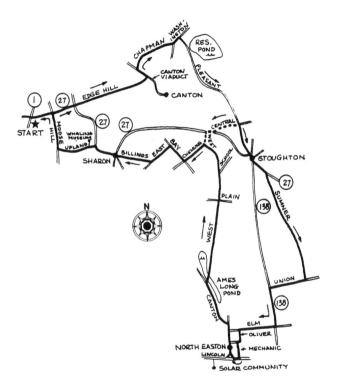

START ★

CHAPMAN

WASH-INGTON

RES. POND

CANTON VIADUCT

PLEASANT

EDGE HILL

CANTON

HILL

HOOSE

WHALING MUSEUM

UPLAND

BILLINGS   EAST   BAY

CHERUNS

SCHOOL

CENTRAL

STOUGHTON

SHARON

N

PLAIN

WEST

138

SUMNER

27

AMES LONG POND

UNION

CANTON

138

ELM

OLIVER

NORTH EASTON

MECHANIC

LINCOLN

SOLAR COMMUNITY

rior. It was built in 1883. Just past the library is an ornate stone church with a tall, slender spire. In the middle of the town's main intersection is a small, rocky terraced park, complete with a stone archway, called the Rockery. It was designed by Olmsted in 1879.

Leaving North Easton, you can go 1/2 mile off the route to visit the largest solar-heated community in New England. The route goes along lovely Ames Long Pond (it seems everything in town is named Ames) and proceeds into the center of Sharon, a pleasant upper-middle-class community with lots of rural land. Just outside town is the Kendall Whaling Museum, a one-man collection of whaling objects and art, unfortunately open only on weekday afternoons. The homestretch brings you past an Audubon sanctuary and the fire tower on top of 530-foot Moose Hill, the highest point in southeastern Massachusetts outside of the Blue Hills.

Directions for the ride: 26 miles

1. Turn right (east) out of parking lot onto Route 27 and go 1 mile to crossroads and stop sign where Route 27 turns right.

2. Go straight at crossroads 2.7 miles to end. At the end, the Canton Viaduct is on your right.

3. Turn left at end and go 1/4 mile to fork where Chapman Street bears right. As soon as you turn, there's a little dam on the right, with the stream flowing from beneath the viaduct.

4. Bear right on Chapman Street and go 1.2 miles to end (Washington Street). If you turn right just after the railroad bridge and go 2/10 mile, you'll come to the unusually fine railroad station.

5. Turn left on Washington Street and go 3/10 mile to Pleasant Street on right. Here the ride turns right, but if you go straight 200 yards you'll come to a beautiful old church and school on the left.

6. Turn right on Pleasant Street and go 4 miles to stop sign (Route 138) in the center of Stoughton. You'll go through two traffic lights about a mile before the stop sign. The short ride turns right at the second light on Central Street.

7. Go straight at stop sign onto Route 138 for 1/10 mile to fork where Route 138 bears right and Route 27 bears left.

8. Bear left on Route 27 and go 3/10 mile to Sumner Street, which bears right (a sign may say "H" for hospital).

9. Bear right on Sumner Street and go 2.6 miles to end.

10. Turn right at end and go 8/10 mile to end (Route 138).

11. Turn left on Route 138 and go 7/10 mile to Elm Street. It's a crossroads with a cemetery on the far right-hand corner.

12. Turn right on Elm Street and go 8/10 mile to Oliver Street on left. You'll pass on your left an arched stone gatehouse designed by H. H. Richardson.

13. Turn left on Oliver Street and go 1/10 mile to Mechanic Street on left.

14. Turn left on Mechanic Street and go 3/10 mile to end. You'll pass the railroad station, built in 1881, on your right, now the headquarters of the Easton Historical Society. Behind the station are the long stone buildings of the Ames shovel factory, recently recycled into offices.

15. Turn right at end. Just ahead is a fork. The little terraced park in the middle of the fork is the Rockery. Here the ride bears right, but if you go straight onto Lincoln Street for a 1/2 mile and turn left on Mahoney Street, you'll come to the solar condominiums.

16. Bear right at fork and go 4/10 mile to Canton Street, which bears left. You'll pass the Memorial Hall, the library, and the stone church on the left. The library is worth going to if it's open.

17. Bear left on Canton Street and go 1.3 miles to West Street, which bears right. You'll go along Ames Long Pond.

18. Bear right on West Street, crossing the lake over a causeway, and go 1.7 miles to crossroads and stop sign (Plain Street).

19. Go straight at crossroads. After 7/10 mile School Street (unmarked) bears right, but go straight on West Street 8/10 mile to Chemung Street, which bears left uphill at a wooded traffic island.

20. Bear left on Chemung Street and go 6/10 mile to crossroads and stop sign (Bay Road).

21. Turn right at crossroads and go 4/10 mile to East Street on left. There's a fantastic ice cream place at the intersection.

22. Turn left on East Street and go 7/10 mile to Billings Street, which bears right.

23. Bear right on Billings Street and go 1 mile to crossroads in the center of Sharon at traffic light (Route 27 goes straight and right). Notice the fine white church on the far side of the intersection.

24. Go straight at crossroads onto Route 27. After 1/2 mile the road curves sharply right at large traffic island with a house on it.

25. At the far end of the traffic island, make a U-turn to the left, then immediately bear right downhill on Upland Road, a narrow lane (sign may say Kendall Whaling Museum). Go 2/10 mile to where Upland Road curves sharply left and Everett Road turns right. Here the ride bears left, but if you turn right for 200 yards you'll come to the Whaling Museum.

26. Bear left, staying on Upland Road, and go 9/10 mile to end. Here the ride turns right, but the entrance to the Moose Hill Audubon Sanctuary is 50 feet to your left.

27. Turn right at end and go 1.4 miles to end (Route 27). Just after you turn right, a narrow lane on the left leads 1/2 mile to the fire tower on top of Moose Hill. Depending on the friendliness of the ranger on duty, you may or may not gain access to the tower.

28. Turn left on Route 27 and go 4/10 mile to Ground Round on left.

Directions for the ride: 16 miles

1. Follow directions for the long ride through number 5.

2. Turn right on Pleasant Street and go 3.3 miles to Central Street, at the second traffic light (sign may say Norman Everett Square).

3. Turn right on Central Street and go 1 mile to West Street, on left immediately after the Stoughton Water Works, an ornate building dated 1892.

4. Turn left on West Street and go 3/10 mile to fork (Chemung Street, unmarked, bears right uphill).

5. Bear right on Chemung Street and go 6/10 mile to crossroads and stop sign (Bay Road).

6. Follow directions for the long ride from number 21 to the end.

57. Sharon–Easton–Norton–Mansfield–Foxboro

Number of miles: 15 (32 with Easton-Norton-Foxboro extension)
Terrain: Flat.
Food: None on the short ride. Grocery and snack bar in
  Mansfield. Snack bar at end.
Start: Shaw's Plaza, South Main Street, Sharon, just east of Route
  95 at the South Main Street–Mechanic Street exit (exit 8).

On this ride you'll explore a delightfully rural, lake-dotted area ten miles west of Brockton. Flat terrain, smooth secondary roads, and a spin along the shore of Massapoag Lake in Sharon make for relaxed pedaling. The longer ride passes the gracious old campus of Wheaton College in Norton.

The ride starts from Sharon, an attractive, upper-middle-class community. It has a few housing developments, but most of the town is still rural. The focal point of the community is refreshingly unspoiled Massapoag Lake, most of its shoreline graced by handsome older homes. You'll follow the lakeshore for half its perimeter and then head through woods and farmlands into Easton. At the town line you'll pass Borderlands State Park, an idyllic expanse of meadows and woodland surrounding Leach Pond, with paths looping around its shore. The park headquarters is a magnificent stone mansion that formerly belonged to the Ames family, whose legacy is concentrated in nearby North Easton.

The long ride heads farther south through prosperous farmlands into Norton, one of the most pleasantly rural towns within commuting distance of Boston. In the center of town is Wheaton College, a small, high-quality women's school with a traditional, tree-shaded campus of stately ivy-covered buildings. At the center of the campus is a perfect little pond. Just north of the campus is the Norton Reservoir, another good-sized lake that you'll skirt briefly. The return to Sharon passes through the rural eastern edges of Mansfield and Foxboro.

Directions for the ride: 32 miles

1. Turn right (northeast) out of parking lot and go 6/10 mile to Wolomolopoag Street on your right.

2. Turn right on Wolomolopoag Street and go 1.5 miles to end (East Foxboro Street).

3. Turn left at end and go 1.5 miles to fork where one road bears left and Beach Street goes straight.

4. Continue straight at fork. You'll immediately see Massapoag Lake on your right. Go 9/10 mile to end.

5. Turn right at end. Just ahead is a little rotary. Continue straight, following the lake, for 4.5 miles to crossroads and stop sign (Rockland Street on left). Here the short ride turns right and the long ride goes straight. The entrance to Borderlands State Park is 1 mile before the crossroads, marked by an inconspicuous wooden sign on left. The Ames mansion is just beyond the entrance.

6. Go straight at crossroads 1.3 miles to end.

7. Turn right at end and go 1.2 miles to South Street on left. The main road curves sharply right at the intersection.

8. Turn left on South Street and go 2/10 mile to crossroads and stop sign (Foundry Street, Route 106). • *CAUTION:* South Street is bumpy.

9. Cross Route 106 and go 3/10 mile to end.

10. Turn left at end and go 3/10 mile to end (Bay Street).

11. Turn right on Bay Street and go 4.8 miles to Myles Standish Industrial Park Road on right, just after the Route 495 overpass. You'll pass Winneconnet Pond on your right about a mile before the intersection.

12. Turn right on Myles Standish Industrial Park Road and go 3/10 mile to first right, North Boundary Road. Turn right and go 2.2 miles to crossroads and stop sign (Plain Street).

13. Turn left at crossroads and go 8/10 mile to end (Pine Street).

14. Turn right at end and go 1/2 mile to Route 123. Just before Route 123, Wheaton College is on your left. The campus is worth visiting.

15. Cross Route 123 onto Elm Street and go 8/10 mile to end (Reservoir Street).

16. Turn right on Reservoir Street. You'll immediately see the Norton Reservoir on your left. Go 1/2 mile to Cobb Street, which bears right. There's a snack bar on the far side of the intersection.

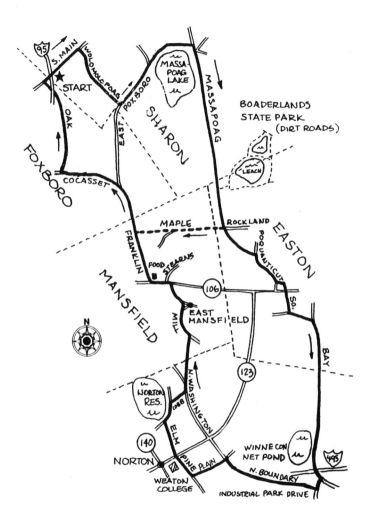

START

MASSA-POAG LAKE

BOADERLANDS STATE PARK (DIRT ROADS)

LEACH

SHARON

MASSAPOAG

EASTON

MAPLE   ROCKLAND

POQUANTICUT

COCASSET

FOXBORO

OAK

S. MAIN

WOLOMOLC POAG

EAST FOXBORO

FRANKLIN

FOOD   STEARNS

106

MILL

EAST MANSFIELD

MANSFIELD

N

So.

BAY

123

N. WASHINGTON

NORTON RES.

LONB

ELM

PINE PLAIN

140

NORTON

WEATON COLLEGE

WINNE CON NET POND

N. BOUNDARY

INDUSTRIAL PARK DRIVE

495

17. Bear right on Cobb Street and go 1/2 mile to end.

18. Turn left at end and go 3/10 mile to fork shortly after the bridge over Route 495.

19. Bear right at fork and go 1.4 miles to end (Mill Street).

20. Turn left on Mill Street. After 1/2 mile, at a little green, Cherry Street turns right, but bear left, staying on the main road. Just ahead is a stop sign.

21. Bear left at stop sign and go 1/2 mile to end (Route 106).

22. Turn left on Route 106 and go 4/10 mile to Franklin Street on right, at traffic light. There's a grocery on the right just before the corner.

23. Turn right on Franklin Street and go 2.1 miles to fork where Cocasset Street bears left and East Street bears right.

24. Bear left on Cocasset Street and go 1 mile to Oak Street on right, at blinking light.

25. Turn right on Oak Street and go 2.1 miles to end.

26. Turn right at end and go 1/2 mile to shopping center on right.

Directions for the ride: 15 miles

1. Follow the directions for the long ride through number 5.

2. Turn right at crossroads and go 1.6 miles to crossroads and stop sign (Franklin Street).

3. Turn right on Franklin Street and go 9/10 mile to fork where Cocasset Street bears left and East Street bears right.

4. Follow directions for the long ride from number 24 to the end.

58. North Attleboro–Plainville–Foxboro–Mansfield

Number of miles: 15 (25 with Plainville–Foxboro extension)
Terrain: Gently rolling, with one short hill.
Food: McDonald's in Plainville. Grocery and restaurant in
   Foxboro. Country store in Mansfield. Snack bar at end.
Start: Triboro Plaza, Toner Boulevard in North Attleboro, just west
   of Route 95. From Route 95, take the Route 152 exit (exit 5).
   Turn right at end of exit ramp. Plaza is just ahead on right.

On this ride we explore the pleasantly rural, lake-dotted countryside just north of Attleboro, midway between Boston and Providence. Immediately heading into pleasant countryside, you'll pass
the North Attleboro National Fish Hatchery, a fascinating spot to
visit. Unfortunately it's open only weekdays from 8 a.m. to 3:30 p.m.
From here you'll go along the shores of three unspoiled ponds in
quick succession—Greenwood Lake, Turnpike Lake, and Lake
Mirimichi. The latter two are in Plainville, a pleasant rural town
consisting mainly of woods, farmland, and orchards. The stretch
from Lake Mirimichi to Foxboro brings you along winding, narrow
lanes bobbing up and down little rises through dense forest. Foxboro is an attractive town with two fine churches and a well-kept
green forming a central square. A landmark in the town is a small,
ornate, churchlike building that was built as a Civil War memorial
and for many years served as the town library. From Foxboro, the
northern tip of the ride, you'll head south past well-kept small farms
and over a ridge into Mansfield, a compact mill town surrounded
by rural countryside. You won't go into the center of town. From
here it's a short ride back to the start past Greenwood Lake.

Directions for the ride: 25 miles
   1. Turn left out of the *east* side of the parking lot onto John
Dietsch Road, paralleling Route 95 on your right, and go 1.2 miles
to wide crossroads (Larsen Way). A sign at the intersection may
point left to Landry Avenue.
   2. Turn left on Larsen Way for 3/10 mile to end (Landry Avenue), and then right for 7/10 mile to end (Route 152). Now turn

right on Route 152 for 6/10 mile to Bungay Road on left, at a large traffic island (sign may say to National Fish Hatchery).

3. Turn sharp left on Bungay Road and go 1/2 mile to end (Mansfield Road on left). You'll pass the North Attleboro National Fish Hatchery on your left, worth visiting if it's open. Every year its hours are reduced.

4. Turn left on Mansfield Road and go 9/10 mile to Plain Street on the left.

5. Turn left on Plain Street and go 1.7 miles to end (Kelley Boulevard, Route 152). You'll pass Greenwood Lake on your left.

6. Turn right on Route 152 and go 2/10 mile to traffic light (Route 106). Here the short ride turns right and the long ride turns left.

7. Turn left on Route 106 and go 4/10 mile to crossroads (George Street).

8. Turn right at crossroads and go 1/2 mile to Route 1, at stop sign.

9. Turn right on Route 1 and go 4/10 mile to Shepard Street, which bears right.

10. Bear right on Shepard Street, following the shore of Turnpike Lake, and go 4/10 mile to end (Route 152).

11. Turn left on Route 152 and go 4/10 mile to Mirimichi Street on right.

12. Turn right on Mirimichi Street. After 4/10 mile the main road curves sharply to the right and a dead-end road goes straight. Bear right and go 1.9 miles to end. You'll go across Lake Mirimichi.

13. Turn left at end and go 3/10 mile to Mill Street on right.

14. Turn right on Mill Street and go 1.3 miles to fork where Prospect Street bears left.

15. Bear left on Prospect Street and go 8/10 mile to end.

16. Turn right at end and go 9/10 mile to end (Route 140).

17. Turn right on Route 140. Just ahead you'll come to the green on your left in the center of Foxboro. Stay on Route 140 for 1/10 mile to end of green. When you get there, notice the small, stone, churchlike Civil War memorial in front of you.

18. Turn right at end of green on South Street and go 2.3 miles to crossroads where North Grove Street bears left uphill.

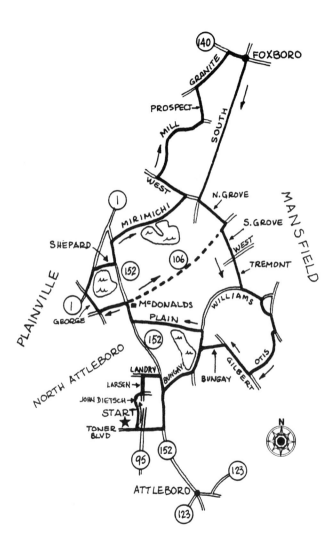

FOXBORO

140

GRANITE

PROSPECT

SOUTH

MILL

WEST

N. GROVE

MANSFIELD

MIRIMICHI

S. GROVE

1

SHEPARD

106

WEST

152

TREMONT

PLAINVILLE

1

McDONALDS

WILLIAMS

GEORGE

PLAIN

152

OTIS

NORTH ATTLEBORO

BUNGAY

GILBERT

LANDRY

LARSEN

BUNGAY

JOHN DIETSCH

START

TONER
BLVD

N

95

152

123

ATTLEBORO

123

333

19. Bear left at crossroads on North Grove Street and go 6/10 mile to end, up a tough hill. At the top, glance behind you for a nice view.

20. Turn right at end and go 1/10 mile to South Grove Street on left, immediately after the bridge over Route 495.

21. Turn left on South Grove Street and go 6/10 mile to crossroads and stop sign.

22. Go straight at crossroads onto Tremont Street 9/10 mile to end (merge left at stop sign).

23. Bear left at end and go 4/10 mile to end.

24. Bear right at end and go 3/10 mile to end.

25. Turn right at end. Just ahead, Otis Street turns right just before a railroad overpass.

26. Turn right on Otis Street and go 1.2 miles to end. There's a country store on your left at the beginning.

27. Turn right at end and go 9/10 mile to fork where Bungay Road bears left.

28. Bear left at fork and go 3/10 mile to end.

29. Turn left at end and go 6/10 mile to Bungay Road on right. (There are two Bungay Roads, one in Mansfield and one in North Attleboro.)

30. Turn right on Bungay Road and go 1/2 mile to end (Route 152).

31. Bear left on Route 152 and go 1.3 miles to traffic light (sign may say to Route 95).

32. Turn right at light and go 1/2 mile back to Triboro Plaza on right.

Directions for the ride: 15 miles

1. Follow directions for the long ride through number 6.

2. Turn right at traffic light on Route 106 and go 2.5 miles to South Grove Street on right, just before the bridge over Route 495.

3. Turn right on South Grove Street and go 6/10 mile to crossroads and stop sign.

4. Follow directions for the long ride from number 22 to the end.

59. Norton–Taunton

Number of miles: 13 (28 with Taunton extension)
Terrain: Flat.
Road surface: 4/10 mile of hard-packed dirt road near the
    beginning.
Food: Country store in Norton. Country store in North Rehoboth.
Start: Fernandes Supermarket, Route 123 in Norton, just west of
    Route 140.

Midway between Taunton and Attleboro, about thirty miles south of
Boston, is a very enjoyable area for biking. The terrain is nearly
level, with an extensive network of little-traveled country roads
looping past ponds and prosperous farmland. The region is far
enough from Boston to be completely rural, with no infiltration of
suburban development.

The ride starts from Norton, one of the most pleasantly rural
towns within commuting distance of Boston, and a graceful New
England classic. The centerpiece of the community is Wheaton College, a high-quality women's school with a lovely campus graced by
elegant, ivy-covered wood and brick buildings. A small pond with a
footbridge across it adds to the beauty of the setting. Adjacent to
the campus is a stately white church and a handsome brick turn-of-
the-century library.

Just north of town you'll ride along most of the perimeter of the
Norton Reservoir. You'll pass the Norton Flea Market, among the
largest in New England, and the Great Woods Performing Arts Center, which is the summer home of the Pittsburgh Symphony Or-
chestra and the scene of many popular concerts. Just ahead you'll
go through the small lakeside community of Norton Grove. After a
few miles of woods and farmland you pass Winneconnet Pond,
Watson Pond, and Lake Sabbatia in quick succession. Across from
the latter pond is the Paul A. Dever School, a state institution for
children who have mental disabilities and a port of embarkation for
troops during World War II. Watson Pond and Lake Sabbatia are just
over the town line in Taunton, a city of 40,000 covering a wide area
in the southeastern part of the state. The city, best known for the

manufacture of fine silver products, is rural around its outer edges. You'll bike through the fringe of the built-up area and then quickly get back into the undeveloped western edge of the city. The return run to Norton brings you through a fine mixture of woods, farmland, and old wooden houses, with a spin through Wheaton College at the end.

Directions for the ride: 28 miles

1. Turn left (east) out of the parking lot onto Route 123 and go 2/10 mile to Route 140 on left. Just beyond the intersection is Wheaton College, which you'll go through at the end of the ride.

2. Turn left on Route 140 and go 2.7 miles to Reservoir Street on right, just before the bridge over Route 495. As soon as you turn left on Route 140, notice the handsome brick library on your left. Just past the Norton Reservoir you pass the Norton Flea Market. Just before the intersection you'll pass the Great Woods Performing Arts Center on your left.

3. Turn right on Reservoir Street and go 1.4 miles to Cobb Street on left (snack bar at intersection). Continue straight for 1/2 mile to Elm Street on left. There is a store at the intersection.

4. Turn left on Elm Street and go 4/10 mile to Cross Street on your left, immediately after a silver factory.

5. Turn left on Cross Street and go 7/10 mile to end. The last 4/10 mile is dirt, but it's hard-packed and should be rideable. A little dam is on the left just past the factory.

6. Turn left at end and go 4/10 mile to Newcomb Street on right.

7. Turn right on Newcomb Street and go 1.1 miles to crossroads (dirt road if you go straight).

8. Turn right at crossroads and go 6/10 mile to end (Route 123).

9. Turn right on Route 123 and go 6/10 mile to Leonard Street on left, just before the bridge over Route 495.

10. Turn left on Leonard Street and go 1 mile to end. At the end the short ride turns right and the long ride turns left.

11. Turn left at end. Just ahead, Burt Street is on your left, but curve right, staying on the main road. Continue 6/10 mile to end (Bay Road).

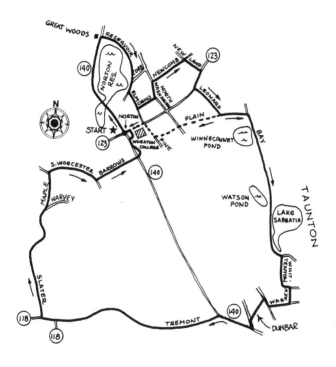

GREAT WOODS

RESERVOIR

140

NORTON RES.

COBB

ELM

NEW

123

NEWCOMB

LAND

NORTH WASHINGTON

LEONARD

CROSS

N

NORTON

PLAIN

START ★

123

WHEATON COLLEGE

PINE

WINNECONNET POND

BAY

S. WORCESTER

BARROWS

140

MAPLE

HARVEY

WATSON POND

TAUNTON

LAKE SABBATIA

SLATER

WHIT-TENTON TPKE.

118

TREMONT

140

WASH

DUNBAR

118

12. Turn right on Bay Road and go 3.5 miles to a road that bears right at the end of a pond on your left. The main road curves sharply left at the intersection over a small bridge. A sign at the intersection may say Benjamin's. On this stretch you'll pass Winneconnet Pond, Watson Pond, and finally Sabbatia Lake. There's a small state park with a beach at Watson Pond. The Dever State School is on your right across from Sabbatia Lake.

13. Bear right on this road and go 8/10 mile to fork at a traffic island (the road bearing left goes over a little bridge).

14. Bear right at fork and go 3/10 mile to end (Warren Street).

15. Turn right on Warren Street and go 6/10 mile to end.

16. Turn right at end and go 1/10 mile to where the main road turns left onto Dunbar Street.

17. Turn left on Dunbar Street and go 1/2 mile to end.

18. Turn left at end and go 1/10 mile to end (Route 140).
• *CAUTION:* Bumpy road.

19. Turn right on Route 140 and go 7/10 mile to Tremont Street, which bears left (sign may say LaSallette).

20. Bear left on Tremont Street. After 3/10 mile, Worcester Street bears right, but curve left, staying on Tremont Street. Continue 4.3 miles until you come to Route 118, which turns left and also goes straight ahead at the intersection. There's a country store on your left shortly before Route 118.

21. Continue straight onto Route 118 for 1/4 mile to your first right.

22. Turn right on this road and stay on the main road 2.3 miles to fork where Harvey Street bears right and Maple Street bears left. Bear left for 8/10 mile to fork immediately after railroad tracks. Notice the unusual Gothic-style wooden building in the middle of the fork.

23. Bear right at fork and go 9/10 mile to Barrows Street on left, just before railroad tracks.

24. Turn left on Barrows Street and go 1.2 miles to wide crossroads and stop sign (Route 140).

25. Cross Route 140 and go 6/10 mile to end (Route 140 again).

26. Turn right on Route 140 and go 2/10 mile to Howard Street on right.

27. Turn right on Howard Street. This is a one-way street in the opposite direction; walk your bike. Just ahead the road turns 90 degrees left. The main campus of Wheaton College is on your right, with the pond about 200 yards in. Continue along Howard Street 1/10 mile to end (Route 123) or walk across the campus to Route 123.

28. Turn left on Route 123 and go 3/10 mile to supermarket on right.

Directions for the ride: 13 miles

1. Follow directions for the long ride through number 10.

2. Turn right at end of Leonard Street and go 1.2 miles to crossroads and stop sign (South Washington Street).

3. Go straight at crossroads 8/10 mile to end (Pine Street).

4. Turn right on Pine Street and go 1/2 mile to crossroads and stop sign (Route 123).

5. Turn left on Route 123. As soon as you turn left, Wheaton College is on your left. Go 1/2 mile to supermarket on right.

60. The Bridgewater Ride: West Bridgewater–East Bridgewater–North Middleboro–Bridgewater

Number of miles: 21 (29 with North Middleboro extension)
Terrain: Gently rolling, with one hill.
Food: Grocery stores or restaurants in the towns.
Start: Center Shopping Plaza, junction of Routes 28 and 106, West Bridgewater, 2 miles east of Route 24.

The three Bridgewaters, just south of Brockton and about thirty miles south of Boston, mark the transition between suburbia to the north and an extensive rural area to the southeast, encompassing nearly all the land down to the Cape Cod Canal and New Bedford. As you head south and southeast from Brockton, the landscape acquires characteristics unique to the southeastern portion of the state—sandy soil, scrub pine, cranberry bogs, generally flat and often swampy terrain, and cedar-shingled houses with peaked roofs. This landscape provides some of the most scenic and easiest bicycling in the state on a superb network of well-maintained country lanes and secondary roads. Most of southeastern Massachusetts has a tidy, prosperous look that is subtly pleasing. This ride is the closest to Boston that offers some of the ambience of this section of the state.

The ride starts from West Bridgewater, a pleasant community with some tract housing toward the Brockton line (which you won't go through) and lots of undeveloped land. You'll quickly cross into East Bridgewater, which is somewhat more rural. The center of town is beautiful, if you can somehow ignore the broad slash of Route 18 that bisects it. The large green is framed by an unusually graceful white church and a handsome old schoolhouse. Heading east of town you'll go through broad farms and past unspoiled Robbins Pond. You'll now start seeing cranberry bogs as you pass through the eastern edge of Halifax, one of the most thoroughly rural towns within commuting distance of Boston, and then into Bridgewater itself, which lies south of its East and West companions. The town center is a New England classic, with a small green smack in the middle of Route 18, framed by a compact row of old

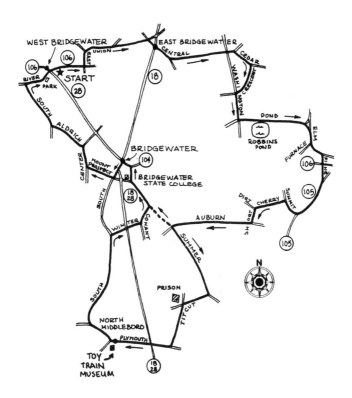

business buildings, a fine church, and an ornate Victorian brick library built in 1881. Adjoining the center of town is the campus of Bridgewater State College, the earliest state college in Massachusetts, with attractive red-brick buildings. From Bridgewater it's not far back to West Bridgewater on back roads. Just before the end you'll pass a beautiful park along the Town River, originally the site of a factory during the 1800s.

The long ride heads farther south through broad sweeps of farmland bordered by stately rows of shade trees. Looming in the distance on a hilltop is the Bridgewater Correctional Institution, a grim, turreted monstrosity resembling a medieval fortress, strangely out of place in this pastoral setting. You'll go right by the prison and then follow the Taunton River into North Middleboro, a charming, unspoiled village. Its small green is framed by a graceful yellow wooden church with a clock tower, a white, pillared mansion, and a classic old schoolhouse. North Middleboro is also home to the wonderful A&D Toy Train Museum, which has a large collection of toy trains in operating order from all over the world. From here you'll have a fine run past farms and meadows to Bridgewater, where you'll pick up the route of the short ride.

Directions for the ride: 29 miles

1. Turn right out of parking lot onto Route 106, heading east, and go 9/10 mile to crossroads (East Street).

2. Turn left on East Street and go 4/10 mile to fork (Union Street bears right).

3. Bear right on Union Street. After 1/2 mile, North Central Street bears left, but continue straight 1 mile to crossroads and stop sign (Central Street).

4. Turn right at crossroads. Just ahead is a traffic light (Route 18). Cross Route 18 and go 3/10 mile to fork at the East Bridgewater town green.

5. Bear left at fork (still Central Street) and stay on the main road 1.8 miles to crossroads and traffic light.

6. Go straight at light 2/10 mile to fork (Central Street bears left; Cedar Street bears right).

7. Bear right on Cedar Street and go 1/2 mile to Crescent Street on right.

8. Turn right on Crescent Street and go 1 mile to crossroads and stop sign (Washington Street). Here is an unfortunate example of suburban development—twenty years ago open farmland, now an ugly strip of crackerbox houses. Fortunately, suburbia ends here, at least for now.

9. Turn left at crossroads and go 8/10 mile to another crossroads (Pond Street).

10. Turn left on Pond Street and go 1.8 miles to fork, staying on the main road. It's after Hudson Street on left. You'll pass Robbins Pond.

11. Bear right at fork and go 1/2 mile to another fork (Furnace Street bears right).

12. Bear left at fork and go 4/10 mile to Pine Street, which bears right. It's your second right.

13. Bear right on Pine Street. After 100 yards you'll cross Route 106. Continue straight 1/2 mile to end (merge to right into Route 105).

14. Bear right on Route 105 and go 1.2 miles to fork (Summit Street bears right).

15. Bear right on Summit Street, which immediately curves sharply right. Continue 4/10 mile to end (merge right).

16. Bear right at end and go 2/10 mile to Cherry Street on left.

17. Turn left on Cherry Street and go 9/10 mile to fork, where Short Street bears left and a dirt road bears right.

18. Bear left on Short Street and go 3/10 mile to end (Auburn Street).

19. Bear right on Auburn Street. After 1.5 miles, Laurel Street turns right, but curve left on the main road. Continue 2/10 mile to crossroads and stop sign. Here the short ride turns right and the long ride turns left.

20. Turn left at crossroads and go 1.8 miles to Titicut Street on right. You'll see the prison on your right.

21. Turn right on Titicut Street and go 6/10 mile to crossroads immediately before the prison.

22. Bear left at crossroads (still Titicut Street) and go 1 mile to end. You'll cross the Taunton River shortly before the end.

23. Turn right at end and go 3/10 mile to traffic light (Routes

28 and 18).

24. Go straight at light 8/10 mile to fork at the North Middleboro green where the main road bears right. The A&D Toy Train Museum is on your left just before the fork. Notice the fine old buildings in the graceful village.

25. Bear right at fork and go 6/10 mile to another fork just after you cross the Taunton River (South Street bears right).

26. Bear right on South Street and go 2.3 miles to another fork (Winter Street bears right).

27. Bear right on Winter Street and go 4/10 mile to Route 18, at stop sign.

28. Cross Route 18 and go 4/10 mile to end.

29. Turn left at end and go 1/2 mile to end (merge left at bottom of hill).

30. Bear left at end and go 9/10 mile to fork (Grove Street bears left). Bridgewater State College is in front of you.

31. Bear right at fork and go 2/10 mile to end (Route 104).

32. Turn left on Route 104 and go 2/10 mile to traffic light (Routes 18, 28, and 104).

33. Turn left at light. This is the center of Bridgewater. Just ahead, Routes 28 and 18 bear left, but continue straight on Route 104 for 1/10 mile to crossroads (Grove Street on left, Mount Prospect Street on right). Notice the old library on right.

34. Turn right on Mount Prospect Street and go 1/2 mile to end.

35. Turn right at end and go 4/10 mile to Aldrich Road on left, just before a church on left.

36. Turn left on Aldrich Road. After 7/10 mile the main road bears left and Bedford Street turns right. Bear left and go 1/10 mile to end.

37. Turn right at end and go 1 mile to end, immediately after a little bridge.

38. Turn right at end. After 2/10 mile, the road curves sharply left and there's a delightful riverfront park on your right. Continue 2/10 mile to Route 28. The shopping center is on the far side of Route 28.

Directions for the ride: 21 miles

    1. Follow directions for the long ride through number 19.

    2. Turn right at crossroads and stop sign. Go 1.5 miles to fork where Grove Street bears left. In front of you is Bridgewater State College.

    3. Follow directions for the long ride from number 31 to the end.

61. Middleboro–Halifax

Number of miles: 16 (25 with Halifax loop)
Terrain: Flat.
Food: Grocery store in Halifax.
Start: Oliver Mill Park, Route 44 in Middleboro, 3 miles east of
Route 25.

On this ride you explore the lakes and broad expanses of farmland
midway between Boston and the Cape Cod Canal and about ten
miles inland from the coast. The area is far enough from Boston,
about thirty-five miles, to be completely rural. Very flat terrain, good
secondary roads without much traffic, and fine rural scenery make
bicycling in this region a pleasure. A section of the ride parallels
Great Cedar Swamp, an extensive wetland bordered by large, prosperous farms.

The ride starts from the outskirts of Middleboro at Oliver Mill
Park, site of an industrial enterprise dating back to the 1700s. It
included a gristmill, sawmill, forge, and other operations. The area
has recently been landscaped and the old stone channel for the
Nemasket River restored. In the early spring, this is a prime spot to
watch the annual herring run, when millions of the fish swim up
the rivers to their spawning grounds. Shortly after you leave the
park you'll pass a magnificent white church on a splendid green in
the middle of nowhere. You'll now head toward Halifax, passing a
couple of cranberry bogs and skirting Great Cedar Swamp on
pretty, narrow lanes. Halifax is one of the most rural communities
within commuting distance of Boston, consisting primarily of
woods, cranberry bogs, swampland, and Monponsett Pond. The
town center is a gem, with a fine, white, pillared town hall and old
schoolhouse. Just north of town you'll thread across Monponsett
Pond along a causeway splitting the lake in half. From here you'll
make a loop, passing unspoiled Stetson Pond, going along the far
side of Monponsett Pond, and arriving back in Halifax. The return
trip to Middleboro goes along Route 105, one of the best numbered
routes in the state for biking. This section is narrow, well surfaced,
almost traffic-free, and passes through magnificent open farmland.

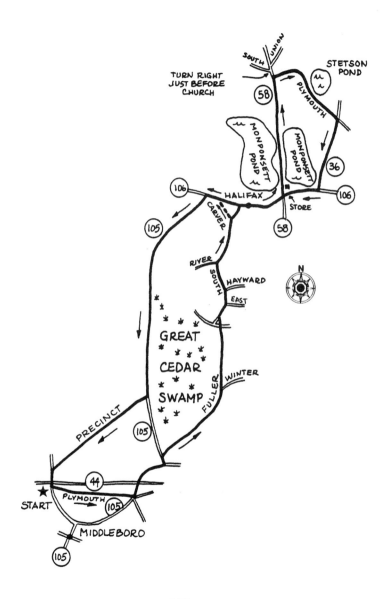

Directions for the ride: 25 miles

1. From the parking lot, go straight ahead opposite the entrance onto Plymouth Street, which parallels Route 44. Go 1.4 miles to stop sign at a five-way intersection (Route 105).

2. Turn left on Route 105 and go 2/10 mile to traffic light (Route 44), passing a classic white church on left.

3. Cross Route 44 and go 7/10 mile to where Route 105 turns left.

4. Turn left, staying on Route 105, and go 2/10 mile to Fuller Street, which bears right.

5. Bear right on Fuller Street and go 1.5 miles to fork where Winter Street bears right.

6. Bear left at fork (still Fuller Street). After 1.4 miles you'll come to a crossroads. Continue straight 4/10 mile to fork (East Street bears right; South Street bears left).

7. Bear left on South Street and go 3/10 mile to where Hayward Street bears right and the main road curves left.

8. Bear left on main road and go 7/10 mile to where River Street turns left and the main road curves right.

9. Bear right on main road and go 1 mile to fork where Carver Street bears left and South Street bears right. Here the short ride bears left and the long ride bears right.

10. Bear right on South Street and go 3/10 mile to end (Route 106).

11. Turn right on Route 106 and go 1 mile to traffic light (Route 58). Notice the pillared town hall on left just after you get on Route 106.

12. Turn left on Route 58 and go 2.7 miles to a road on right immediately before an unattractive modern church. You'll cross Monponsett Pond. If you come to the fork where Route 58 bears left and Union Street bears right, you've gone 100 yards too far.

13. Turn right just before church and go 1.4 miles to crossroads and stop sign (Route 36). You'll pass Stetson Pond on left.

14. Turn right on Route 36 and go 1.7 miles to end (Route 106).

15. Turn right on Route 106 and go 7/10 mile to traffic light (Route 58).

16. Cross Route 58 and go 1.6 miles to Route 105 (Thompson Street) on left.

17. Turn left on Route 105. After 3 miles you'll come to a crossroads (River Street). Continue straight 2.1 miles to Precinct Street on right.

18. Turn right on Precinct Street and go 2 miles to end.

19. Turn left at end and go 2/10 mile to traffic light (Route 44). The park is on the far side of the intersection.

Directions for the ride: 16 miles

1. Follow directions for the long ride through number 9.

2. Bear left on Carver Street and go 4/10 mile to end (Route 106).

3. Bear left on Route 106 and go 2/10 mile to Route 105 (Thompson Street) on left.

4. Follow directions for the long ride from number 17 to the end.

Chapter 6

Southeastern Massachusetts

Numbers on this map refer to rides in this book.

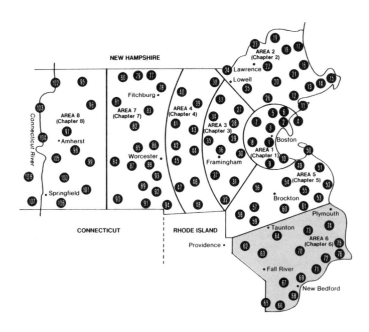

62. Seekonk–Rehoboth

Number of miles: 15 (28 with southern extension)
Terrain: Gently rolling, with one hill. The long ride has an
additional hill.
Food: Two country stores in Rehoboth.
Start: Seekonk High School, corner of Arcade Avenue and Ledge
Road in Seekonk , 7/10 mile north of Route 44.
How to get there: From the north, exit south from Route 95
onto Route 1A (a Holiday Inn is at the interchange). Go 1
mile to the third traffic light (Central Avenue). Turn left on
Central Avenue and go 1 mile to end (Route 152). Turn right
on Route 152 and go 3.4 miles to Arcade Avenue on left, just
before Route 152 goes between two ponds. Turn left on
Arcade Avenue and go 6/10 mile to school on right. If you're
coming from Route 195, exit north onto Route 114A. After 1
mile, Route 114A bears left, but go straight onto Arcade
Avenue 1 mile to traffic light (Route 44). Cross 44 and go
7/10 mile to school on left.

Just east of Providence is a very rural, gently rolling area that provides superb bicycling. An extensive network of well-paved, narrow
country lanes winds past large farms, a couple of ponds, and rustic,
weathered old barns and farmhouses. The center of Rehoboth is a
gem, with a perfect little dam and millpond, a fine small church,
and a graceful brick building called Goff Memorial that holds the
town library and hosts a classical music festival during the summer.
The only problem with Rehoboth is that it has more dogs per acre
than any other place I've ever cycled. You should carry some sort of
dog repellent and not hesitate to use it.

The ride starts off from Seekonk, a residential suburb of Providence that quickly becomes rural toward its eastern edge. You'll
bike past gentleman farms and large, gracious homes, and then
cross into Rohoboth, where you'll head to Rehoboth Village, the
center of town, through a pastoral landscape of gently rolling farmland. The return run to Seekonk leads through more of this landscape. The long ride heads farther east and south through an even

more rural area. You'll go along the Warren Upper Reservoir and follow the beautiful valley of the Palmer River, lined with large farms. Just ahead you'll pass Shad Factory Pond, a small millpond with a nice dam. From here you've a short ride back to the start.

Directions for the ride: 28 miles

1. Turn left out of south end of parking lot onto Ledge Road (don't get onto Arcade Avenue). You'll immediately come to Arcade Avenue at stop sign. Cross Arcade Avenue and go 3/10 mile to fork (Greenwood Avenue, a dead-end road, bears left).

2. Bear right at fork (still Ledge Road). After 2/10 mile Hope Street bears right, but continue straight for 7/10 mile to end (merge to right just before Route 44).

3. Turn sharply left at end, up a gradual hill, and go 4/10 mile to Prospect Street on left.

4. Turn left on Prospect Street and go 1.4 miles to fork where Walker Street bears left and Prospect Street bears right. It's after Woodward Avenue on left.

5. Bear right at fork (still Prospect Street) and go 1/2 mile to another fork, where the main road curves right and a small lane (Davis Street) bears left.

6. Curve right on main road for 1 mile to end.

7. Turn right at end (this is Pine Street) and go 2.2 miles to end.

8. Turn left at end of Pine Street and go 3/10 mile to fork where the main road bears slightly left.

9. Bear left at fork and go 3/10 mile to crossroads (River Street).

10. Bear left at crossroads down a little hill. Go 7/10 mile to end (Danforth Street).

11. Turn right on Danforth Street and go 3/10 mile to wide crossroads and stop sign (Route 44).

12. Cross Route 44 and go 8/10 mile to fork (County Street bears right; Bay State Road bears left). You'll go through Rehoboth Village just before the fork.

13. Bear right at fork and go 3/10 mile to crossroads and blinking light (Route 118). Here the short ride turns right and the long ride goes straight.

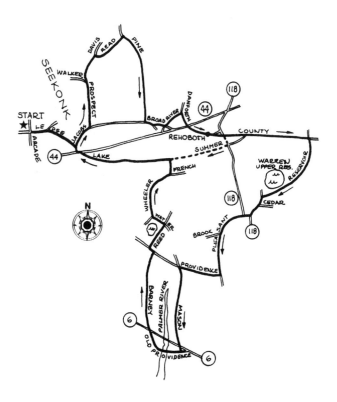

SEEKONK

START

WALKER

DAVIS
READ
PINE

PROSPECT

LEE
ARCADE
44
JACOB
LAKE

BROAD RIVER
DANFORTH
44
118

REHOBOTH
SUMMER
COUNTY

WARREN
UPPER RES.

RESERVOIR

N

FRENCH

WHEELER
WATER
4
REED

118

CEDAR

BROOK
PLEASANT
118

PROVIDENCE

BARNEY
PALMER RIVER
MASON

6

OLD PROVIDENCE
6

14. Cross Route 118 onto County Street and go 2.2 miles to crossroads and stop sign at top of hill. There's a country store at the crossroads.

15. Turn right at crossroads and go 2 miles to end (Gorham Street). You'll pass a fire tower on your left at top of hill. Then there's a nice downhill run to the Warren Upper Reservoir on your right.

16. Turn left on Gorham Street and go 2/10 mile to end (merge right at stop sign onto Cedar Street).

17. Bear right on Cedar Street and go 6/10 mile to stop sign (Route 118). At the intersection, Route 118 turns right and also goes straight.

18. Turn right on Route 118. Just ahead Route 118 turns right, but continue straight. Go 7/10 mile to fork where Brook Street bears right and the main road, Pleasant Street, bears left.

19. Bear left on the main road and go 1 mile to Providence Street on right, just beyond fire station on right.

20. Turn right on Providence Street and go 1.3 miles to Mason Street, which turns sharply left at a traffic island.

21. Make a sharp left on Mason Street and go 1.9 miles to Route 6, at stop sign.

22. Cross Route 6 • *CAUTION* here. Go 1/10 mile to end (Old Providence Road).

23. Turn right at end and go 1 mile to Route 6, at stop sign. The bridge over the Palmer River is a delightful spot.

24. Cross Route 6 diagonally. • *CAUTION* again. Go 1.9 miles to end.

25. Turn left at end and go 1/10 mile to your first right, Reed Street.

26. Turn right and go 6/10 mile to crossroads and stop sign (Water Street). You'll pass Shad Factory Pond and the dam on your left.

27. Turn left on Water Street and go 3/10 mile to fork at bottom of hill, at traffic island.

28. Bear right at fork and go 1.1 miles to another fork, where Wheeler Street bears left. It's after Lake Street on right.

29. Bear left on Wheeler Street and go 3/10 mile to end.

30. Turn left at end. After 3/10 mile, the main road curves left and Pond Street turns right. Stay on main road for 1.7 miles to end (merge left onto Route 44).

31. Bear left on Route 44, immediately turn right on Jacob Street, and then immediately bear left at fork on Ledge Road. Go 1.2 miles to crossroads and stop sign (Arcade Avenue).

32. Cross Arcade Avenue. The school is just ahead on right.

Directions for the ride: 15 miles

1. Follow directions for the long ride through number 13.

2. Turn right on Route 118 and go 3/10 mile to crossroads (Elm Street on left, Summer Street on right).

3. Turn right on Summer Street. After 9/10 mile, School Street bears left, but bear slightly right, staying on Summer Street. Continue 6/10 mile to fork.

4. Bear slightly right at fork (still Summer Street). After 6/10 mile, the main road curves left and Pond Street turns right. Stay on main road for 1.7 miles to end (merge left into Route 44).

5. Follow directions 31 and 32 of long ride.

63. Swansea–Somerset–Dighton–Rehoboth

Number of miles: 17 (30 with Rehoboth extension)
Terrain: Gently rolling, with one moderate hill and one steep one.
Food: Grocery in Dighton. McDonald's at end.
Start: McDonald's, Route 6, Swansea, 3 miles west of Route 138 and 1/2 mile east of Route 195 (exit 3). The McDonald's is in a shopping center.

This ride takes you exploring the gently rolling countryside along the west bank of the lower Taunton River, the major river in the southeastern part of the state. The route parallels the river for several miles and then returns along the ridge rising just inland from the west bank. The long ride heads farther west into farm country and then finishes with a relaxing run along Mount Hope Bay, the broad estuary at the mouth of the river.

You'll start from Swansea, a pleasant rural community midway between Fall River and Providence, and just far enough from either to have so far avoided suburban development. The center of town boasts a handsome stone town hall with a clock tower, built in 1890, and a fine stone library next door.

From Swansea you'll traverse a low ridge into Somerset, which lies along the Taunton River across from Fall River. Most of Somerset is suburban, but you'll bike through the older and less-developed northern portion of town. You'll follow the river on a narrow street lined with fascinating old wooden buildings in a wide variety of architectural styles, and then continue along the water into an increasingly rural landscape to the center of Dighton, another attractive riverfront town extending westward into gently rolling farm country.

In Dighton you'll head back toward Swansea along a ridge a short distance inland from the riverbank, with impressive views of the river and the surrounding landscape. The longer ride heads farther inland to Rehoboth, a beautiful rural town of broad farms and winding, wooded roads. You'll cross briefly into a little strip of Rhode Island to the shore of Mount Hope Bay, just back over the Massachusetts line. After a scenic, curving run along the shore, you've a short ride back to the start.

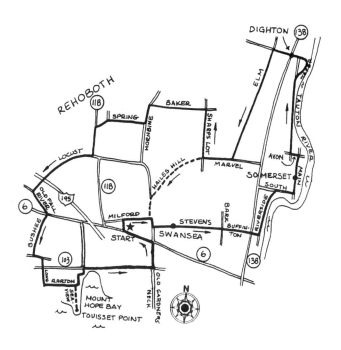

DIGHTON (138)

REHOBOTH (118)

SPRING   BAKER

HORNBINE

SHARPS LOT

ELM

TAUTON RIVER

LOCUST

HALES HILL

MARVEL   AVON

MAIN

(118)   SOMERSET

SOUTH

OLD FALL RIVER

(195)

MILFORD

STEVENS

BARK

BUFFIN-
TON

RIVERSIDE

6

(6)   START   SWANSEA

BUSHEE

(103)

6

(138)

RARTON

SEA VIEW

LONG

OLD GARDNERS NECK

MOUNT
HOPE BAY

TOUISSET POINT

N

357

Directions for the ride: 30 miles

1. Turn right out of *back* of parking lot onto Milford Road, which parallels Route 6 one block north of it, and go 6/10 mile to end (Hortonville Road). • *CAUTION:* There are speed bumps when you leave the parking lot. Ride around the sides.

2. Turn right on Hortonville Road and go 2/10 mile to Main Street on left, at traffic light.

3. Turn left on Main Street and go 2.8 miles to traffic light at bottom of hill (County Street, Route 138). Just after you turn left there's a little dam on your left. Then, just ahead, you'll pass the handsome stone Swansea town hall and library.

4. Cross Route 138 and go 3/10 mile to end. The Taunton River is in front of you.

5. Turn left at end and go 4/10 mile to fork where the main road bears right along the river.

6. Bear right at fork, following the river, and go 1.1 miles to diagonal crossroads where South Street bears right up a little hill.

7. Bear right on South Street and go 4/10 mile to end (Main Street).

8. Turn left on Main Street and go 1/2 mile to Avon Street on left. As soon as you turn left, notice the pillared mansion on the left. Farther on you'll pass a varied mixture of fascinating old buildings on both sides of the street.

9. Turn left on Avon Street and go 100 yards to end, at traffic island.

10. Turn right at end and go 2.6 miles to Water Street on your right. It's a little lane that comes up just after a small concrete bridge.

11. Turn right on Water Street and go 6/10 mile to Route 138, at stop sign and blinking light. This is the center of Dighton.

12. Cross Route 138 and go 4/10 mile to crossroads (Elm Street). You'll pass a grocery on the right.

13. Turn left on Elm Street and go 3 miles to end (Marvel Street on right). As soon as you turn left, a lovely dam is on your right. Then you'll climb a steep hill. As you're going down the far side there's a crossroads—continue straight ahead. Farther on you'll go along a ridge with fine views of the river to your left.

14. Turn right on Marvel Street and go 1 mile to crossroads and blinking light (Sharps Lot Road). Here the short ride goes straight and the long ride turns right.

15. Turn right on Sharps Lot Road and go 1.7 miles to cross-roads (Baker Road on left).

16. Turn left at crossroads and go 1.6 miles to end. Opposite the intersection is the Hornbine School, a one-room wooden schoolhouse. It was built during the 1830s and used until 1934.

17. Turn left at end and go 1/2 mile to Spring Street on right.

18. Turn right on Spring Street and go 1 mile to fork (main road bears left).

19. Bear left at fork and go 2/10 mile to end (Route 118).

20. Turn left on Route 118 and go 8/10 mile to end, where a big water tower stands on the right. Route 118 turns left here.

21. Turn right at end onto Locust Street and go 1.8 miles to end.

22. Turn left at end and go 8/10 mile to end (merge into Route 6).

23. Bear left on Route 6 and immediately turn right on a small road (Bushee Road). • *CAUTION* here. Go 1.4 miles to end (School-house Road).

24. Turn left on Schoolhouse Road and go 2/10 to Long Lane on right, at traffic island.

25. Turn right on Long Lane and go 2/10 mile to crossroads and stop sign (Route 103).

26. Cross Route 103. After 8/10 mile, the road turns 90 degrees left onto Barton Avenue. Continue 1.8 miles to traffic light (Route 103). When you come to Mount Hope Bay the road twists and turns, but stay on the main road until you come to Route 103. If you wish, you can turn right immediately before the bay onto Seaview Avenue, which parallels the water 1 mile to a dead end, and then backtrack to Barton Avenue. The massive building across the bay is the coal-fueled Brayton Point power plant.

27. Turn right on Route 103 and go 1.3 miles to blinking light at top of hill (Old Gardners Neck Road).

28. Turn left on Old Gardners Neck Road (• *CAUTION* here) and go 9/10 mile to Route 6, at traffic light.

29. Turn left on Route 6 and go 9/10 mile to McDonald's on right.

Directions for the ride: 17 miles

1. Follow directions for the long ride through number 14.

2. Continue straight at blinking light and go 1.8 miles to end (merge left at stop sign).

3. Bear left at stop sign (don't go through the intersection onto Wood Street) and go 1/2 mile to Milford Road on right.

4. Turn right on Milford Road and go 6/10 mile to shopping center on left. You enter the shopping center from the back, just as you left it. • *CAUTION:* Watch out for speed bumps as you enter parking lot.

64. Profile Rock and Dighton Rock: Taunton–Berkley–Assonet–North Dighton

Number of miles: 13 (24 with Profile Rock-Dighton Rock extension)
Terrain: Gently rolling, with one moderate hill.
Road surface: 4/10 mile of dirt road on the long ride that can be avoided.
Food: Country store in Berkley. The delightful Assonet Inn, Assonet. Burger place at end.
Start: McDonald's in shopping center on Route 44 in Taunton, just east of Warner Boulevard. It's about 1.5 miles west of the center of town.

The region just south of Taunton, along the east bank of the Taunton River, is ideal for bicycling. Country lanes wind through a fairly flat landscape of farms and woodland, with some stretches along the river. You'll go through the pleasingly rural town centers of Berkley and Assonet, and then through North Dighton, an unusually attractive mill village in the middle of nowhere. On the ride you investigate two unique landmarks—Profile Rock, a large boulder with a striking resemblance to an Indian's profile, and Dighton Rock, on which are inscriptions of disputed origin.

The ride starts from Taunton, a city of 40,000 best known for the manufacture of fine silver products. In the downtown area (not on the route) is the majestic, domed Bristol County courthouse standing proudly over a grassy square. At the beginning of the ride you'll pass the massive nineteenth-century plant of the F. B. Rogers Silver Company stretching along the riverbank. As soon as you cross the river you get into gently rolling countryside with broad farms. It's not far to Berkley, a pretty village with an unusually large green. From here you'll proceed to Profile Rock, where a short path leads to a spot from which the profile is best seen. Just downhill from the rock is the attractive mill village of Assonet, which is part of Freetown. The Assonet River is dammed into a tiny millpond with a fine dam at its end. You'll follow the river, where you'll pass the Assonet Inn, a rambling Victorian building with broad porches.

It looks elegant but inside is an informal, old-fashioned restaurant serving good food at reasonable prices.

Leaving Assonet you'll traverse a hillside with fine views of the Taunton River, which widens into an estuary as it flows between Taunton and Fall River. A short pedal across broad meadows brings you to Dighton Rock State Park, a lush, grassy area along the riverbank. The rock itself is enclosed in a small museum open from April through September. Its strange pictographs are clearly visible; their origins have been attributed to a Portuguese explorer (the most generally accepted theory), Vikings, Phoenicians, and Indians.

After you leave Dighton Rock, another carefree run follows the river on a narrow lane; then you'll cross it over the narrow, steel-trussed Berkley Bridge, one of the more picturesque spots in south-eastern Massachusetts. From here you make a brief run to North Dighton, one of the more unusual mill villages in the state. Completely surrounded by farmland, a massively grim brick mill on one side of the road contrasts with a large, well-kept green and fine old homes on the other. From here, it's a couple of miles back to Taunton through broad farms.

Directions for the ride: 24 miles

1. Turn left out of west side of parking lot onto Warner Boulevard. Just ahead is a crossroads (Cohannet Street).

2. Turn left on Cohannet Street. Just ahead a road bears right, but continue straight for 1/2 mile to crossroads and stop sign.

3. Turn right at crossroads and go 9/10 mile to end (Route 138).

4. Turn left on Route 138 and go 3/10 mile to Fifth Street, which bears right under railroad bridge.

5. Bear right on Fifth Street and go 2/10 mile to end.

6. Turn left at end, passing the Rogers Silver Company, and go 3/10 mile to your first right, which crosses the Taunton River.

7. Turn right. Immediately after the bridge, turn right again and then immediately bear left, staying on the main road. Go 1.7 miles to North Main Street on your left. A restaurant with a large parking lot is on the corner.

8. Turn left on North Main Street and go 1.2 miles to fork at the Berkley town green. Here the short ride bears right and the long

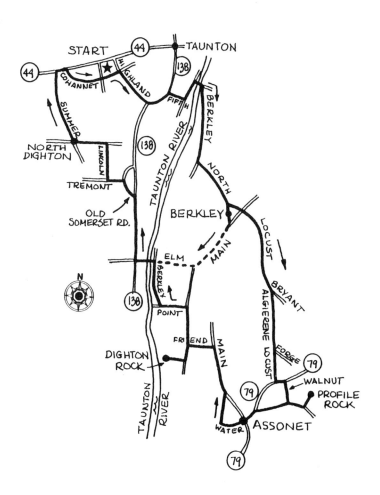

ride bears left. Notice the small brick library in the middle of the fork.

9. Bear left at fork and go less than 2/10 mile to crossroads and stop sign.

10. Go straight at crossroads onto Locust Street 1.8 miles to fork shortly beyond the overpass over Route 24. At the fork, Algerene Street bears right and Bryant Street bears left.

11. Bear right on Algerene Street. After 1.2 miles, Forge Road bears left, but continue straight on Locust Street 1/2 mile to end (Mill Street, Route 79). There's a nice dam and an old mill on your left just before the end.

12. Turn left at end and go 100 yards to Walnut Street on right.

13. Turn 90 degrees right on Walnut Street and go 3/10 mile to end (Elm Street).

14. Turn left at end and go 3/10 mile to the entrance to Profile Rock on left, at a long, grassy traffic island.

15. Turn left onto entrance road and go 2/10 mile to end. From here a path leads about 100 yards to the viewpoint for the rock.

16. Leaving the rock, turn right at end of entrance road. Go 6/10 mile to stop sign (merge left into Route 79).

17. Bear left at stop sign. As you turn, notice the dam on your right. Go 1/10 mile to crossroads and stop sign. This is Assonet.

18. Go straight at crossroads onto Water Street 9/10 mile to end, at top of hill. The Assonet Inn is on your right just beyond the crossroads.

19. Bear left at end and go 9/10 mile to Friend Street on left (sign may say State Park).

20. Turn left on Friend Street and go 8/10 mile to end (Bay View Avenue).

21. Turn left at end and go 3/10 mile to the entrance to Dighton Rock on your right. It's about 6/10 mile to the museum and picnic area on the bank of the river.

22. Leaving Dighton Rock, turn left at end of entrance road. Go 1 mile to Point Street on left. It's your first left.

23. Turn left on Point Street and go 7/10 mile to Berkley Street on right. A 3/10-mile stretch of dirt road lies along here. (You

Profile Rock, Assonet.

could avoid it by continuing straight on Bay View Avenue to end and then turning left. You'd miss a delightful run along the Taunton River.)

24. Turn right on Berkley Street and go 9/10 mile to crossroads and stop sign (Elm Street).

25. Turn left at crossroads, crossing the river, and go 7/10 mile to stop sign and blinking light (Route 138). The bridge is currently blocked off to cars, but you can get your bike across.

26. Turn right on Route 138 and go 1 mile to Old Somerset Road, which bears left.

27. Bear left on Old Somerset Road and go 2/10 mile to Tremont Street on left.

28. Turn left on Tremont Street and go 3/10 mile to Lincoln Avenue on right.

29. Turn right on Lincoln Avenue and go 7/10 mile to end (Spring Street). A picturesque little dam is on the right just before the end.

30. Turn left on Spring Street. After 4/10 mile, go straight ahead, passing a long mill on your right and a green on your left. Continue 2/10 mile to diagonal crossroads at end of mill (Summer Street bears right). This is North Dighton.

31. Bear right on Summer Street and go 1.4 miles to end (Route 44).

32. Turn right on Route 44 and go 2/10 mile to Cohannet Street on right.

33. Turn right on Cohannet Street and go 8/10 mile to crossroads and stop sign. (The bridge at the beginning is currently blocked off to cars, but you can get your bike across. If it becomes impassable or is torn down, simply stay on Route 44 for 9/10 mile to shopping center on right.)

34. Turn left at stop sign. Shopping center is just ahead on right.

Directions for the ride: 13 miles

1. Follow the directions for the long ride through 8.

2. Bear right at fork and go 1.2 miles to another fork, where Bay View Avenue bears left and the main road bears right.

3. Bear right, staying on main road, and go 1.4 miles to stop sign and blinking light (Route 138). You'll cross the Taunton River. The bridge is currently blocked off to cars, but you can get your bike across.

4. Follow directions for the long ride from number 26 to the end.

65. Westport–Tiverton, Rhode Island– Little Compton, Rhode Island

Number of miles: 20 (34 with Tiverton–Little Compton extension)

Terrain: Gently rolling, with one tough hill.

Food: Country store in Adamsville. Country store in Little Compton.

Start: Supermarket on Main Road, Westport, just north of the town hall.

How to get there: From Route 195, exit south onto Route 88 and go about 5 miles to Charlotte White Road, at traffic light. Turn right and go 4/10 mile to crossroads (Main Road). Turn left on Main Road and go 1.5 miles to supermarket on left.

The southwestern corner of coastline directly south of Fall River, extending into Rhode Island along the broad Sakonnet River, has some of the most ideal and idyllic bicycling in the state. The region is a pedaler's paradise of untraveled country lanes winding past salt marshes, snug, cedar-shingled homes with immaculately tended lawns, trim picket fences, and broad meadows sloping down to the bay.

The ride starts from Westport, a slender town stretching from east of Fall River all the way down to the coast. The Westport River, a broad tidal estuary, bisects the town, and you'll be exploring the thin strip of land between the river and the Rhode Island border. You'll ride across sweeping expanses of farmland to the tiny village of Adamsville, which lies in Little Compton, Rhode Island, 100 yards over the state line. In the town are a country store in a rambling old wooden building, a little millpond, and a monument to the Rhode Island Red breed of poultry. From Adamsville you'll head south to the most southwesterly bit of coast in Massachusetts, an unspoiled strand framed by salt ponds and stately, cedar-shingled homes. At its eastern tip, guarding the mouth of the Westport River, is the exclusive summer colony of Acoaxet. From here you have an excellent run back to Adamsville along the West Branch of the Westport River, and a short spin through farms to the starting point.

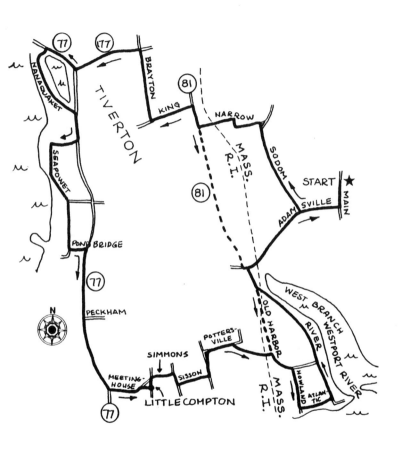

77 77

BRAYTON

TIVERTON

NANAQUAKET

81

KING

NARROW

MASS. R.I.

SODOM

START ★

SEAPOWET

81

ADAMSVILLE

MAIN

POND BRIDGE

77

N

PECKHAM

WEST BRANCH

OLD HARBOR

RIVER

WESTPORT RIVER

POTTERS-VILLE

SIMMONS

MEETING-HOUSE

SISSON

HOWLAND

MASS. R.I.

ATLANTIC

LITTLE COMPTON

77

369

The long ride heads west into the little strip of Rhode Island south of Fall River lying along the mile-wide Sakonnet River, which is the easternmost section of Narragansett Bay. The landscape is beautiful as you hug the river on narrow country lanes and then climb onto a ridge with dramatic views of broad meadows sloping down to the shore. Just ahead is the center of Little Compton, the finest traditional New England village in Rhode Island. The long green is framed by a classic white church, a delightful country store, and an old cemetery where Elizabeth Pabodie, daughter of John and Priscilla Alden and the first white girl born in New England, is buried. From here you'll wind through gently rolling, open farmland to Adamsville, where you'll pick up the short ride for the run to Acoaxet.

Directions for the ride: 34 miles

1. Turn left (south) out of parking lot and go 1/2 mile to Adamsville Road on right.

2. Turn right on Adamsville Road and go 8/10 mile to Sodom Road on right.

3. Turn right on Sodom Road and go 2.1 miles to traffic island where the main road curves sharply right.

4. Go straight at traffic light and immediately turn left at end on Narrow Avenue. Go 1.6 miles to end (Route 81). Shortly before the end you'll cross the state line into Tiverton, Rhode Island. The short ride turns left on Route 81 and the long ride turns right.

5. Turn right on Route 81 and go 4/10 mile to King Road on left.

6. Turn left on King Road and go 1 mile to Brayton Road on right. It's your second right.

7. Turn right on Brayton Road and go 1.8 miles to crossroads and blinking light (Bulgarmarsh Road, Route 177).

8. Turn left on Route 177 and go 1.8 miles to end (Route 77). There's a great downhill run at the end.

9. Turn right on Route 77 and go 1/2 mile to Nannaquacket Road, on left.

10. Turn left on Nannaquacket Road, crossing a little bridge, and go 1.6 miles to end (merge into Route 177).

11. Bear right on Route 177 and go 1/2 mile to Seapowet Road on right.

12. Turn right on Seapowet Road and go 2.2 miles to fork.

13. Bear right at fork and go 1.3 miles to your first left (Pond Bridge Road), just past top of hill.

14. Turn left on Pond Bridge Road and go 1/2 mile to end (Route 77).

15. Turn right on Route 77 and go 3.6 miles to a road that turns left at a traffic island (a sign may say to the Commons). After about 1.5 miles you'll pass the Sakonnet Vineyards, a commercial winery, on your left.

16. Turn left at traffic island and go 6/10 mile to fork.

17. Bear right at fork and go 2/10 mile to end, in the center of Little Compton.

18. Turn left at end and go 1/10 mile to your first right (Simmons Road).

19. Turn right on Simmons Road and go 6/10 mile to a traffic island, where the main road curves sharply left and a smaller road turns right.

20. Turn right at traffic island and go 3/10 mile to William Sisson Road on left.

21. Turn left on William Sisson Road and go 6/10 mile to end.

22. Turn left at end and go 6/10 mile to fork, where one branch bears right and the other goes straight.

23. Bear right at fork and go 9/10 mile to another fork, where the main road bears right at a traffic island.

24. Bear right on the main road and go 8/10 mile to end. You cross back into Massachusetts just before the end.

25. Turn right at end and go 1/2 mile to Howland Road on right.

26. Turn right on Howland Road and go 1.1 miles to Atlantic Avenue on left, just before the ocean.

27. Turn left on Atlantic Avenue and go 7/10 mile to end, in the village of Acoaxet. Here the ride turns left, but if you turn right a dirt road leads 1/2 mile through the dunes to a high boulder at the tip of the point between the Westport River and the ocean. There's a great view from the boulder.

28. Turn left at end of Atlantic Avenue. After 3.3 miles you'll merge to the right at stop sign. Bear right and go 1/2 mile to end, in the village of Adamsville. At the end, notice the unique, three-story white tower on the right. It covers a well. On the left-hand corner is a plaque commemorating the Rhode Island Red breed of poultry. Abraham Manchester's, opposite you, is a good lunch spot.

29. Turn right at end and go 2.5 miles to end (Main Road).

30. Turn left on Main Road and go 1/2 mile to supermarket on right, just beyond the town hall. There's an ice cream place here, too.

Directions for the ride: 20 miles

1. Follow directions for the long ride through number 4.

2. Turn left on Route 81 and go 3.3 miles to end, in the village of Adamsville.

3. Turn left at end and go 100 yards to your first right. A plaque commemorating the Rhode Island Red breed of poultry is on the near corner, and an unusual, three-story wooden tower, covering a well, is on the far corner. Abraham Manchester's, on your left, is a good lunch spot.

4. Turn right on this road and go 1/2 mile to fork, where one road bears left and the other goes straight up a steep hill.

5. Go straight up the hill 2.2 miles to Howland Road on right.

6. Follow directions for the long ride from number 26 to the end.

66. Westport–Horseneck Beach

Number of miles: 11 (22 with Horseneck Beach extension)
Terrain: Gently rolling, with one tough hill.
Food: Snack bar just beyond Horseneck Beach. Grocery just before end.
Start: Westport High School, Main Street in Westport. From Route 24, head east on Route 195 for two miles to Route 88. Go south on Route 88 for 3.5 miles to Old County Road, at traffic light. Turn right at light and go one block to end. Turn left and the school is just ahead on right. It's best to park at the lot at the far end of the school.

If you draw a line from Fall River to New Bedford and chip away the urban areas, everything south of that line is an absolute paradise for biking. This is a gently rolling landscape of little-traveled country roads winding past snug, cedar-shingled homes with trim picket fences and flawless lawns, and broad meadows sloping gently down to wide tidal rivers and salt marshes. This ride takes you exploring the heart of this area, heading along the east bank of the East Branch of the Westport River, a broad tidal estuary, and returning along the west bank. You'll stay within the borders of Westport, a slender town stretching from Route 195 to the ocean at Horseneck Beach, among the most unspoiled in the state. With its splendid harbor and the broad reaches of both the East and West branches of the river, Westport is an active boating center.

The ride starts from the top of the broad, gradual hillside stretching along the river and heads down to its narrow northern end. The ride down to Horseneck is delightful and when you reach the ocean, the road hugs the shoreline for nearly a mile. Just before the public portion of the beach, you can bike onto a narrow pendant of land that extends a mile into Buzzards Bay. At the end of the beach, you'll enjoy superb views of the harbor from the bridge across the mouth of the river. Near the end you'll go along the top of the ridge that runs along the west bank of the river, enjoying splendid views of the river below and the neighboring ridge on the other side.

373

Directions for the ride: 22 miles

1. Turn left out of parking lot and go 1/10 mile to Old County Road on right, at blinking light.

2. Turn right on Old County Road and go 1/10 mile to traffic light (Route 88).

3. Cross Route 88 and go 1.4 miles to Pine Hill Road on right, at top of tough hill.

4. Turn right on Pine Hill Road. Go 2.1 miles to where Pine Hill Road bears right shortly after Riverview Drive on right.

5. Bear right (still Pine Hill Road) and go 1.4 miles to crossroads and stop sign (Hix Bridge Road). Here the short ride turns right and the long ride goes straight.

6. Go straight at crossroads. After 5 miles the road turns 90 degrees to the right along the ocean. (Just before this point is the Bayside Restaurant on the right, a great lunch spot.) Continue 8/10 mile to Route 88 on right, immediately after John Reed Road. The ride turns right on Route 88, but if you continue straight for 1/2 mile you'll cross a dramatic causeway with open ocean on both sides. On the far side of the causeway is Gooseberry Neck, a narrow pendant protruding into the bay.

7. Turn right on Route 88 and go 3.2 miles to traffic light (Drift Road). • *CAUTION:* The metal-grate bridge shortly before the light is very slippery when wet. If the road is wet, walk across. For a side trip, you can turn left immediately before the bridge and go 1/2 mile along the harbor to the Westport Yacht Club.

8. Turn right on Drift Road and go 3.3 miles to crossroads and stop sign (Hix Bridge Road).

9. Go straight for 3.7 miles to fork with a small green in the middle. The little square building on the green is a powder house built in 1812.

10. Bear right at fork and go 100 yards to end. This is the small village of Head of Westport. At the end, there's a grocery on your right.

11. Turn left at end and go 9/10 mile to Route 88. This is a long, steady hill—the same hill that you went down at the beginning.

12. Cross Route 88 and go 1/10 mile to end.

13. Turn left at end. The school is just ahead on right.

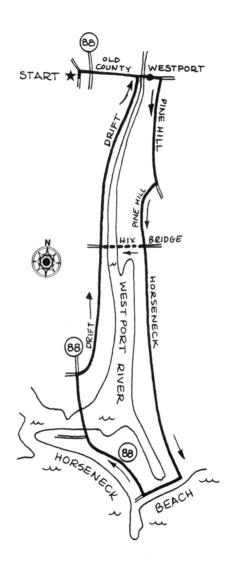

START ★

88

OLD COUNTY

WESTPORT

DRIFT

PINE HILL

PINE HILL

N

HIX BRIDGE

HORSENECK

WEST PORT RIVER

88

DRIFT

88

HORSENECK

BEACH

Directions for the ride: 11 miles

1. Follow directions for the long ride through number 5.

2. Turn right on Hix Bridge Road and go 1 mile to crossroads (Drift Road). The bridge over the river is a pretty spot.

3. Turn right on Drift Road and go 3.7 miles to a fork with a small green in the middle. The little square building on the green is a powder house built in 1812.

4. Follow directions for the long ride from number 10 to the end.

67. North Dartmouth–Freetown–Westport

Number of miles: 15 (25 with Freetown extension)
Terrain: Gently rolling, with two long, gradual hills and one short, steep one.
Food: Grocery in Westport. Fast-food places on Route 6 near end.
Start: K-Mart, Faunce Corner Road in North Dartmouth. It's just north of Route 6 across from the North Dartmouth Mall. From Route 195 take the Faunce Corner–North Dartmouth exit (exit 12) and turn south at end of exit ramp. Go 1 mile to K-Mart on left.

This ride takes you exploring the surprisingly rural area midway between Fall River and New Bedford. The region is an attractive mixture of forest and farmland, including a broad, open ridge with fine views. Smooth secondary roads help make this an enjoyable ride. The architectural highlight of the ride is the bold, strikingly modern campus of Southeastern Massachusetts University (SMU), the major educational facility for this part of the state.

The ride starts from North Dartmouth, the section of town near the University and along the Route 6 commercial strip, and heads north into farm country. After two miles you're on top of a high, open ridge with sweeping views to the east. Just ahead is a small hilltop reservoir within an embankment. As you head toward Westport you'll enjoy a run along Noquochoke Lake and pass the back of Lincoln Park, an old-fashioned amusement park with a big roller coaster. The small village of Head of Westport is a delight, with a stream flowing between grassy banks and some graceful old Colonial-style homes. From here it's a gradual climb to the SMU campus, crowning a broad hill. The main road looping around the perimeter of the campus is worth following. From SMU it's a short trip back to the start.

Directions for the ride: 25 miles

1. Turn right (north) out of parking lot and go 2.6 miles to crossroads and stop sign (Old Fall River Road). This is a long but very gradual climb. At the crossroads the short ride turns left and the long ride goes straight.

2. Go straight at crossroads 1.5 miles to end (High Hill Road). You'll pass the High Hill Reservoir on your right, hidden behind a tall embankment. Just beyond the reservoir a road bears left, but go straight.

3. Turn left on High Hill Road (sign may say to Freetown). After 7/10 mile, Pine Island Road bears left, but continue straight 1.4 miles to crossroads (Quanapoag Road).

4. Go straight at crossroads 1.3 miles to Chipaway Road, which turns sharply right while you're going uphill.

5. Make a sharp right on Chipaway Road and go 1.9 miles to crossroads and stop sign (Quanapoag Road on right, Braley Road on left).

6. Turn right at crossroads and go 2 miles to another crossroads and stop sign (Bullock Road).

7. Go straight at crossroads 1.7 miles to another crossroads and stop sign (Collins Corner Road).

8. Turn right on Collins Corner Road and go 2.2 miles to end.

9. Turn right at end and go 3/10 mile to end. At the intersection, notice the fine church on your right. This is the tiny village of Hixville.

10. Turn left at end. After 2/10 mile Hixville Road bears left, but go straight on Reed Road 3 miles to traffic light (Route 6). You'll pass Noquochoke Lake and then on your left you'll pass the Trollheim Gallery, a strange-looking, gaily painted establishment with unusual sculptures beside it.

11. Cross Route 6 and go 1.9 miles to end. • *CAUTION* crossing Route 6. Shortly after crossing Route 6 you'll see the Lincoln Park roller-coaster on your right. At the end the ride turns left, but if you turn right 100 yards you'll see a grocery store and the beautiful stream flowing through the village of Head of Westport.

12. Turn left at end of Reed Road and go 3.9 miles to end (Old Westport Road on left). You'll tackle a short hill at the beginning; then you climb very gradually to the SMU campus.

13. Turn left on Old Westport Road and go 1/2 mile to traffic light (Route 6). Cross Route 6. The K-Mart is just ahead on right. • *CAUTION* crossing Route 6—it's a very busy intersection.

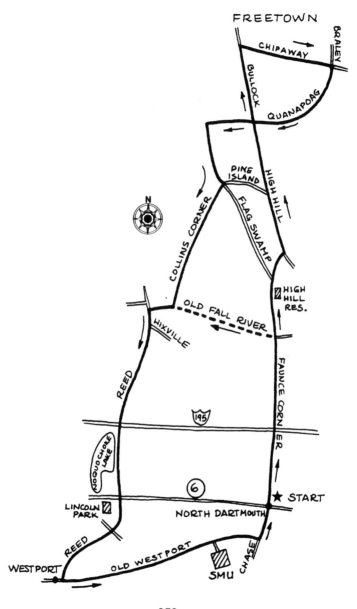

FREETOWN

BRALEY

CHIPAWAY

BULLOCK

QUANAPOAG

PINE ISLAND

HIGH HILL

N

COLLINS CORNER

FLAG SWAMP

HIGH HILL RES.

OLD FALL RIVER

HIXVILLE

REED

FAUNCE CORNER

195

AQUOUCHOKE LAKE

6

LINCOLN PARK

★ START

NORTH DARTMOUTH

REED

OLD WESTPORT

CHASE

WESTPORT

SMU

379

Directions for the ride: 15 miles

    1. Same as direction number 1 for the long ride.

    2. Turn left at crossroads onto Old Fall River Road. Go 2.3 miles to end. You'll come to a great downhill run halfway along this stretch. At the end, notice the fine church on your right. This is the tiny village of Hixville.

    3. Follow directions for the long ride from number 10 to the end.

68. Dartmouth

Number of miles: 18 (27 with southwestern loop, 29 if you visit Demarest Lloyd Memorial State Park)

Terrain: Flat, with a couple of gradual, easy hills

Food: Grocery and restaurant in Padanaram. Numerous restaurants on Route 6 near end.

Start: North Dartmouth Library on Tucker Road, just south of Route 6. From Route 195 take exit 12 (the Faunce Corner–North Dartmouth exit), and turn south at the end of the ramp. Go 1 mile to Route 6. Turn left on Route 6 and take your first right on Tucker Road. The library is just ahead on your left.

Dartmouth, an extensive oceanfront town south and west of New Bedford, offers ideal biking on numerous back roads. The landscape is flat, with broad stretches of farmland and salt marshes. The ride starts in North Dartmouth, commercial center of the town and home of Southeastern Massachusetts University (SMU). The bold, modern campus is about 1 mile off the route. You'll head down to the picturesque village of Padanaram on Apponagansett Bay, with antique shops and fine old homes. From here, you'll cross the bridge over the bay and enjoy a run along its shore. The marvelous Children's Museum, one of the best in New England, is a mile off the route. From Padanaram you'll work your way to the southern coast and the tiny village of Russells Mills on winding, wooded roads. You'll pass the Lloyd Center for Environmental Studies, dramatically located on Buzzards Bay at the mouth of the Slocum River. Nature trails wind through the grounds, and there's a spectacular view from the top of the main building.

The long ride heads farther into Dartmouth to the Westport line, passing broad, well-tended farms. Demarest Lloyd Memorial State Park is about 1 mile from the route and worth visiting. It's a lovely expanse of woods and shoreline, with a good beach that doesn't get such crowds as nearby Horseneck Beach does.

Directions for the ride: 27 miles

1. Turn left out of the parking lot, heading south on Tucker Road, and go 2.9 miles to Russells Mills Road on left, at the bottom of a long, very gradual hill. A snack bar is on the corner.

2. Turn left on Russells Mills Road and go 1.2 miles to Elm Street on right, immediately before the brick police station on left.

3. Turn right on Elm Street and go 1.3 miles to crossroads in the center of Padanaram (Bridge Street).

4. Turn right on Bridge Street, which crosses the bay, and go 4/10 mile to Smith Neck Road on left. Here the ride turns left, but if you continue straight for 1 mile you'll come to the Children's Museum on your left.

5. Turn left on Smith Neck Road, following the bay. After 1.8 miles a road turns right, but bear slightly left on the main road. Go 1.4 miles to Little River Road on right (dead end if you go straight). You'll pass an ice cream stand shaped like a milk bottle on your right.

6. Turn right on Little River Road and go 3.3 miles to fork and traffic island, at stop sign at bottom of hill. • *CAUTION:* Watch for sand at the intersection. After 1.6 miles, you'll pass the Lloyd Center for Environmental Studies on your left. The main building is 1/10 mile down the dirt entrance road.

7. Bear left at the traffic island and then immediately bear right. Go 8/10 mile to Tannery Lane, which bears left. Here the short ride goes straight and the long ride bears left.

8. Bear left on Tannery Lane and immediately turn left at end. Go 1.9 miles to fork where the main road curves left (becoming Barney's Joy Road) and another road bears right. Curve left for 8/10 miles to end (Allens Neck Road). This is a nice run past broad farms with views of the river to your left. When you come to Allens Neck Road, the ride turns right, but if you turn left you'll come to Demarest Lloyd Memorial State Park after 1.1 miles.

9. Turn right on Allens Neck Road and go 7/10 mile to end (Horseneck Road).

10. Turn left on Horseneck Road and go 7/10 mile to Division Road on right.

11. Turn right on Division Road and go 2.7 miles to Slades Corner Road on right. Division Road runs along the border of Dartmouth and Westport.

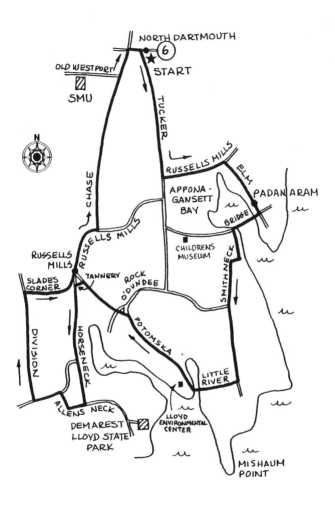

NORTH DARTMOUTH

⑥

OLD WESTPORT

SMU

START

TUCKER

N

CHASE

RUSSELLS MILLS

ELM

PADANARAM

APPONA-
GANSETT
BAY

BRIDGE

RUSSELLS MILLS

RUSSELLS
MILLS

TANNERY

ROCK
O'DUNDEE

CHILDRENS
MUSEUM

SMITH NECK

SLADES
CORNER

DIVISION

HORSENECK

POTOMSKA

LITTLE
RIVER

ALLENS NECK

DEMAREST
LLOYD STATE
PARK

LLOYD
ENVIRONMENTAL
CENTER

MISHAUM
POINT

12. Turn right on Slades Corner Road and go 1.5 miles to end (merge left; Horseneck Road is on right). This is the tiny village of Russells Mills. There's a wonderful country store at the intersection.

13. Bear left at end and go 1 mile to Chase Road on left, just after the public works building on right.

14. Turn left on Chase Road and go 4 miles to traffic light (Route 6). If you'd like to visit SMU, turn left after 3.5 miles on Old Westport Road and go 1 mile to the strikingly modern campus on your left.

15. Turn right on Route 6 and go 1/10 mile to Tucker Road, your first right.

16. Turn right on Tucker Road. The library is just ahead on your left.

Directions for the ride: 18 miles

1. Follow the directions for the long ride through number 7.

2. Bear right at fork, up short hill, and go 100 yards to end (Russells Mills Road). This is the tiny village of Russells Mills.

3. Turn right on Russells Mills Road and go 9/10 mile to Chase Road on left, just after the public works building on the right. Chase Road is a fairly wide road with a stripe down the middle.

4. Follow directions for the long ride from number 14 to the end.

69. Whales and Wharves: Fairhaven–New Bedford–Acushnet

Number of miles: 14 (25 with New Bedford extension)
Terrain: Flat, with one short hill on the longer ride.
Food: Numerous groceries and snack bars. McDonald's at end.
Start: McDonald's, Route 6, Fairhaven, 1 mile east of the bridge
from New Bedford. From Route 195, exit south on Route 240
and go 1.2 miles to Route 6, at traffic light. Turn right on
Route 6 and McDonald's is just ahead on left.

With the exception of Boston and its nearby suburbs, this is the
only urban ride in this book. That's because New Bedford is a very
special city. Several facets make it an exciting place to explore—it
boasts the largest fishing fleet on the East Coast; a historic port
district painstakingly restored to match its glory days in the nineteenth century, when it was the whaling capital of the world; a
splendid shoreline; and a vivid ethnic flavor, primarily Portuguese.
The mansions of the whaling captains and ornate Victorian homes
line the brow of the hill that slants back from the Acushnet River.
The Whaling Museum is outstanding and holds a half-size replica
of a whaling ship, the largest ship model in the world. Across from
the museum is the Seaman's Bethel, a simple church built in 1832
with a pulpit shaped like the prow of a ship. Also of interest is a
glass museum housed in a magnificent granite mansion; the imposing city hall; and the handsome granite library, which has a
collection of whaling logbooks.

Overshadowed by its better-known neighbor across the
Acushnet River, Fairhaven is one of the most graceful and visually
appealing towns in the state. The town bears the stamp of Henry
Huttleston Rogers, a local boy who made a fortune in oil and then
donated money to construct an outstanding collection of public
buildings. Thousands of motorists whizz through the town on
Route 195 or Route 6, the main drag, never seeing the real
Fairhaven hidden a half mile south. The center of town boasts the
Millicent Library, one of the most beautiful in the state, a turreted
stone structure built in 1893. It houses a collection of Mark Twain's

manuscripts and letters. Across from the library stands the handsome town hall, symmetrically flanked by two churches, and on the same block stands a third church, the majestic Unitarian Memorial Church, built in 1904 in English Gothic style. And if all this weren't enough, just outside of town is the most ornate high school in the state, a marvelous building soaring onward and upward like some Elizabethan castle. It was built in 1906 and is another Rogers gift.

Fairhaven has its own whaling history, because many of the New Bedford whaling ships were built and maintained in the town. Today a fascinating collection of boatyards and wharves lines the river, with fine views of New Bedford across the water. Just south of town, elegant old homes lie along the shore. Fairhaven comes to a peninsula at its southern tip, on which are Fort Phoenix, a park that was a Revolutionary fort, and a state beach.

The ride starts off by heading north into farm country for a few miles, a refreshing contrast to the urban areas to come, and then curves south into Acushnet, a residential suburb just north of Fairhaven. From here the short ride follows the Fairhaven waterfront down to Fort Phoenix and then returns north through the center of town.

The long ride crosses the river into New Bedford, where you'll bike through the historic district and then along the crest of the hill on County Street, which has many of the elegant whaling-era homes. At the southern end of the city you'll enjoy a relaxing run along the rim of the two-mile-long peninsula leading to Clark Point. At its tip is Fort Taber, a granite building dating from before the Civil War. One of its designers was Robert E. Lee, a United States colonel at the time. From here you'll go up the ocean side of the peninsula and then by the fishing docks. You'll cross the bridge into Fairhaven and rejoin the route of the short ride for a tour of that town's waterfront and magnificent town center.

Directions for the ride: 25 miles

1. Turn left out of the east side of the parking lot and immediately cross Route 6 at traffic light, heading north. Go 4/10 mile to crossroads (Bridge Street).

2. Turn right on Bridge Street. Just ahead, cross Route 240 at traffic light. Continue 1.5 miles to end.

386

Millicent Library, Fairhaven.

3. Turn left at end and go 1.6 miles to Mattapoisett Road on left. New Boston Road curves right at the intersection. Here the ride turns left, but if you bear right for 1/10 mile you'll see a fine little pond on your left.

4. Turn left on Mattapoisett Road and go 1.5 miles to end (Hathaway Road on left, Mendall Road on right).

5. Turn left on Hathaway Road. After 1.3 miles the main road curves sharply right, then sharply left in quick succession. After curving sharply left, go 3/10 mile to your fourth left, James Street. It's just after house number 36 on left.

6. Turn left on James Street and go 1/2 mile to end (Pembroke Avenue). You are going through Acushnet.

7. Turn right at end and go 2/10 mile to end (South Main Street).

8. Turn left on South Main Street and go 8/10 mile to fork where the main road bears right at blinking light. Bear right and go 7/10 mile to fork at a little triangular green.

9. Bear right at fork. Immediately ahead is a traffic light (Howland Street). Here the short ride goes straight and the long ride turns right.

10. Turn right at light on Howland Street and go 1.2 miles to County Street, at stop sign. It's immediately after a modern brick school on left. (You'll pass an old brick school on left before the modern one.) You'll go through three traffic lights after crossing the Acushnet River into New Bedford.

11. Turn left on County Street and go 4/10 mile to end. This is a congested lower-middle-class neighborhood of three- and four-story wooden tenements. Be prepared for choice comments about your means of transportation from the children and young people milling about on the sidewalks.

12. At end, jog left and then immediately right (still County Street). After 9/10 mile you'll come to Kempton Street (Route 6 East) at traffic light. Continue 2/10 mile to William Street on left, opposite the old high school, now the school administration building. The tenements give way to ornate whaling-era homes, many with widow's walks and cupolas.

13. Turn left on William Street and go 4/10 mile to end (Water Street). This is the heart of historic New Bedford. Halfway down

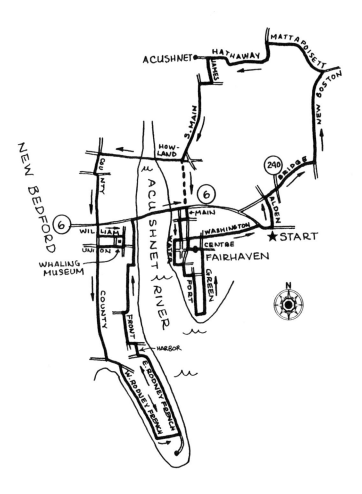

ACUSHNET

HATHAWAY

MATTAPOISETT

JAMES

NEW BEDFORD

S. MAIN

HOW-LAND

COUNTY

ACUSHNET RIVER

NEW BOSTON

240

BRIDGE

6

ALDEN

6

← MAIN

★ START

WILLIAM

WASHINGTON

UNION

CENTRE

FAIRHAVEN

WHALING MUSEUM

WATER

FORT

GREEN

COUNTY

N

FRONT

HARBOR

E. RODNEY FRENCH

W. RODNEY FRENCH

you'll pass the library on your right, facing city hall on your left, across the street from each other. A statue of a whaleman stands on the lawn of the library. The last part of William Street is cobblestone, and you'll want to walk your bike. Two blocks before the end, the glass museum is just to your left on Second Street. One short block before the end on your right is Johnnycake Hill, where you'll find the Whaling Museum and Seaman's Bethel. As you're heading down William Street, you'll see the pillared Greek Revival building in front of you. It was built in 1831 as a bank.

14. Turn right on Water Street and go 100 yards to crossroads and stop sign (Union Street). Here the ride turns right, but you can chop off 9 miles by turning left, going down the waterfront, turning left again, going 2/10 mile to the Route 6 bridge, and carrying your bike up the stairs on your left. Turn right at top of stairs and cross the bridge to Fairhaven. Go the first traffic light, Main Street, and resume with direction number 25.

15. Turn right on Union Street and go 4/10 mile back to County Street, at traffic light at top of hill. Notice the Gothic-style stone church on your right at the corner.

16. Turn left on County Street and go 1.4 miles to end. The whaling mansions in turn give way to tenements as you progress into the south end of the city.

17. Turn left at end of County Street and go 2/10 mile to traffic light. There's a high seawall on your right.

18. Bear right at light on West Rodney French Boulevard, an excellent run along the ocean. After 1.4 miles the road turns inland 90 degrees left. Continue 4/10 mile to end. If you go straight where the road turns left, you'll see some earth-covered bunkers full of mysterious tunnels and chambers. You'll need a flashlight to explore them. When you get to the end the ride turns left, but if you turn right for 3/10 mile you'll come to Fort Taber.

19. Turn left at end, following the ocean on your right. After 1.6 miles the road curves sharply inland. Continue 1/10 mile to Harbor Street on right, immediately after the clock tower on right.

20. Turn right on Harbor Street and go 2/10 mile to end. The street passes between two old mills and under a bridge connecting them.

21. Turn left at end and go 1/10 mile to end.

New Bedford.

22. Turn right at end and go 3/10 mile to end.

23. Turn right at end, following the harbor. After 7/10 mile the main road curves 90 degrees right and then left in quick succession. Continue 4/10 mile to the Route 6 bridge, where a stairway on your left goes up to Route 6. The last 4/10 mile before the bridge goes by the docks of the fishing fleet and the boats to Martha's Vineyard and Cuttyhunk Island. The docks are fascinating to explore. Just before the bridge you'll go underneath an overhead walkway with a good view of the docks from the top. • *CAUTION:* Just before the footbridge are dangerous diagonal railroad tracks; please dismount.

24. Carry your bike up the stairs to Route 6. Turn right at top of stairs and go 8/10 mile to the second traffic light on the Fairhaven side of the bridge (Main Street). Be sure to get a look at the high school on the far left-hand corner of the intersection.

25. Turn right on Main Street and go one block to Bridge Street.

26. Turn right on Bridge Street and go one block to Middle Street.

27. Turn left on Middle Street, following the harbor. Go 3/10 mile to the first crossroads (Washington Street).

28. Turn right at crossroads and immediately left on Water Street, following the harbor. After 3 blocks the road turns 90 degrees left. Continue 1 block to end (Main Street).

29. Turn right on Main Street and go 2/10 mile to crossroads and stop sign (Fort Street).

30. Turn right on Fort Street, still following the water, and go 1/2 mile to end, at ocean. Here you'll see Fort Phoenix and the state beach.

31. Turn left at ocean and then immediately left on Green Street. Go 8/10 mile to Centre Street, just after magnificent church on left.

32. Turn left on Centre Street and go 3 blocks to crossroads and stop sign (Main Street). You'll pass the town hall on your right and the library on your left. It's worth your time to take a look at the inside of the library.

33. Turn right on Main Street and go 1 block to Washington Street.

34. Turn right on Washington Street and go 1 mile to end (Route 6).

35. Bear right on Route 6. McDonald's is just ahead on right.

Directions for the ride: 14 miles

1. Follow directions for the long ride through number 9.

2. Go straight at traffic light 1 mile to Route 6, at traffic light. The amazingly ornate high school is on your left at the intersection.

3. Cross Route 6 and go one block to Bridge Street.

4. Follow directions for the long ride from number 26 to the end.

70. Land o' Lakes: Lakeville–Freetown–Acushnet–Rochester

Number of miles: 16 (27 with Freetown–Acushnet–Rochester extension).

Terrain: Gently rolling, with two short hills.

Food: Snack bar in Acushnet. Grocery in Rochester.

Start: Savas Plaza, a small shopping center on Route 18 in Lakeville, 4 miles south of Route 44. From Route 495, exit south on Route 18 and go 4 miles to shopping center on right. It's just south of where Route 105 turns left heading north.

Ten miles north of New Bedford is a cluster of large, unspoiled lakes surrounded by woods, prosperous farms, and a few cranberry bogs. Lightly traveled roads threading between the lakes make this one of the nicest regions for biking in southeastern Massachusetts.

The ride starts from the rural town of Lakeville, which is accurately named. Most of Assawompset Pond and adjacent Long Pond, two of the largest lakes in the state, lie within its borders. Lakeville is unusual in that it has no distinct town center; the closest approximation is where the ride starts. Next to the starting point is the combination town hall and fire station, housed in a handsome brick building with a bell tower. A little beyond is a fine church overlooking the water. You start off by going along the shore of Assawompset Pond, which, along with most of the other lakes in the area, supplies Taunton and New Bedford with water. Shortly you'll weave between Great Quittacas and Little Quittacas Ponds, both surrounded by pine groves. On the south shore of Little Quittacas Pond is the graceful stone New Bedford Waterworks building; just ahead, the lane carves through a perfectly groomed, symmetrical row of trees.

For a few miles you'll ride past small farms and a couple of cranberry bogs on narrow lanes. Then you'll cross the New Bedford Reservoir to the little village of Long Plain, which is surrounded by broad farms. It contains a museum of local history housed in a fine Victorian building dated 1875. A little farther along you'll pass Sni-

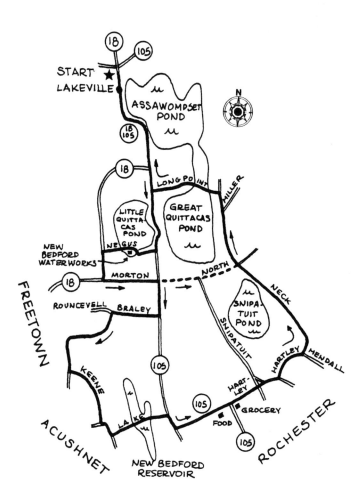

patuit Pond and bike across the gracefully curving causeway between Great Quittacas Pond and Assawompset Pond. At the end you'll go along the latter pond back to the start.

Directions for the ride: 27 miles

1. Turn right (south) out of parking lot and go 2.6 miles to where Route 18 turns right and Route 105 goes straight. Assawompset Pond is on your left. Notice the brick town hall just after you leave the lot.

2. Go straight on Route 105 for 2.1 miles to Negus Way, which bears right at bottom of little hill. You'll pass Little Quittacas Pond on your right.

3. Bear right on Negus Way, following the water, and go 1.1 miles to end (Route 18). You'll pass the New Bedford Water Works.

4. Turn left on Route 18 and go 1/2 mile to where Route 18 curves sharply right and a smaller road goes straight.

5. Go straight on smaller road and then immediately turn left at end on Morton Road. Go 1.1 miles to crossroads and stop sign (Route 105, Braley Hill Road). Here the short ride goes straight and the long ride turns right.

6. Turn right on Route 105 and go 1/2 mile to your first right, Doctor Braley Road.

7. Turn right and go 1 mile to fork where Rouncevell Drive bears right and the main road curves sharply left.

8. Curve left on main road. After 1.6 miles the paved road turns 90 degrees left and a dirt road goes straight. Stay on paved road 1.8 miles to end (Peckham Road).

9. Turn left on Peckham Road and go 1/4 mile to Lake Street on left.

10. Turn left on Lake Street and go 1 mile to end (Route 105). You'll cross the New Bedford Reservoir.

11. Turn right on Route 105 and go 2/10 mile to where Robinson Road (still Route 105) turns left. You'll pass the Long Plain Museum on your right. A snack bar is on the right immediately after the intersection.

12. Turn left on Route 105 and go 1.5 miles to where Route 105 turns right and Hartley Road goes straight.

13. Go straight on Hartley Road. After 7/10 mile you'll come to a crossroads. Go straight 2/10 mile to fork.

14. Bear left at fork and go 6/10 mile to another fork (sign may say Middleboro to left).

15. Bear left at fork and go 3.1 miles to crossroads and stop sign. You'll go along Snipatuit Pond.

16. Go straight at crossroads on Neck Road. After 1.5 miles, Miller Street bears right, but go straight 3/10 mile to Long Point Road on left.

17. Turn left on Long Point Road and go 2 miles to end (Route 105).

18. Turn right on Route 105 and go 3.1 miles to shopping center on left, just before Route 105 bears right.

Directions for the ride: 16 miles

1. Follow directions for the long ride through number 5.

2. Cross Route 105. After 8/10 mile Snipatuit Road bears right, but continue straight downhill for 1.3 miles to crossroads (Neck Road).

3. Turn left at crossroads. After 1.5 miles, Miller Street bears right, but continue straight 3/10 mile to Long Point Road on left.

4. Follow directions 17 and 18 for the long ride.

71. Mattapoisett–Rochester

Number of miles: 18 (30 with northern loop)
Terrain: Flat or gently rolling.
Food: Great country store in Rochester.
Start: A&P, Route 6, Mattapoisett, just east of North Street. From Route 195, take the Mattapoisett exit and go 1 mile to Route 6. Turn left on Route 6. The A&P is just ahead on left.

The cranberry bog country of southeastern Massachusetts provides some of the finest biking in the state. On this ride you explore a sample of that country just inland from Buzzards Bay, midway between New Bedford and the Cape Cod Canal. The area is very rural but with a tidiness about it—the trim appearance of cozy, cedar-shingled homes behind picket fences and stone walls; broad fields bordered by rustic wooden fences; and the close-cropped, reddish-hued cranberry bogs surrounded by pine groves. Smooth, lightly traveled, narrow lanes and back roads spin their web across the landscape, connecting a bog here, a pond there, and a gracious old cedar-shingled farmhouse around the bend.

The ride starts from Mattapoisett, an elegant, well-preserved harborfront town on Buzzards Bay. At one time a shipbuilding center, the waterfront is now lined with attractive wooden homes, a few tastefully designed shops, and a fine park complete with bandstand overlooking the harbor. Leaving town, you'll head into a peaceful landscape of woods and prosperous farms to Rochester, an unspoiled rural village. The center consists of a good country store and a large green, framed by a stately Gothic-style church and the old wooden town hall. Beyond Rochester you enter the cranberry bog country, with runs along Blackmore Pond and Mary's Pond for variety. The return trip to Mattapoisett is a smooth run passing small farms and fine old wooden homes.

Directions for the ride: 30 miles

   1. Turn left (east) out of parking lot and go 1/2 mile to a road that bears right.

   2. Bear right on this road and go 2/10 mile to crossroads and stop sign.

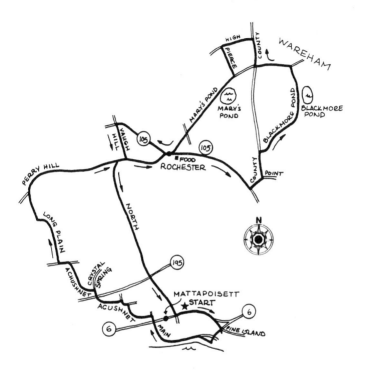

3. Turn right at crossroads and go 1/4 mile to another crossroads (Ned's Point Road on left, Beacon Street on right).

4. Go straight ahead. Just before the water the road turns 90 degrees right. Continue 2/10 mile to end (merge left).

5. Bear left at end, following the water, and go 8/10 mile to Route 6, at traffic light.

6. Cross Route 6. Just ahead the main road curves 90 degrees left on Acushnet Road. Stay on main road 4/10 to end.

7. Turn left at end (still Acushnet Road). Just ahead, the main road curves sharply right and then sharply left in quick succession. Continue 1/2 mile to where Acushnet Road turns left, immediately after the Route 195 overpass.

8. Turn left on Acushnet Road and go 1.5 miles to Long Plain Road on right, just after the road turns 90 degrees left. This is a beautiful run—and the rest of the ride is just like it!

9. Turn right on Long Plain Road and go 2.2 miles to end (merge right). You'll pass through a wooded area where the trees arch across the road in a vaulted green canopy.

10. Bear right at end and go 3.3 miles to stop sign (merge into Route 105). Here the short ride turns sharply left and the long ride bears right.

11. Bear right on Route 105. The country store is just ahead on your right. If you don't want to stop there now, you'll go by it again toward the end of the ride. Continue on Route 105 for 2.2 miles to County Road on left, just before the Route 195 overpass.

12. Turn left on County Road. After 4/10 mile, Point Road bears right, but curve left on the main road. Go 1/2 mile to Blackmore Pond Road on right (sign may say to Wareham Boat Yard).

13. Turn right on Blackmore Pond Road and go 2.6 miles to end. You'll pass Blackmore Pond on your right.

14. Turn left at end and go 8/10 mile to crossroads (County Road).

15. Turn right on County Road and go 1 mile to High Street on left (sign may say to Outdoor World).

16. Turn left on High Street and go 9/10 mile to Pierce Street on left.

17. Turn left on Pierce Street and go 1 mile to end (Mary's Pond Road).

18. Turn right at end and go 2.1 miles to crossroads. Continue straight 6/10 mile to end (merge into Route 105). You'll pass Mary's Pond on your left; then you'll go by a picturesque old wooden mill on the left, opposite a smaller pond. When you come to Route 105, the country store is just to your left.

19. Bear right on Route 105. A little ahead is a fork. Bear right, staying on Route 105, and go 1.5 miles to crossroads (Vaughn Hill Road). Just after the fork is the distinctive Gothic-style church overlooking the Rochester town green.

20. Turn left on Vaughn Hill Road and go 1.1 miles to end.

21. Turn right at end and go 1/10 mile to Mattapoisett Road on left.

22. Turn left on Mattapoisett Road. After 3 miles Crystal Spring Road bears right, but continue straight 1.6 miles to traffic light (Route 6).

23. Turn left on Route 6. The A&P is just ahead on left.

Directions for the ride: 18 miles

1. Follow directions for the long ride through number 10. Here the short ride turns sharply left on Route 105, but if you bear right, a great country store is just ahead on your right.

2. Make a sharp left on Route 105. You'll immediately see the distinctive Gothic-style church and the Rochester town green on your left. Go 1.5 miles to crossroads (Vaughn Hill Road).

3. Follow directions for the long ride from number 20 to the end.

72. Marion Ride

Number of miles: 17
Terrain: Flat.
Food: Grocery and restaurant at the center of town.
Start: Church at corner of Route 105 and County Road in
Marion, just north of Route 195.

This a one-town ride on which you explore Marion, one of the series of graceful waterfront communities along Buzzards Bay between the Rhode Island border and the Cape Cod Canal. Midway between New Bedford and the Canal along both sides of Sippican Harbor, Marion is a yachting center and the site of Tabor Academy, a prestigious boys' private school. The expansive harbor divides the town into two portions, with the center of town on the western shore. Just south of town is Converse Point, a long, slender peninsula with mansions and estates along the tip. On the eastern shore of the harbor is Sippican Neck, a much larger peninsula, more than three miles long, rimmed with estates and large, gracious homes. One of the estates, Great Hill, matches anything to be found along the Massachusetts coast. It comprises its own 300-acre subpeninsula, with a majestic mansion overlooking the bay, narrow lanes hugging the shore, and a hill 125 feet high with spectacular views. Unfortunately, the estate is open only on weekdays from 8 a.m. to 4 p.m. It's worth doing this ride during the week just to see the estate.

The ride starts off by going through the unspoiled, untouristed center of town, with a handsome white Victorian town hall, several fine churches, and well-kept, cedar-shingled homes and shops. You'll bike along the splendid shoreline, passing Tabor Academy with its large, impressive Tudor-style main building directly on the water. From here you'll swing over to Sippican Neck, bike to its tip along smooth, traffic-free roads, and return along its opposite shore, passing the Great Hill estate.

Directions for the ride

1. Turn right out of parking lot and immediately turn left on Route 105. Go 7/10 mile to fork where Front Street bears left and Spring Street bears right.

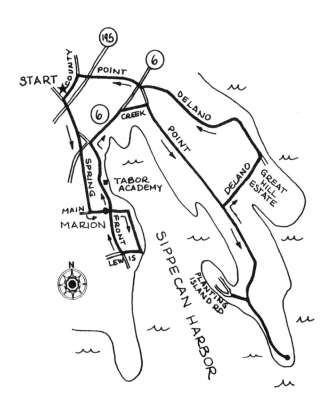

START

195

6

COUNTY

POINT

6

CREEK

DELANO

POINT

DELANO

GREAT
HILL
ESTATE

SPRING

TABOR
ACADEMY

MAIN

MARION

FRONT

LEWIS

N

SIPPECAN HARBOR

PLANTING
ISLAND RD

2. Bear right on Spring Street and go 2/10 mile to Route 6, staying on the main road.

3. Cross Route 6 and go 9/10 mile to end (Main Street). At the end the town hall is on your right.

4. Turn left on Main Street and go 2/10 mile to crossroads and stop sign (Front Street).

5. Cross Front Street and go 8/10 mile to another crossroads and stop sign (Front Street again). The road turns 90 degrees right twice on this stretch, bringing you back to Front Street. Here the ride turns right, but if you go left 2/10 mile you'll come to the town beach.

6. Turn right on Front Street and go 1.4 miles to traffic light (Route 6).

7. Turn right on Route 6 and go 7/10 mile to Creek Road, which bears right.

8. Bear right on Creek Road and go 4/10 mile to end (Point Road).

9. Turn right on Point Road. After 2.6 miles a road turns left into Piney Point and the main road curves sharply right. Continue on main road for 3/10 mile to a narrow lane on right (Planting Island Road).

10. Turn right on the lane, which leads to an island connected to the mainland by a causeway. It's called Planting Island. Go 4/10 mile to the far end of the causeway, where the road becomes private, and backtrack to the main road.

11. Turn right on the main road and go 1 mile to end, at the tip of Sippican Neck. At the very end is a country club where the road becomes private; turn around at this point.

12. At the end, backtrack 2.6 miles to Delano Road on right.

13. Turn right on Delano Road and go 2.7 miles to end (Point Road). After 6/10 mile the road curves sharply left along the ocean. (At this point the entrance to the Great Hill estate is on your right; be sure to explore it if it's open.)

14. Turn right on Point Road and immediately cross Route 6 at traffic light. Go 1 mile to end.

15. Turn left at end and go 3/10 mile to church on right.

73. Cranberry Cruise: Middleboro–Plympton–Carver

Number of miles: 18 (28 with Carver extension)
Terrain: Flat, with a couple of short hills.
Food: Grocery store and snack bar in Plympton. Grocery store in Carver.
Start: Middleboro Plaza, junction of Routes 105 and 28 in Middleboro, just north of Route 495.

This is a tour of the heart of the cranberry-growing country, midway between Taunton and Plymouth. Biking through the bogs, which are crosshatched by narrow, straight channels and have rustic little wooden sheds next to them, is a true pleasure. Narrow, untraveled lanes wind past peaked-roof, cedar-shingled homes and scrub pine from one bog to another across one of the most appealingly rural landscapes in Massachusetts. The nicest time to do this ride is during the harvest season in October, when the berries form a deep red carpet across the land, or during the spring, when the bogs are flooded ponds.

The ride starts from Middleboro, a handsome town with large old wooden homes along the main street leading into the center, a dignified white town hall with a graceful dome, and a stately white church across from it. A fascinating place to visit is the Middleboro Historical Museum, with a display relating to the lives of Tom and Lavinia Thumb, the most famous midgets in history. Lavinia was born in Middleboro. Two miles out of town you'll pass a large green with a magnificent white church standing over it, unusual because it is in splendid isolation. A little farther on is the Eddy Homestead, a Federal-style mansion built by Zachariah Eddy, a prominent local lawyer. From here you'll head along pretty, narrow lanes to Plympton, an unspoiled gem of a town. The long green, with a monument in the middle, is framed by a fine old church and country store. The rest of the ride brings you past dozens of bogs on country lanes, passing through Carver, the number-one cranberry town in the state. The tiny center of town has a little park with a handsome Civil War monument.

Directions for the ride: 28 miles

1. Turn left (north) out of parking lot onto Route 105 and immediately cross Route 28 at traffic light. Go 6/10 mile to another light (Wareham Street on right) in the center of town. The handsome, pillared town hall is on your left shortly before the intersection.

2. Go straight at light 4/10 mile to crossroads where Route 105 turns right. If you want to visit the museum, turn right 1 block past the light on Jackson Street. The museum is just ahead on your left.

3. Turn right, staying on Route 105, and go 1.6 miles to traffic light (Route 44). Just before the light is a magnificent church and green.

4. Cross Route 44. After 7/10 mile, Route 105 turns left, but continue straight 1.4 miles to fork (sign may say Waterville, Plymouth).

5. Bear left at fork and go 2.2 miles to blinking light where the main road curves sharply right and a smaller road turns left. Just beyond the fork, at a crossroads, the Eddy Homestead is on your left.

6. Turn left at blinking light and go 1.2 miles to end (Route 58), in the center of Plympton. Here the short ride turns right and the long ride turns left.

7. Turn left on Route 58 (there's a restaurant if you turn right for 1/10 mile). Go 1/4 mile to Main Street on right, at cemetery. Turn right on Main Street and go 7/10 mile to a road that bears right up a short hill.

8. Bear right on this road and go 3/10 mile to Upland Road, which bears right up another short hill.

9. Bear right on Upland Road and go 1.2 miles to end.

10. Turn right at end and go 1/10 mile to Brook Street on left, at traffic island.

11. Turn left on Brook Street. After 2/10 mile a road bears right, but curve left on the main road. Go 4/10 mile to fork.

12. Bear slightly right at fork up a little hill. After 8/10 mile you'll merge to your right into High Street. Continue 7/10 mile to your first left (Gate Street) at a traffic island.

13. Turn left on Gate Street and go 1/2 mile to end, at stop sign.

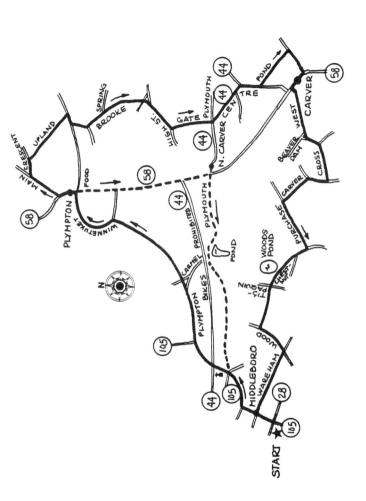

14. Go straight at stop sign and immediately bear left on Route 44. (Don't turn 90 degrees left directly at the stop sign.) Go 1.3 miles to fork where Route 44 bears left and Center Street bears right. Notice the unusual wooden church on your right as soon as you get on Route 44.

15. Bear right at fork and go 1/2 mile to Pond Street on left.

16. Turn left on Pond Street and go 1.1 miles to end.

17. Turn right at end and go 1 mile to end (Route 58).

18. Turn right on Route 58 and go 1/2 mile to West Street on left. This is the center of Carver. A grocery is on the far side of the intersection, and a park with a Civil War monument is on the near side.

19. Turn left on West Street and go 1.1 miles to fork where the main road bears left and Beaver Dam Road bears right.

20. Bear left at fork and go 3/10 mile to another fork (Cross Street bears right).

21. Bear right on Cross Street and go 8/10 mile to end (Popes Point Street).

22. Turn right on Popes Point Street and go 3/10 mile to fork (Carver Street bears left).

23. Bear left on Carver Street and go 9/10 mile to end.

24. Turn left at end and go 1.7 miles to end (Chestnut Street), at traffic island.

25. Turn right on Chestnut Street and go 3/10 mile to where the main road curves left and a narrow lane goes straight.

26. Go straight onto the lane (still Chestnut Street). After 1 mile you'll come to a crossroads (Tisquapin Street). Continue 1.2 miles to end (Wood Street). You'll pass Woods Pond on right.

27. Turn left on Wood Street and go 1.2 miles to diagonal crossroads and stop sign.

28. Turn right at stop sign and go 1.2 miles to traffic light (Route 105), back in the center of Middleboro.

29. Turn left on Route 105 and go 6/10 mile to Route 28, at traffic light. Shopping center is on far side of intersection.

Directions for the ride: 17 miles

1. Follow directions for the long ride through number 6. Here the ride turns right, but it's worth turning left to see Plympton.

Harvesting cranberries in Carver.

2. Turn right on Route 58 and go 2.3 miles to traffic light where Route 44 turns left. Here the ride turns right, but if you turn left on Route 44 for 1/4 mile you'll go through North Carver, another delightful village with a handsome white church.

3. Turn right at traffic light and go 1.6 miles to fork where the main road bears right.

4. Bear right, staying on main road. After 7/10 mile, a road bears right underneath Route 44, but bear slightly left, staying on the main road. Go 2.6 miles to Route 105, at a five-way intersection.

5. Bear slightly left on Route 105 and go 2.4 miles to Route 28, at second traffic light. The shopping center is on the far side of the intersection.

74. Pilgrim's Progress: Plymouth–Carver

Number of miles: 9 (24 with Carver extension, 32 visiting Myles
    Standish State Forest and Edaville Railroad)
Terrain: Gently rolling, with a few short hills.
Food: Country store in South Carver. Snack bar at Edaville
    Railroad.
Start: Shopping center on the north side of Route 44 in
    Plymouth, just west of Route 3.

This is a tour of Plymouth and the scrub-pine and cranberry-bog
country surrounding it. You'll go past or near many of the town's
historic landmarks. Outside of town you'll go through the Myles
Standish State Forest, a large, unspoiled area of pines and ponds,
and then go past the Edaville Railroad, a narrow-gauge railway
looping through a large expanse of cranberry bogs.

The cranberry-growing area is a uniquely beautiful part of the
state to explore by bicycle, especially during the harvest season in
October, when the berries turn the bogs into a crimson carpet.
Surrounded by pines and sandy banks, with little wooden sheds
next to them, the bogs have a trim, rustic appeal. Narrow roads
guide the bicyclist from bog to bog past cedar-shingled, cozy-look-
ing homes.

You'll start the ride by visiting the Pilgrim Monument, a soaring,
Victorian granite statue built in 1889. From here it's just a couple of
blocks to the Commonwealth Winery, which is open for tours and
wine-tastings. Just ahead is the waterfront, where you'll go by Cran-
berrry World, a museum of the cranberry and the cranberry industry. It's free and worth seeing. A little farther along the waterfront
are the Mayflower II and Plymouth Rock. When you see the Mayflower II you'll be surprised at how small it is. Plymouth Rock is just
a plain old rock covered by an ornate pillared portico. Within a
couple of blocks are numerous other attractions and historic buildings, including a wax museum depicting Pilgrim life, the Federal-era
Antiquarian House, and the outstanding Pilgrim Hall Museum, one
of the oldest in the country, founded in 1824. It contains extensive
displays of Pilgrim possessions and artifacts.

Leaving Plymouth you'll head to the Myles Standish State Forest, an extensive wilderness area of scrub pine spreading up and over an endless succession of bubblelike little hills and hollows. Biking through this terrain is a lot of fun if you use your gears properly, roller-coastering down one little hill and over the next one. Several small ponds lie nestled in the pines. Beyond the forest you abruptly enter cranberry-bog country. After a few miles you'll come to the Edaville Railroad, which is touristy but fun. On the grounds is a museum with a fine collection of railroad memorabilia, antique toy trains, fire engines, and antique cars. Beyond Edaville you'll go through a long string of bogs and pass by Savery's Avenue, the first divided highway in America, built in 1861. The road consists of two narrow lanes with pine trees between them and on each side, extending a half mile alongside Route 58.

Directions for the ride: 32 miles

1. Turn left out of parking lot onto Route 44 and go 6/10 mile to Allerton Street on left, one block before traffic light at Route 3A.

2. Turn left on Allerton Street up a short hill. Just ahead, the Pilgrim Monument is on your left. From the monument, continue 2/10 mile to end (Route 3A).

3. At end, jog right and immediately left on Lothrop Street. Go 2/10 mile to end (Water Street), passing Commonwealth Winery on left. • *CAUTION:* It's very bumpy where you cross the railroad tracks. When you come to Water Street the ride turns right, but if you turn left for 100 yards you'll come to Cranberry World, which is free and fascinating.

4. Turn right on Water Street and go 1/4 mile to rotary.

5. Go straight at rotary, paralleling Plymouth Harbor. After 1/4 mile you'll pass the Mayflower II and then Plymouth Rock on your left. Continue past the Rock 1/10 mile to Leyden Street, which bears right uphill.

6. Bear right on Leyden Street and go 1/10 mile to traffic light (Route 3A). Notice the fine old homes along this street.

7. Cross Route 3A and turn immediately left. If you go straight instead of left, you'll go up Old Burial Hill, a well-landscaped cemetery with most of its gravestones dating back to the 1700s. The view from the top of the hill is impressive.

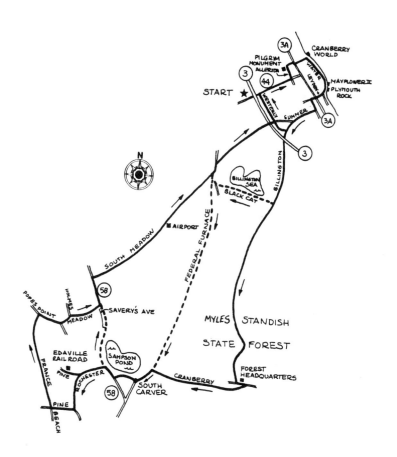

START

N

PILGRIM
MONUMENT
ALLERTON

3A

CRANBERRY
WORLD

MAYFLOWER II
PLYMOUTH
ROCK

3

44

WATER

WESTERLY

SUMMER

LEYDEN

3A

3

BILLINGTON

BILLINGTON
SEA

BLACK CAT

SOUTH MEADOW

AIRPORT

FEDERAL FURNACE

POPES POINT

HOLMES

58

MEADOW

SAVERY'S AVE

MYLES STANDISH

STATE FOREST

FRANCE

EDAVILLE
RAIL ROAD

PINE

ROCHESTER

SAMPSON
POND

58

SOUTH
CARVER

CRANBERRY

FOREST
HEADQUARTERS

PINE
BEACH

8. After turning left, go 1 block to Summer Street on right.
• *CAUTION:* There's a sewer grate with the slots going the wrong way at the intersection.

9. Turn right on Summer Street, passing the Governor Carver Motor Inn on your right, and go 4/10 mile to Billington Street, which bears left downhill. Across from the Inn is a beautifully landscaped park with a restored old gristmill. Bear left on Billington Street and go 1/2 mile to fork.

10. Bear left at fork, going underneath Route 3, and go 1.4 miles to Black Cat Road on right, opposite cranberry bog. Here the 32-mile ride goes straight and the two shorter rides turn right.

11. Continue straight for 6 miles to fork where the main road bears right. Stay on main road for 1 mile to end, where you'll merge left immediately after the State Forest headquarters on your left.

12. Turn sharply right at end, just after the forest headquarters, and go 1.5 miles to fork where Federal Road bears left and the main road bears right. Stay on main road for 1.2 miles to end.

13. Turn left at end and go 4/10 mile to fork. A small grocery store is at the intersection.

14. Bear right at fork and go 6/10 mile to end (Route 58), passing Sampson Pond on your right.

15. Turn right at end and go 2/10 mile to Rochester Road on left (sign may say Edaville Railroad).

16. Turn left on Rochester Road and go 6/10 mile to Pine Street, the second of two roads that bear right (sign says to Edaville Railroad). Here the ride bears left, but if you'd like to visit Edaville, bear right at fork on Pine Street. The Railroad is just ahead on right.

17. Bear left at fork (still Rochester Road) and go 1.1 miles to end (Pine Street on right, East Street on left).

18. Turn right on Pine Street and go 7/10 mile to crossroads (Beach Street on left, France Street on right).

19. Turn right at crossroads and go 3.1 miles to end, at traffic island.

20. Turn right at end and go 7/10 mile to fork (Meadow Street bears left).

21. Bear left on Meadow Street. After 1/2 mile Holmes Street turns left, but bear right, staying on Meadow Street. Go 1.3 miles to end (Route 58). Here the ride goes left, but if you turn right for 2/10 mile you'll come to Savery's Avenue.

414

Jenny Gristmill, Plymouth. A working replica of the first gristmill built in 1636 by the Pilgrims.

22. Turn left on Route 58 and go 7/10 mile to South Meadow Road on right. There may be a sign pointing to the airport.

23. Turn right on South Meadow Road and go 5.2 miles to end. You'll pass the Plymouth Airport on your right.

24. Turn left at end and then immediately bear right at fork. Go 1.8 miles to crossroads immediately after you go over the Route 3 overpass (Westerly Road).

25. Turn left at crossroads and go 4/10 mile to Route 44.

26. Turn left on Route 44. • *CAUTION:* Busy intersection. Shopping center is just ahead on right.

Directions for the ride: 24 miles

1. Follow directions for the long ride through number 10.

2. Bear left at fork, going underneath Route 3, and go 1.4 miles to Black Cat Road on right, opposite cranberry bog.

3. Turn right on Black Cat Road and go 1.7 miles to end (merge into Federal Furnace Road). You'll go past Billington Sea, which is a freshwater lake. At the end of Black Cat Road the 24-mile ride turns sharply left and the 9-mile ride bears right.

4. Turn sharply left on Federal Furnace Road and go 6.7 miles to fork. The South Carver Post Office and a small grocery store are at the intersection.

5. Bear right at fork and go 6/10 mile to end (Route 58), passing Sampson Pond on your right.

6. Turn right on Route 58 and go 3 miles to South Meadow Road on right. There may be a sign pointing to the airport at the intersection. You'll parallel Savery's Avenue on your left after 1.5 miles. It's more pleasant to ride on the Avenue than on the main road.

7. Follow directions for the long ride from number 23 to the end.

Directions for the ride: 9 miles

1. Follow directions for the 32-mile ride through number 10.

2. Turn right on Black Cat Road and go 1.7 miles to end (merge into Federal Furnace Road). You'll go past Billington Sea, which is a freshwater lake.

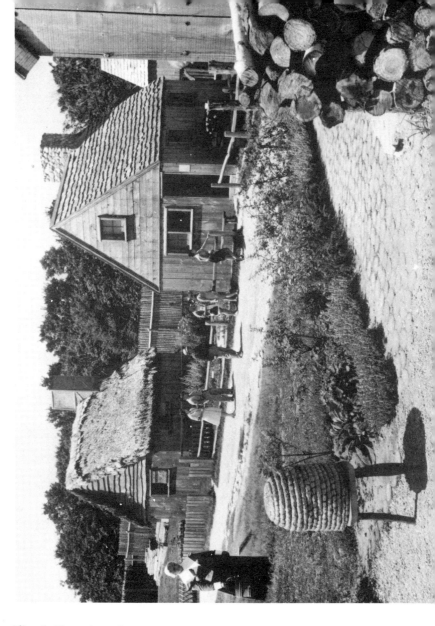

Plimoth Plantation, Plymouth.

3. Bear right on Federal Furnace Road and go 2/10 mile to fork.

4. Bear right at fork and go 1.8 miles to crossroads immediately after you go over the Route 3 overpass (Westerly Road).

5. Turn left at crossroads and go 4/10 mile to Route 44.

6. Turn left on Route 44. • *CAUTION:* Busy intersection. Shopping center is just ahead on right.

75. Southeastern Shore: Manomet–Cedarville–Cape Cod Canal

Number of miles: 16 (34 with Cedarville–Cape Cod Canal extension)

Terrain: Gently rolling, with several short, sharp hills and lots of little ups and downs.

Food: Grocery and snack bar in Manomet. Snack bar in Cedarville. Friendly and McDonald's near the Canal. Cafeteria at Plimoth Plantation.

Start: Plimoth Plantation, Route 3A in Plymouth, 3 miles south of Route 44. From Route 3, take the Plimoth Plantation Highway exit and follow the signs. Park here only if you'll definitely be back before the Plantation closes (currently at 5 o'clock). Allow 5 hours for the long ride and 2.5 hours for the short one. I recommend getting an early start and then visiting the Plantation after the ride.

Another good starting point is the Cape Cod Canal visitor's center parking lot on Route 6 in Bourne (see Ride 76). If you start here, carry your bike down the stairs to the canal service road and begin with direction 13.

The southeastern shoulder of Massachusetts between Plymouth and the Cape Cod Canal provides ideal bicycling through a rural, unspoiled area of scrub pine, lots of lakes, cranberry bogs, a few farms, and refreshingly undeveloped coastline with the exception of White Horse Beach. The long ride goes along a section of the service road hugging the Cape Cod Canal, which is one of the nicest places in the state to bike. The ride has both a cultural highlight and a low point—Plimoth Planation, a superb reconstruction of the original Pilgrim colony, and Pilgrim I, a nuclear power plant.

You'll start from Plimoth Plantation, a successful attempt to portray the village and the style in which the Pilgrims lived in 1627 as accurately as possible. Employees dress in period costume, imitate the Pilgrim's speech as well as it has been determined, raise farm animals, and reenact episodes from the daily life of the colony such as court sessions, trade with the Indians, and military drills.

Leaving the Plantation you immediately enter the delightful landscape of scrub pine and cozy, cedar-shingled homes characteristic of southeastern Massachusetts. The terrain is rolling but in miniature, with little ups and downs that are fun to bike through if you time your shifting properly. You'll pass Little Long Pond and then enjoy a smooth, straight run past cranberry bogs to Manomet, the community where the shoulder of land protrudes farthest out to sea. You'll follow the shore along a steep bluff nearly 100 feet high, and then descend past the access road to the public shore-front behind the Pilgrim I nuclear power plant. It's worth visiting this spot to see what a nuke looks like—a monolithic concrete slab jutting up starkly from the otherwise unspoiled coastline, with the effluent gushing from beneath the building to the ocean along a concrete channel lined with fishermen. An information booth displays booklets extolling the benefits and safety of nuclear energy, and you can decorate your bike with free bumper stickers saying "Know Nukes" and "Build Pilgrim II." From here it's not far along the bay back to the starting point.

The longer ride heads south all the way to the canal through more of this beautiful woods-and-lakes landscape, passing weathered, cedar-shingled homes nestled in pine groves, a country church, and two old cemeteries. Then you'll enjoy an extended run along two-mile-long Great Herring Pond. Just beyond the canal you go through the tiny village of Bournedale, with a small, cupola-topped village hall and a charming country store. At the canal a small pavilion provides an exhibit of its history.

The canal is a visual delight, curving gently between low hills with the graceful span of the Sagamore Bridge in the background. From the canal you'll head back to Plymouth, following the coast. Several small roads diverge from the main road to dip along the water's edge. In Manomet you'll go out to Manomet Point, which provides panoramic views of Cape Cod Bay. You'll go along White Horse Beach, a popular summer resort, and then rejoin the short ride just in time for the run along the Manomet Bluffs.

Directions for the ride: 34 miles

1. From Plimoth Plantation, turn right (south) on Route 3A and go 1/2 mile to Clifford Road, which bears right midway up the hill.

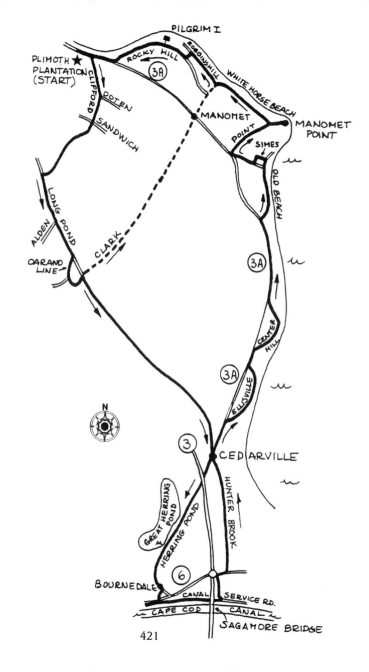

PILGRIM I

PLIMOTH
PLANTATION
(START)

ROCKY HILL

3A

ROBINSHILL

WHITE HORSE BEACH

CLIFFORD

DOTEN

SANDWICH

MANOMET

MANOMET
POINT

Point

SIMES

LONG POND

ALDEN

OLD BEACH

CLARK

OARAND
LINE

3A

CENTER HILL

N

3A

ELLISVILLE

3

CEDARVILLE

GREAT HERRING POND

HUNTER BROOK

HERRING POND

BOURNEDALE

6

CANAL SERVICE RD.

CAPE COD CANAL

SAGAMORE BRIDGE

421

2. Bear right on Clifford Road and go 8/10 mile to fork (Doten Road bears left).

3. Bear right at fork (still Clifford Road) and go 4/10 mile to crossroads and stop sign (Sandwich Road).

4. Cross Sandwich Road. After 7/10 mile Russell Mill Road is on your right, but curve left, staying on the main road. Continue 1.2 miles to end.

5. Turn left at end. After 1 mile there'll be a road on your right (sign may say to Myles Standish State Forest), but again curve left, staying on the main road. Go 1.6 miles to Oar and Line Road, which bears right.

6. Bear right on Oar and Line Road and go 4/10 mile to fork, passing Little Long Pond on right. At the fork the ride bears left, but if you bear right for 100 yards you'll come to a captivating little beach on Long Pond.

7. Bear left at fork and go 4/10 mile to end (Long Pond Road). Here the short ride jogs left and immediately right on Clark Road, and the long ride turns right.

8. Turn right on Long Pond Road and go 4.8 miles to end (merge into Route 3A at stop sign). After 1.2 miles, as you pass a little field on the right with a cedar-shingled home at the back, notice an unusual tower next to the road; it has a wooden top and a stone base.

9. Bear right on Route 3A and go 1/10 mile to fork. This is Cedarville, which is part of Plymouth.

10. Bear right at fork, going underneath Route 3. From Route 3 go 2.8 miles to the Bournedale Village Hall, a picturesque old building with a cupola, on your right. It's 8/10 mile after the end of Great Herring Pond. Just past the village hall, a road turns right opposite the country store.

11. Turn right on this road and go 100 yards to end (Route 6).

12. Cross Route 6. The Cape Cod Canal is in front of you. A small pavilion tells you about the canal. Carry your bike down the stairs to the service road running along the bank of the canal.

13. Turn left on the service road, following the canal on your right. Ahead of you is the Sagamore Bridge. Go 9/10 mile to a fork just before the bridge where the left-hand road bears up a steep hill.

14. Bear left uphill at fork. Go underneath the bridge and into a small parking lot. Turn sharp left out of the lot and go up a moderate hill, paralleling the bridge on your left. Just ahead is a Friendly on your left and a rotary.

15. At rotary, turn immediate right, passing McDonald's on left. Immediately after McDonald's, turn left (sign may say to Route 3A). After 2.6 miles you'll be back in Centerville, where the road becomes Route 3A. Continue 1/2 mile to Ellisville Road, a smaller road that bears right.

16. Bear right on Ellisville Road and go 1.5 miles to end (3A again).

17. Turn right on Route 3A and go 1/4 mile to Center Hill Road, a smaller road that bears right.

18. Bear right on Center Hill Road and go 1.8 miles to end (merge back into Route 3A).

19. Bear right on Route 3A and go 2.5 miles to Old Beach Road on right. If you come to a large pond on your left, you've gone 2/10 mile too far.

20. Turn right on Old Beach Road and go 1.2 miles to fork (Simes Road bears left).

21. Bear left on Simes Road and go 2/10 mile to end. You'll turn 90 degrees left on this stretch.

22. Turn right at end and go 1/4 mile to end.

23. Turn 90 degrees right at end on Point Road (don't bear right on Route 3A). After 9/10 mile you'll come to a little traffic island. Bear slightly right and go 3/10 mile to the tip of Manomet Point.

24. Turn around and backtrack 3/10 mile to the traffic island.

25. Bear right at traffic island, following the ocean along White Horse Beach, and go 1.1 miles to Robbins Hill Road on right. It's your first right after the road curves sharply inland.

26. Turn right on Robbins Hill Road and go 6/10 mile to a large rock in the middle of the road.

27. Turn left immediately after the rock and go 100 yards to end, down a steep hill. • *CAUTION* at bottom.

28. Turn right at end and go 2.4 miles to end (merge into Route 3A). You'll pass the access road to the public shorefront behind the nuclear power plant. It's the third driveway on the right. All three access roads bristle with forbidding signs that say "exclusion area" and other dire warnings, but the third road is public and you won't be shot on sight if you venture down it.

29. Bear right on Route 3A and go 1 mile to Plimoth Plantation on left.

Directions for the ride: 16 miles

1. Follow the directions for the long ride through number 7.

2. At end, jog left and immediately right onto Clark Road. Go 4.4 miles to crossroads and stop sign (Route 3A). Notice the fine white church at the intersection.

3. Cross Route 3A and go 7/10 mile to Robbins Hill Road on left. It's your second left. If you come to the water you've gone 1/10 mile too far.

4. Turn left on Robbins Hill Road and go 6/10 mile to a large rock in the middle of the road.

5. Follow directions for the long ride from number 27 to the end.

76. The Cape Cod Canal Ride: Bournedale– Buzzards Bay–Onset

Number of miles: 14
Terrain: Flat, with one moderate hill at the beginning.
Food: Grocery stores and snack bars in Onset and Buzzards Bay.
Start: Cape Cod Canal visitor's center parking lot, Route 6 in Bourne, on the north side of the canal, across from the Bournedale Lodge Motel. It's 1 mile west of the rotary immediately before the Sagamore Bridge, and 3 miles east of the rotary before the Bourne Bridge, in a valley between two hills. If you're heading east on Route 195, take exit 2 (Route 6), which deposits you at the Bourne Bridge rotary.

• *CAUTION:* This ride has two brief sections on Route 6, a four-lane, undivided, extremely busy highway. The only safe way to go is to walk or ride through the parking lots of the businesses alongside the road, dismounting when necessary. Do not ride on the roadway—it's too dangerous.

This is a relaxing tour along the scenic Cape Cod Canal, the unspoiled woods and inlets just north of it, and the old beach resort of Onset. You'll start from the banks of the canal at the visitor's center, where there's an exhibit on the canal's construction and history. Just inland from the canal is the tiny village of Bournedale, with a charming country store and the little Village Hall, an ornate old building with a cupola. From here you'll head a couple of miles inland along winding, nearly untraveled roads through woods and then along the shore of Buttermilk Bay, one of the many inlets along the edge of Buzzards Bay. You'll then head south to Onset, an old beach resort with some fine Victorian buildings set on a peninsula surrounded by little coves and inlets. Onset is not Hyannisport—it's middle-class rather than elegant, a little congested, a little faded—but it's not sleazy. The views of neighboring peninsulas across the gracefully curving shoreline of Onset Bay, instead of just open ocean, give Onset a unique appeal.

From Onset it's a short ride to Buzzards Bay, which is a part of Bourne and the main commercial center for the southeastern corner of the state south of Plymouth. Here you'll get onto the service road beside the Cape Cod Canal, one of the most enjoyable places to bicycle in Massachusetts. The road is blocked off to motor vehicles, completely flat, and hugs the bank of the canal for its entire length. As a waterway the canal is beautiful, curving gently between low wooded hills, of uniform width (about 200 yards), and crossed by the spidery steel spans of the Bourne and Sagamore highway bridges, as well as the striking vertical-lift railroad bridge that you'll see when you get onto the service road. In good weather the canal is alive with pleasure boats and some sleek yachts, and if you're lucky you may see an enormous barge or cargo ship chugging along.

Directions for the ride

1. Go to the west end of the parking lot and head inland at blinking light. Go 100 yards to end, where there's a country store. This is the village of Bournedale.

2. Turn left at end and go 1/10 mile to fork (Bournedale Road bears left). Immediately before the fork, the Bournedale Village Hall is on your left.

3. Bear left downhill at fork and go 2.2 miles to end, at a large, triangular traffic island. Shortly before the end you'll pass a farm on the left with an unusual stone tower.

4. Bear right at end and go 1/10 mile to Old Head of the Bay Road, a smaller road that bears left.

5. Bear left on Old Head of the Bay Road and go 1/2 mile to end (merge back into main road). You'll go along Little Buttermilk Bay.

6. Bear left at end and go 8/10 mile to Pine Ridge Road, a smaller road that bears left. You'll pass a cranberry bog on your right and Buttermilk Bay on your left.

7. Bear left on Pine Ridge Road, following the bay, and go 1/2 mile to end.

8. Turn left at end and go 9/10 mile to end (merge into Route 6).

9. Bear right on Route 6 and go 3/10 mile to traffic light (sign may say to Onset, Point Independence). Here you will turn left by making a jug-handle turn—you bear right just before the light and

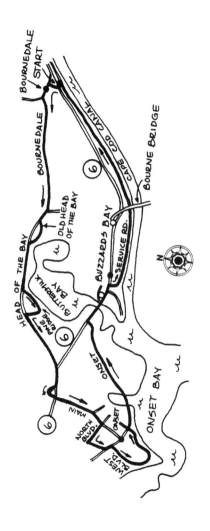

427

cross the highway at right angles. • *CAUTION:* See caution notice at beginning of ride—don't bike on travel portion of Route 6.

10. Make jug-handle left turn at light onto Main Avenue. • *CAUTION:* Bad railroad tracks as soon as you cross Route 6. Go 7/10 mile to drawbridge. Curve right on the main road immediately after drawbridge and go 100 yards to crossroads (North Boulevard on right).

11. Turn right on North Boulevard. On your right is Muddy Cove, an offshoot of Onset Bay, which is in turn an offshoot of Buzzards Bay. After 1/4 mile the main road turns 90 degrees left. Continue less than 2/10 mile to end (merge left).

12. Bear left at end and go 1/10 mile to West Boulevard on right, immediately after playground on right.

13. Turn right on West Boulevard and go 9/10 mile to crossroads and stop sign, following the shore of Onset Bay. This is a pleasant run around the Onset peninsula and along Onset Beach.

14. Turn right at crossroads and go 1.9 miles to Route 6, at traffic light.

15. Turn right on Route 6 and go 1/2 mile to rotary immediately after bridge over inlet. • *CAUTION:* Walk or ride through the parking lots along the *westbound* side of the highway, against the traffic. Cross the bridge using the sidewalk (there's no sidewalk on the eastbound side). Walk across Route 6 immediately after the bridge. You may have to wait a long time for a break in the traffic or for a courteous driver to let you across.

16. Go straight at rotary (don't bear left). Just ahead is a traffic light where Academy Avenue turns right. Immediately after the light, turn right into parking lot, passing the old Buzzards Bay train station on your right. In front of you is the magnificent vertical-lift railroad bridge across the canal, built in 1935, one of the highest bridges of this type in the country. Just past the train station the parking lot turns to dirt. Continue 100 yards to the canal, where you'll pick up the beginning of the service road. You'll have to walk your bike around a barricade meant to keep out cars.

17. Follow the service road along the canal 3.7 miles until you come to several flights of stairs going up the embankment on your left. The stairs lead to the parking lot you started from.

Chapter 7

Central Massachusetts

Numbers on this map refer to rides in this book.

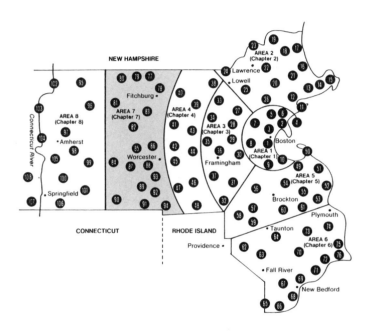

77. Ashby–Ashburnham–New Ipswich, New Hampshire–Greenville, New Hampshire

Number of miles: 15 (32 with New Ipswich–Greenville extension)

Terrain: Hilly. The toughest hills are in the first half of the ride.

Road surface: 1/4 mile of dirt road near beginning of the ride.

Food: None en route for the short ride. Grocery in New Ipswich. Grocery and restaurant in Greenville. Grocery at end.

Start: Corner of South Road and Route 119 in the center of Ashby. Park on South Road, because of the No Parking signs on Route 119.

This is a fascinating and very scenic tour of the rugged hills and pristine little towns north of Fitchburg in the region straddling the Massachusetts–New Hampshire border. The first eight miles are challenging, but after that the terrain is delightfully rolling, with some fine views from the tops of broad, open ridges. The twin towns of New Ipswich and Greenville, only two miles apart, contrast dramatically with each other. New Ipswich is a museum-piece rural town with an outstanding Federal-era mansion, and Greenville is a classic, well-maintained mill town.

The ride starts from Ashby, a fine little town with a classic white church and green and a rambling, wooden Victorian town hall. Outside of town you'll go along two undeveloped reservoirs and then head west into Ashburnham, up and over steep hills with inspiring views at the top. The return to Ashby brings you through a very rural landscape of woods and small farms along narrow country roads.

The long ride heads north into New Hampshire, skirting the base of 1,830-foot Mount Watatic, second highest mountain in the state east of the Connecticut River. Just over the border is the elegant, perfectly preserved village of New Ipswich. Gracing the center of town are two stately white churches (one of them recycled into an office building), rambling white wooden homes with dark shutters, a miniature wooden library, and a handsome brick schoolhouse at the head of a large green. And if this isn't enough, the

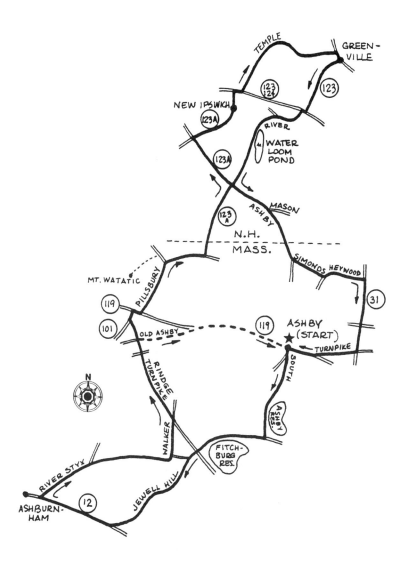

pride of the village is the Barrett House, an elegant Federal-era mansion built in 1800 and stocked with impressive period furnishings. It is administered by the Society for the Preservation of New England Antiquities and is open afternoons from June 1 to October 15.

From New Ipswich you take a short run to Greenville, a beautiful and unusually graceful old mill town. You first see it from a hillside spread out beneath you in its entirety. In the center of town is a fine Gothic-style church, gracious brick and wooden homes, the elegant Red Brick Inn, and an impressive, high dam. A mile outside of town, in splendid isolation, is a marvelous five-story Victorian mill that's more like a castle. The return to Ashby is a delight, following the dammed-up Souhegan River and then traversing open ridges with fine views.

Directions for the ride: 32 miles

1. Head south on South Road and go 1/10 mile to fork.

2. Bear left at fork (still South Road) and go 1.7 miles to end. You'll pass the Ashby Reservoir near the end.

3. Turn right at end and go 1.2 miles to crossroads and stop sign. You'll go along the Fitchburg Reservoir.

4. Go straight at crossroads 2/10 mile to fork.

5. Go straight up the hill at fork (don't bear right). After 8/10 mile, at top of tough hill, the road becomes dirt for 1/4 mile. • *CAUTION:* The last hundred yards of the dirt stretch go down a steep hill. *Walk* your bike—it's unsafe to ride. After the road becomes paved again, continue 1.5 miles to end (merge into Route 12). • *CAUTION:* This road has some steep downhill pitches with bumpy spots, and a sharp curve to the right midway down the first hill. Take it easy. This is the worst road on the ride, so don't get discouraged.

6. Bear right on Route 12 and go 1.2 miles to River Styx Road, which turns sharply right (it's a hairpin turn). After 1/2 mile there's a small parking area on the left at a pretty little dam and millpond. When you get to River Styx Road, the ride turns right, but if you go straight 3/10 mile, you'll come to the center of Ashburnham, another classic New England town. There's a grocery here.

7. Make a sharp right on River Styx Road and go 9/10 mile to fork.

8. At fork go straight downhill (don't bear left uphill). Go 1.5 miles to where Walker Road bears slightly left and another road turns right.

9. Bear slightly left on Walker Road and go 7/10 mile to a diagonal crossroads and stop sign.

10. Bear left at crossroads and go 1.6 miles to a small crossroads, then continue straight 3/10 mile to a second crossroads (Old Ashby Road). There's a small house on the right at the far side of the intersection. Here the short ride turns right and the long ride goes straight.

11. Cross Old Ashby Road and go 1/2 mile to end (merge into Route 101).

12. Bear right on Route 101 and go 1/10 mile to end (Route 119).

13. Turn right on Route 119 and go 100 yards to Pillsbury Road on left.

14. Turn left on Pillsbury Road and go 1 mile to fork. On your left is Mount Watatic. If you bear left at the fork for 3/10 mile, a path bearing left climbs 1 mile to the summit. A lookout tower is at the top, and a ski area is on the northeast slope.

15. Bear right at fork (still Pillsbury Road) and go 6/10 mile to your first left (West Road).

16. Turn left on West Road (it becomes Route 123A at the New Hampshire line) and go 1.8 miles to crossroads and stop sign.

17. Turn left at crossroads (still Route 123A) and go 1.3 miles to another crossroads (Smithville Road).

18. Turn right at crossroads (still Route 123A) and go 1.4 miles to end (Routes 123 and 124). Toward the end you'll go through New Ipswich, New Hampshire, and pass the Barrett House on your left. Just before the end there's a church on your right that has been recycled into offices. If you look to your right immediately after the church, you'll see the stately brick Appleton Academy standing proudly over the green.

19. Turn right on Routes 123 and 124, go 100 yards, and turn left. Go 2.5 miles to end, at stop sign, at bottom of steep hill. This is Greenville. At the brow of the hill, notice the Gothic-style church on your left.

20. Bear right at bottom of hill and bear right again on Route 123 immediately after the bridge. There's an impressive dam on your right at the bridge. Go 1.6 miles to end.

21. Turn right at end and then immediately turn left uphill on River Road. Go 6/10 mile to fork where the main road bears left and a smaller road, Old County Road, goes straight.

22. Bear left on the main road and go 1.7 miles to crossroads and stop sign. You'll pass Water Loom Pond on your left.

23. Turn left at crossroads and go 1 mile to fork at top of long, gradual hill. It's after Whittemore Road, a small road that bears right.

24. Bear right at fork and go 1.4 miles to another fork that comes up suddenly as you're going down a little hill. You are now back in Massachusetts.

25. Bear left at fork onto a smaller road and go 1 mile to end (merge left).

26. Bear left at end and go 8/10 mile to end (Greenville Road, Route 31).

27. Turn right on Route 31 and go 1.5 miles to blinking light (Turnpike Road). It's your third crossroads.

28. Turn right on Turnpike Road and go 9/10 mile to end (merge into Route 119).

29. Bear right on Route 119 and go 4/10 mile to South Road on left, in the center of Ashby.

Directions for the ride: 15 miles

1. Follow directions for the long ride through number 10.

2. Turn right on Old Ashby Road and go 1 mile to end (Route 119).

3. Turn right on Route 119 and go 2.3 miles to South Road on right, in the center of Ashby. A couple of hundred yards before the end, notice the old Victorian town hall on your left.

78. Fitchburg–Ashby

Number of miles: 17 (23 with Trap Falls extension)
Terrain: Hilly.
Food: Grocery store in Ashby. Restaurants at end.
Start: Central Plaza, Route 12, Fitchburg, 3 miles north of Route 2.

The rolling hills north of Fitchburg offer challenging but very scenic biking on a mazelike network of narrow, winding roads. Once you get a mile north of Fitchburg, the area is very rural, with only the tiny town of Ashby interrupting the large, sparsely populated expanses of woods and hilltop farms.

Fitchburg, a thriving industrial city of 40,000 lying in the steep valley of the North Nashua River, does not have the shabby appearance of some other mill cities in New England. The downtown area, with many fine nineteenth-century buildings flanking the main street in close formation, has recently had a facelift. A steady supply of local money has provided the city with an impressive library, civic center, planetarium, and art museum.

Fitchburg is also an active bicycling center, with several good bike shops and a thriving bicycle club. On the weekend of the Fourth of July the city holds one of the major bicycle races in the country, attracting top-caliber contestants such as Eric Heiden and the Stettina brothers. If you've never seen a bike race it's an exciting event to watch, with the racers traveling around and around a short course in a tight cluster, leaning into the corners at gravity-defying angles, and constantly jockeying for position—all at an average speed of 25 miles per hour.

Hemmed in by steep hills, Fitchburg is amazingly compact. Within a mile of downtown, which you'll go through at the beginning of the ride, you're in the woods. There's a long, steady climb out of town to a broad, rolling plateau to the north. At the top you'll go past the Fitchburg and Ashby Reservoirs to the picture-book New England village of Ashby, with a pair of graceful old churches framing the small green and a handsome Victorian town hall of wood.

From Ashby you'll wind across rolling hills and small farms to Trap Falls, a picturesque little waterfall where the water cascades around both sides of a large rock. You'll return to Fitchburg along a high, open ridge with spectacular views and then enjoy a long downhill run back into the city.

Directions for the ride: 23 miles

1. Turn right out of parking lot. Just ahead is a traffic light where Route 12 bears left.

2. Turn right at traffic light and cross railroad bridge to another light at far end of bridge.

3. Turn left at end of bridge and go 4/10 mile through the downtown area to where the road widens, with a green in the middle. Continue straight 2/10 mile to traffic light at end of green (Route 31).

4. At end of green turn left on Route 31. Go 2/10 mile to where Route 31 turns left and another road goes straight.

5. Continue straight 3/10 mile to fork where West Street bears left and Ashburnham Hill Road bears right uphill.

6. Bear right on Ashburnham Hill Road and go 6/10 mile to another fork where Williams Road bears left. This is a long, steep climb. At the top of the steep part, notice the old town pound on your right. It's a small stone enclosure about four feet high.

7. Bear right at fork and go 7/10 mile to another fork where Ashby West Road bears right.

8. Bear right on Ashby West Road. After 2/10 mile there's a crossroads. Continue straight 2.2 miles to end. You'll pass the Scott Reservoir on your left. • *CAUTION:* There's a steep, curving descent near the end.

9. Turn left at end and go 1.5 miles to crossroads. Just before the end the Fitchburg Reservoir is on your right, nestled among the pines.

10. Turn right at crossroads and go 4/10 mile to fork (Richardson Road bears right).

11. Bear right on Richardson Road and go 8/10 mile to a road that turns left at a traffic island. You'll go along the north shore of the Fitchburg Reservoir.

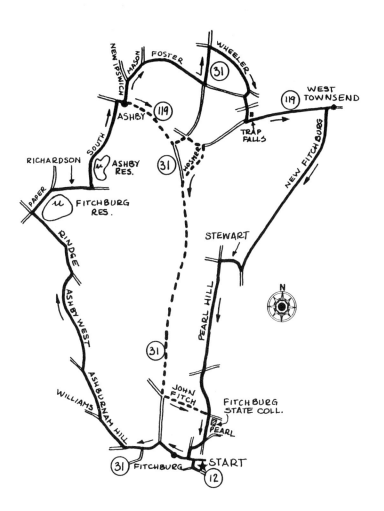

NEW IPSWICH
MASON
FOSTER
WHEELER
31
WEST TOWNSEND
119
ASHBY
119
TRAP FALLS
RICHARDSON
SOUTH
ASHBY RES.
31
HOSMER
NEW FITCHBURG
PAPER
FITCHBURG RES.
RINDGE
STEWART
ASHBY WEST
PEARL HILL
ASHBURNHAM HILL
31
WILLIAMS
N
JOHN FITCH
FITCHBURG STATE COLL.
PEARL
31
FITCHBURG
START
12

437

12. Turn left on this road and go 1.8 miles to end (Route 119), in the center of Ashby. Just after you turn you'll pass the Ashby Reservoir. When you come to the end, the handsome town hall is 200 yards to your left on Route 119. The short ride turns right on 119, and the long ride jogs right on 119 and then immediately left.

13. Turn right on Route 119 and then immediately left on New Ipswich Road. Go 3/10 mile to fork at bottom of hill.

14. Bear right at fork and go 3/10 mile to another fork.
• *CAUTION:* Bumpy downhill.

15. Bear right at fork and go 1.2 miles to crossroads and stop sign (Greenville Road, Route 31).

16. Turn left on Route 31 and go 8/10 mile to crossroads (Dump Road on left, Wheeler Road on right).

17. Turn right on Wheeler Road and go 1.2 miles to fork.

18. Bear right at fork and go 1/10 mile to another fork.

19. Bear left at fork and go 1/10 mile to crossroads and stop sign.

20. Go straight at crossroads 1/10 mile to end (merge into Route 119).

21. Turn sharp left on Route 119. Trap Falls is immediately ahead on your left. Continue on Route 119 for 1.7 miles to New Fitchburg Road on right, opposite church on left. Shortly before the intersection there's a little grocery store on the right, followed by an unusual circular wooden house. This is West Townsend.

22. Turn right on New Fitchburg Road and go 3.4 miles to Stewart Road, which turns very sharply right. This is a pleasant run through deep pine woods, passing a state recreation area.

23. Make a very sharp right on Stewart Road and go 3/10 mile to crossroads (Pearl Hill Road on left).

24. Turn left on Pearl Hill Road and go 2.1 miles to end (merge to your right at bottom of long, steady hill). You'll have a long, steady climb to the top of a ridge with magnificent views.

25. Bear right at end. You'll immediately come to a fork where Fisher Road bears right downhill. Bear *left* at fork and go 8/10 mile to crossroads and blinking light (John Fitch Highway).

26. Go straight at crossroads 6/10 mile to another crossroads and stop sign (Pearl Street bears right). You'll go through the campus of Fitchburg State College.

27. Bear right on Pearl Street and go 2/10 mile to end.

28. Turn left at end and go 3/10 mile to end.

29. Turn left at end and then immediately right at traffic light, crossing railroad bridge.

30. Turn left at end of bridge. Central Plaza is just ahead on left.

Directions for the ride: 17 miles

1. Follow directions for the long ride through number 12.

2. Turn right on Route 119 and go 1.5 miles to where Route 119 turns left and Route 31 goes straight.

3. Turn left, go 1/10 mile, and then turn right, staying on Route 119. Go 3/10 mile to your first right (sign may say Damon Pond).

4. Turn right on this road. Immediately ahead on your right is Damon Pond, a great place for a swim on a hot day. Continue beyond Damon Pond 6/10 mile to end (merge into Route 31). Shortly after the pond, you'll have to walk your bike around a barrier to keep out cars.

5. Bear left on Route 31 and go 3.7 miles to crossroads (John Fitch Highway).

6. Turn left on John Fitch Highway and go 8/10 mile to another crossroads, at blinking light (North Street on right).

7. Turn right at crossroads and go 6/10 mile to crossroads and stop sign (Pearl Street bears right). You'll go through Fitchburg State College.

8. Follow directions for the long ride from number 27 to the end.

79. Ashburnham Ride

Number of miles: 13 (20 with New Hampshire border extension)
Terrain: Rolling, with one tough hill at the very beginning.
Food: None en route.
Start: Junction of Routes 12 and 101 in the center of
   Ashburnham. Park on Route 12 or at the IGA supermarket on
   north side of road.

This is a tour of a wooded area along the New Hampshire border
dotted with ponds. You start from the center of Ashburnham, an
appealing New England town with a stately old church commanding the hillside just west of the center. The town is built around
Cushing Academy, a prestigious preparatory school founded in
1865 with an extensive campus of impressive old buildings. In the
northeast corner of the town is Mount Watatic, second highest
peak in the state east of the Connecticut River, with an elevation of
1,832 feet. (Mount Wachusett is the highest.) Just outside of town
you'll bike along the shore of Upper Naukeag Lake, undeveloped
except for a handful of gracious, tree-shaded old homes. Within a
few miles you'll go along Lower Naukeag Lake and Sunset Lake on
winding roller-coaster roads, and then head back to Ashburnham
with a repeat run along Upper Naukeag Lake, this time in the opposite direction.

   The long ride heads farther north through dense woodland
punctuated by a few small farms for variety and pokes just a bit
into New Hampshire. The return to Ashburnham skirts the base of
Mount Watatic and leads by two additional ponds—Wallace Pond
just as you cross back into Massachusetts, and Winnekeag Lake
close to the end. Just before you arrive in town you'll pass an old
spring with pure, ice-cold water.

Directions for the ride: 20 miles

   1. Head west on Route 12. After 3/10 mile you'll come to
School Street on your left. Cushing Academy is 200 yards down this
street. Continue uphill on Route 12 for 1/10 mile to your second
right, at traffic island.

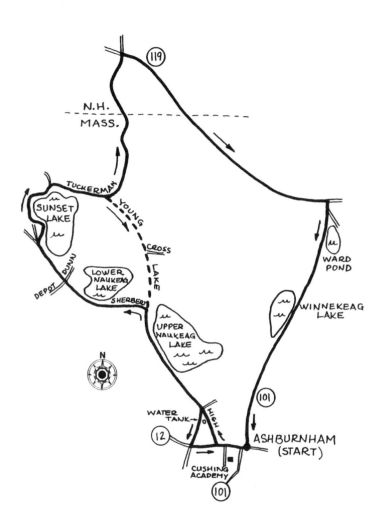

2. Turn right at traffic island. After 1/2 mile you'll pass an unusual round, concrete water tank on your left. Continue straight 1.8 miles to your second left, shortly after the Naukeag Hospital on right. (The first left is a sharp left.) You'll go along Upper Naukeag Lake.

3. Turn left on this road and go 1.9 miles to crossroads and stop sign.

4. Go straight at crossroads for 7/10 mile to small bridge. Immediately after the bridge the road is very bumpy for 50 yards and then becomes dirt. At this point there's a paved road on your right.

5. Turn 90 degrees right on paved road (don't bear right up steep hill). Just ahead you'll see Sunset Lake on your right. Go 3/10 mile to fork where the main road bears right.

6. Bear right at fork, staying on main road and following the shore of the lake. Go 1 mile to fork with three large rocks in the middle. This is a fine run along the water with lots of little ups and downs.

7. Bear right at fork. Just ahead is another fork where the main road bears left. Stay on main road for 7/10 mile to another fork (Young Road bears right). Here the short ride bears right and the long ride bears left.

8. Bear left at fork. After 8/10 mile, the main road curves left at traffic island. Stay on main road for 2.6 miles to crossroads and stop sign (Route 119). The last mile of this stretch is in Rindge, New Hampshire.

9. Turn right on Route 119 and go 5.2 miles to Route 101 on your right. You'll pass Wallace Pond on your right and then skirt the base of Mount Watatic on your left.

10. Turn right on Route 101 and go 4 miles to Route 12, in the center of Ashburnham. Shortly after you turn onto this road you'll pass Ward Pond on your left; then you'll go along Winnekeag Lake on your right. A half mile before the end a spring is on your right, with the water flowing from a pipe into a large metal catchbasin. It's safe to drink and delicious—enjoy it!

Directions for the ride: 13 miles

1. Follow directions for the long ride through number 7.

2. Bear right on Young Road and go 1.4 miles to another fork where the main road bears right.

3. Bear right, staying on main road, and go 2.5 miles to fork with the concrete water tank in the middle. You'll go along Naukeag Lake again, this time in the opposite direction.

4. Bear right at fork, passing the water tank on your left, and go 4/10 mile to crossroads and stop sign at bottom of hill (Route 12). • *CAUTION* approaching intersection.

5. Turn left on Route 12 and go 9/10 mile back to center of Ashburnham. This is a fast downhill run.

80. Cathedral of the Pines Ride: Winchendon– Rindge, New Hampshire

Number of miles: 20
Terrain: Rolling, with several moderate hills and one tough one.
Food: Country store in Rindge. Groceries and restaurants at end.
Start: Toy Town Plaza (also called Winchendon Shopping Center), junction of Routes 12 and 202 in Winchendon.

On this ride you explore a very rural, primarily wooded area of low hills around Lake Monomonac, largest in the vicinity. You'll head several miles north of the state line through the stately hilltop town of Rindge to the Cathedral of the Pines, one of New England's true beauty spots, and return to Winchendon on back roads by way of the classic New England village of Winchendon Center.

The ride starts in Winchendon, a small, compact mill town that for years was the country's prime producer of wooden toys, especially rocking horses. Most of the original toy factories have been demolished and the few remaining mills now house diversified industries.

From Winchendon you'll head north across the New Hampshire border along narrow wooded roads to Rindge, a graceful old hilltop town with a traditional New England church and green, a country store, and a fine red-brick Victorian library. From here you're not far from the Cathedral of the Pines, one of New England's most beautiful attractions. The Cathedral is a nondenominational chapel set in a grove of pines on top of a hill with a magnificent view of Mount Monadnock and its neighboring peaks. A tall, delicate bell tower stands at the entrance to the grove. The Cathedral was founded in 1945 by Douglas and Sybil Sloane, who lived in the farmhouse at its entrance, as a memorial to their son, a pilot who was shot down over Germany during World War II.

From the Cathedral you'll head back to Winchendon with a run along the shore of Lake Monomonac. Just before the end you'll go through the tiny hilltop village of Winchendon Center, with a beautiful old church standing proudly above a little green, and enjoy a fast downhill run back into town.

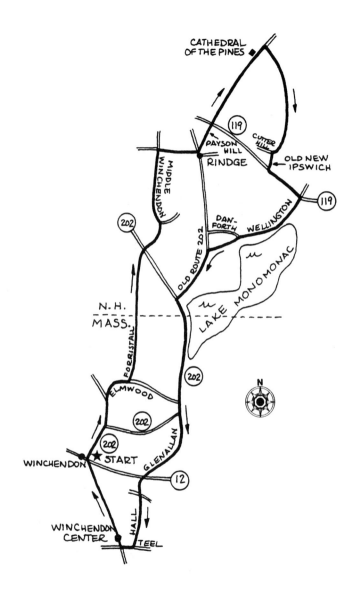

CATHEDRAL
OF THE PINES ◆

119

PAYSON
HILL

CUTTER
HILL

RINDGE

OLD NEW
IPSWICH

202

MIDDLE
WINCHENDON

DAN-
FORTH

WELLINGTON

119

OLD ROUTE 202

LAKE MONOMONAC

N. H.

MASS.

N

FORRISTALL

202

ELMWOOD

202

202

WINCHENDON

★ START

GLENALLAN

12

HALL

WINCHENDON
CENTER

TEEL

445

Directions for the ride

1. Turn right out of parking lot onto Route 202, heading north. Go 4/10 mile to where Route 202 turns right and Center Street bears slightly left.

2. Bear left on Central Street and go 4/10 mile to fork where North Central Street bears left and Elmwood Road bears slightly right (almost straight).

3. Bear right on Elmwood Road and go 7/10 mile to fork where the main road bears left and a smaller road goes straight.

4. Bear left on the main road and go 2.4 miles to a wide crossroads and stop sign (Route 202.) You are now in New Hampshire.

5. Cross Route 202 and go 6/10 mile to where Lord Brook Road turns right and Middle Winchendon Road bears left.

6. Bear left on Middle Winchendon Road and go 1 mile to crossroads.

7. Turn right at crossroads and go 7/10 mile to end, at the church in the center of Rindge. There's a country store on the right just before the end. At the end, notice the fine old library 100 yards down the hill to your right.

8. Bear left at end on Payson Hill Road, passing an old cemetery on your right (don't turn sharply left uphill). Go 1/2 mile to traffic light at bottom of steep hill (Route 119). • *CAUTION* here.

9. Cross Route 119 and go 1.5 miles to the Cathedral of the Pines on your left, midway up steep hill. Be sure to go up to the altar at the far end of the chapel to enjoy the view of the Monadnock Range.

10. Leaving the Cathedral, turn left up the hill. At the top there's a road on your right.

11. Turn right at top of hill and go 1.9 miles to traffic island where Old New Ipswich Road turns left and Cutter Hill Road bears slightly right down a steep hill. There's an unmarked road on the left 1/2 mile before the intersection.

12. Turn left on Old New Ipswich Road and go 2/10 mile to end (Route 119).

13. Turn left on Route 119 and to 6/10 mile to crossroads (Wellington Road).

14. Turn right on Wellington Road and stay on the main road 1.2 miles to fork. You'll parallel the shore of Lake Monomonac 200 yards to your left.

15. Bear left at fork and go 1/2 mile to end.

16. Turn left at end and go 8/10 mile to end (Route 202).

17. Turn left on Route 202 and go 1.7 miles to where Route 202 curves sharply to the right and Glenallan Street goes straight. There's an exquisite run along the lakeshore on this stretch.

18. Go straight onto Glenallan Street 1.6 miles to traffic island immediately after railroad tracks.

19. Bear right at traffic island and immediately cross Route 12 onto a narrow lane (Hall Road). Go 3/10 mile to crossroads. The Winchendon School, a coeducational preparatory school, is on your right on the far side of the golf course.

20. Go straight at crossroads 9/10 mile to end (Teel Road). This is a steady but very gradual hill. • *CAUTION:* The road is very bumpy, with wheel-eating potholes.

21. Turn right on Teel Road and go 2/10 mile to crossroads at top of hill. This is Winchendon Center.

22. Turn right at the green on top of hill. Notice the graceful old church on your left and the fine view to your right. Go 1.5 miles to end (Route 12). This is a fine downhill run. At the bottom, there's a little millpond on your right and two old mills on your left.

23. Cross Route 12 onto Route 202. The shopping center is on your right at the far side of the intersection.

81. Athol–Royalston–Phillipston–Petersham

Number of miles: 21 (34 with Phillipston–Petersham extension)
Terrain: Hilly.
Food: Country store in South Royalston. Country store in
Petersham (long ride).
Start: Burger King on Route 2A in Athol, just west of the center
of town. The large parking lot in back of the building is out
of harm's way.

This is a tour of the wooded hills northeast of the Quabbin Reservoir, passing through a trio of unspoiled, classic New England towns. A highlight of the tour is Doane Falls, a beautiful waterfall maintained by the Trustees of Reservations. The terrain is hilly but most of the hills are gradual. Only two hills are really steep, and they are fairly short. Numerous small farms and a couple of open ridges with fine views add variety to the landscape.

The ride starts in Athol, an old mill town on the Millers River, straight out of the Industrial Revolution, with the grim, fortresslike mills forming a nearly unbroken wall along the river for several blocks. The main industry is the manufacture of tools. In the compact downtown area, three- and four-story Victorian commercial buildings line both sides of the main street.

From Athol you'll head north, passing Tully Lake and Dam. Just ahead is Doane Falls, one of the state's unspoiled and nearly unknown beauty spots. A spectacular chain of small waterfalls, separated by deep, crystal-clear pools, flows through a wooded gorge from beneath a graceful arched stone bridge. From the falls it's not far to Royalston, one of the most elegant classic towns in the state. Commandingly located atop a hill, the town boasts a large green framed by a stately white church and gracious old wooden homes.

From Royalston you'll have a fast downhill run into South Royalston, another attractive little town with an old wooden church and schoolhouse. You'll now head along a couple of open ridges to the tiny hamlet of Phillipston, which has an old church, a cemetery, a school, and not much else. Phillipston's main claim to fame is the Baldwin Hill Bakery, major producer for the Northeast of good, old-

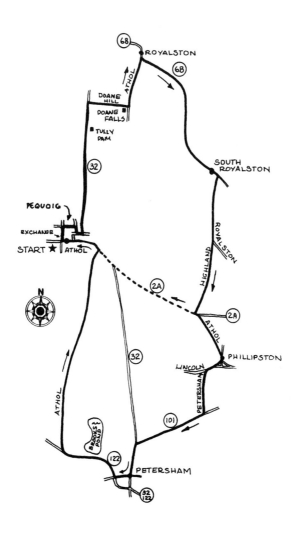

fashioned stone-ground bread without the additives, preservatives, and refined-down-to-nothing flour. The bakery is about a mile off the route, and you're welcome to visit it if you call before coming.

A few miles beyond Phillipston is the dignified hilltop town of Petersham (pronounced Peters'm), with a large green accented by a bandstand, traditional white church, ornate stone library, and the attractive Maria Assumpta Academy, formerly a resort hotel. The return run to Athol leads past small farms and along a high ridge, with a fast downhill run at the end.

The short ride bypasses Phillipston and Petersham, taking a direct route back to Athol along Route 2A past the Phillipston Reservoir. There's an exhilarating downhill run at the end.

Directions for the Ride: 34 miles

    1. Turn right (east) out of the parking lot onto Route 2A and go 100 yards to traffic light.

    2. Turn left at light on Exchange Street and go 3/10 mile to crossroads at base of steep hill (Pequoig Avenue).

    3. Turn right on Pequoig Avenue and go 4/10 mile to end.

    4. Turn right at end of Pequoig Avenue and go 50 yards to end (Route 32).

    5. Turn left on Route 32. Just ahead, Route 32 turns left.

    6. Turn left (still Route 32) and go 3.9 miles to unmarked road on right. It's the first right after you pass Tully Lake and Dam on your right. A sign may say to Royalston, Tully Camping Area.

    7. Turn right on this road and go 1.2 miles to end, at top of steep hill. At the end you'll see an arched stone bridge on your right. Below the bridge is Doane Falls—don't miss it!

    8. Turn left at end, heading north from the falls, and go 1.9 miles to end (merge onto Route 68), in Royalston. The ride turns right on Route 68, but go straight 100 yards to see the town center, one of the finest in the state.

    9. Turn right on Route 68 and go 4.5 miles to a road that bears right uphill just after you cross the Millers River in South Royalston, at the bottom of a magnificent downhill run.

    10. Bear right up the hill and go 2.1 miles to fork where the right-hand branch goes uphill. This is a pleasant run along a ridge with fine views.

    11. Bear right uphill at fork and go 2.1 miles to end (Route

2A). Here the short ride turns right and the long ride turns left.

12. Turn left on Route 2A and then immediately bear right downhill on Athol Road. Go 1.8 miles to end (merge to your right).

13. Bear right at end and go 1/10 mile to a three-way fork. This is Phillipston. Notice the fine old church on your left.

14. Bear right at fork and go 2/10 mile to another fork where the main road bears left and Lincoln Road goes straight.

15. Bear left, staying on the main road, and go 1.8 miles to end (Route 101), at a large grassy traffic island.

16. Bear right on Route 101 and go 3.1 miles to end (Route 32).

17. Turn left on Route 32 and go 1.1 miles to crossroads and blinking light at the center of Petersham (West Street on right). A country store is on the left.

18. Turn right at crossroads and go 6/10 mile to another crossroads (Route 122). • *CAUTION:* It comes up while you're going down a steep hill.

19. Turn right on Route 122 and go 2.2 miles to a road that bears right. It's your first paved road.

20. Bear right on this road and go 6 miles to end (Route 2A). • *CAUTION:* Route 2A comes up suddenly at bottom of steep hill.

21. Turn left on Route 2A and go 1.4 miles to the Burger King on your left, just beyond downtown Athol. It's a fast downhill run back into town.

Directions for the ride: 21 miles

1. Follow the directions for the long ride through number 11.

2. Turn right on Route 2A and go 4.7 miles to the Burger King on left, just beyond downtown Athol.

82. Barre–Templeton–Hubbardston

Number of miles: 25
Terrain: Hilly.
Food: Groceries and restaurants in Templeton and Barre.
Start: Center of Barre, which is 20 miles northwest of Worcester
on Route 122. Park wherever it's legal.

This ride is a tour of the wooded, very rural hill country east of the
Quabbin Reservoir and passes through three unspoiled New England
towns. Barre is almost on a timberline—south of the town is
primarily open farmland, but north of the town is primarily forest.
The wooded landscape does not provide the spectacular vistas you
find from atop the open ridges farther south, but this is a peaceful
ride on narrow, winding roads through a remote area, with an occasional view from a ridge.

The ride starts from Barre, a fine example of the many pristine
New England towns sprinkled across Worcester County. A large
green ornamented with a bandstand forms a nucleus where several
roads come together like spokes. Adjoining the green is a compact
business block, the traditional white church, and a marvelous, rambling Victorian hotel. From Barre you'll head along twisting roads to
Templeton, another handsome town situated on top of a ridge. Like
Barre, Templeton sports a large, well-trimmed green framed by a
fine white church and old wooden homes. From Templeton you'll
proceed to the little crossroads town of Hubbardston, the smallest
and most rural of the three communities. On the return trip to
Barre, you can go 1 mile off the route to visit spectacular Barre
Falls Dam, which spans a rocky gorge carved by the Ware River.

Directions for the ride
1. Head north out of Barre on School Street (currently unmarked, but a sign may say to Williamsville, Templeton). It passes
between a white wooden house on the right and a car dealer on
the left, one block north of Route 62. Go 1.5 miles to fork where
main road bears right. You'll go down and then up a steep hill.

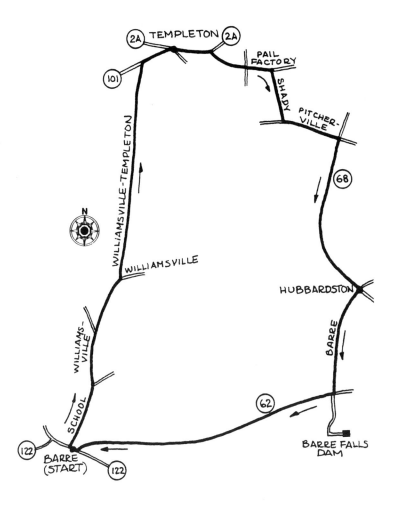

TEMPLETON

2A   2A

101

PAIL FACTORY

SHADY

PITCHER-VILLE

WILLIAMSVILLE-TEMPLETON

N

WILLIAMSVILLE

68

HUBBARDSTON

WILLIAMS-VILLE

BARRE

SCHOOL

62

BARRE FALLS DAM

122

BARRE (START)

122

2. Bear left at fork and go 1.3 miles to another fork, where the main road goes straight and a smaller road bears left.

3. Continue straight on the main road and go 1 mile to another fork (Williamsville Road bears right; Williamsville–Templeton Road bears left).

4. Bear left on Williamsville–Templeton Road and go 5.5 miles to end (merge to right into Route 101). You'll skirt the shore of Williamsville Pond and then ascend onto a ridge with a fine view.

5. Bear right on Route 101, up steep hill, and go 4/10 mile to end (merge into Route 2A). This is the center of Templeton.

6. Bear right on Route 2A and go 6/10 mile to your first right, at a small traffic island with a telephone pole in the middle.

7. Bear right on this road and go 1.1 miles to crossroads and stop sign.

8. Go straight at crossroads onto Pail Factory Road. Go 4/10 mile to your first right, which comes up while you're going downhill just after the road curves sharply to the left.

9. Turn right on this road and go 1.2 miles to end.

10. Turn left at end and go 1.3 miles to a wide crossroads and stop sign (Route 68).

11. Turn right on Route 68 and go 3.6 miles to crossroads and blinking light at the center of Hubbardston (Elm Street on right). A sign may say to Barre, 7 miles.

12. Turn right at crossroads and go 2.7 miles to crossroads and stop sign (Route 62). Here the ride turns right, but if you go straight ahead 1 mile you'll come to Barre Falls Dam.

13. Turn right on Route 62 and go 4.4 miles to the center of Barre. You get hit with a long, steep hill at the end. • *CAUTION:* On this stretch is a metal-grate bridge that is slippery when wet; there is a real danger of falling on this grating. Please *walk* across.

83. Mount Wachusett Challenge: West Boylston–Princeton–Sterling

Number of miles: 34 (30 if you don't go to summit)
Terrain: Guess!
Food: Grocery store and snack bar in Princeton and Sterling. Because the ride is demanding, you should carry food with you.
Start: Picnic area at the fork of Routes 12 and 140 in West Boylston, just north of the bridge over the Wachusett Reservoir. Park at side of road.

The area between Worcester and Fitchburg is dominated by 2,006-foot Mount Wachusett, the highest point in Massachusetts east of the Connecticut River. The symmetrical, gently rounded mountain, with no other mountains nearby, is a landmark for miles around. The long climb to the summit, a net gain in elevation of 1,600 feet from the starting point, offers a difficult but rewarding challenge to the adventuresome cyclist. The view from the summit, a nearly 360-degree panorama, is among the state's most spectacular. The breathtaking descent drops nearly 600 feet in the first mile, a gradient of more than 10 percent.

The ride starts from the western edge of the Wachusett Reservoir, elevation 390 feet, and follows its slender western arm to Oakdale, a small village in West Boylston. From here, you'll climb gradually to Princeton, elevation 1,200 feet, along lightly traveled Route 31. The ascent does not become steep until the last quarter mile into Princeton.

Princeton is an elegantly classic New England town crowning a hillside with a proud old church, Victorian town hall, and handsome clock-towered library poised above the large, sloping green. Before the turn of the century, Princeton was a fashionable summer resort with rambling Victorian hotels, including one on the summit of Mount Wachusett. Unfortunately, none remain. The smaller but equally gracious Country Inn at Princeton, on the ridge just north of town, provides today's visitor with a glimpse of that bygone era.

From Princeton, you'll ride along the eastern flank of the mountain, enjoying sweeping views to the east. At the beginning of the summit road is a visitor's center with exhibits on the history of the mountain and the native wildlife. The summit road climbs 800 feet in 3 miles, with most of the elevation gain in two steep sections in the first and last half mile. A succession of hotels stood on the summit until 1970, when the last one burned. The only thing up there now is a fire tower, which is not open to the public, along with a couple of radio towers.

The descent is a thriller. When you get to the end of the summit road, there's more coming—the main road drops another 400 feet in the next mile. You'll now pedal along lovely narrow roads, passing prosperous farms and orchards, to the attractive valley town of Sterling, which is best known as the locale of "Mary Had a Little Lamb." A small white statue of a lamb on the green commemorates the nursery rhyme. From Sterling you'll return to the start, passing through woods and farmland along lightly traveled secondary roads.

Directions for the ride

1. Head north on Route 140, paralleling the western arm of the reservoir on your left. As soon as you start, notice the Old Stone Church, built in 1890, on your left. It was recently restored after years of neglect. Go 1.3 miles to where Route 140 curves sharply right at yield sign, in Oakdale. Continue 1/10 mile to Laurel Street on left.

2. Turn left on Laurel Street and go 3.3 miles to end (Route 31).

3. Turn right on Route 31 and go 5.5 miles to Route 62, at blinking light in the center of Princeton. There's a small snack bar on your right on the far side of the intersection, and a country store if you turn left on Route 62 for 2/10 mile. This is a good spot to eat, because the summit road begins in 3 miles.

4. Cross Route 62, following the green on your left up a steep hill. Notice the red-brick, turreted town hall, built in 1884, and the elegant stone library, built in 1883, at the head of the green. Go 3.2 miles to the summit road on left (sign may say Mount Wachusett State Reservation). If you decide not to go to the summit, continue straight downhill for 1.7 miles to end (Route 140), and resume with direction number 9.

5. Turn left on the summit road. The visitor's center is just ahead on your left. Be sure to get water here. Continue 2.9 miles to

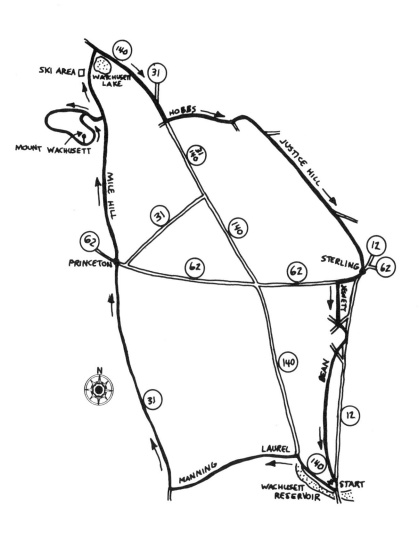

SKI AREA

WACHUSETT LAKE

140

31

HOBBS

JUSTICE HILL

MOUNT WACHUSETT

MILE HILL

140

31

140

12

62

PRINCETON

62

62

STERLING

62

JEWETT

N

140

BEAN

31

12

LAUREL

140

MANNING

WACHUSETT RESERVOIR

START

a road on left that climbs steeply (sign says to summit). Turn left for 2/10 mile to summit.

6. Backtrack 2/10 mile to end. Turn left and descend very steeply for 8/10 mile to end.

7. Turn right and go 6/10 mile to end, at the entrance to the state reservation.

8. Turn left and go 1.7 miles to end (Route 140). The first mile is a wonderful descent on smooth, aptly named Mile Hill Road. At the bottom, the Mount Wachusett Ski Area is on your left. There's a snack bar in the base lodge open all year. When you come to Route 140, Wachusett Lake is on your right.

9. Turn right on Route 140 and go 2.4 miles to second crossroads, Hobbs Road (sign on right may say to Shady Lane Greenhouse).

10. Turn left on Hobbs Road and go 1.5 miles to fork where the road on the left bears up a steep hill.

11. Bear left at fork and go 1 mile to another fork, where one road bears left and the other goes straight. It comes up while you're going downhill. The first half mile of this section climbs steeply—a piece of cake compared to Mount Wachusett. There are good views to your right as you ascend the hill.

12. Continue straight at fork (don't bear left). After 2.6 miles a road bears left, but continue straight on the main road for 1.5 miles to end, in Sterling (merge into Routes 12 and 62). Just before the end, you'll go along the green on your left.

13. Bear right at end and go 1/10 mile to fork where Route 12 bears left and Route 62 bears right.

14. Bear right on Route 62 and go 4/10 mile to Jewett Road on left.

15. Turn left on Jewett Road and go 1 mile to end, at five-way intersection.

16. Turn 90 degrees left at end (don't turn sharply left), and go 1/4 mile to end (merge onto Route 12).

17. Bear right on Route 12 and go 1/10 mile to Bean Road, which bears right.

18. Bear right on Bean Road and go 1/4 mile to a diagonal crossroads. Continue straight for 2.4 miles to end (merge onto Route 12).

19. Bear right on Route 12 and go 2/10 mile to starting point.

84. Covered-Bridge Ride: Ware–Hardwick–Gilbertville

Number of miles: 16 (28 with northern loop)
Terrain: Hilly.
Food: Country store in Hardwick. Grocery and snack bar in Gilbertville. McDonald's at end.
Start: McDonald's, Route 32, Ware, 1/2 mile southwest of Route 9.

The section of Massachusetts between Worcester and the Quabbin Reservoir provides challenging but extremely scenic cycling. This is a very rural area of high, open ridges with spectacular views, dotted with unspoiled, picture-book New England towns. The cycle of touch climb, plateau atop a ridge, and exhilarating descent repeats itself as you wind through the inspiring landscape on untraveled back roads. On this ride you explore the area fairly close to the reservoir, passing through the classic village of Hardwick and then across one of only two covered bridges in the state east of the Connecticut River (the other is in Pepperell).

You start from Ware, a nineteenth-century mill town right out of the Industrial Revolution. Most of the mills have factory outlets selling to the public, making Ware one of the prime bargain centers in New England for clothing, woolen goods, and sportswear. The majority of the mills are clustered in one massive complex called the Industry Yard on Route 9 just east of downtown.

From Ware you quickly head into ridge country to Hardwick, a beautiful classic town among the many spread across Worcester County. The large, well-kept green is framed by two graceful old churches facing each other, and by the handsome, white, pillared town hall. From Hardwick you'll traverse a ridge with inspiring views and enjoy a long descent into Gilbertville, a small, attractive mill town with a magnificent stone church. In Gilbertville you'll cross the Ware River over the covered bridge and return to Ware across yet another ridge along the narrowest of country lanes.

The longer ride makes a loop north of Hardwick through more ridge-and-valley country. As you head north out of Hardwick you come closer to Quabbin Reservoir and catch glimpses of it far below. At the northern tip of the ride, you can go a quarter of a mile off the route to the water's edge. From here, you'll return to Hardwick along ridges with fine views.

Directions for the ride: 28 miles

1. Turn left out of parking lot and just ahead take your first left (a sign may say to Route 9, Belchertown). Go 1/10 mile to end (Route 9).

2. Turn right on Route 9 and go 1/10 mile to your first left (Barnes Street).

3. Turn left on Barnes Street. Immediately ahead is a fork where the right-hand branch goes uphill. Bear left at fork and go 3/10 mile to end. There are gates at the beginning and end of this road; if they are closed, walk your bike around them. Don't worry about the sign that says "Public water supply, no trespassing"—it refers to the grounds, not the road.

4. Bear left at end and go 2/10 mile to fork (Greenwich Road bears right). You'll pass an attractive little dam on your right.

5. Bear right at fork, passing a cemetery on your left, and go 2.3 miles to Hardwick Pond Road, which bears right.

6. Bear right on Hardwick Pond Road and go 3.5 miles to end (merge head-on into Route 32A). This is a winding narrow lane. A mile after you bear right you'll pass a music camp on your left. From here you'll ascend gradually onto a ridge with fine views.

7. Go straight onto Route 32A for 1.2 miles to a crossroads in the center of Hardwick (Greenwich Road on left). Here the short ride turns right and the long ride continues straight.

8. Continue straight on Route 32A for 4/10 mile to fork (North Road bears right). Just beyond the crossroads on your left is an ornate brick library with a cupola.

9. Bear left at fork (still Route 32A) and go 4.8 miles to crossroads at the bottom of a long hill (a sign may say to Barre). The road on the right is paved and the road on the left is dirt. Here the ride turns right, but if you turn left for 3/10 mile you'll come to the eastern arm of the Quabbin Reservoir.

10. Turn right at bottom of hill and go 9/10 mile to fork (right-hand branch goes uphill). It's a steady climb to the fork.

11. Bear right uphill and go 1/2 mile to Spring Hill Road on right, at top of hill.

12. Turn right on Spring Hill Road. After 5 miles you'll merge

460

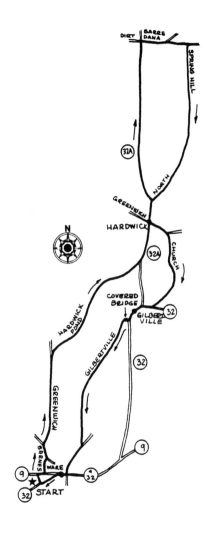

461

left onto Route 32A. Bear left for 4/10 mile back to the crossroads in the center of Hardwick (Greenwich Road on right). A mile after you turn onto Spring Hill Road, as you're climbing a long hill, look behind you to the right for a magnificent view.

13. Turn left in the center of Hardwick. As soon as you turn, a country store is on your right. Go 1/2 mile to fork where Church Street bears right uphill.

14. Bear right on Church Street and go 2.8 miles to end (merge into Route 32). This is another pleasant, narrow lane, climbing onto a ridge with great views. To the left you can see the high water tower of the former Pioneer Valley Academy, a Seventh-Day Adventist school in New Braintree, 4 miles away. After you crest the ridge, a relaxing downhill run takes you to the Ware River Valley.

15. Bear right on Route 32 and go 2/10 mile to end, in Gilbertville.

16. Bear left at end (still Route 32). After 2/10 mile you'll cross the Ware River. Continue 2/10 mile to your first right, Bridge Street (sign may say Covered Bridge). You can see the bridge from the corner. Here the ride turns right, but you'll find a magnificent stone church if you go straight 200 yards.

17. Turn right on Bridge Street and cross the covered bridge, one of only ten remaining in Massachusetts. Continue 3.1 miles to end (merge to your right while going downhill). This road is so narrow that two cars would have trouble passing. You'll climb onto a ridge with fine views on both sides.

18. Bear right at end and go 8/10 mile to traffic light (Route 9). This is a nice downhill run.

19. Turn right on Route 9 and go 2/10 mile through the center of Ware to Route 32, which bears left.

20. Bear left on Route 32 and go 4/10 mile to McDonald's on right.

Directions for the ride: 16 miles

1. Follow directions for the long ride through number 7.

2. Turn right at crossroads. As soon as you turn a country store is on your right. Go 1/2 mile to fork where Church Street bears right uphill.

3. Follow directions for the long ride from number 14 to the end.

Ware River Bridge, Gilbertville.

85. Central Massachusetts Spectacular: North Brookfield–New Braintree–Barre–Oakham

Number of miles: 32
Terrain: Hilly.
Food: Grocery and snack bar in Barre.
Start: Supermarket on Route 67, North Brookfield, just south of the center of town.

The rolling, open hills, ridges, and valleys midway between Worcester and Springfield provide some of the most inspiring scenery in Massachusetts. Of all the rides in the book, this one is my favorite. The terrain is challenging—a recurrent cycle of steep climbs and exhilarating descents—but the panoramic vistas from atop every hill will more than reward your efforts. Here is rural countryside at its best: rambling old farmhouses, weathered red barns with woodpiles neatly stacked beside them, stone walls zigzagging across broad, sloping fields where cows and horses graze. Dotting this Currier-and-Ives landscape are unspoiled museum-piece towns and hamlets, hardly changed since the 1800s.

The ride starts from one of these towns, North Brookfield, a New England jewel with a stately old church and green, a handsome stone library, and an ornate Victorian town hall built in 1864. When the Rolling Stones needed a place to practice for their 1981 American tour, they chose North Brookfield. From here you'll bike across ridgetops and along two delightful ponds to Oakham, a pristine hilltop hamlet buried off the beaten path among a maze of back roads. No one would ever find it except by accident. A graceful white church, fine stone library, schoolhouse, and old cemetery comprise the village center. From Oakham you'll wind your way on deserted country lanes to the larger town of Barre, also a New England classic. The extensive green, ornamented with a bandstand in the center, forms a nucleus from which eight roads radiate like spokes. Adjoining the green are a stately wooden church, an old town hall, a compact little business block, and a rambling Victorian building with wide porches, formerly a resort hotel, now a

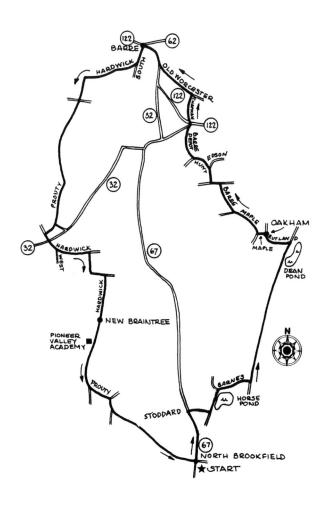

boarding house. From Barre you'll traverse more ridges with sweeping views to the nearly depopulated hamlet of New Braintree. The center of town has a fine white church, an old cemetery, a tiny post office, a handful of weathered farmhouses, and not much else. Just south of town the landscape is jarred by the starkly modern Pioneer Valley Academy, formerly run by the Seventh-Day Adventists. Its enormous water tower can be seen for miles. From here, we're soon back to North Brookfield, biking through magnificently rolling, open farmland.

Directions for the ride

1. Turn right out of parking lot onto Route 67, heading north, and go 2.2 miles to Stoddard Road on right. It's the second right once you get out of town.

2. Turn right on Stoddard Road and go 9/10 mile to end (merge right at bottom of hill). The road snakes down a broad hillside with a fine view. You'll pass the elegant Long View Farm, where the Rolling Stones practiced for their 1981 tour.

3. Turn sharply left at bottom of hill (*CAUTION* here), and go 7/10 mile to end (Barnes Road). You'll pass Horse Pond on your right.

4. Bear right on Barnes Road and go 1.1 miles to end.

5. Turn left at end and go 3.7 miles to Rutland Road, which turns sharply left (sign may say to Oakham Center). It comes up 4/10 mile after you pass Dean Pond on your right.

6. Make a sharp left on Rutland Road. After 7/10 mile the road curves sharply to the right up a steep hill. Just ahead, at the top, Maple Street is on your left. This is the center of Oakham.

7. Turn left on Maple Street and go 1/10 mile to your first right.

8. Turn right (still Maple Street) and go 8/10 mile to fork (Barre Road bears right).

9. Bear right on Barre Road and go 8/10 mile to end (Old Turnpike Road).

10. Turn left at end and go 2/10 mile to Hunt Road on right. A country store is at the intersection.

11. Turn right on Hunt Road and go 1/2 mile to fork.

12. Bear left downhill at fork and go 3/10 mile to another fork. Notice the unusual stone tower on your right.

13. Bear right at fork and go 1 mile to end (merge to your right). From the top of the hill you can see Mount Wachusett, the highest mountain in central Massachusetts, elevation 2,006 feet.

14. Bear right at end and go 1/10 mile to Route 122. Notice the dam on your right.

15. Cross Route 122, heading steeply uphill. You bear left as you go through the intersection. Go 9/10 mile to end.

16. Turn left at end and go 1.2 miles to second crossroads.

17. Continue straight at crossroads up steep hill 1/10 mile to Route 122.

18. Bear right on Route 122 and go 7/10 mile into the center of Barre. Follow Route 122 alongside the green, passing the bandstand on your left.

19. At the far end of the green, turn sharply left. Just ahead you'll pass the Victorian-style hotel on your right. Continue 6/10 mile to a road on your right while you're going uphill (sign may say to Hardwick, 6 miles).

20. Turn right on this road and go 1.5 miles to crossroads. • *CAUTION:* No stop signs for all four roads. You'll pass a farm with stately rows of trees on both sides of the road.

21. Go straight at crossroads 3.8 miles to fork just after a long downhill run with magnificent views. At the fork, Shunpike Road bears left and Prouty Road bears right.

22. Bear right at fork and go 3/10 mile to end, at bottom of hill. • *CAUTION* here—the end comes up suddenly.

23. Turn left at end and go 1/10 mile to crossroads and stop sign (Route 32).

24. Cross Route 32. After 3/10 mile, West Street bears right, but continue straight 9/10 mile to your next right, which crosses a small bridge.

25. Turn right on this road. After 6/10 mile the main road curves 90 degrees left uphill. Continue 1/2 mile to your first right, at a spot where the hill levels off a bit. Notice the white, pillared mansion on your left at the intersection.

26. Turn right on this road and go 3.2 miles to fork at bottom of long hill (Prouty Road bears left). You'll go through New Braintree and pass the former Pioneer Valley Academy.

27. Bear left at fork and go 6/10 mile to another fork with a traffic island in the middle.

28. Bear right at fork and go 2/10 mile to another fork where the main road curves left.

29. Bear left at fork and follow the main road 2.6 miles back to Route 67, in the center of North Brookfield. There's a steep climb into town.

30. Turn right on Route 67. The supermarket is just ahead on your left.

86. Worcester–Paxton–Holden–Rutland

Number of miles: 16 (33 with Paxton–Rutland extension, 27
   with shortcut)
Terrain: Hilly.
Food: Grocery stores and snack bars in the towns.
Start: CVS Pharmacy on Pleasant Street in the western part of
   Worcester, just east of Route 122 (Chandler Street). From
   Route 290, head west on Route 122. After 2 miles you'll pass
   Worcester State College. Continue nearly one mile to traffic
   light where Route 122 turns left and Pleasant Street turns
   right. Turn right, and the CVS is just ahead on left. There's
   plenty of parking on the side of the building.

Just northwest of Worcester is a prime area for cycling. It has
wooded hills interspersed with ponds and reservoirs, occasional
open ridges with fine views, and unspoiled towns that haven't yet
become suburban. Worcester is fortunate to be a relatively compact
city with almost no suburban sprawl beyond its borders. Within a
mile of the start you're in wooded countryside before you even
cross the city line.

The ride starts from the Tatnuck section of Worcester, near its
western edge, and almost immediately enters forested landscape.
Just off the route near the beginning is the Cascade, a steep, rocky
ravine that becomes a dramatic waterfall after heavy rain and a
delicate, icy fairyland in the winter. Just beyond the city line you'll
enjoy a long, exhilarating run beside the Holden Reservoirs, go
across the Kendall Reservoir, and arrive in Holden, an attractive
community with two graceful old churches and a Federal-era mansion framing the center of town. From Holden you'll head south
back toward Worcester along Chaffin Pond, enjoy a long downhill
run to the shore of Indian Lake, and return to the start through
gracious residential neighborhoods.

The long ride heads farther west and north to the graceful old
town of Paxton. Although less than ten miles from downtown Worcester, Paxton remains an unspoiled New England gem of a town
with a stately white church, an old town hall, fine white wooden

homes, and the gracious Paxton Inn, all clustered around the village center. From Paxton you'll head north over hill, dale, and ridge to Rutland, another refreshingly unspoiled town crowning a hilltop. From Rutland you'll thread your way to Holden along a labyrinth of winding, roller-coastering lanes. In Holden you'll pick up the short ride and follow it back to Worcester.

Directions for the ride: 33 and 27 miles

1. Turn right onto Pleasant Street and go 1/10 mile to traffic light (Mower Street on right). Turn right at light and go 2/10 mile to fork (Olean Street bears right).

2. Bear right on Olean Street and go 2.9 miles to fork where South Road bears left uphill. This is a beautiful run along the Holden Reservoirs. If you're taking the ride after a heavy rain, be sure to visit the Cascade. After bearing right on Olean Street, take your first left on Fernside Road. Go to end, turn right and immediately left, and go to end. Turn right and go 3/10 mile to Cascade on left. Backtrack to Olean Street.

3. Bear left on South Road and go 1 mile to end (Route 31). At the end, the short ride turns right on Route 31 and the long ride turns left.

4. Turn left on Route 31 and go 1.6 miles to end, at stop sign and blinking light.

5. Turn left at end (still Route 31) and go 2/10 mile to where Route 31 turns right onto Maple Street.

6. Turn right, staying on Route 31, and go 1/2 mile to end (Route 56). This is Paxton. The center of town is on your left. Notice the fine church to your left at the intersection.

7. Turn right on Route 56 and go 4.7 miles to end (Route 122A), in the center of Rutland. Here the 33-mile ride turns left, but you can shorten the route by 6 miles if you turn right on Route 122A, go 1.7 miles to Bond Road on right at the Holden town line, and resume with direction number 12.

8. Turn left on Route 56 and 122A. Just ahead, Route 56 turns right and Route 122A goes straight.

9. Turn right on Route 56 and go 3.3 miles to Campbell Street on right, 1/2 mile after pond on right. There's a great downhill run out of Rutland.

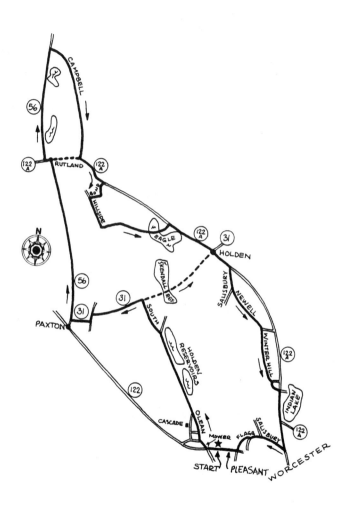

471

10. Turn right on Campbell Street. After 1.8 miles you will merge to your right. Bear right and go 1.5 miles to end (Route 122A).

11. Turn left on Route 122A and go 1 mile to Bond Road on right, at the Holden town line.

12. Turn right on Bond Road and go 7/10 mile to end (Hillside Road).

13. Turn left on Hillside Road and go 3.1 miles to fork immediately after you pass between two ponds.

14. Bear left at fork and go 2/10 mile to end (Route 122A).

15. Turn right on Route 122A and go 1.5 miles to traffic light (Route 31) in the center of Holden. Just before the light you'll pass two graceful churches and a Federal-era mansion on your left.

16. Cross Route 31 and go 7/10 mile to Salisbury Street, which bears right at traffic light.

17. Bear right on Salisbury Street and go 7/10 mile to Newell Road, which bears left just after a pond on your right.

18. Bear left on Newell Road and go 1.2 miles to fork (Winter Hill Road bears right). You'll pass Chaffin Pond on your left, back a little from the road.

19. Bear right on Winter Hill Road and go 1.3 miles to fork at bottom of long, steep hill. At the fork Parkton Road bears left.

20. Bear right at fork and go 1/10 mile to end, at stop sign. Turn left downhill and go 2/10 mile to crossroads and stop sign (Route 122A, Grove Street).

21. Turn right on Route 122A and go 7/10 mile to traffic light where Route 122A bears left and Forest Street goes straight. Indian Lake is on your left.

22. Go straight at light onto Forest Street 7/10 mile to end, at stop sign (merge left on Salisbury Street).

23. Turn sharply right on Salisbury Street and go 9/10 mile to fork (Flagg Street bears left).

24. Bear left on Flagg Street and go 4/10 mile to another fork.

25. Bear right at fork (still Flagg Street) and go 1/2 mile to crossroads and stop sign (Pleasant Street).

26. Turn right on Pleasant Street and go 4/10 mile to CVS on right.

Dairy farm in Rutland.

Directions for the ride: 16 miles

1. Follow directions for the long rides through number 3.

2. Turn right on Route 31 and go 2.5 miles to traffic light (Route 122A). This is the center of Holden. At the intersection, notice the two fine churches and the Federal-era mansion to your left on Route 122A.

3. Turn right on Route 122A and go 7/10 mile to Salisbury Street, which bears right at traffic light.

4. Follow directions for the long rides from number 17 to the end.

87. The Brookfields Ride: East Brookfield–Brookfield–West Brookfield–North Brookfield

Number of miles: 26 (22 omitting western loop)
Terrain: Delightfully rolling, with several short hills and one tough one.
Food: Groceries and restaurants in the towns.
Start: Park on Route 9 beside Lake Lashaway in the center of East Brookfield.

On this ride you explore the four similarly named towns midway between Worcester and Springfield. The surrounding landscape, a harmonious mixture of magnificent rolling farmland, wooded hills, ridges with inspiring views, and several lakes, promises biking at its best along a wide-ranging network of rural lanes and lightly traveled secondary roads. The terrain is not as hilly as the more rugged ridge country surrounding it.

The ride starts in East Brookfield, smallest and least distinctive of the quartet, attractively located along the shore of Lake Lashaway. A couple of miles out of town is a fine run along Quaboag Pond, largest lake in the area, followed by another run beside Quacumquasit Pond (say it three times fast). From here you'll ascend gradually onto a hillside with magnificent views across the well-groomed fields of estates and horse farms. Just ahead you'll cross the Quaboag River and climb a short hill into the classic New England village of Brookfield. The long, slender green is framed by two dignified churches, an ornate brick Victorian library, and fine old homes. Just off the green, the compact business block is a relic from the turn of the century.

Leaving Brookfield, you'll climb onto another ridge with fine views and descend into West Brookfield, most elegant of the four towns. The long, triangular green, highlighted by a fountain in the middle, is surrounded by a fine church and gracious wooden and brick homes. Just west of town you'll make a circuit around Wickaboag Pond and thread your way between rolling hills to North Brookfield, yet another New England gem of a town, with a traditional white church and green, a graceful stone library, and an ornate Victorian town hall with a bell tower, built in 1864. A statue on the green honors the soldiers killed in the War of the Rebellion, the official Union name for the Civil War.

From North Brookfield you'll enjoy a relaxing downhill run through orchards back to the shore of Lake Lashaway and East Brookfield.

Directions for the ride

1. Head west on Route 9 and go 2.1 miles to Quaboag Street on left. It's your first left after the Brookfield town line, and it immediately crosses a railroad bridge.

2. Turn left on Quaboag Street and go 2.1 miles to West Sturbridge Road on right, at top of hill. You'll go along Quaboag Pond on your right.

3. Turn right on West Sturbridge Road and go 1.7 miles to fork.

4. Bear right at fork and go 7/10 mile to a road that bears right after you pass Quacumquasit Pond on your left.

5. Bear right on this road and go 2.1 miles to end, where you'll merge to the right at bottom of hill (no stop sign here).

6. Bear right at end and go 1/10 mile to fork where the main road bears right. Stay on main road for 1/10 mile to end (merge into Route 148 at stop sign).

7. Bear right on Route 148. After 6/10 mile you'll cross a railroad bridge. Continue straight on Route 148 for 1/2 mile to end (Route 9), going along the Brookfield town green. Notice the Victorian library on the right at beginning of green. If you turn right halfway down the green, there's a grocery and snack bar.

8. Turn left on Route 9 and go 6/10 mile to West Brookfield Road, which bears right.

9. Bear right on West Brookfield Road and go 1.7 miles to end (merge into Route 9). This is another pleasant road climbing onto a ridge with fine views, passing fields bordered by graceful rows of shade trees.

10. Bear right on Route 9 and go 3/10 mile to end of green in West Brookfield (Route 67 turns sharp right). Here you can chop 4 miles off the ride by turning sharply right on Route 67, going 1.2 miles to Hunt Road on left, and resuming with direction number 15.

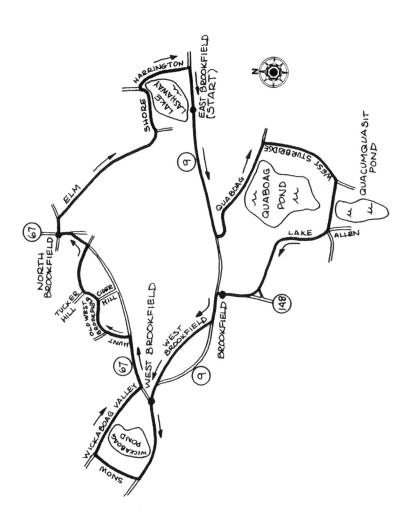

11. Continue straight on Route 9 for 1.8 miles to Snow Road on right. You'll pass Wickaboag Pond on your right. If you come to the Salem Cross Inn (a well-known, elegant restaurant), you've gone 2/10 mile too far.

12. Turn right on Snow Road and go 1.2 miles to end.

13. Turn right at end and go 1.9 miles to end (Route 67), staying on main road.

14. Turn left on Route 67 and go 1 mile to Hunt Road on left.

15. Turn left on Hunt Road and go 1/2 mile to fork (Old West Brookfield Road bears right).

16. Bear right at fork and go 6/10 mile to another fork.

17. Bear left at fork and go 2/10 mile to another fork (Tucker Hill Road bears left).

18. Bear right at fork and go 8/10 mile to crossroads (Route 67).

19. Turn left on Route 67 and go 1/2 mile to stop sign at top of hill.

20. Turn left at stop sign (still Route 67) and go 1/10 mile to crossroads, immediately after the church. This is North Brookfield.

21. Turn right at crossroads and go 2/10 mile to fork.

22. Bear right at fork. After 2.6 miles the main road curves sharply left at bottom of long hill. stay on main road 1/10 mile to fork, at traffic island (North Street turns right).

23. Bear left at fork and go 8/10 mile to a road on your right that crosses a small bridge. Just after the fork you'll see Lake Lashaway on your right.

24. Turn right on this road. After 1 mile Harrington Lane, a dead-end road, bears right. Bear left on main road and go 1/10 mile to end (Route 9).

25. Turn right on Route 9 and go 8/10 mile back to start.

88. West of Worcester: Leicester–Spencer–Paxton

Number of miles: 13 (25 with Paxton extension)
Terrain: Hilly.
Food: Groceries and restaurants in the towns.
Start: Leicester town green, Route 56, just north of Route 9. Park
on Main Street, which runs along the south side of the green.

The region just west of Worcester, a harmonious mixture of rolling
farmland and woods dotted with ponds, provides very scenic biking
on a network of traffic-free rural roads. Although close to the city,
the area is pleasantly rural, because Worcester is fortunate in not
being surrounded by dreary, sprawling suburbs. In addition to the
countryside, two landmarks highlight this ride: a Trappist monastery and the fine Moore State Park.

The ride starts from the handsome hilltop town of Leicester.
Although its town center is only seven miles from downtown Worcester, Leicester is a surprisingly unspoiled rural community. The
large rectangular green is framed by an impressive stone church
and the campus of Becker Junior College. From Leicester you'll
head past Cedar Meadow Pond and Stiles Reservoir to Spencer, an
attractive, compact mill town clinging to steep hillsides. A magnificent old church, a nineteenth-century brick business block, fine old
Victorian homes, and an ornate wooden hotel give charm to the
town.

A few miles north of town is one of the state's more unusual
places of interest, Saint Joseph's Abbey, a Trappist monastery. As
you approach the Abbey, a sign warns you that women are not
permitted on the grounds of the monastery proper. With this policy,
it may seem surprising that the Trappists have managed to exist
since medieval times. The church, which is open to the public (including women), is a large, impressive stone building with its interior shrouded in nearly total darkness. Inside, the silence is
overpowering. The monks sing Gregorian chants at their services
every couple of hours throughout the day, beginning with vigils at
3:30 in the morning. To listen to these slow, unaccompanied intona-
tions in the darkness is a haunting experience. At the entrance to

the grounds is a gift shop selling recordings of Gregorian chants, religious articles, and jams and preserves made by the monks. A monk in full, flowing robes, grim and gaunt as a cadaver, minds the shop.

A few miles beyond the monastery is a brighter spot, Moore State Park. Here a stream cascades in a file of waterfalls past a beautifully restored old mill. Above the mill is a small millpond. From here it's not far to the graceful town of Paxton, another mostly rural community less than ten miles from downtown Worcester. A traditional wooden church, an old town hall, some fine, white wooden homes, and the elegant Paxton Inn grace the center of town. From Paxton you have an enjoyable run back to Leicester along the shores of several ponds.

Directions for the ride: 25 miles

1. Head west from the green and immediately merge head-on into Route 9. Proceed west on Route 9 for 1/2 mile to Rawson Street on left, just beyond the Castle Restaurant on your right. Notice the handsome stone library on your right just after you get onto Route 9.

2. Turn left on Rawson Street. After 1.1 miles Burncoat Street turns right, but bear slightly left on the main road. Go 1.1 miles to crossroads (Greenville Street). A long, tough hill faces you near the beginning of this stretch.

3. Turn left on Greenville Street and go 8/10 mile to end.

4. Turn right at end and go 1/2 mile to fork. You'll go along the Stiles Reservoir.

5. Bear left at fork, following the water on your left, and go 6/10 mile to end.

6. Turn right at end and go 3/10 mile to your first right, Marble Road.

7. Turn right on Marble Road and go 1.3 miles to where Ash Street bears right and the main road continues straight.

8. Bear right on Ash Street and go 7/10 mile to end. A little pond is at the end on your left.

9. Turn left at end (still Ash Street). After 1.3 miles there's a crossroads and stop sign. Continue 1/10 mile to end (Route 9). At the end is a beautiful old church to your right on Route 9. The short

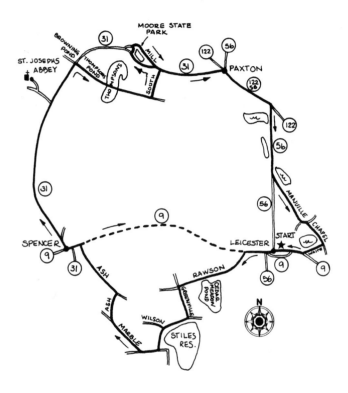

MOORE STATE PARK

BROWNING POND

ST. JOSEPHS ABBEY

THOMPSONS POND

(31)

MILL

SOUTH

(31)

(122) (56)

PAXTON

(122) (56)

(122)

(56)

MANVILLE

CHAPEL

(56)

(31)

(9)

SPENCER

(9)

(31)

ASH

LEICESTER

START

(9)

(9)

(56)

RAWSON

GREENVILLE

CEDAR MEADOW POND

ASH

WILSON

MARBLE

STILES RES.

N

ride turns right on Route 9 and the long ride turns left.

10. Turn left on Route 9 and go 3/10 mile to second traffic light, at bottom of steep hill, where Route 31 (Pleasant Street) turns right. This is the center of Spencer. Notice the fine Victorian homes along Route 9 and the ornate hotel at the corner of Route 31.

11. Turn right on Route 31 and go 2/10 mile to fork (Route 31 bears left).

12. Bear left, staying on Route 31, and go 3.7 miles to the entrance road to Saint Joseph's Abbey on left. It's 9/10 mile up a steady hill to the Abbey church.

13. Continue on Route 31 for 1.3 miles to crossroads (Browning Pond Road on left, Thompson Pond Road on right).

14. Turn right at crossroads up a steep hill. After 3/10 mile, at the top of the hill, a road bears right, but continue straight ahead. Go 1.5 miles to South Street, on left.

15. Turn left on South Street and go 7/10 mile to end (Route 31).

16. Turn left on Route 31 and go 1/2 mile to Black Hill Road, which bears right while you're going downhill.

17. Bear right on Black Hill Road and go 2/10 mile to bridge. Be sure to look to your right at the bridge; there's a fine view of the waterfall and the old mill in Moore State Park.

18. Just after the bridge, make a hairpin right turn onto a narrow lane that passes through a pair of stone pillars. The lane is blocked off to cars. You'll have to walk your bike; there's a "no vehicles" sign at the other end of the lane. You wouldn't want to ride up that hill anyway. (At the intersection, *don't* turn 90 degrees right onto Brigham Road, a dirt road.) Follow the lane through Moore State Park for 1/2 mile to end (merge left onto Route 31).

19. Bear left on Route 31 and go 1.3 miles to traffic light in the center of Paxton (Route 122). Turn right on Route 122 and go 1.3 miles to crossroads where Route 56 (Reservoir Drive) turns right.

20. Turn right on Route 56 and go 1.8 miles to Manville Street, which bears left along a reservoir. It's shortly after a crossroads. You'll pass two reservoirs bordered by stately groves of pines.

21. Bear left on Manville Street, following the water on your left, and go 1.5 miles to end, at stop sign.

22. Turn left at end and go 100 yards to fork (Chapel Street bears right).

23. Bear right at fork and go 1/2 mile to Waite Street on right, just beyond Waite Pond.

24. Turn right on Waite Street and go 4/10 mile to end (Route 9).

25. Bear right on Route 9 and go 2/10 mile to where Route 9 curves left and Main Street bears right up a hill.

26. Bear right on Main Street 4/10 mile to the Leicester green, on top of hill.

Directions for the ride: 13 miles

 1. Follow directions for the long ride through number 9.

2. Turn right on Route 9 and go 4.8 miles to Route 56, at traffic light.

3. Turn left on Route 56 and immediately turn right on Main Street. The green is on your left.

89. Old Sturbridge Village Ride: Sturbridge–Brimfield–Warren–Brookfield

Number of miles: 20 (30 with Warren-Brookfield extension)
Terrain: The short ride is rolling, with one long, steady hill. The long ride has two additional tough climbs.
Food: Grocery and snack bar in Brimfield. Burger King at end. The long stretch between Brimfield and the end has no facilities; bring some food with you.
Start: Burger King, Route 20, Sturbridge, just east of Old Sturbridge Village.

The magnificent ridge, valley, and lake country of south-central Massachusetts provides superb bicycling on a network of nearly untraveled country roads, with spectacular vistas spread before you as you crest each ridge. The ride passes through Brimfield, one of the numerous classic New England towns dotting the middle of the state.

The ride starts adjacent to Old Sturbridge Village, an outstanding historical restoration, among the best in the country. If you've never been there it would be worthwhile to set aside several hours before or after the ride to visit it. With painstaking historical research and attention to detail, Old Sturbridge Village recreates life in a rural early nineteenth-century New England community as closely as possible. No power mowers trim the green—sheep do the job just as effectively. Dirt paths become muddy when it rains and dusty in the summer heat, just as in 1800, when the luxury of blacktop hadn't diffused to the country towns. In the ramshackle little shops and outbuildings, apprentices dressed in historically accurate garments learn and apply traditional unmechanized crafts and trades like spinning yarn, making watertight casks, tanning leather, blacksmithing, and cabinetmaking. No attempt has been made to artificially glamorize the village or dress it up. As in most post-Revolutionary small towns, it has only one impressive house which belonged to the community's most prominent family; everyone else lived in simple, sparsely furnished cottages, scratching a living from the soil, a small business, or a trade.

Spring plowing at Old Sturbridge Village.

Old Sturbridge Village also has several galleries exhibiting artifacts from everyday life in early New England, a fascinating garden of medicinal and culinary herbs, and a full range of educational programs.

The success of Old Sturbridge Village has spawned several other attractions, including a doll museum, an antique auto museum, Saint Anne's Shrine with a collection of Russian icons, and too many overpriced antique and crafts shops.

From Sturbridge you'll head into lake country, going along the Brimfield Reservoir. Just off the route is East Brimfield Dam, holding the waters in place. A couple of miles ahead you'll pass beautiful Holland Pond, where you can take a swim. Next you go through a valley to the elegant old town of Brimfield. The larger-than-average green is framed by a graceful white church, rambling old wooden homes, and an ornate pink-purple Victorian town hall. From Brimfield you'll head north past Sherman Pond into inspiring ridge-and-valley country. It's a long climb to the top of the ridge, but you'll be rewarded by sweeping views of the rolling, open countryside. The return to Sturbridge leads mainly downhill on smooth roads through the little village of Fiskdale, with its uniquely ornate Victorian main building of brick. A short ride along Route 20 takes you back to Old Sturbridge Village.

The longer ride heads farther north into more rural, equally spectacular ridge-and-valley country. In Brookfield you'll bike past gracious horse farms, with views of Quaboag Pond and distant hills in the background, and then hug the shore of Quacumquasit Pond. The return to Sturbridge leads through woods and small farms along a quiet country road.

Directions for the ride: 30 miles

1. Turn right (west) out of parking lot onto Route 20 and go 3 miles to Holland-East Brimfield Road on your left, at the far end of the Reservoir (sign may say to Holland, 4 miles). After slightly more than 1 mile, you'll see the Victorian building in the center of Fiskdale, newly renovated into shops and offices. Just after the building, Saint Anne's Shrine is on your right up a short hill. To visit East Brimfield Dam, turn left 6/10 mile beyond Route 148 on River-

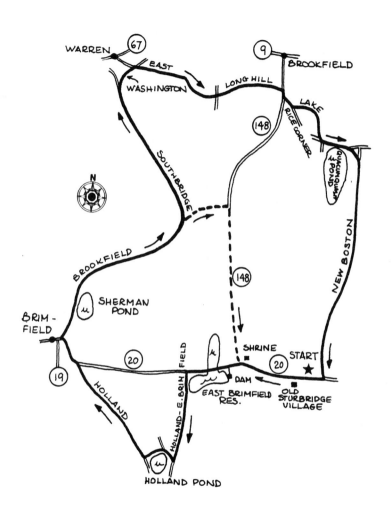

WARREN (67)
EAST
WASHINGTON
LONG HILL
(9) BROOKFIELD
LAKE
RICE CORNER
(148)
QUACUMQUASIT POND
SOUTHBRIDGE
N
BROOKFIELD
NEW BOSTON
SHERMAN POND
BRIM-FIELD
(148)
(20)
HOLLAND - E. BRIM FIELD
SHRINE
START
(20)
OLD STURBRIDGE VILLAGE
DAM
EAST BRIMFIELD RES.
(19)
HOLLAND
HOLLAND POND

487

view Avenue, opposite a motel. The dam is 1/4 mile ahead.

2. Turn left on Holland-East Brimfield Road and go 2.1 miles to a small lane that turns very sharply right. It's immediately after telephone pole number 34 on the right.

3. Make a sharp right onto the lane and go 3/10 mile to fork. Holland Pond is on your left. • *CAUTION:* Most of this road is dirt with loose rocks. It's safest to walk.

4. Bear left at fork, following the pond, and go 1/2 mile to end.

5. Turn right at end and go 3 miles to end (merge into Route 20).

6. Bear left on Route 20 and go 4/10 mile to traffic island with a monument in the middle. Just before the intersection, notice the old wooden windmill on your left. At the monument the ride turns right, but it's worth going straight 200 yards to see the lovely Brimfield town green and the unique Victorian town hall. There's also a grocery and snack bar opposite the green, the last food stop of the ride.

7. Bear right at monument on Brookfield Road and go 4.4 miles to fork where Southbridge Road bears left. You'll pass Sherman Pond and then make the long ascent to the top of the ridge. At the fork the short ride bears right and the long ride bears left.

8. Bear left on Southbridge Road and go 3.7 miles to another fork (Washington Road bears right). It comes up at the bottom of a long downhill run. After a tough climb at the beginning, this is a magnificent run along ridges with panoramic views.

9. Bear right on Washington Road and go 3/10 mile to another fork (East Street bears right uphill). Here the ride bears right, but if you turn sharply left downhill 1/2 mile you'll come to the center of Warren, an old mill town with stores and restaurants. Then it's a tough climb back to where you are now.

10. Bear right uphill on East Street and go 4.6 miles to end (Route 148), at a traffic island. Halfway along this stretch you'll come to a crossroads and stop sign while going downhill—go straight ahead. • *CAUTION:* This road has a couple of steep downhills with bumpy spots. Take it easy.

11. Turn right on Route 148 and immediately bear left on Rice Corner Road. Go 2/10 mile to fork (Lake Road bears left).

12. Bear left on Lake Road and go 2.1 miles to end. This is an inspiring run along a hillside past estates and horse farms, with views of Quaboag Pond below.

13. Turn left at end and go 7/10 mile to fork. In the middle of the fork is a large traffic island with trees on it. You'll pass Quacumquasit Pond on your right.

14. Bear right at fork and go 3.8 miles to end (Route 20).

15. Turn right on Route 20 and go 3/10 mile to Burger King on right.

Directions for the ride: 20 miles

1. Follow directions for the long ride through number 7.

2. Bear right at fork and stay on the main road 1.2 miles to end (Route 148).

3. Turn right on Route 148 and go 3.7 miles to end (merge into Route 20).

4. Bear left on Route 20 and go 1.4 miles to Burger King on left. • *CAUTION:* Route 20 is very busy. Be very careful making the left turn into the parking lot at the end.

90. Brimfield–Holland–Union, Connecticut–Wales

Number of miles: 14 (32 with Union extension)
Terrain: The short ride is rolling, with one tough hill. The long ride is hilly.
Food: Country store in Holland (long ride). Restaurant in Union, Connecticut, just over the state line (long ride). Country store in Wales. Grocery and snack bar in Brimfield, at end.
Start: Route 20 in Brimfield, opposite the green, just west of Route 19 South. Park at side of road.

The southern boundary area of Massachusetts, midway between Worcester and Springfield, has some of the most rural and remote countryside in the state east of the Connecticut River. This is an area of rugged, wooded hills separated by spring-fed lakes and ponds, and populated with only a handful of tiny, pristine towns. This ride makes a circuit of four towns, passing several ponds along the way.

The ride starts from Brimfield, a stately old town with a larger-than-average green, a graceful white church, a marvelous purple Victorian town hill, and several antique shops. The town hosts a giant flea market three times a year: on Mother's Day, July 4, and in the middle of September.

From Brimfield you'll head south to Holland, which consists primarily of summer cottages along the shore of the Hamilton Reservoir. You'll enjoy a relaxing run along the water to the metropolis of Union, Connecticut, which is solely a church and green. From here you'll straddle the Massachusetts-Connecticut border on twisting country lanes, eventually making a long, gradual descent to the Staffordville Reservoir. After biking beside this long, slender lake you'll arrive in Wales, a quiet village on the shore of Lake George. Wales hosts an old-fashioned country fair in August. The final leg back to Brimfield brings you over a high ridge with farms on top and fine views, with a great downhill run at the end.

The short ride weaves through wooded hills from Holland directly to Wales, with a run along Lake George.

Road obstruction in Holland.

Directions for the ride: 32 miles

1. Head east on Route 20 and go 1/2 mile to Holland Road, which bears right. Notice the old wooden windmill on your right just beyond the Route 19 traffic light.

2. Bear right on Holland Road and just ahead bear left at fork (sign may say to Holland). Go 4.2 miles to crossroads (Sturbridge Road on left, Stafford Road on right). Here the short ride turns right and the long ride goes straight. If you turn left after 3.1 miles on Pond Beach Road for 2/10 mile you'll come to a beach on Holland Pond.

3. Continue straight at crossroads. After 9/10 mile a smaller road bears right, but curve left on main road. Go 2.4 miles to a road on your left that crosses over Route 84. There's a nice run along the Hamilton Reservoir on this section.

4. Turn left across the highway 1/10 mile to end.

5. Turn right at end and go 2.3 miles to where the road runs head-on into Route 190, and Route 171 turns left.

6. Go straight onto Route 190 for 2.4 miles to Stickney Hill Road, which makes a sharp right shortly after the Route 84 interchange. You'll pass the Union church and green just after getting onto Route 190.

7. Turn sharply right on Stickney Hill Road (don't turn 90 degrees right on Webster Road) and go 1.5 miles to fork. A long, steep descent comes just before the fork.

8. Bear right at fork and go 3.5 miles to crossroads (Stafford-Holland Road on right, New City Road on left).

9. Turn left at crossroads and go 4.5 miles to end (merge into Route 19). This is a pleasantly winding wooded lane heading mostly downhill. Halfway along you'll pass New City Pond on your left.

10. Turn sharply right on Route 19 and go 5.9 miles to a stone monument, where Route 19 curves right and Haynes Hill Road bears left up a hill. At the beginning of this stretch you'll parallel the Staffordville Reservoir; then you'll pass Lake George on your right and go through the center of Wales.

11. Bear left on Haynes Hill Road, heading uphill. Go 3.1 miles to crossroads at bottom of long hill (Route 19). • *CAUTION* here—

492

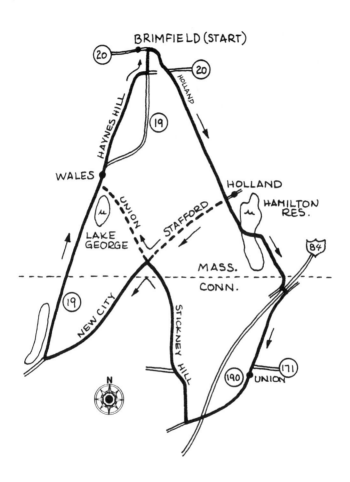

BRIMFIELD (START)

20

20

HOLLAND

HAYNES HILL

19

WALES

UNION

HOLLAND

HAMILTON RES.

STAFFORD

LAKE GEORGE

84

MASS.

CONN.

19

NEW CITY

STICKNEY HILL

N

190

UNION

171

there is no stop sign. There are some fine views from the top of the ridge.

12. Turn left on Route 19 and go 6/10 mile to Route 20, in center of Brimfield. Your starting point is to the left.

Directions for the ride: 14 miles

1. Follow directions number 1 and 2 for the long ride.

2. Turn right at crossroads on Stafford Road and go 3.1 miles to another crossroads (road on right goes up a short, steep hill).

3. Turn right at crossroads and go 2 miles to end (Route 19), in Wales. Just before the end you'll go along Lake George.

4. Turn right on Route 19 and go 6/10 mile to a stone monument where Route 19 curves right and Haynes Hill Road bears left up a hill.

5. Follow directions number 11 and 12 for the long ride.

91. Southbridge–Woodstock, Connecticut

Number of miles: 14 (24 with Woodstock extension)
Terrain: Very rolling, with several short, steep hills.
Food: None en route. McDonald's at end.
Start: McDonald's, Route 131, Southbridge, in shopping center
1.5 miles east of the center of town.

This ride has us explore the very rural, very rolling ridge-and-valley country straddling the Massachusetts-Connecticut border roughly midway between Worcester and Springfield. Steep-sided wooded ridges, running north to south, become more open and rounded as you head south into Connecticut. The long ride passes through the magnificent hilltop town of Woodstock, Connecticut.

You start from the small industrial city of Southbridge, one of the most attractive mill towns in Massachusetts. Southbridge is a one-industry town—optical products—with the factories of the largest company, American Optical, lining the banks of the Quinebaug River in a seemingly endless row. The company's main building is a massive yet graceful Victorian structure resembling an Elizabethan castle. American Optical was founded in 1833, making the city the first producer of optical goods in the country. In the downtown area, graceful Victorian buildings of brick line the wide, gently curving main street, which leads up a hill to a large, graceful church standing proudly over the town.

From Southbridge you'll head south through open farmland and along unspoiled Morse Pond into Connecticut. After a few miles on country lanes winding past old barns and broad fields, you cross back into Massachusetts and follow the crest of a high ridge with spectacular views. The descent back into Southbridge is a screamer.

The long ride heads farther south into Connecticut to the unspoiled hilltop town of Woodstock, a classic New England jewel. Framing the large green are the traditional white church, the handsome old wooden main building of Woodstock Academy, and the Bowen House, a marvelous pink Gothic mansion. Also called Roseland Cottage, it was built in 1846 by Henry C. Bowen, a businessman who invited Presidents Grant, Hayes, Harrison, and McKinley there for Fourth of July gatherings. Now run by the Society for the Preservation of New England Antiquities and open to the public afternoons from June to October, the mansion has period furnishings and a private bowling alley, one of the earliest in the country.

Beyond Woodstock you'll weave through inspiring, very rolling farmland and rejoin the short ride just in time to enjoy the high ridge and fast descent into Southbridge.

Directions for the ride: 24 miles

1. Turn left out of parking lot onto Route 131 and go 1/4 mile to Ashland Avenue on right. Route 131 curves sharply left at the intersection.

2. Turn right on Ashland Avenue and go 3/10 mile to end (Route 169).

3. Turn left on Route 169. After 2.8 miles you'll enter Connecticut just after you pass Morse Pond on the right. Continue 2.4 miles to English Neighborhood Road, which turns sharply right almost at bottom of hill just before blinking light (Route 197). Here the short ride makes a sharp right and the long ride goes straight.

4. Go straight on Route 169 and just ahead cross Route 197. Go 1/10 mile to fork where Route 169 bears slightly right (sign may say to Pomfret).

5. Bear right, staying on Route 169. After 3.1 miles you'll pass the Bowen House, also called Roseland Cottage, on your right opposite the Woodstock town green. Continue 4/10 mile to Plaine Hill Road, which bears slightly right where Route 169 curves left downhill. There's a magnificent view to the left at the intersection.

6. Bear slightly right on Plaine Hill Road and go 1/2 mile to end (Route 171), at bottom of steep hill. • *CAUTION* here.

7. Turn right on Route 171 and go 2.7 miles to crossroads (Coatney Hill Road on right and dirt road on left).

8. Turn right on Coatney Hill Road and go 1.2 miles to crossroads and stop sign.

9. Go straight at stop sign onto Center School Road and go 3/10 mile to end (Center Road).

10. Turn right on Center Road and go 1.1 miles to diagonal crossroads and stop sign (Route 197).

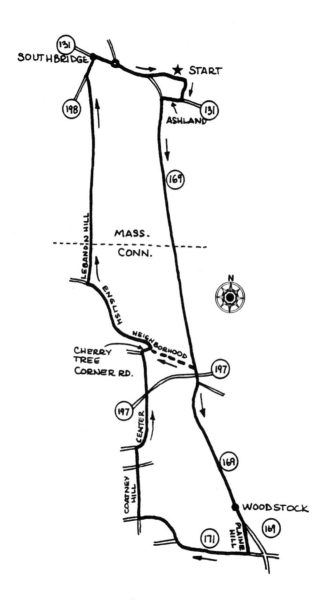

131

SOUTHBRIDGE

198

★ START

131

ASHLAND

169

MASS.
CONN.

LEBANON HILL

ENGLISH

N

NEIGHBORHOOD

CHERRY
TREE
CORNER RD.

197

197

CENTER

169

WOODSTOCK

COATNEY HILL

PLAINE HILL

169

171

497

11. Cross Route 197 onto Lyon Hill Road and go 9/10 mile to fork (Cherry Tree Corner Road bears right).

12. Bear right on Cherry Tree Corner Road and go 1/10 mile to end.

13. Turn left at end. After 3/10 mile you'll come to a fork where the main road bears left. Stay on main road for 1.5 miles to Lebanon Hill Road on right, at top of long, very gradual hill. A brick ranch house is on the corner.

14. Turn right on Lebanon Hill Road and go 3.8 miles to where Everett Street bears right and Elm Street goes straight, just after you enter the built-up section of Southbridge. At the Massachusetts line there's a granite marker dated 1906. Shortly before the intersection you'll have a thrilling downhill run.

15. Go straight on Elm Street 1/2 mile to end (Route 131), in downtown Southbridge. Just before the end, notice the castlelike town hall on the right, built in 1888, and the clock-towered fire station on the left. When you come to Route 131, the main business district is on your left.

16. Turn right on Route 131 and go 4/10 mile to rotary. At the rotary, glance to your left and see the castlelike main building of American Optical Company.

17. Bear right at rotary onto Routes 131 and 169. Go 6/10 mile to fork, where Route 131 goes straight and Route 169 bears right uphill. The Quinebaug River is on your left.

18. Go straight on Route 131 for 4/10 mile to McDonald's on left.

Directions for the ride: 14 miles

1. Follow directions for the long ride through number 3.

2. Turn sharp right on English Neighborhood Road. After 1.4 miles you'll come to a fork where the main road bears left. Stay on main road for 1.5 miles to Lebanon Hill Road on right, at top of long, very gradual hill. A brick ranch house is on the corner.

3. Follow directions for the long ride from number 14 to the end.

Southbridge.

92. Hill and Gully Rider: Dudley–Charlton

Number of miles: 24
Terrain: Hilly.
Food: Grocery and pizza place in Charlton.
Start: Shopping center on Airport Road, Dudley, just north of
Route 197, 2 miles west of downtown Webster. An alternate
starting point, closer to the Worcester area, is the small
shopping center on Route 31 in Charlton, 1 mile south of
Route 20. Directions for the Charlton start are at the end.
The Dudley start offers the advantage that most of the
second half of the ride is downhill.

The rolling, rural countryside between Worcester and Springfield
consists primarily of high, open ridges that provide some of the
most spectacular bicycle riding in the state. This ride tours the
southeastern portion of the region, ascending and descending from
one ridge to another on smooth, lightly traveled roads with sweeping vistas around every bend. The graceful New England hilltop
towns of Charlton and Dudley add to the appeal and variety of the
ride.

The ride starts from Dudley, a two-faced town with old, grim
mills on the Quinebaug River that forms the border with Webster,
and the classic town center three miles to the west, surrounded by
broad expanses of farmland. You'll go past the massive granite
Stevens Mill, built in 1864, and head into the ridge country to
Charlton, among the most appealing and spectacularly located central Massachusetts towns. The handsome church, turn-of-the-century brick schoolhouse, town hall, and an old cemetery crown the
top of a hill with superb views to the west. From here you'll head
south to Dudley on Route 31, absolutely a paradise for biking. Three
miles out of town is the Dresser Hill Dairy, with some of the best ice
cream in Worcester County. From here you'll climb onto more open
ridges with inspiring vistas, dip downhill, climb and dip some more,
and finally enjoy a thrilling two-mile descent into the Quinebaug
Valley.

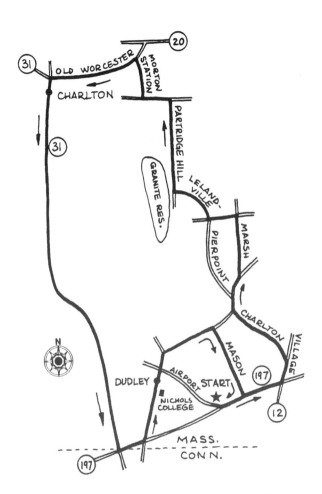

20

31

OLD WORCESTER

MORTON STATION

CHARLTON

31

PARTRIDGE HILL

GRANITE RES.

LELAND-VILLE

PIERPOINT

MARSH

CHARLTON

VILLAGE

MASON

N

DUDLEY

AIRPORT

START

197

NICHOLS COLLEGE

12

MASS.

CONN.

197

Near the end of the ride you'll climb one more hill to the gracious town center of Dudley. It consists primarily of Nichols College, which is mainly a business school. Adjoining the campus are some handsome old homes and a distinctive brick church with a tall, slender clock tower. From here it's a short downhill ride to the end.

Directions for the ride: Dudley start

1. Turn left out of parking lot and immediately bear left onto Route 197. Go 1.1 miles to traffic light where Route 12 turns right and Village Street turns left.

2. Turn left on Village Street and go 3/10 mile to Charlton Road, which bears left. You'll pass underneath a section of the massive Stevens Mill, built in 1864.

3. Bear left on Charlton Road and go 2.2 miles to Marsh Road, which bears left just before top of hill. It's 6/10 mile after Pierpoint Road on left.

4. Bear left on Marsh Road and go 1.4 miles to crossroads and stop sign. There's a steep but short climb to the top of a ridge with fine views.

5. Turn left at crossroads and go 6/10 mile to another crossroads and stop sign, midway up a sharp hill.

6. Turn right at crossroads and go 7/10 mile to top of hill, where the main road curves sharply right and another road turns left.

7. Curve right on main road. The Granite Reservoir is on your left, set back a short distance from the road. Go 2.3 miles to end.

8. Turn left at end and go 1/2 mile to Morton Station Road on right. It comes up as you start go to downhill—don't whizz past it.

9. Turn right on Morton Station Road and go 1/2 mile to end.

10. Turn left at end and go 1.5 miles to crossroads and stop sign (Route 31). You'll pass an orchard on your right as soon as you turn left. When you get to Route 31, a grocery and pizza place are on the far side of the intersection.

11. Turn left on Route 31 and go 8.1 miles to crossroads and blinking light at bottom of long hill (Route 197). At the beginning of this stretch you'll go through the center of Charlton. The Dresser Hill Dairy is 3 miles ahead on your right, atop a ridge. Immediately after the dairy, go straight (don't bear right downhill).

12. Turn left on Route 197 and go 1/2 mile to crossroads (sign may say to Nichols College).

13. Turn left at crossroads and go 1.4 miles to crossroads and stop sign shortly after Nichols College and brick church on left. It's a tough climb to the college.

14. Go straight at crossroads 2/10 mile to fork.

15. Bear right at fork and go 7/10 mile to a road on right (sign may say Wysocki Square). It comes up immediately after Mason Road Extension on left.

16. Turn right on this road and go 1.4 miles to crossroads and stop sign (Route 197, West Main Street).

17. Turn right on Route 197 and go 3/10 mile to Airport Road, which bears right.

18. Bear right on Airport Road. The parking lot is just ahead on right.

Directions for the ride: Charlton start (small shopping center on Route 31)

1. Turn right (south) onto Route 31 and go 8.1 miles to crossroads and blinking light at bottom of long hill (Route 197). After 3 miles you'll pass the Dresser Hill Dairy on your right, atop a ridge. Immediately after the dairy, go straight (don't bear right downhill).

2. Follow directions number 12 through 16 for the ride starting in Dudley.

3. Turn left on Route 197 and go 8/10 mile to traffic light where Route 12 turns right and Village Street turns left.

4. Follow directions number 2 through 10 for the ride starting in Dudley.

93. Auburn–Sutton–Oxford–Charlton–Leicester

Number of miles: 20 (31 with Charlton–Leicester extension)
Terrain: Hilly.
Food: Grocery and restaurants in Oxford. Country store in
     Leicester.
Start: Auburn Plaza, Route 12, Auburn, just west of Route 290
     and 1/2 mile northeast of Route 20.

This is a tour of rolling farm country, dotted with lakes, south and a
little west of Worcester. Although close to the city, the region is
delightfully rural because, unlike Boston and Springfield, Worcester
has no dreary suburbs despoiling the surrounding area. Biking in
this part of the state is challenging because the landscape is hilly,
but you'll be rewarded with fine views from ridgetops, narrow lanes
twisting past old barns and grazing cattle, and several stretches
along ponds.

You start from Auburn, Worcester's closest approximation to a
bedroom suburb, and immediately head into undeveloped countryside. You'll go along Ramshorn and Stockwell ponds, and up and
over ridges with fine views to Oxford; a pleasant community best
known as the birthplace of Clara Barton, founder of the American
Red Cross. From Oxford it's an easy run back to Auburn along a
valley.

The long ride heads farther west into the rolling hills and ridges
of Charlton and then Leicester (pronounced Lester). Just before the
end is a delightful run along the Dark Brook Reservoir, bordered by
a stately grove of pines.

Directions for the ride: 31 miles

1. Turn right out of parking lot onto Route 12 and go 2/10
mile to Faith Avenue on right, just before Route 290.

2. Bear right on Faith Avenue and go 1/2 mile to Route 20.

3. Cross Route 20 onto Oxford Street. • *CAUTION:* Watch traffic. Go 1.2 miles to Cedar Street on left.

4. Turn left on Cedar Street and go 6/10 mile to end (merge to
right).

504

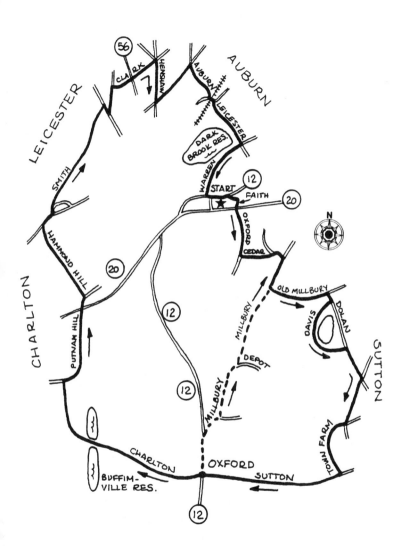

5. Bear right at end, crossing railroad tracks, and go 2/10 mile to end.

6. Turn right at end and go 6/10 mile to Old Millbury Road, which turns sharply to the left shortly after top of hill.

7. Turn sharply left on Old Millbury Road and go 1.8 miles to Dolan Road on right. It comes up while you're going downhill.

8. Turn right on Dolan Road and go 2/10 mile to Davis Road on right.

9. Turn right on Davis Road and go 1.8 miles to end. You'll climb a tough hill and then descend to the shore of Ramshorn Pond.

10. Turn right at end and go 6/10 mile to crossroads and stop sign at bottom of hill.

11. Turn right at stop sign and go 1.2 miles to Town Farm Road, a crossroads where the road on the right goes up a very steep hill.

12. Turn right at crossroads up the hill—I won't blame you for walking it—and go 1.1 miles to end. At the top of the hill you'll be rewarded by a panoramic view of rolling green hillsides.

13. Turn right at end and go 3.6 miles to traffic light (Route 12) in the center of Oxford. After a short climb, you'll relax on a gradual downhill run with fine views. When you come to Route 12, notice the handsome red-brick town hall on the far side of the intersection. The short ride turns right on Route 12 and the long ride goes straight.

14. Cross Route 12 and go 3.9 miles to end, at stop sign. There's a long, tough hill toward the end of this section, after you cross the Buffumvile Reservoir.

15. Turn right at end and go 1.5 miles to Route 20, a four-lane highway.

16. Cross Route 20 diagonally (• *CAUTION* here) and go 1/10 mile to fork.

17. Bear left at fork and go 1.5 miles to end (merge to your right shortly after the bridge over the Massachusetts Turnpike).

18. Bear right at end and go 4/10 mile to Smith Road, which bears left just after railroad bridge.

19. Bear left on Smith Road, go 100 yards to fork, and bear left again. Go 2 miles to end. • *CAUTION:* The end comes up suddenly while you're going downhill.

20. Turn right at end and go 1/10 mile to River Street, which turns sharply left. A country store is at the intersection.

21. Turn sharply left and go 3/10 mile to Clark Street on right. You'll pass a fine white church on your left.

22. Turn right on Clark Street and go 1/2 mile to crossroads and stop sign (Route 56).

23. Cross Route 56 and go 6/10 mile to traffic island at bottom of hill (sign may say Patrick M. Lorditch Square).

24. Turn sharply right at traffic island up steep hill and go 1 mile to crossroads and stop sign.

25. Turn sharply left at crossroads and go 1.5 miles to Auburn Street, a small diagonal crossroads where the road on the right turns sharply right. It comes up very suddenly while you're going downhill—don't whizz past it.

26. Turn sharply right on Auburn Street and go 1.1 miles to end, at railroad bridge.

27. Turn left at end, going under railroad bridge. Immediately after the bridge, turn right and go 1.1 miles to crossroads and stop sign.

28. Turn right at crossroads and go 1.1 miles to end (Route 12). You'll go along the Dark Brook Reservoir at the beginning.

29. Turn left on Route 12. Auburn Plaza is just ahead on right.

Directions for the ride: 20 miles

1. Follow the directions for the long ride through number 13.

2. Turn right on Route 12 and go 1.1 miles to Millbury Boulevard, which bears right at a blinking light immediately after police station on right.

3. Bear right on Millbury Boulevard and go 4/10 mile to where Millbury Boulevard turns left, immediately after railroad tracks.

4. Turn left (still Millbury Boulevard) and go 9/10 mile to fork immediately after the Route 395 access road. • *CAUTION:* There are diagonal railroad tracks on this section, and there's another set of tracks at the fork.

5. Bear left at fork onto Millbury Road. After 1.1 miles Old Millbury Road bears right, but continue straight on the main road. Go 6/10 mile to your first left, South Street.

6. Turn left on South Street and go 2/10 mile to fork immediately after railroad tracks (Cedar Street bears left).

7. Bear left on Cedar Street and go 6/10 mile to end.

8. Turn right at end and go 1.2 miles to Route 20.

9. Turn left on Route 20. (• *CAUTION:* Busy intersection.) Go 4/10 mile to the *back* of the shopping center on right. • *CAUTION:* There's a speed bump when you turn into the shopping center.

94. Tri-State Tour: Webster–Douglas–Pascoag, Rhode Island–Thompson, Connecticut

Number of miles: 19 (33 with Pascoag–Thompson extension)
Terrain: Rolling, with one tough hill.
Food: Small grocery at Sutton Falls Campground, Sutton, open
   during camping season. Grocery and snack bar in Pascoag.
Start: Friendly Ice Cream, Route 12, Webster, just west of Route
   395.

This is a tour of the very rural, mostly wooded, lake-studded countryside surrounding the point where Massachusetts, Rhode Island,
and Connecticut meet. The terrain is not as hilly as in the surrounding areas. The lightly traveled backroads, winding through the
woods and along several ponds, promise enjoyable and peaceful
bicycling.

The ride starts in Webster, a small and rather bleak mill city on
the French River just north of the Connecticut line. You'll immediately head into rolling, wooded countryside to the tiny village of
West Sutton and pass Sutton Falls, a small dam with a little covered
bridge above it. Just ahead are pleasant runs along Manchaug Pond
and then the Whitin Reservoir. From here it's a short way to the
graceful, classic New England village of Douglas, with stately white
church, old cemetery, and triangular green.

From Douglas you'll follow a smooth secondary road to the
attractive little mill town of Pascoag, in the northwestern corner of
Rhode Island. With massive granite and brick Victorian mills
straight out of the Industrial Revolution, Pascoag is typical of the
many mill villages hugging the fast-flowing rivers throughout
Rhode Island. Unfortunately, the largest mill burned to the ground
in 1980 after being set afire by a local teenager. Leaving Pascoag,
you'll skirt the Wilson Reservoir and then climb gradually to the top
of Buck Hill, one of Rhode Island's highest points.

You now speed down two steep hills into the northwestern
corner of Connecticut. After about three miles of narrow lanes
you'll cross back into Webster, and return into town along the shore
of Lake Chargoggagoggmanchaugagoggchaubunagungamaug,

which in the Nipmuc Indian language means, "I fish on my side, you fish on your side, and nobody fishes in the middle." If it hasn't been stolen, a sign spelling out the name of the lake may greet you as you cross the state line.

The short ride heads directly from Douglas back to Webster without leaving Massachusetts. There's a great downhill run at the end.

Directions for the ride: 33 miles

1. Turn left (east) out of parking lot. Just ahead, go straight at traffic light onto Route 16. Go 3/10 mile to Sutton Road on left, immediately after the Route 395 underpass.

2. Turn left on Sutton Road and go 3/10 mile to where Sutton Road turns right and Cudworth Road goes straight.

3. Turn right (still Sutton Road) and go 3.8 miles to end. You'll pass Nipmuck Pond on your right.

4. Turn right at end. After 2/10 mile, Douglas Road bears right uphill, but bear slightly left downhill, staying on the main road. Go 1 mile to Manchaug Road on right (a sign may say Sutton Falls Campground). It's your second right, and it comes up almost at the bottom of a long downhill.

5. Turn right on Manchaug Road. After 8/10 mile, watch for the Sutton Falls Campground on your right, with its fine little dam and covered bridge. A small grocery store here is open during camping season.

6. From the campground, continue 1.5 miles to a fork where a smaller road bears left and Torrey Road continues straight down a steep hill.

7. Go straight down the hill for 3/10 mile to Holt Road, which bears right at pond.

8. Bear right on Holt Road and go 1.3 miles to fork (Wallis Street bears right).

9. Bear right at fork (don't turn sharp right) and go 1.2 miles to another fork. There is 1/10 mile of dirt road when you cross the pond.

10. Bear slightly left and go 7/10 mile to end (merge right; no stop sign).

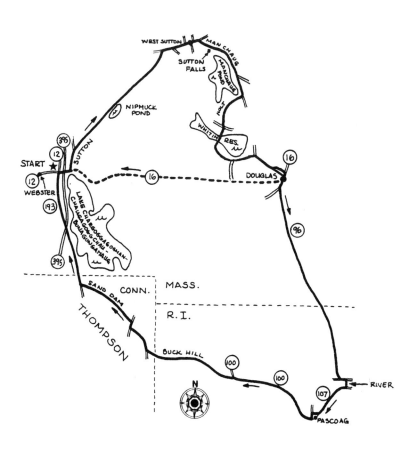

511

11. Bear right at end and go 6/10 mile to fork where the main road bears left.

12. Bear left on the main road and go 4/10 mile to another fork at church on right. This is Douglas.

13. Bear right at fork and go 1/10 mile into Route 16. Immediately ahead is a blinking light where Route 16 turns right. Here the short ride turns right onto Route 16 and the long ride goes straight.

14. Go straight where Route 16 turns right. Immediately ahead is a fork, where Route 96 bears left.

15. Bear left on Route 96 and go 6.6 miles to stop sign where the main road bears left. Continue 1/10 mile to River Street on right.

16. Turn right on River Street and go 1/10 mile to end (Route 107).

17. Bear right on Route 107 and go 1.4 miles to end, opposite a supermarket in the center of Pascoag, Rhode Island. Route 107 twists and turns, but stay on the main road. Just before the end you'll cross a stream with a small waterfall on your left.

18. Turn left at end, in front of supermarket, and go one block to end (Route 100).

19. Turn right on Route 100. After 100 yards Route 100 turns 90 degrees right (sign may say to Zamborano Hospital). Continue on Route 100 for 3.2 miles to Buck Hill Road, a smaller road that bears left (sign may say to Buck Hill Campground). About 1 mile out of Pascoag you'll pass a wonderful old red country schoolhouse on your right. Then you'll go by the Wilson Reservoir.

20. Bear left on Buck Hill Road and go 1/10 mile to fork.

21. Bear left at fork and go 3 miles to end (merge to right at bottom of second long downhill). You are now in Connecticut.
• *CAUTION:* Both descents are steep and bumpy; take it easy.

22. Bear right at bottom of hill and go 1.2 miles to end. Notice the old church, built in 1841, at the intersection.

23. Turn right at end and go 1/10 mile to fork (Sand Dam Road bears left).

24. Bear left on Sand Dam Road and go 2 miles to end (Route 193).

25. Bear right on Route 193 and go 3 miles to the third traffic light (Routes 16 and 12).

26. Turn left on Routes 16 and 12. Friendly is just ahead on right.

Directions for the ride: 19 miles

   1. Follow directions for the long ride through number 13.

   2. Turn right at blinking light on Route 16 and go 7 miles to Friendly on right. It's just past the traffic light after the Route 395 underpass. You'll have a great downhill run coming into Webster.

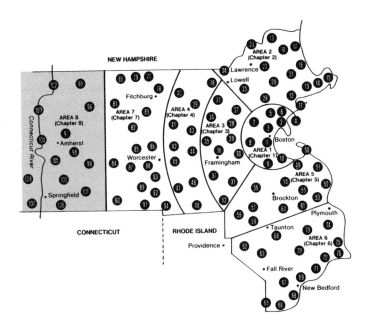

Chapter 8:

The Connecticut Valley

Numbers on this map refer to rides in this book.

95. Wilderness Experience: Orange–Erving–Northfield–Warwick

Number of miles: 31 (sorry, no short ride)
Terrain: Hilly.
Food: Groceries and snack bars in the towns.
Start: Junction of Routes 122 and 2A in the center of Orange. Park where legal at side of road. An alternate starting point is at the corner of Route 63 and Warwick Avenue in the center of Northfield.

If the name of this ride conjures up images of a Sierra Club expedition with packhorses and pickaxes, it's not that bad. But almost. You'll explore an area that's about as backwoods as you can get in Massachusetts—the nearly uninhabited hill country just east of the Connecticut River and just south of the New Hampshire border. Biking in these parts is challenging but exciting, with the long climbs balanced by thrilling descents and inspiring mountain scenery. And just when you need a rest or a bite to eat, along comes an unspoiled rural town.

The ride starts from Orange, a small, compact mill town on the Millers River. You'll follow the valley from Orange to Erving, a small town dominated by a giant paper mill, and then head north into the mountains. This is a long but fairly gradual climb, punctuated by a few steep pitches and occasional open spots, where you get views of the neighboring hillsides. The descent into Northfield is a thriller, dropping 800 feet in two miles to broad farms with a backdrop of mountains on the west bank of the Connecticut River.

Northfield is an elegant town poised proudly on a hillside overlooking the river. The community is unusual in that it has no real town center, just a long stretch of gracious old white homes, churches, schools, and an impressive stone library, tastefully spaced along the main street. From Northfield you once again climb to the base of 1,600-foot Mount Grace, the state's third-highest mountain east of the Connecticut. Suddenly you arrive in Warwick, a totally unspoiled New England gem of a town in the middle of nowhere. A country store, white wooden town hall, the rambling old Warwick Inn, an old schoolhouse, and a graceful white church on top of the hill cluster around the village center.

Just beyond Warwick you'll ascend onto an open ridge with spectacular views; then once again the fun begins with the long descent back to Orange on narrow, well-paved roads. As you approach the floor of the valley, woodland gradually gives way to widening farmland.

Directions for the ride

1. Head west on Route 2A for 3.3 miles to end (Route 2).

2. Turn left on Route 2 and go 1.7 miles to Church Street on right, immediately after the Erving town hall and fire station on right (sign may say to Erving State Forest). • *CAUTION:* Route 2 is very heavily traveled.

3. Turn right on Church Street and stay on the main road 7.6 miles to end (Routes 10 and 63), in Northfield. The descent into Northfield is magnificent, on a good, smooth road.

4. Turn right on Routes 10 and 63. Go 4/10 mile to crossroads and blinking light (Warwick Avenue). Here the ride turns right, but it's worth going straight a short distance to see the handsome stone library and some of the gracious old homes in this town.

5. Turn right on Warwick Avenue and go 7/10 mile to crossroads and fork.

6. Bear left at fork and go 6.4 miles to end (merge left at stop sign). Midway along this stretch, a unique round wooden house perches on the hillside to your left.

7. Bear left at end. Just ahead is a fork where the main road bears left. Stay on main road for 6/10 mile to crossroads and stop sign (Route 78) in the center of Warwick. Just before the end, a trail on the left leads 1.5 miles to the top of Mount Grace, where there's a lookout tower.

8. Cross Route 78 and go 1.6 miles to crossroads (Hasting Heights Road on right goes up a sharp hill).

9. Turn right at crossroads and go 4.1 miles to your second paved right (Wheeler Avenue), at top of hill. Your first right comes up at the bottom of a long downhill—go straight here. Just after you turn right at the crossroads, as you're climbing the hill, glance behind you for an inspiring view. When you get to Wheeler Avenue,

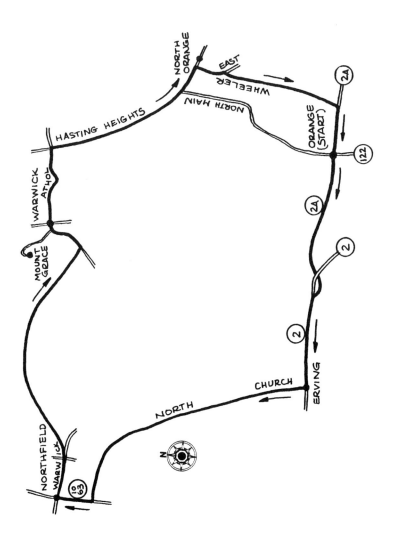

NORTH ORANGE

EAST

WHEELER

2A

NORTH MAIN

HASTING HEIGHTS

ORANGE (START)

122

WARWICK ATHOL

2A

MOUNT GRACE

2

2

CHURCH

ERVING

NORTH

NORTHFIELD WARWICK

N

10 63

the ride turns right, but if you go straight 3/10 mile you'll come to the tiny hamlet of North Orange, with a stately old church.

10. Turn right on Wheeler Avenue and go 6/10 mile to fork.

11. Bear right at fork (still Wheeler Avenue) and go 3 miles to end (Route 2A).

12. Turn right on Route 2A and go 1 mile to traffic light in the center of Orange. You'll pass the handsome, pillared Eastern Star Home (it's for the elderly) on your right. At the light, a handsome church and the old town hall are just up the hill to the right.

Rural scene in Spencer.

96. Orange–Wendell–Shutesbury–New Salem

Number of miles: 21 (31 with Shutesbury–New Salem extension)
Terrain: Hilly.
Road surface: 4/10 mile of dirt road on the 21-mile ride.
Food: Country store in Wendell; it may be closed. Restaurant in
    New Salem.
Start: Junction of Routes 122 and 2A in the center of Orange.
    Park where legal at side of road.

This is a tour of the remote, isolated hill country northwest of the
Quabbin Reservoir. The region is sparsely populated, with rugged,
wooded hills and tiny, perfectly preserved hamlets almost unchanged since the century gone by. As you bike along the narrow,
twisting roads, you're just as likely to encounter horses and cows
in the road as cars.

The ride starts in Orange, a compact mill town on the Millers
River. It is best known for its airport, which is the major center for
skydiving in the state. From Orange you'll head through deep
woods and small farms to the tiny hilltop hamlet of Wendell. A
miniature town hall, library, church, and school cluster around the
green, all in need of a little upkeep.

From Wendell you'll enjoy a relaxing downhill run to Lake
Wyola, where you can take a swim, and proceed to Shutesbury,
another pristine hilltop hamlet consisting of an elegant white
church, a tiny post office, several rambling old homes, and not
much else. From Shutesbury you'll scream downhill to the watershed of the Quabbin Reservoir and then proceed to New Salem, a
marvelous museum-piece of a town, set just far enough from the
main road that the only way anyone would find it would be by
accident. Fronting the large green are a splendid church, an old
wooden town hall, and a wonderful old schoolhouse on top of the
hill. The return leg to Orange brings you along the shore of Lake
Mattawa. Just off the route you can visit the Bears Den, a steep
gorge with a stream cascading over the rocks.

The short ride bypasses Shutesbury by taking a remote back
road from Wendell to New Salem.

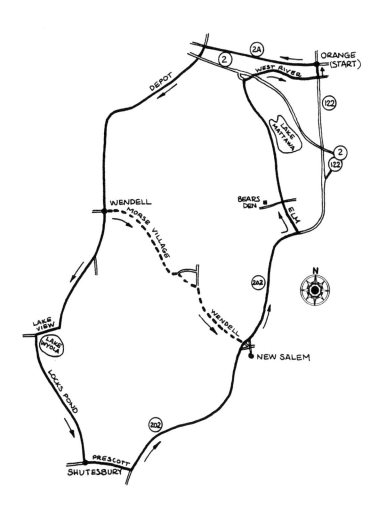

Directions for the ride: 31 miles

1. Head west on Route 2A and go 2.7 miles to crossroads (sign may say to Wendell Center, 5 miles).

2. Turn left at crossroads and go 4.6 miles to crossroads in the center of Wendell, at the top of a long, gradual hill. In Wendell the short ride turns left and the long ride continues straight.

3. Go straight at the center of Wendell 1.3 miles to fork where the main road bears right and a smaller road bears slightly left. There's a country store on the left shortly after you leave Wendell.

4. Bear right, staying on the main road. After 2 miles the road turns 90 degrees right onto Lake View Road. Continue 8/10 mile to Locks Pond Road on left, just after Lake Wyola.

5. Turn left on Locks Pond Road and go 4 miles to end, in the center of Shutesbury. There's a long gradual hill at the beginning; then it levels off.

6. Turn left at end and go 1.3 miles to end (Route 202). This is a terrific downhill run.

7. Turn left on Route 202 and go 5 miles to crossroads and blinking light (sign may say to New Salem Center). There's a long, steady climb on this section.

8. Turn right at blinking light, and after 100 yards bear right uphill, at the five-way intersection. Go 3/10 mile to the top of the hill in New Salem, then backtrack to Route 202.

9. Turn right on Route 202 and go 2.8 miles to Elm Street, which turns sharply left (sign may say to North New Salem). As soon as you turn onto Route 202 you'll pass a restaurant. After 1/2 mile, a small turnoff on your right provides a fine view. Most of this stretch is downhill.

10. Turn sharply left on Elm Street. After 8/10 mile there's a crossroads. Here the ride goes straight, but if you turn left 4/10 mile you'll come to the Bears Den on your right. Watch for a small dirt turnoff beside the road. A trail leads from the turnoff a short distance to the gorge.

11. From the crossroads, continue straight 3.4 miles to end (West River Street). A nice run along Lake Mattawa is along here.

12. Turn right on West River Street and go 1.5 miles to traffic light in center of Orange (Route 122).

13. Turn left on Route 122 and go 2/10 mile to Route 2A.

Directions for the ride: 21 miles

1. Follow directions number 1 and 2 for the long ride.

2. In the center of Wendell, turn left on Morse Village Road. After 2.3 miles the road turns to dirt. Immediately ahead is a fork.

3. Bear right at fork and go 4/10 mile to end (paved road at end.)

4. Turn right at end and go 1.9 miles to wide crossroads (Route 202).

5. Cross Route 202 and go 100 yards to a five-way intersection. Bear right uphill and go 3/10 mile to the top of the hill in New Salem, then backtrack to Route 202.

6. Follow directions for the long ride from number 9 to the end.

97. Amherst–Leverett–Shutesbury

Number of miles: 21 (31 with North Leverett–Shutesbury extension)
Terrain: Hilly.
Food: Grocery stores and restaurants in Amherst at the end. Country store in North Leverett (31-mile ride).
Start: Amherst Shoppers Park on University Drive, Amherst, just north of Route 9 and 7/10 mile west of the center of town. There's a traffic light at the corner of Route 9 and University Drive.

The wooded hills between the Connecticut River and the Quabbin Reservoir provide challenging but rewarding cycling. This is a remote, very sparsely populated area, with a few tiny pristine villages and several ponds. From Amherst you'll gain 1,000 feet in elevation as you wind your way through deep valleys up to Shutesbury; then it's all downhill back to Amherst.

Amherst (pronounced Ammerst), on top of a gradual rise at the eastern edge of the Connecticut Valley, is the largest community between Worcester and Springfield. With three colleges—University of Massachusetts, Amherst College, and Hampshire College— Amherst is the largest true "college town" in the state. During the school year, the students outnumber the residents. The three institutions are totally different in appearance and character. The massive campus of the University of Massachusetts, with more than 25,000 students, dominates the town with its sprawling, ever-growing expanse of new high-rise buildings virtually burying the smaller number of older, traditional ones. Amherst College, in contrast, is a perfect example of the gracious, traditional New England campus and is in the center of town. Amherst College matches the Ivy League schools in prestige and difficulty of getting admitted. Hampshire College, surrounded by farmland and orchards two miles south of town, was founded in 1970 and has a stark, ultramodern campus. Hampshire is the most unstructured and experimental of the three schools and has maintained much of the atmosphere of student activism prevalent during the early 1970s.

Old coke oven in Leverett.

Leaving Amherst, you'll bike through a blend of farm country and woodland to the tiny villages of Leverett and North Leverett. Leverett is the home of Leverett Craftsmen and Artists, one of the major centers in New England for teaching and working on traditional rural crafts. In North Leverett you can visit some coke ovens dating from the 1800s and a dramatic waterfall just off the route.

Beyond North Leverett you'll climb steadily to the unspoiled hilltop village of Shutesbury, elevation 1,225 feet. It consists of a splendid church, a minuscule post office, a few rambling old homes, and that's about all. From here you finally get paid for all the work you've done up to now—it's a relaxing gradual downhill run on good roads almost all the way back to Amherst.

The short ride bypasses North Leverett and Shutesbury, but comes within a mile of the latter village if you'd like to see it.

Directions for the ride: 31 miles

1. Turn left (north) out of the parking lot onto University Drive. After 3/10 mile you'll come to a traffic light. Continue straight 8/10 mile to end (Massachusetts Avenue). The University of Massachusetts campus is on your right.

2. Turn left on Massachusetts Avenue and go 8/10 mile to end.

3. Turn right at end and go 1.8 miles to traffic light (Route 116).

4. Cross Route 116 onto Route 63. Go 3/10 mile to another light, where Route 63 turns left.

5. Go straight at light 4/10 mile to State Street, which bears left downhill.

6. Bear left on State Street and go 4/10 mile to crossroads and stop sign (Sand Hill Road).

7. Continue straight at crossroads 6/10 mile to end. Just beyond the crossroads, you'll pass a small pond on your left. This is Factory Hollow Pond, also called Puffers Pond, a favorite swimming hole for University of Massachusetts students.

8. Turn left at end and immediately left again on Leverett Road. (The short ride turns left at end but then continues straight ahead.) Stay on the main road 2.6 miles to fork where the left-hand

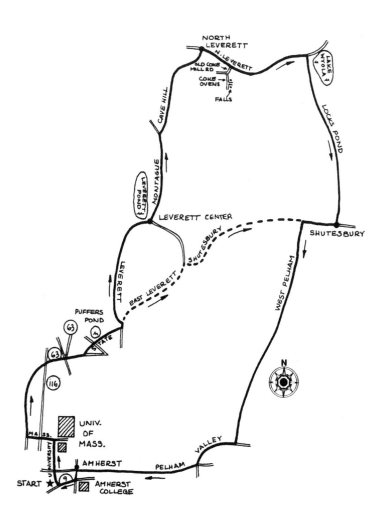

NORTH LEVERETT

N. LEVERETT

LAKE WYOLA

OLD COMB MILL RD

COMB OVENS

FALLS

CAVE HILL

LOCKS POND

MONTAGUE

LEVERETT POND

LEVERETT CENTER

SHUTESBURY

SHUTESBURY

LEVERETT

EAST LEVERETT

WEST PELHAM

PUFFERS POND

63

STATE

63

116

N

UNIV. OF MASS.

MASS.

VALLEY

UNIVERSITY

AMHERST

PELHAM

START ★

9

AMHERST COLLEGE

branch bears up a short, steep hill with a church on top. This is the tiny village of Leverett Center.

9. Bear left at fork and go 2 miles to another fork (Cave Hill Road bears right). You'll pass the crafts center, a long red wooden building, on your right shortly after you bear left up the hill.

10. Bear right on Cave Hill Road and go 2.3 miles to end (North Leverett Road). There is a long, tough climb at the beginning. When you get to the end you're in North Leverett, another tiny community. At the end, there's a small dam on your left and a rickety little country store on your right.

11. Turn right on North Leverett Road and stay on the main road for 3.4 miles to Locks Pond Road on right (sign may say to Shutesbury Athletic Club). Lake Wyola is on the far side of the intersection. If you'd like to visit the coke ovens and waterfall, turn right after 1.1 miles on Old Coke Kiln Road, a dirt road, and go 1/10 mile to fork. Bear left, staying on dirt road, and after 2/10 mile you'll see the large, white conical ovens on your left. If you bear left just beyond the ovens, the waterfall is 100 yards ahead on your right.

12. Turn right on Locks Pond Road and go 4 miles to end. There's a long but fairly gradual climb at the beginning; then the road levels off. At the end is Shutesbury, 1,000 feet higher than the starting point. Now the fun begins.

13. Turn right at end and go 9/10 mile to West Pelham Road on left. It's your second left.

14. Turn left on West Pelham Road and go 4.7 miles to end (Valley Road). After a short climb at the beginning it's a nearly unbroken downhill run all the way to end.

15. Turn right at end and go 1.3 miles to crossroads and stop sign. This stretch is also all downhill. • *CAUTION:* Watch for bumpy spots.

16. Turn right at crossroads and go 2.6 miles to traffic light in the center of Amherst, at top of hill (Pleasant Street).

17. Turn left at light on South Pleasant Street and go 2/10 mile to another light (Route 9). Amherst College is on the far side of the intersection on the left. The elegant old campus is worth visiting.

18. Turn right on Route 9 (left if you visited Amherst College) and go 7/10 mile to traffic light at bottom of hill (University Drive).

19. Turn right on University Drive. The shopping center is just ahead on your left.

Directions for the ride: 21 miles

1. Follow the directions for the short ride through number 7.

2. Turn left at end and go 2.1 miles to Shutesbury Road, which turns right at traffic island at top of short hill (signs may say to Lake Wyola, Shutesbury, Route 202).

3. Turn right on Shutesbury Road and go 3.3 miles to West Pelham Road on right. After the initial steep pitch comes a long, gradual climb; you ascend from 400 to 1,100 feet. At the intersection the ride turns right, but it's worth continuing straight 9/10 mile to visit the tiny hilltop town of Shutesbury.

4. Turn right on West Pelham Road and go 4.7 miles to end (Valley Road). After a short climb at the beginning, it's a nearly unbroken downhill run all the way to the end.

5. Follow the directions for the long ride from number 15 to the end.

98. Amherst–Belchertown

Number of miles: 18 (27 with Belchertown extension)
Terrain: Rolling, with several short, steep hills and a long, gradual climb into Belchertown on the longer ride.
Food: Grocery and restaurants in Belchertown. McDonald's across the road from end.
Start: Mountain Farms Mall, Route 9, Hadley, 2 miles west of the center of Amherst and 4 miles east of Route 91.

On this ride you explore the rolling, rural countryside on the eastern edge of the Connecticut Valley. You'll start by heading east across gently rising farmland with views of the spectacular Holyoke Range rising abruptly from the valley floor. After a couple of miles you'll come into South Amherst, a still-unspoiled village with a graceful white church and a large green. From here, you'll proceed on narrow backroads to Belchertown, among the most gracious towns in the Pioneer Valley. The magnificent town green, accented by a bandstand in the middle, is a quarter mile long and is framed by several fine churches and large, old wooden homes. Just behind the green is an old cemetery with many gravestones dating back to the 1700s. The town hosts an old-fashioned country fair each June.

Just outside of town you'll go through the Belchertown State School, an institution for children with disabilities. Numerous brick Victorian buildings are spread across the campuslike grounds. From here, you'll return to the start on secondary roads through prosperous, rolling farmland with views of the Holyoke Range in the distance.

The short ride bypasses the center of Belchertown by taking a shortcut at Arcadia Lake.

Directions for the ride: 27 miles

1. Turn right (south) out of the east side of the parking lot onto South Maple Street. Go 4/10 mile to crossroads and stop sign.

2. Go straight at crossroads 7/10 mile to another crossroads (Moody Bridge Road).

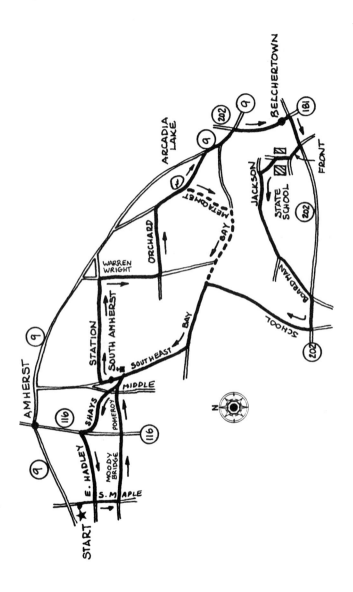

3. Turn left at crossroads and go 1.5 miles to crossroads and stop sign (Route 116).

4. Cross Route 116 and go 8/10 mile to another crossroads and stop sign (Middle Street). This is South Amherst.

5. Cross Middle Street. Just ahead, turn sharply left in front of the church on Southeast Street and go 1/10 mile to Station Road on right.

6. Turn right on Station Road and go 2 miles to crossroads and stop sign at top of hill (Warren Wright Road). This is a beautiful run through broad farms with mountains in the background.

7. Turn right at crossroads and go 1.4 miles to another crossroads (Orchard Street). • *CAUTION:* Diagonal railroad tracks at bottom of hill—walk your bike across them.

8. Turn left on Orchard Street and go 1.3 miles to end (merge right on Federal Street).

9. Bear right at end and go 1/2 mile to fork (Metacomet Street bears right). Arcadia Lake is on your left. At the fork the short ride bears right and the long ride bears left.

10. Bear left at fork and go 7/10 mile to end (merge into Route 9) • *CAUTION:* Another set of diagonal railroad tracks.

11. Bear right on Route 9 and go 1.3 miles to traffic light (Route 202).

12. Bear right on Route 202 and go 9/10 mile to crossroads in the center of Belchertown, where Route 202 turns right and Route 181 goes straight.

13. Turn right on Route 202 and go 6/10 mile to crossroads and blinking light (Front Street on right). A sign may say Belchertown State School. This is a fast, smooth downhill run.

14. Turn right on Front Street and go 2/10 mile to fork.

15. Bear right at fork. Just ahead is another fork, where the main road bears left and Elm Street bears right.

16. Bear left, staying on the main road, and go 3/10 mile to end, at stop sign.

17. Turn left at end. As soon as you turn, you're cheered by a magnificent view of the Holyoke Range. Go 1.4 miles to fork.

18. Bear left at fork and go 1.5 miles to crossroads and stop sign (Route 202, East State Street). You'll pass through broad fields bordered by a stately row of trees.

19. Bear right on Route 202 and go 7/10 mile to crossroads (School Street).

20. Turn right on School Street and go 3.2 miles to end. Shortly after turning, you'll pass Saint Hyacinth Seminary, run by the Franciscan Fathers, on your left, and Forge Pond on your right.

21. Turn left at end and go 2.8 miles to Southeast Street on right.

22. Turn right on Southeast Street and go 1.9 miles to fork at the South Amherst green. At the fork, notice the fine white church on your right, built in 1825.

23. Bear left at fork on Shays Street and go 1.1 miles to end (merge into Route 116). Look for good views of the Holyoke Range to your left.

24. Bear right on Route 116 and go 3/10 mile to East Hadley Road on left, immediately after bridge. Just before the intersection an old wooden building is on your right. It was formerly a gristmill and is now an antique shop.

25. Turn sharply left on East Hadley Road and go 1.8 miles to crossroads.

26. Turn right at crossroads and go 4/10 mile to mall on left.

Directions for the ride: 18 miles

1. Follow the directions for the long ride through number 9.

2. Bear right at fork onto Metacomet Street and go 9/10 mile to end (Bay Road).

3. Turn right on Bay Road and go 3 miles to Southeast Street on right.

4. Follow the directions for the long ride from number 22 to the end.

99. The Quabbin Reservoir Ride: Belchertown–Bondsville–Ware

Number of miles: 29
Terrain: Hilly.
Food: McDonald's in Ware. Groceries and restaurants in Belchertown.
Start: Route 202, Belchertown, opposite the green. Park at side of road. If you're coming from the east, an alternate starting point is the McDonald's on Route 32 in Ware, 1/2 mile southwest of Route 9. Directions for the ride starting in Ware are at the end of the ride.

This is a tour of the southern shore of the Quabbin Reservoir, by far the largest lake in Massachusetts, with spectacular runs along Goodenough Dike and Winsor Dam, the massive, half-mile-long embankments holding the water in its place. South of the reservoir is magnificent, rolling farmland.

You'll start from the elegant, classic New England town of Belchertown, among the finest in the Pioneer Valley. The magnificent green, highlighted by a bandstand in the middle, is a quarter of a mile long and is framed by several fine churches and large, old wooden homes. Just behind the green is an old cemetery with many gravestones dating back to the 1700s. Belchertown hosts an old-fashioned country fair in June.

From Belchertown, you'll head south through rolling farmland and orchards to the little valley town of Bondsville, which straddles the Belchertown-Palmer line along the Swift River. From here you'll follow the delightful valley of the Ware River, with views of rugged hills on both sides, to Ware, a nineteenth-century mill town straight out of the Industrial Revolution. Ware is one of the great bargain centers for clothing and sportswear in New England; most of the mills have factory outlets. The majority of the mills are clustered in one enormous complex called the Industry Yard.

Beyond Ware comes the exciting part of the ride, as you follow the southern shore of the Quabbin Reservoir back to Belchertown. Physically, the reservoir is impressive, fifteen miles long and dotted

Quabbin Reservoir.

with rugged, mountainous islands rising steeply from the water like dorsal fins. The uninhabited Prescott Peninsula splits the reservoir into two unequal parts, the western arm a long, slender ribbon less than a mile wide. Access to the water is limited, because most of the shoreline consists of cliffs and steep hills rising directly from the water's edge. The Quabbin was created in 1939 and 1940 by damming the Swift River, flooding five small villages. Its waters flow eighty miles through an elaborate system of aqueducts to supply the Boston metropolitan area, passing through the Wachusett Reservoir, the state's second-largest lake, en route.

You first encounter the reservoir at the 2,000-foot-long Goodenough Dike and then climb 400 feet to the handsome stone lookout tower atop Quabbin Hill, elevation 1,025 feet. From the observation deck a spectacular view of the entire reservoir unfolds in front of you. On a clear day you can easily see Mount Monadnock, forty miles to the north. The watershed is a breeding ground for bald eagles, and if you're very lucky you may see one glide past. From the tower it's all downhill to 125-foot-high Winsor Dam, the second-largest earth dam east of the Mississippi (the largest is Saluda Dam in South Carolina). After the spectacular run across the top of the dam, it's a short way back to Belchertown.

Directions for the ride: Belchertown start

1. Head south on Route 202, following the Belchertown green on your left. Just ahead, at the end of the green, is a crossroads where Route 202 turns right and Route 181 goes straight.

2. Go straight onto Route 181 for 2.1 miles to Cold Spring Road, a small road that bears left at top of hill (sign may say Swift River Club). There's a relaxing downhill run out of Belchertown.

3. Bear left on this road and go 7/10 mile to fork. This is a delightful run past farms and orchards.

4. Bear right at fork and go 1.2 miles to end (Route 181). You'll ascend onto a ridge with panoramic views.

5. Turn left on Route 181. After 1.3 miles, Route 181 turns left. Stay on Route 181 for 3/10 mile to end. This is Bondsville.

6. Turn right at end (still Route 181) and go 2/10 mile to end, facing a church. Route 181 bears slightly right at the intersection.

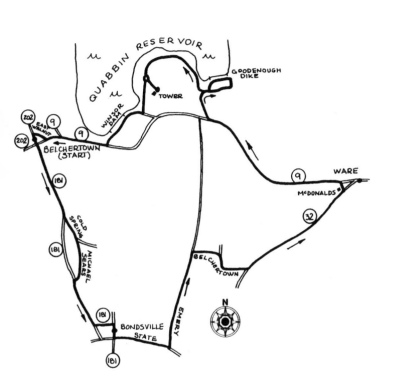

QUABBIN RESERVOIR

GOODENOUGH DIKE

TOWER

WINSOR DAM

202 9 EAST WALNUT

202 9

BELCHERTOWN (START)

WARE

9

McDONALDS

181

COLD SPRING

181 MICHAEL SEARS

32

BELCHERTOWN

181

BONDSVILLE STATE

EMERY

181

N

7. Turn left in front of the church and go 1.5 miles to Emery Street on left, at bottom of hill after railroad tracks and immediately before bridge.

8. Turn left on Emery Street and go 2.5 miles to a road on right that goes down a steep hill. It's the first right after the airport. • *CAUTION:* Diagonal railroad tracks after 6/10 mile.

9. Turn right on this road and go 6/10 mile to end (merge to your right). • *CAUTION:* Bumpy road.

10. Bear right at end and go 9/10 mile to end (Route 32).

11. Turn left on Route 32 and go 2.2 miles to a street on your left just past McDonald's (sign may say to Route 9, Belchertown). Here the ride turns left, but if you'd like to visit the mill outlets, stay on Route 32 for 7/10 mile. The mills are just east of downtown Ware.

12. Turn left after McDonald's and go 1/10 mile to end (Route 9).

13. Turn left on Route 9 and go 3.9 miles to a road that bears right through a pair of stone pillars about 50 yards ahead.

14. Bear right on this road and go 8/10 mile to fork (sign may say to Goodenough Dike).

15. Bear right at fork. After 1/10 mile a road bears left, but bear slightly right downhill. Go 1.6 miles to end, first passing below the dike and then biking along the top of it. You'll have a steep climb from the picnic area below the dike to the level of the reservoir.

16. Turn right at end and go 1/10 mile to fork (sign may say to Winsor Dam).

17. Bear right at fork and go 2.5 miles to rotary, up a long, tough hill.

18. Go two-thirds of the way around the rotary and head uphill 3/10 mile to summit. The view from the observation tower is magnificent.

19. From the summit, backtrack 3/10 mile to the rotary.

20. Turn sharply left at the rotary, following the sign to Winsor Dam, and go 1.4 miles to end. This is an exhilarating downhill run.

21. Turn right at end and immediately curve right on the main road. Go 1.1 miles to end (Route 9), going along the top of Winsor Dam.

22. Turn right on Route 9 and go 2 miles to fork, where Route 21 bears left and Route 9 bears right.

23. Bear left on Route 21 and go 1/2 mile to East Walnut Street on right.

24. Turn right on East Walnut Street and go 3/10 mile to Route 202 (North Main Street) at top of hill.

25. Turn left on Route 202. The Belchertown green is on your left.

Directions for the ride: Ware start (McDonald's, Route 32)

1. Turn left out of parking lot and just ahead take your first left (sign may say to Route 9, Belchertown). Go 1/10 mile to end (Route 9).

2. Follow directions number 13 through 24 for the ride starting in Belchertown.

3. Turn left on Route 202 and go 2/10 mile to crossroads at the end of the Belchertown green, where Route 202 turns right and Route 181 goes straight.

4. Follow directions number 2 through 11, back to McDonald's on left.

100. Ludlow–Belchertown–Three Rivers

Number of miles: 17 (22 with Belchertown–Three Rivers
    extension)
Terrain: Gently rolling, with one long, tough hill and one
    moderate hill.
Food: Grocery and restaurant in Three Rivers (22-mile ride).
    Friendly at end.
Start: Friendly Ice Cream, Route 21, Ludlow, opposite the
    entrance and exit ramps for the Massachusetts Turnpike.

The region northeast of Springfield, consisting of rolling farmland
and low, forested hills, provides relaxing bicycling on a network of
lightly traveled backroads. Ludlow is an old industrial town with an
enormous nineteenth-century mill complex stretching half a mile
along the Chicopee River. The ride starts from the outskirts of town
and immediately heads north into rolling farm country with views
of the Holyoke Range rising in the background. You'll cut across a
wooded ridge into Belchertown, where you'll descend into a beautiful valley with expansive, gently rolling farms and orchards. Suddenly you enter the small mill town of Three Rivers, where the
Ware and Quaboag Rivers join to form the Chicopee, which flows
into the Connecticut River at Springfield. From here you'll parallel
the Chicopee River to a fine old dam with a spillway 40 feet high;
behind it the river is backed up into an unspoiled pond. On the
return trip to Ludlow, you can detour to Ludlow State Forest, which
commands the top of 720-foot Minechoag Mountain. There's a
magnificent view from the lookout tower on the summit, but check
first at the bottom to see if it's open. The summit is less than a mile
from the route. It's a steep climb, but worth the effort if the tower is
open.

The short ride bypasses Three Rivers to take a more direct
route back to Ludlow. You'll pass the Springfield Reservoir, part of
the water supply for Springfield, and then bike through the part of
Ludlow that was its center before the town became industrialized,
with a distinctive church and old cemetery.

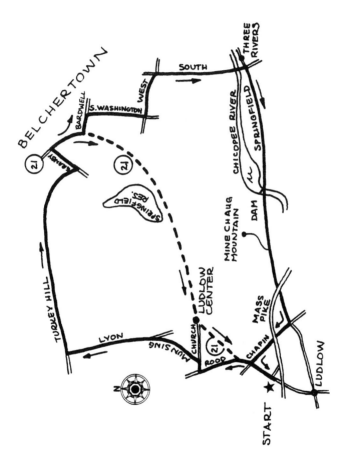

BELCHERTOWN

THREE RIVERS

SOUTH

WEST

S. WASHINGTON

BARDWELL

21

GRANBY

21

SPRINGFIELD RES.

CHICOPEE RIVER

SPRINGFIELD

DAM

MINE CHAUG MOUNTAIN

LUDLOW CENTER

CHURCH

MASS PIKE

TURKEY HILL

LYON

MUNSING

ROOD

21

CHAPIN

LUDLOW

N

START

Directions for the ride: 22 miles

1. Turn left (north) out of parking lot onto Route 21 and go 8/10 mile to Rood Street, which bears left. There's a great fruit and vegetable stand at the intersection.

2. Bear left on Rood Street and go 7/10 mile to Church Street on right.

3. Turn right on Church Street and go 2/10 mile to Munsing Street, which bears left.

4. Bear left on Munsing Street and go 1 mile to end (merge left into Lyon Street).

5. Bear left on Lyon Street and go 1.9 miles to end. You pass through inspiring, rolling farmland, with glimpses of the Holyoke Range in the distance. The peak with the distinctive sharp dropoff is Long Mountain.

6. Turn right at end. After 3.5 miles you'll come to a fork where the left-hand branch (Granby Road) is dirt. Bear right, staying on the paved road, and go 1/2 mile to a road that turns sharply left (it's a dirt road if you bear right). For the first 2 miles of this stretch you climb gradually, with two steep pitches; then you'll enjoy a downhill run to the intersection. • *CAUTION:* The beginning of the downhill section has bumpy spots.

7. Turn sharply left at the intersection and go 9/10 mile to end (Route 21).

8. Turn right on Route 21 and go 7/10 mile to your first left (Bardwell Street). Here the short ride continues straight and the long ride turns left.

9. Turn left on Bardwell Street and go 4/10 mile to your first right, South Washington Street.

10. Turn right on this road and go 1.3 miles to crossroads (West Street). This is beautiful, open farmland.

11. Turn left at crossroads and go 9/10 mile to crossroads and stop sign.

12. Turn right at crossroads and go 2.1 miles to crossroads and stop sign just after bridge (Springfield Street). From the bridge there's a fascinating view of the Chicopee River as it flows between two old mills. At the crossroads the ride turns right, but if you turn left, stores and restaurants are just ahead in the center of Three Rivers.

13. Turn right on Springfield Street. After 2.4 miles, watch for a grassy embankment on your right, just as you start to go downhill. Behind the embankment is the dammed-up Chicopee River, a perfect spot for a picnic. The dam is just to your left. As you start down the hill, you can see the dam from the road, and you'll pass an old brick pumping station on your left. At the bottom of the hill you'll cross the river itself over the Red Bridge.

14. From the bridge, continue 2.5 miles to traffic light (Chapin Street). If you'd like to tackle Minechoag Mountain, turn right 1.2 miles after the bridge onto Tower Road. After 4/10 mile of steep uphill, the paved road bears right and a dirt path, blocked off to cars, goes straight. Follow the path 4/10 mile to tower, which may or may not be open. As of this writing there is a fence around the tower, but the gate is unlocked.

15. Turn right on Chapin Street and go 1.1 miles to Route 21, at traffic light.

16. Turn left on Route 21 and go 1/2 mile to Friendly on right.

Directions for the ride: 17 miles

1. Follow directions for the long ride through number 8.

2. Continue straight on Route 21 for 6.6 miles to Friendly on right. You'll pass the Springfield Reservoir on your right. A mile and a half beyond the reservoir you'll go through the old center of Ludlow.

101. Wilbraham–Monson–Hampden

Number of miles: 17 (22 with Monson extension)
Terrain: Hilly.
Food: Grocery and restaurant in Monson (22-mile ride). Grocery in Hampden. Drugstore selling soda and snacks in Wilbraham.
Start: Small shopping center on Crane Park Drive in center of Wilbraham, just east of Main Street. From the junction of Routes 20 and 21 in Springfield, head east on Route 20 for 3.5 miles until you see Post Road Place, a small shopping center, on your right. Just past it, bear right at a traffic island and then immediately right on Main Street. Go 2.1 miles to Crane Park Drive on left, shortly after the Wilbraham and Monson Academy. If you're coming from the east, Main Street bears left from Route 20, five miles west of Route 32 North in Palmer, shortly after you go under a railroad bridge. If you're coming from the east, you can save driving by starting from the supermarket on Route 32 in the center of Monson (22-mile ride only). Directions for the Monson start are at the end of the ride.

The rounded hills beyond the Connecticut Valley east of Springfield provide challenging but dramatic bicycling on good roads. This is an area of long climbs but equally long descents, with fine views from the tops of the ridges. The ride starts from Wilbraham, a well-to-do suburb of Springfield that lies partly in the valley and partly along the steep hills rising from its eastern edge. The town is more rural than suburban. The center of town is graced by the handsome campus of Wilbraham and Monson Academy, a prestigious preparatory school. The town is also the site of the main office of the Friendly Ice Cream Corporation, whose restaurants are in every town of any size throughout the state. You may have noticed Friendly's floral "Welcome to Wilbraham" greeting planted on a hillside as you're driving west on the Massachusetts Turnpike.

As you leave Wilbraham you'll immediately climb onto Wilbraham Mountain, the high ridge forming the eastern edge of the Con-

Back road in Hampden.

necticut Valley. It's a long ascent but the view from the top is superb. On a clear day you can see far beyond Springfield to the Berkshires. After enjoying the spectacular run along the top of the ridge, you'll head mostly downhill through a mixture of woods and rolling farmland to the quiet crossroads town of Hampden. Hampden is best known as the home of Thornton Burgess, one of America's best-known writers of animal stories. His house, built in 1742, stands next to the Laughing Brook Educational Center and Wildlife Sanctuary, run by the Massachusetts Audubon Society. In the center of town stands Academy Hall, a splendid old schoolhouse built in Greek Revival style. Leaving Hampden, you'll once again climb onto the ridge through open farmland and descend steeply back into Wilbraham.

The longer ride heads farther east to the small mill town of Monson (pronounced Munson). As mill towns go, Monson is one of the most attractive in the state, with a graceful white church, a handsome Victorian stone library, and an ornate granite town hall with a clock tower, built in 1884. Leaving Monson, you wind gradually uphill through fine, rolling, pastoral countryside. You'll be rewarded with some fine views and a smooth downhill run into Hampden.

Directions for the ride: 22 miles

1. At the end of Crane Park Drive, turn right on Main Street and go 1/10 mile to Mountain Road on right. Notice the beautiful stone church on the far corner. Just beyond the church is the impressive main building of Wilbraham and Monson Academy.

2. Turn right on Mountain Road and go 1.4 miles to end (Ridge Road). This is a long, steady climb.

3. Turn right on Ridge Road and go 1.7 miles to end. To your right are unsurpassed views of the Connecticut Valley across the lawns of expensive homes.

4. Turn left at end and go 3.1 miles to stop sign at bottom of hill. Just after you turn left there's an exciting downhill run on smooth pavement—enjoy it! At the stop sign the short ride turns sharply right and the long ride goes straight.

5. Continue straight at stop sign 2.3 miles to another stop sign, where you merge head-on into Route 32 in Monson. Notice

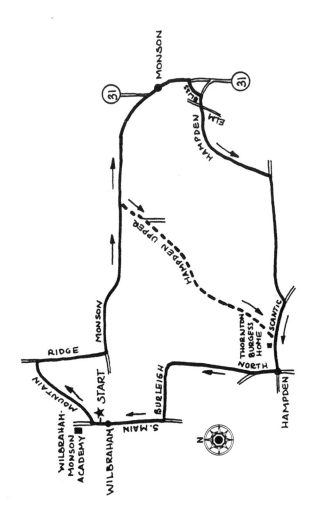

MONSON

31

31

ELM

HAMPDEN

MONSON

HAMPDEN UPPER

RIDGE

MONSON

SCANTIC

THORNTON BURGESS HOME

NORTH

WILBRAHAM-MONSON ACADEMY

START

MOUNTAIN

BURLEIGH

S. MAIN

HAMPDEN

WILBRAHAM

N

the ornate Victorian library, built in 1881, on your right at the intersection.

6. Go straight onto Route 32 for 9/10 mile to Bliss Street on right, just after a red-brick mill on your left. You'll pass the tall Victorian town hall on your left.

7. Turn right on Bliss Street and go 2/10 mile to end (merge right).

8. Bear right at end, going between a pair of ancient, grim mills. Just beyond the mills is a crossroads (Elm Street).

9. Cross Elm Street onto Hampden Road and go 2.4 miles to where the main road curves 90 degrees to the right. You'll start off with a long, steady climb; then the road levels off, winding through magnificent, rolling countryside.

10. Curve right, staying on the main road, and go 3 miles to end (Scantic Road).

11. Turn right on Scantic Road and go 1/2 mile to stop sign.

12. Continue straight at stop sign and go 1/2 mile to crossroads in the center of Hampden (North Road on right). Thornton Burgess's home, a small gray cottage, is on your right just past the Laughing Brook Educational Center. At the crossroads the ride turns right, but there's a grocery if you go straight 2/10 mile.

13. Turn right on North Road and go 4/10 mile to fork.

14. Bear right at fork (still North Road) and go 1.8 miles to where the road curves 90 degrees left onto Burleigh Road. This is a long, tough climb, but you're rewarded with fine views.

15. Turn left on Burleigh Road and go 1.4 miles to end.
• *CAUTION:* Steep, bumpy downhill—take it easy.

16. Turn right at end and go 2 miles to Crane Park Drive on right, back in Wilbraham. Notice the fine old homes as you come into the town.

17. Turn right on Crane Park Drive into shopping center.

Directions for the ride: 17 miles

1. Follow directions for the long ride through number 4.

2. Turn sharply right at stop sign and go 4/10 mile to fork (main road bears right).

3. Bear right at fork and stay on main road 4.5 miles to crossroads in the center of Hampden (North Road on right). Most of this section is a relaxing, gentle downgrade. Half a mile before Hampden the road curves sharply to the right, and you'll pass the Laughing Brook Educational Center. Just beyond it on the right is the Thornton Burgess Home, a small gray cottage.

4. Follow directions for the long ride from number 13 to the end.

Directions for the ride: Monson start (Supermarket on Route 32)

1. Turn right out of parking lot, heading south on Route 32 and go 6/10 mile to Bliss Street on right, just after a red-brick mill on your left. Notice the handsome Victorian town hall on your left.

2. Follow directions for the 22-mile ride from number 7 through 16.

3. Continue straight past Crane Park Drive 1/10 mile to Mountain Road on right. Notice the beautiful stone church on the far corner. Just beyond the church is the impressive main building of Wilbraham and Monson Academy.

4. Follow directions for the 22-mile ride from number 2 through 5.

5. Go straight onto Route 32 for 3/10 mile to supermarket on right.

102. Turners Falls–Gill–Northfield–Millers Falls

Number of miles: 23 (29 with Northfield loop)
Terrain: Rolling, with several hills.
Road surface: 1.1 miles of hard-packed dirt road, which can be
    avoided.
Food: Grocery and restaurants in Northfield. Grocery and snack
    bar in Millers Falls. Stores and restaurants in Turners Falls, at
    end.
Start: IGA Supermarket on Main Street in Turners Falls, just
    south of downtown. From Route 2, turn south at traffic light
    that is 3 miles east of Route 91 and 3.5 miles west of the
    French King Bridge. Go 1 mile to the IGA on your right.

This ride takes you exploring the Connecticut Valley just south of
the Vermont and New Hampshire borders. The valley in this region
is rugged and narrow, with steep hills rising almost at the water's
edge, and thinly populated. Surprisingly, this remote area is home
to two magnificently situated preparatory schools only four miles
apart—Mount Hermon on the west bank of the river and Northfield
on the east bank. The two schools are administered together and
are collectively called the Northfield-Mount Hermon School. Mount
Hermon is for boys and Northfield is for girls.

The ride starts from Turners Falls, an attractive mill town right
out of the nineteenth century. For a fuller description, see the Turners Falls-Deerfield-Sunderland-Montague ride. As you leave the
town you'll cross the Connecticut River above an impressive dam
and immediately head into rugged hill country to the tiny valley
village of Gill. The village center has a country store, church, an old
cemetery, a few old wooden homes, and not much else. Two miles
beyond Gill, you suddenly come upon the Mount Hermon campus,
impressive as any in New England, with gracious red-brick buildings spread along a broad hillside overlooking the river, and surrounded by miles of farmland and forest. Beyond Mount Hermon,
you skirt the edge of the valley to the New Hampshire border, passing some broad farms.

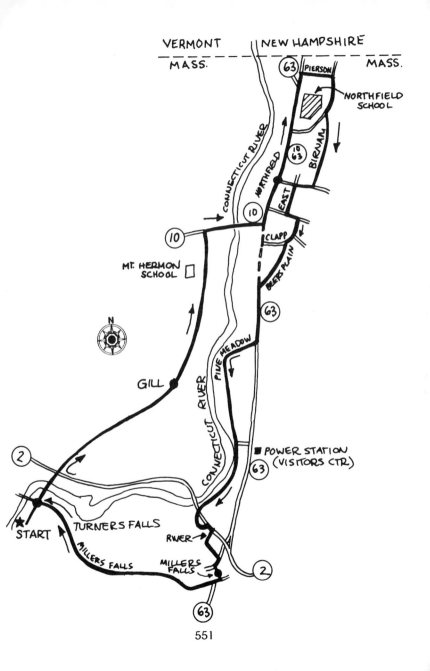

VERMONT — NEW HAMPSHIRE

MASS. — MASS.

⑥③ PIERSON

NORTHFIELD SCHOOL

CONNECTICUT RIVER

BIRNAM

¹⁰/⁶³

NORTHFIELD

① EAST

⑩

CLAPP

BEERS PLAIN

⑥③

MT. HERMON SCHOOL

N

PINE MEADOW

GILL

CONNECTICUT RIVER

POWER STATION (VISITORS CTR)

⑥③

②

TURNERS FALLS

START

MILLERS FALLS

RIVER

MILLERS FALLS

②

⑥③

551

When you get to the east bank, the Northfield campus, another imposing group of handsome stone buildings on a hillside over the river, is just off the route. The town of Northfield is a New England jewel, with gracious old homes, several fine churches, and a couple of former Victorian resort hotels spaced along the main street. The elegant stone library is a New England classic. Below Northfield, you'll bike through large expanses of rich farmland extending to the water's edge. You'll pass an underground hydroelectric power plant with a fascinating visitor's center. The facility offers boat trips on the Connecticut River from June to October. Near the end of the ride you'll go through Millers Falls, a fascinating old mill town whose main industry is paper manufacture. The town is also the home of Renovators Supply Company, which manufactures old-fashioned–style fittings and supplies for renovating old houses.

Directions for the ride: 29 miles

1. Turn left (north) out of the parking lot and go 9/10 mile to traffic light just after the bridge across the Connecticut River (Route 2). You will now make a small loop along the river and return to this same intersection in about a mile.

2. Turn right on Route 2 and immediately (at the same intersection) turn right on Bridge Street, heading back toward the river. Go 6/10 mile to end (Route 2 again).

3. Turn left on Route 2 and go 3/10 mile to traffic light.

4. Turn right at light and go 6.5 miles to a wide crossroads (Route 10) about 1 mile beyond the Mount Hermon campus. You'll start off with a long, steady climb, followed by a fast descent into Gill. Beyond Gill is rolling, open farmland with views of the mountains on the east bank of the river.

5. Turn right on Route 10 and go 1.2 miles to end. Route 10 turns left here. At this point the short ride turns right and the long ride turns left.

6. Turn left and follow Route 10 for 2.9 miles to Pierson Road on right.

7. Turn right on Pierson Road and go 1/2 mile to end (Winchester Road).

8. Turn right on Winchester Road and go 6/10 mile to a road that bears left at a traffic island, opposite the Northfield School. The gracious campus is worth exploring.

9. Bear left on this road (Birnam Road) and go 1.5 miles to end.

10. Turn right at end and go 1/4 mile to crossroads and stop sign (East Street).

11. Turn left on East Street and go 4/10 mile to end.

12. Turn left at end and go less than 2/10 mile to your first right.

13. Turn right. After 1/2 mile the main road bears slightly right at a traffic island. Stay on main road for 2/10 mile to fork (Lucky Clapp Road bears right).

14. Bear left at fork and go 7/10 mile to end (Route 63).

15. Turn left on Route 63 and go 1.4 miles to Pine Meadow Road on right.

16. Turn right on Pine Meadow Road and go 2.4 miles to where the road becomes dirt. • *CAUTION:* There are bad diagonal railroad tracks on this section. (If you want to avoid the dirt road, turn left after 2.1 miles and go back to Route 63. Turn right and go to Millers Falls. Resume with direction number 23, heading straight uphill where Route 63 bears left).

17. Follow dirt road for 6/10 mile to where it becomes paved again and continue 1/10 mile to crossroads. Here the ride goes straight, but if you turn right there's a lovely picnic area on the riverbank. If you'd like to visit the fascinating visitors center of the Northeast Utilities hydroelectric plant, turn left at crossroads and go 2/10 mile to Route 63. Turn right and immediately left, and go 1/10 mile to visitors center on right. Behind the center is Northfield Mountain, an extensive area with 25 miles of trails and a lake on top. It's a popular place for cross-country skiing.

18. Go straight at crossroads, following the river on your right. After 4/10 mile the road becomes dirt again. The dirt stretch is 1/2 mile long.

19. When the pavement resumes, continue 9/10 mile to end (Route 2). You'll go underneath the high French King Bridge where Route 2 crosses the river. Just after the bridge, a small lane turns right and crosses the mouth of the Millers River over a rickety little bridge, currently blocked off to cars. It's a picturesque spot.

20. Turn right (east) on Route 2 and go 1/10 mile to River Road on right (sign may say to Millers Falls, Amherst).

21. Turn right and go 9/10 mile to end (Route 63), in Millers Falls.

22. Turn right on Route 63 and follow it 4/10 mile to where Route 63 bears left and another road goes straight ahead up a short, steep hill. Route 63 turns left and then right on this stretch, so follow the signs. If you go straight at the first point where Route 63 turns left, Renovators Supply is just ahead, in an old mill on the riverbank.

23. Continue straight up the hill and go 4.3 miles to traffic light (Avenue A) in the center of Turners Falls.

24. Turn left at light and go 3/10 mile to IGA on right. As you pull into the lot, notice the magnificent church on your left just ahead.

Directions for the ride: 23 miles

1. Follow directions for the long ride through number 5.

2. Turn right at end on Route 63 and go 2.4 miles to Pine Meadow Road on right.

3. Follow directions for the long ride from number 16 to the end.

103. Turners Falls–Deerfield–Sunderland– Montague

Number of miles: 24

Terrain: Gently rolling, with a couple of short hills. The optional climb to the Poet's Seat is moderately difficult; the optional climb up South Sugarloaf Mountain is very difficult.

Food: Groceries or restaurants in the towns.

Start: IGA Supermarket on Main Street in Turners Falls, just south of downtown. From Route 2, just south at a traffic light that is 3 miles east of Route 91 and 3.5 miles west of the French King Bridge. Go 1 mile to the IGA on your right.

This ride has us explore a beautiful segment of the Connecticut Valley where it is narrowed by hills rising close beside the river-bank. South of the bridge between Deerfield and Sunderland, the valley is generally wide and filled with broad tobacco farms, but as you head north of the bridge, it becomes progressively narrower all the way to the Vermont–New Hampshire line. The ride has a historical highlight: Old Deerfield, a restored community of gracious homes and inns dating from the eighteenth and early nineteenth centuries.

You start from Turners Falls, an attractive mill town with a compact business section of ornate brick Victorian buildings lining the unusually wide main street. On the cross streets are brick row houses that seem transplanted from an English industrial city. A magnificent brick church on a hillside stands proudly over the town. Just outside of town you cross the Connecticut River and enter the valley of the Deerfield River, a major tributary. You can detour 1 mile to the Poet's Seat, a ledge perched 350 feet above the river, offering a fine view of Greenfield, the larger twin city of Turners Falls, and of the Connecticut River. A short run brings you to Historic Deerfield, a wonderful example of how an early community can be restored to its original grandeur. It's not as well known as Old Sturbridge Village, but it is equally fascinating. You can visit the houses singly or in various combinations. In the center of the village is the elegant Deerfield Inn; a handsome brick church; a spacious green; and the large, gracious campus of Deerfield Academy, a prestigious boys' preparatory school. Also in the village is the Memorial Hall Museum, which houses a collection of artifacts and relics spanning the long history of the community.

From Old Deerfield you'll follow the gently rolling valley of the Deerfield River, with soft, green hills in the distance, and then traverse a small ridge back to the Connecticut River. For a real workout you can tackle the steep climb up South Sugarloaf Mountain, where one of the finest views in the state—the entire sweep of the Pioneer Valley all the way down to Springfield—unfolds before you. You cross the river into the graceful rural town of Sunderland and pass beneath the spreading branches of the largest sycamore tree in New England. From here you'll parallel the river on the east bank along back roads through rich farmland, and pass a splendid waterfall en route.

Directions for the ride:

1. Turn right out of the parking lot and go 2 miles to fork, immediately after the bridge over the Connecticut River. As you leave the lot, notice the handsome church on your left. At the fork the ride bears left, but if you'd like to visit the Poet's Seat, which is 1.2 miles off the route, bear right at the fork onto Mountain Road. Go 8/10 mile to a narrow lane that bears right at top of hill, and bear right 4/10 mile to lookout tower. • *CAUTION:* The lane leading down from the tower is very bumpy.

2. Bear left at fork and go 1 mile to traffic island where Routes 5 and 10 turn left. (Routes 5 and 10 also go straight at this intersection.)

3. Turn left on Routes 5 and 10. Go 1.3 miles to your first right (sign says Historic Deerfield).

4. Turn right into Historic Deerfield. After 1/10 mile, the main road curves 90 degrees to the left. Continue on the main road 9/10 mile to end, at traffic island (Mill Village Road bears right).

5. Bear right on Mill Village Road and go 2.3 miles to an intersection, at top of short hill, where the main road curves left and another road turns right. Mill Village Road is a lovely lane through prosperous broad farms, with a run along the Deerfield River.

6. Curve left on the main road and go 1 mile to busy cross-

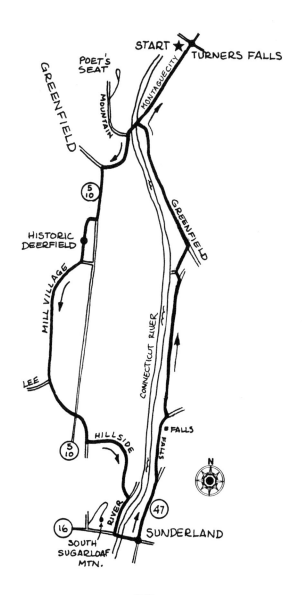

START ★ TURNERS FALLS

POET'S SEAT

GREENFIELD

MOUNTAIN

MONTAGUECITY

5 10

HISTORIC DEERFIELD

GREENFIELD

MILL VILLAGE

CONNECTICUT RIVER

LEE

HILLSIDE

5 10

FALLS

FALLS

N

RIVER

16

47

SOUTH SUGARLOAF MTN.

SUNDERLAND

roads (Routes 5 and 10). The two hump-shaped mountains in front of you are North Sugarloaf Mountain, elevation 791 feet, and South Sugarloaf Mountain, elevation 652 feet.

7. Cross Routes 5 and 10. Go 7/10 mile to Hillside Road on left. It's immediately after house number 389 on right.

8. Turn left on Hillside Road and go 1.7 miles to end, at bottom of hill. A moderate climb is followed by a relaxing downhill run to the valley floor.

9. Turn right at end and go 1.4 miles to end (Route 116). This is a beautiful run along the riverbank, with broad farms on the right ending abruptly at the steep side of Sugarloaf Mountain. At Route 116 the ride turns left, but if you'd like to tackle South Sugarloaf, the summit is 1.2 miles off the route. To get to the top, turn right on Route 116 and go 4/10 mile to your first right. Turn right and then immediately turn right again uphill to the summit. You climb 450 feet in 8/10 mile, for an average grade of 11 percent. • *CAUTION:* On the return trip it's essential to take it easy. On one extremely steep pitch, at the hairpin turn, you should walk your bike—most bicycle brakes simply are not designed for these conditions.

10. Turn left on Route 116, crossing the river, and go 4/10 mile to traffic light (Route 47) in the center of Sunderland.

11. Turn left on Route 47 and go 1.4 miles to Falls Road, a smaller road that bears left. Just after you get onto Route 47, notice the enormous sycamore tree on your left; it's the largest in New England.

12. Bear left on Falls Road and go 1.8 miles to fork just beyond the Montague town line where Old Sunderland Road bears right uphill and the main road bears left. Just before the town line there's a beauty of a natural waterfall on your right.

13. Bear left on main road for 2.7 miles to an unmarked road that bears left at traffic island. It's just after North Taylor Hill Road on your right.

14. Bear left. After 2/10 mile the main road curves sharply left. Continue 1/10 mile to fork (dead-end road bears left).

15. Bear right at fork and go 6/10 mile to end (merge left).

16. Bear left and go 2.9 miles to end.

17. Turn right at end and go 1.8 miles to IGA on left. There's a magnificent church on the right just before the end.

104. Tobacco Road: Northampton–Hatfield–Sunderland–Hadley

Number of miles: 28

Terrain: Flat. The optional climb up South Sugarloaf Mountain is very difficult.

Food: Grocery and snack bar in Sunderland. Stores and restaurants in Northampton, at end.

Start: Route 9 in Northampton opposite Smith College. Park at side of road or on a side street. If you're coming from the south on Route 91, get off at the Route 5 exit. Go north on Route 5 for 1 mile to Route 9. Turn left on Route 9 and go 1/2 mile to Smith College.

The heart of the Pioneer Valley, midway between the Connecticut and Vermont–New Hampshire borders, is the prime tobacco-growing region of Massachusetts. The valley here is broad and flat, with long, weathered tobacco sheds standing guard over the wide, sweeping fields, and with mountains rising in the distance.

Northampton, a city of 30,000, is one of the most attractive communities for its size in New England. In the downtown area, the unusually wide main street is lined with gracious, ornate buildings from the nineteenth century: churches, the county courthouse, city hall, the Forbes Library, old commercial buildings, and many others. Adjacent to downtown is Smith College, largest of the "Seven Sisters" schools, with 2,500 students. The tree-shaded campus mixes gracious buildings in many architectural styles. Behind the campus the Mill River flows over a beautiful little dam with a footbridge just below it.

From Northampton you'll head into tobacco country to Hatfield, among the finest of the Pioneer Valley towns, graced by a stately white church built in 1849, a handsome brick library, and old wooden homes. Many of the homes have plaques saying when they were built. Some go back to the 1700s. From Hatfield you'll continue along the river to Sunderland, another gracious New England town. For a real challenge, you can climb South Sugarloaf Mountain and gaze in wonder at a spectacular vista with few equals in the state as the broad sweep of the Pioneer Valley unfolds for miles before you.

From Sunderland you'll parallel the river through extensive tobacco farms to the tiny village of North Hadley, with two old churches and a country store. Just ahead is the Porter-Phelps-Huntington House, an outstanding eighteenth-century residence, elaborately furnished by six generations of a prominent family. A little farther on is the center of Hadley, yet another New England jewel of a town with the traditional wooden church and a fine old town hall. The Hadley Farm Museum, displaying early farm implements and other artifacts spanning the long history of the valley, is worth visiting. Just beyond Hadley, you'll cross the river back into Northampton.

Directions for the ride

1. Head west on Route 9 and go 1.3 miles to North Elm Street, which bears right opposite the Cooley-Dickinson Hospital.

2. Bear right on North Elm Street and go 3/10 mile to crossroads.

3. Turn right at crossroads and go 3/10 mile to end (Bridge Road).

4. Turn right on Bridge Road and then immediately left on Hatfield Street. Go 6/10 mile to end (merge into Routes 5 and 10).

5. Bear left on Routes 5 and 10. Go 1.1 miles to a road on your right that crosses the highway (a sign may say to Route 91, Hatfield).

6. Turn right on this road and go 9.2 miles to fork. Beyond Hatfield you'll see the distinctive hump of Mount Sugarloaf across the tobacco farms.

7. Bear right at fork and go 4/10 mile to end (Route 116). Here the ride turns right, but for a real challenge you can climb South Sugarloaf. Turn left on 116 and go 3/10 mile to your first right. Turn right and immediately turn right again uphill. It's 8/10 mile to the summit, and you climb 450 feet, for an average grade of 11 percent. The view is absolutely worth the climb, even if you walk your bike.
• *CAUTION:* There is one extremely steep pitch as you're going down, just before the hairpin turn. You should walk your bike on

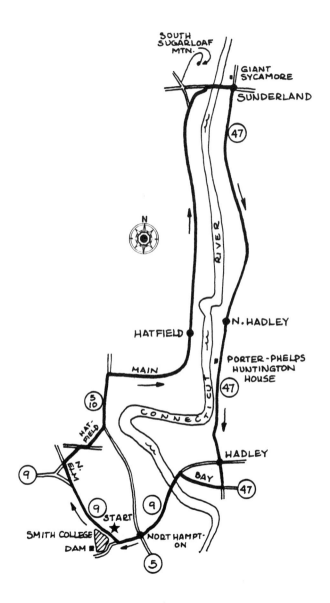

SOUTH
SUGARLOAF
MTN.

GIANT
SYCAMORE

SUNDERLAND

(47)

N

RIVER

N. HADLEY

HATFIELD

PORTER-PHELPS
HUNTINGTON
HOUSE

MAIN

(47)

5
10

CONNECTICUT

HAT-
FIELD

HADLEY

N. ELM

BAY

(47)

(9)

(9)

(9)

START

SMITH COLLEGE

NORTHAMPT-
ON

DAM

(5)

this section, because even good bike brakes may not be enough to handle the gradient.

8. Turn right on Route 116 and go 1/2 mile to traffic light just beyond the bridge (Route 47). Here the ride turns right, but if you turn left for 1/10 mile you'll see the largest sycamore tree in New England on your left.

9. Turn right on Route 47 and go 9.5 miles to traffic light (Route 9) in the center of Hadley. After about 6.5 miles you'll go through the tiny village of North Hadley. Just past Mount Warner Road in North Hadley a picturesque little dam is on your left. A mile beyond the dam, the Porter-Phelps-Huntington House is on your right.

10. Continue straight on Route 47 for 1/2 mile to crossroads and blinking light where Route 47 turns left.

11. Turn right at crossroads and go 1.1 miles to end (Route 9).

12. Turn left on Route 9 and go 2.3 miles back to start. At the end, be sure to see the little dam behind Smith College.

105. The Dinosaur Ride: Hadley–Granby–South Hadley

Number of miles: 11 (25 with South Hadley-Granby extension)
Terrain: Gently rolling, with two tough hills. The optional climb up Mount Holyoke is very challenging.
Food: McDonald's at end, across the road. Groceries and restaurants in South Hadley (long ride).
Start: Mountain Farms Mall, Route 9, Hadley. It's 3 miles east of Route 91 and 2 miles west of the center of Amherst.

On this ride you explore the countryside surrounding the Holyoke Range, a prominent feature of the Pioneer Valley. The mountains lie on an east-west axis six miles long, averaging 800 to 900 feet high. The highest point, Mount Norwottock, has an elevation of 1,106 feet. The range is broken in the center by a steep defile known as the Notch. A road leads to the summit of Mount Holyoke, the westernmost peak, which provides a magnificent view of the valley's broad sweep, and the silvery ribbon of the Connecticut River curving through it for miles.

The ride starts midway between Hadley and Amherst and immediately heads across broad farms with dramatic views of the Holyoke Range in the background. You'll ascend into the Notch, a steady half-mile climb, and enjoy the run down the other side. Shortly after the Notch you'll come to Nash's Dino Land, a rocky ledge that preserves dinosaur footprints. Just ahead is a true beauty spot of this state: the Aldrich Mill, a weathered wooden building with a massive water wheel dating from the 1830s.

From here you have a short ride to Granby, a New England gem of a town, with a large green framed by the traditional white church, Victorian town hall, and stately wooden homes. Just outside of town you'll pass the Granby Dinosaur Museum, with its fascinating collection of dinosaur tracks, fossils, and minerals. You'll now proceed to South Hadley, another gracious old town. It's centerpiece is the magnificent campus of Mount Holyoke College, oldest women's college in the country, founded in 1837. The extensive campus, in part designed by Frederick Law Olmsted, has two ponds, a delightful little dam, and a wealth of impressive stone and brick Gothic-style buildings.

From South Hadley you'll parallel the Connecticut River to Hadley, passing Skinner State Park, in which is the summit of Mount Holyoke. The climb is grueling but the view will make it worth your while. The center of Hadley is another New England jewel, with a handsome old town hall, traditional white church, and fine old homes. The Hadley Farm Museum, in the center of town, displays early farm implements and other artifacts. A little farther on you can visit the Porter-Phelps-Huntington House, among the finest eighteenth-century houses in the state. Built in 1752, it holds an impressive collection of furnishings owned by six generations of one family.

Directions for the ride: 25 miles

1. Turn right (south) out of the east side of the parking lot onto South Maple Street and go 4/10 mile to a crossroads and stop sign.

2. Go straight at crossroads 1.9 miles to end (Bay Road). Here the short ride turns right and the long ride turns left.

3. Turn left on Bay Road and go 1.1 miles to end (Route 116).

4. Turn right on Route 116 and go 2.9 miles to Aldrich Street, which turns sharply left (a sign may say Nash Dino Land). It's a steady half-mile climb to the top of the Notch, where you'll pass the well-guarded Federal Reserve Records Center.

5. Turn sharply left on Aldrich Street and go 7/10 mile to fork. You'll pass Nash Dino Land on your left and, just ahead, the Aldrich Mill on your right. Opposite the mill is a fine dam.

6. Go straight at fork (don't bear right) and go 2/10 mile to end. The millpond is on your left.

7. Turn right at end and go 1/10 mile to small crossroads (Aldrich Street on right).

8. Turn left at crossroads and go 7/10 mile to crossroads and stop sign (Easton Street).

9. Cross Easton Street and go 1.3 miles to end (Route 202), in the center of Granby. In front of you is the wooden Victorian town hall.

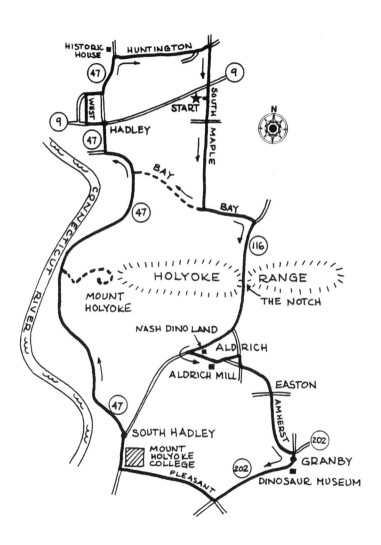

HISTORIC HOUSE
HUNTINGTON
47
9
WEST
HADLEY
9
47
START
SOUTH MAPLE
N
BAY
47
BAY
116
HOLYOKE RANGE
THE NOTCH
MOUNT HOLYOKE
CONNECTICUT RIVER
NASH DINO LAND
ALDRICH
ALDRICH MILL
EASTON
AMHERST
202
47
SOUTH HADLEY
MOUNT HOLYOKE COLLEGE
202
GRANBY
PLEASANT
DINOSAUR MUSEUM

10. Turn right on Route 202 and go 1.7 miles to traffic light (Pleasant Street). Just after you get on 202, notice the graceful little library on your left. Just ahead, also on the left, is the Dinosaur Museum.

11. Turn right on Pleasant Street and go 1.8 miles to end (College Street, Route 116).

12. Turn right on Route 116, passing Mount Holyoke College on your right, and go 1/2 mile to Route 47 on left. It's immediately after a small green on your left.

13. Turn left on Route 47 and go 7.1 miles to blinking light, where Route 47 turns right on Middle Street. If you'd like to tackle Mount Holyoke, turn right after 3.5 miles at the sign for Skinner State Park. You'll have a steady 2-mile climb with some very steep pitches and gain 700 feet of elevation.

14. Turn right on Middle Street (still Route 47) and go 1/2 mile to traffic light (Route 9) in the center of Hadley. The Hadley Farm Museum is on your right at the intersection.

15. Turn left on Route 9 and go 4/10 mile to crossroads (West Street), which runs beside a long, slender green.

16. Turn right on West Street, following the green on your left, and go 1/2 mile to end (North Lane).

17. Turn right on North Lane and go 3/10 mile to end (Middle Street, Route 47). The Connecticut River is behind the embankment on your left.

18. Turn left on Route 47 and go 1.2 miles to Huntington Road on right. Here the ride turns right, but if you go straight 3/10 mile you'll come to the Porter-Phelps-Huntington House on your left.

19. Turn right on Huntington Road and go 1.7 miles to end (merge left at stop sign into Rocky Hill Road). After you crest the hill there's a good view of the University of Massachusetts campus.

20. Bear left on Rocky Hill Road and go 1/10 mile to crossroads (North Maple Street).

21. Turn right on North Maple Street and go 1 mile to traffic light (Route 9). The mall is on the far side of the intersection on your right.

Directions for the ride: 11 miles

1. Follow directions number 1 and 2 for the long ride.

Roger Johnson's Bicycle Museum, Hadley.

2. Turn right on Bay Road and go 1.7 miles to end (Route 47).

3. Turn right on Route 47 and go 6/10 mile to blinking light where Route 47 turns right on Middle Street.

4. Follow directions for the long ride from number 14 to the end.

106. Longmeadow–East Longmeadow–Somers, Connecticut

Number of miles: 19 (30 with eastern hills extension, 15 with shortcut)

Terrain: Gently rolling, with one hill. The 30-mile ride has an additional steady climb 1.5 miles long.

Food: None until near the end of the ride. Better bring your own.

Start: Junction of Routes 5 and 192 in Longmeadow, 2 miles south of the Route 5 exit from Route 91. Park on Route 192.

The gently rolling farmland southeast of Springfield, with views of the rugged hills several miles to the east across broad fields, provides relaxed and very scenic biking on a wealth of lightly traveled secondary roads. The ride starts from the center of Longmeadow, Springfield's most prosperous suburb. The town is well named—the green is so long it's practically a meadow. Its half-mile length makes it the longest green in the state. It is also one of the most gracious, lined on both sides with handsome old homes dating back to the 1800s and earlier, a graceful church, and two old brick schools. The Storrs Parsonage, built in 1786, and the Colton House, built in 1734, are both open by appointment.

From Longmeadow you'll head along quiet suburban streets to East Longmeadow, another pleasant residential community, best known as the home of Milton Bradley, the games company. Tours of the plant are available. As you head east out of town and then south across the Connecticut line, the landscape becomes more and more rural, with broad sweeps of farmland and views of the mountains in the distance. You'll go past the Connecticut state prison, incongruously located in the midst of acres of rolling farmland.

The long ride offers a real workout by heading eastward beyond the valley into the wooded hills. You'll climb 500 feet to a plateau dotted with small farms and then enjoy the long, gradual descent back into the valley. The return to Longmeadow leads through gently rolling farmland with inspiring views of the mountains you've just conquered.

The fifteen-mile ride takes a more direct route from East Longmeadow back to the end and is not quite so rural.

Directions for the ride: 30 miles

1. Head north on Route 5 and go 1 mile to Converse Street on right, at traffic light.

2. Turn right on Converse Street and go 2.3 miles to end (Dwight Road).

3. Bear right on Dwight Road and go less than 2/10 mile to traffic light (Maple Street on left).

4. Turn left on Maple Street and go 1.3 miles to the center of East Longmeadow, where seven roads come together. Here the 15-mile ride turns right onto Route 186 and the two longer rides continue straight.

5. Continue straight, crossing Route 83 onto Pleasant Street. After 9/10 mile, the main road curves sharply right at bottom of hill. Stay on the main road for 9/10 mile to crossroads and blinking light (Parker Street).

6. Turn right on Parker Street and go 1.9 miles to stop sign and blinking light (Hampden Road).

7. Continue straight 6/10 mile to end. Notice the old church to your right at the intersection.

8. Turn left at end and then immediately bear left on Mill Road. (The 19-mile ride bears right, staying on the main road). Go 1.7 miles to end (Somers Road).

9. Turn right on Somers Road and go 1.1 miles to fork (Isaac Bradway Road bears left).

10. Bear left on Isaac Bradway Road and go 4/10 mile to end, at stop sign.

11. Bear left uphill at end. After 6/10 mile, Root Road bears right, but bear slightly left, staying on the main road. Go 1.9 miles to end (Old Springfield Road on left, Mountain Road on right). Most of this section is a long, steady climb with some steep pitches. If you turn right at the crossroads on top of the hill on Camp Road, a dirt road, you'll find a little pond after 1/10 mile. It's a great spot to rest after the long climb.

12. Turn right at end and go 1.9 miles to crossroads and stop

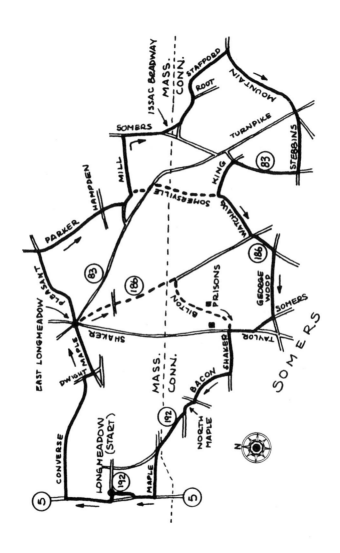

571

sign (Turnpike Road). This is a fine downhill run. Notice the unusual castle-like stone house on your left, about halfway down.

13. Cross Turnpike Road and go 1/10 mile to fork (Stebbins Road bears right).

14. Bear right on Stebbins Road and go 1 mile to crossroads and stop sign (Springfield Road, Route 83).

15. Turn right on Route 83 and go 1.5 miles to a small crossroads (King Road on left, Grist Mill Terrace on right).

16. Turn left on King Road and go 1.1 miles to end (Watchaug Road).

17. Turn left on Watchaug Road and go 1 mile to crossroads and stop sign where Route 186 goes straight. This is a magnificent run through broad farms, with the mountains in the distance.

18. Go straight at crossroads onto Route 186 for 1/2 mile to another crossroads (George Wood Road).

19. Turn right on George Wood Road and go 1.3 miles to crossroads and stop sign (Somers Road).

20. Turn right on Somers Road and go 2/10 mile to end (Taylor Road). The buildings at the top of the hill to your right are a Connecticut state prison.

21. Turn right on Taylor Road and go 4/10 mile to crossroads and stop sign (Shaker Road on left).

22. Turn left at crossroads and go 8/10 mile to Bacon Road on right.

23. Turn right on Bacon Road and go 7/10 mile to end (North Maple Street).

24. Turn right on North Maple Street and go 3/10 mile to fork where North Maple Street bears right and Brainard Road goes straight.

25. Bear right at fork and go 9/10 mile to diagonal crossroads (Maple Road) immediately after the state line.

26. Bear left on Maple Road and go 1.5 miles to end (Route 5).

27. Turn right on Route 5 and go 1.2 miles to Route 192. When you get to the green, there's less traffic if you take the road along the right-hand side of the green.

Directions for the ride: 19 miles

1. Follow directions for the 30-mile ride through number 7.

2. Turn left at end and immediately bear right at fork, staying on main road. Go 4/10 mile to end (Route 83).

3. Turn left at end and then immediately right on Somersville Road. Go 2.5 miles to crossroads and stop sign. This is a magnificent run past broad farms with views of the distant mountains.

4. Follow the directions for the 30-mile ride from number 18 to the end.

Directions for the ride: 15 miles

1. Follow directions for the 30-mile ride through number 4.

2. In the center of East Longmeadow, turn 90 degrees right on Prospect Street, Route 186 (don't turn sharply right on Shaker Road). Go 7/10 mile to crossroads and blinking light (Chestnut Street).

3. Cross Chestnut Street and go 1.7 miles to Bilton Road, which turns sharply right just beyond the Connecticut line. You'll climb a long, gradual hill, passing expensive homes; then you'll enjoy a relaxing downhill run with views of the mountains.

4. Turn sharp right on Bilton Road and go 2.1 miles to crossroads and stop sign. You'll pass a Connecticut state prison on your left and then another on your right.

5. Go straight at crossroads 8/10 mile to Bacon Road on right.

6. Follow directions for the 30-mile ride from number 23 to the end.

107. Agawam–Southwick–Suffield, Connecticut

Number of miles: 20 (30 with Southwick loop)
Terrain: Gently rolling, with a few short hills.
Food: Many stores and restaurants in Agawam. Stores and
    restaurants just off the route in Southwick (long ride).
Start: McDonald's, Southgate Plaza, Route 75, Agawam, 1 mile
    south of Route 57. If you're coming from the west on Route
    57, you can't exit directly onto Route 75. Instead, turn right
    just after the high school on your left onto Mill Street and go
    1/2 mile to Route 57. Turn right on Route 57 to plaza.

This ride takes you exploring the prosperous farm country on the
west bank of the Connecticut River, straddling the Massachusetts-
Connecticut border just southwest of Springfield. As you head farther west, you get into tobacco country, with long, weathered
tobacco sheds silhouetted against broad, flat, open fields.

The ride starts in Agawam, a middle-class suburb of
Springfield, best known for Riverside Park, largest amusement park
in New England. As you head west, the countryside quickly becomes rural rather than suburban. Suffield, Connecticut, is a town
of extensive, gently rolling farms with some fine homes. Although
close to Springfield, it has not become suburban and, we can hope,
will remain that way. From Suffield you'll cross back into Agawam,
go past Riverside Park with its convoluted roller-coaster, and enjoy
a two-mile run right along the Connecticut River.

The longer ride heads farther west into tobacco country and to
Southwick, which you've probably noticed on maps because the
town dips several miles below the otherwise straight southern border between Massachusetts and Connecticut. The jog stems from a
boundary dispute that Massachusetts won in 1642. You'll go across
the Congomond Lakes, a chain of three ponds separated by narrow
necks of land. In the center of town, just off the route, is a handsome church built in 1824 and the Southwick Inn, an old-fashioned
restaurant in an early wooden building.

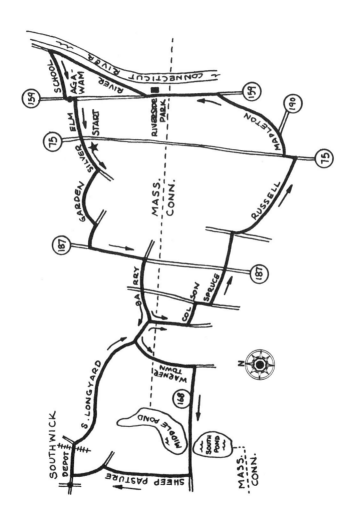

Directions for the ride: 30 miles

1. Turn left out of north side of parking lot onto Silver Street. Go 7/10 mile to Garden Street on right.

2. Turn right on Garden Street. After 1.1 miles, Garden Street runs into Poplar Street. Continue straight on Poplar Street 4/10 mile to end (Shoemaker Lane).

3. Turn right at end and go 3/10 mile to end (South Westfield Street, Route 187). • *CAUTION:* The first quarter mile is bumpy.

4. Turn left on Route 187 and go 1.6 miles to crossroads (Barry Street).

5. Turn right on Barry Street and go 8/10 mile to crossroads and stop sign (South-West Street).

6. Go straight at crossroads 7/10 mile to fork (Rising Corner Road bears left). Here the short ride bears left and the long ride bears right.

7. Bear right at fork and go 3/10 mile to end, at top of little hill.

8. Turn left at end and go 1.3 miles to a road on your right, just before a stop sign. This is a splendid run past broad farms and weathered wooden tobacco sheds.

9. Turn right on this road and then immediately go straight onto Route 168. Go 2.6 miles to Sheep Pasture Road on right, about 1/2 mile after you pass between two ponds and just as you start to climb a short hill. The two ponds are part of the Congomond Lakes chain—South Pond is on your left and Middle Pond is on your right. A grocery is on your right shortly before the intersection.

10. Turn right on Sheep Pasture Road and go 1.9 miles to end.

11. Turn left at end and go 1/2 mile to end (Depot Street). Here the ride turns right, but if you turn left for 2/10 mile you'll come to the center of Southwick. The Southwick Inn looks elegant, but it's informal and a good place for a bite.

12. Turn right on Depot Street and go 3/10 mile to fork where Powdermill Road bears left and South Longyard Road bears right. Bear right on South Longyard Road and go 2.8 miles to fork (Rising Corner Road bears left). This is a beautiful run through tobacco fields.

13. Bear left downhill at fork and go 3/10 mile to another fork (North Stone Street bears right). Yes, you were here before; you've just finished the western loop and are now rejoining the short ride

14. Bear right at fork and go 6/10 mile to Colson Street on left.

15. Turn left on Colson Street and go 1/2 mile to end (Ratley Road).

16. Turn right on Ratley Road and go less than 2/10 mile to Spruce Street on left.

17. Turn left on Spruce Street and go 7/10 mile to crossroads and stop sign (North Grand Street, Route 187).

18. Cross Route 187 and go 9/10 mile to end, at top of short, steep hill.

19. Turn right at end and then immediately bear left at fork on Russell Avenue. Just ahead, curve left downhill on the main road. Go 2.2 miles to end (Route 75).

20. Turn left on Route 75, passing fine old homes, and go 2/10 mile to Route 190 (Mapleton Avenue) on right.

21. Turn right on Mapleton Avenue and go 6/10 mile to fork where Route 190 bears right and Mapleton Avenue bears left. Notice the sweeping views of the valley on your right.

22. Bear left at fork (still Mapleton Avenue) and go 1.8 miles to end (merge into East Street, Route 159).

23. Bear left on Route 159 and go 1.8 miles to River Road, which bears right at traffic light. You'll pass Riverside Park on your right.

24. Bear right on River Road and go 2.3 miles to School Street, which turns sharply left. This is a relaxing run along the river.

25. Turn sharp left on School Street and go 1.3 miles to end (Main Street, Route 159).

26. Turn left on Main Street and go 1/10 mile to Elm Street on right, at traffic light.

27. Turn right on Elm Street. After 1/2 mile, Elm Street bears right, but continue straight on Silver Street 4/10 mile to Route 75. The shopping center is on the far side of the intersection.

Directions for the ride: 20 miles

    1. Follow directions for the long ride through number 6.

    2. Bear left at fork and go 6/10 mile to Colson Street on left.

    3. Follow directions for the long ride from number 15 to the end.

108. I Will Lift Up Mine Eyes Unto the Hills: Westfield–Montgomery–Westhampton– Southampton

Number of miles: 20 (36 with Montgomery–Westhampton extension)

Terrain: The short ride is gently rolling, with one tough hill. The long ride is the toughest in the book, with two steep climbs more than 1 mile long, and several shorter hills.

Food: Grocery and restaurant just off the route in Southampton. Grocery at junction of Routes 112 and 66 in Huntington (long ride). Howard Johnson's at end.

Start: Friendly Ice Cream, Routes 10 and 202 in Westfield, opposite the exit and entrance ramps for the Massachusetts Turnpike.

Just northwest of Springfield, delightful bicycling abounds in the small valley tucked between the East Mountain–Mount Tom range on the east and the rugged, wooded hill country on the west. Lying in the small watershed of the Manhan River, the valley presents a harmonious blend of broad, gently rolling farms and stands of woodland, with views of the surrounding hills across the fields.

The ride starts on the outskirts of Westfield, a small industrial city best known as the home of Columbia bicycles (tours of the plant are available). You'll immediately head into farm country as you wind along the western edge of the valley on back roads to the handsome town of Southampton, with its magnificent old white church and a brick turn-of-the-century library. From here you'll head on through prosperous farmland to Pequot Pond and return to Westfield, skirting the base of East Mountain.

The long ride challenges the cyclist with a taste of the rugged hill country that extends across the western quarter of the state. As you struggle across the steep, nearly unpopulated landscape, you'll understand why the hill towns were the last part of the state to be settled. Leaving the valley, you'll climb nearly 1,000 feet to the tiny, unspoiled hilltop town of Montgomery, complete with little red schoolhouse, a traditional white church, and wooden courthouse built in 1849. From here you'll revel in a screaming downhill run t‹

578

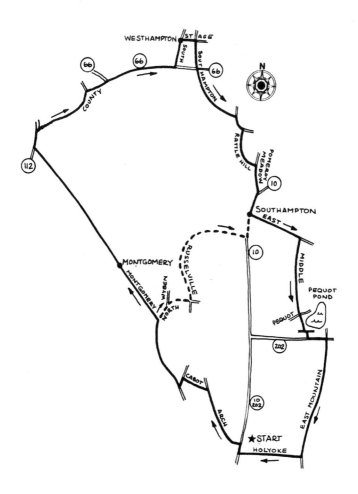

the Westfield River, only to face another long climb to get to West-hampton. This is another New England gem of a town, with a digni-fied white church commanding the hillside, a small well-kept green, and a white, pillared town hall. Beyond Westhampton is a relaxing downhill run into Southampton, with spectacular views of the Mount Tom range. In Southampton you'll pick up the short ride and follow it past Pequot Pond back to Westfield.

Directions for the ride: 36 miles

1. Turn left out of the parking lot onto Routes 10 and 202, and just ahead turn right on Arch Road after Howard Johnson's. Go 1.6 miles to Cabot Road, which bears left just after the Agway plant.

2. Bear left on Cabot Road and go 7/10 mile to end.

3. Turn left at end and go 2/10 mile to end, at stop sign.

4. Turn sharp right at end and go 2 miles to fork (North Road, unmarked, bears right). Here the short ride bears right and the long ride bears left.

5. Bear left at fork and go 7 miles to end (Route 112). It's a steady climb to Montgomery; you ascend 600 feet in 2 miles. Al-most at the top, at the crossroads, is a little, red, one-room school-house on the left, built in 1867. A mile farther on you'll pass the church and courthouse on the right. From here it's a breathtaking downhill plunge to the Westfield River. • *CAUTION:* There are some sharp curves toward the bottom—don't let yourself go too fast.

6. Bear right on Route 112 and go 6/10 mile to County Road, which bears right up a steep hill.

7. Bear right on County Road for 2.4 miles to fork where County Road turns right and Searle Road curves left, just before the church. You climb 600 feet in the first 1.2 miles, an average grade of 10 percent.

8. Turn right (still County Road) for 6/10 mile to end, at stop sign (merge head-on into Route 66). Go straight on Route 66 for 3 miles to a road on your left at bottom of hill (sign may say to Westhampton, 1 mile).

9. Turn left on this road and go 1.3 miles to Stage Road on right, at the church. This is the gracious village center of West-hampton. Notice the small, pillared, town hall on your left at the intersection.

10. Turn right on Stage Road and go 1/2 mile to crossroads almost at bottom of hill.

11. Turn right at crossroads and go 1.2 miles to crossroads and stop sign (Route 66).

12. Cross Route 66. As soon as you cross, there's a fruit stand on your right and a magnificent view of the valley on your left. Go 2.3 miles to end (Lead Mine Road).

13. Turn right at end and go 3/10 mile to Rattle Hill Road (unmarked) on right.

14. Turn right on Rattle Hill Road and go 1.2 miles to end (Pomeroy Meadow Road). Look for fine views of the Mount Tom Range to your left. The main road curves sharply left downhill near the end of this stretch.

15. Turn right on Pomeroy Meadow Road and go 1/2 mile to end (Route 10).

16. Bear right on Route 10 and go 1/2 mile to East Street on left, immediately before traffic light. There's a stately white church just beyond the intersection on your right.

17. Turn left on East Street and go 1.9 miles to Middle Road on right, at top of hill.

18. Turn right on Middle Road and go 2 miles to crossroads and stop sign (Pequot Road).

19. Cross Pequot Road and go 1/2 mile to end. Pequot Pond is on your left.

20. Jog left and immediately right at end, and go 100 yards to Route 202.

21. Turn left on Route 202 and go 7/10 mile to crossroads and blinking light (East Mountain Road), just before the Holyoke town line. You'll pass a state-run beach on your left.

22. Turn right at crossroads and go 2.9 miles to Holyoke Road on right, immediately after you go underneath the Massachusetts Turnpike and a railroad bridge.

23. Turn right on Holyoke Road and go 1.9 miles to end (Route 202 and 10).

24. Bear right on Routes 202 and 10. Friendly Ice Cream is just ahead on right.

Directions for the ride: 20 miles

1. Follow directions for the long ride through number 4.

2. Bear right at fork on North Road and go 3/10 mile to fork

581

(Wyben Road bears slightly left).

3. Bear right at fork (still North Road), and go 8/10 mile to crossroads and stop sign.

4. Turn left at crossroads and go 3.7 miles to end (Route 10). You'll climb a tough hill, but you're rewarded with a panoramic view of the valley when you get past the top.

5. Turn left on Route 10 and go 7/10 mile to traffic light (East Street on right). Shortly before the light a handsome brick library is on your right, and at the intersection a beautiful white church is on your left.

6. Turn right on East Street and go 1.9 miles to Middle Road on right, at top of hill.

7. Follow directions for the long ride from number 18 to the end.

About the Author

Howard Stone grew up in Boston, went to college in Maine and Illinois, and returned to his native New England, where he is now a librarian at Brown University. Howard is the touring director of the Narragansett Bay Wheelmen, the major bicycle club for southeastern Massachusetts and Rhode Island, and is the author of *Short Bike Rides in Rhode Island*, also published by The Globe Pequot Press. He has done extensive bicycle touring, including a cross-country trip from Newport, Oregon, to Newport, Rhode Island, in 978.

583

**Other outdoor recreation books
from the same publisher**

Short Bike Rides:
In Connecticut
On Long Island
On Cape Cod, Nantucket and the Vineyard
In New Jersey
In Rhode Island

Short Nature Walks:
In Connecticut
On Cape Cod and the Vineyard
On Long Island

Available at your bookstore or direct from the publisher. For a free catalogue or to place an order, call 1-800-243-0495 (in Connecticut, call 1-800-962-0973) or write to The Globe Pequot Press, Box Q, Chester, CT 06412.